Educational Research

An Introduction

Educational Research
An Introduction

BY WALTER R. BORG

CHAIRMAN, BUREAU OF EDUCATIONAL RESEARCH
UTAH STATE UNIVERSITY

DAVID MC KAY COMPANY, INC.

NEW YORK

EDUCATIONAL RESEARCH: AN INTRODUCTION

COPYRIGHT © 1963 BY DAVID MC KAY COMPANY, INC.

FIRST EDITION JUNE 1963
REPRINTED AUGUST 1965
MAY 1967
NOVEMBER 1969

C6170056-8

LIBRARY OF CONGRESS CATALOG CARD NUMBER: 63–15884

MANUFACTURED IN THE UNITED STATES OF AMERICA

To

Harold Carter

Who first set my foot on the path of research

Preface

This textbook aims at an elementary treatment of those aspects of educational research specifically needed by the Master's degree candidate in education. In planning this book, I have attempted to cover the minimum essentials needed to carry the student through the entire research process—from locating his problem to writing the thesis. Every effort has been made to make the presentation simple and practical. Much information of interest to more advanced researchers has been omitted in order that the student may concentrate on those concepts and methods essential to the beginner. I have tried to give the student specific procedures so that he can carry out the steps in his research project with relatively little additional training or information. I have avoided specific information only when it seemed impractical. For example, there seems little justification in presenting details on thesis style and format because most colleges have either adopted one of the published style manuals or developed one of their own that the student must follow. On the other hand, a detailed system for preparing note cards has been presented because the student is usually left to his own devices in this area and often arrives at an awkward and inefficient method of taking notes.

Preparation of a text in research methods poses a problem because it is desirable to give the student a reasonable insight into statistical tools and measurement techniques as they apply to research, while avoiding a general review of the usual classes in elementary statistics and educational evaluation. Therefore, the chapters on these topics assume that the student has taken these introductory courses and emphasize the application of measurement and statistical tools to educational research. An attempt is made to give the student enough information about these tools so that he can recognize situations in which each is appropriate. He will generally find it necessary, however, to go to other sources for details of their application—such as carrying out the steps in a statistical calculation.

In general, I have attempted to organize this text so that material is presented in about the order that the student will use it in developing and carrying out his research project. *The entire book, however, should be studied before the student attempts to plan and carry out his project.* Inasmuch as each phase of a research project is tied rather closely to every other phase, it is not possible to develop a text that permits the student to become fully competent in the initial steps of research before he has gained some knowledge and insight into later steps. He cannot, for example, review the literature adequately until he can evaluate the research of others critically, and this critical evaluation requires knowledge of research design, statistical tools, and, for that matter, insight into almost all aspects of research. Thus, the chapter dealing with critical evaluation has been placed near the end of the book (although in the research sequence, critical evaluation takes place during the review of the literature). Some instructors may wish to assign Chapter 15 immediately after Chapter 3 so that the student will get a complete introduction to reviewing the literature before moving on to the next step in the research sequence. If this approach is taken, however, it will be advisable to have students review Chapter 15 near the end of the course when they will be better able to understand it. Most of the chapters include a section summarizing the most common mistakes made by graduate students in the phase of research dealt with in the chapter. This approach, coupled with the many specific suggestions for procedure such as those dealing with locating a research problem, compiling note cards, and selecting statistical tools, is used in an attempt to make the text useful not only during the time the student takes his research course, but also as a handbook that he can later follow in designing and carrying out his thesis project and any subsequent research projects he may undertake.

Many textbooks contain a great deal of background information and illustrative material that is not essential to the student's understanding of the topic. Because this volume attempts to serve as a handbook as well as a text, brevity has been emphasized and very little material has been included that is not of major importance. Thus, the amount of important information per page is often quite high, and the student will find it difficult to assimilate the information in a single reading. From the standpoint of effective learning, it is recommended that, after a quick reading of the text early in the research course in order to gain perspective, the student try to read a few pages each day, keeping abreast of the instructor's presentation. He should underline or, in some other manner, indicate the most important points and review these points frequently as his reading carries him further into the book. He should make marginal notes to clarify important points, and should mark, for future reference, information that is especially pertinent to his own research plan. Another review of the text will be helpful to the student as he goes through the steps involved in carrying out his own research project. In each step of his research project, the student should pay special attention to the section at the end of the pertinent chapter that lists mistakes often made by graduate students. If he can keep these mistakes well in mind and can avoid most of them in his research project, he may be sure that his research will be well above average.

Inasmuch as this text is far from exhaustive, the student may have to go to other sources for additional information concerning specific aspects of his research. He will find the annotated references helpful in locating such sources. Relatively few references are given for each chapter, but those given are generally among the most useful available. The annotations will in most cases tell the student which reference is most likely to provide the information he needs. If none of the references meets his requirements, he may locate the information he needs by a systematic search of the literature, following the techniques discussed in Chapter 3.

Walter R. Borg

April, 1963

Contents

Figures

Tables

Educational Research
An Introduction

CHAPTER 1

Education as a Science

A NEW SCIENCE

Education did not begin to emerge as a science until the start of the twentieth century, although a few stirrings were evident during the latter 1800's. Scientific progress is based to a large degree upon the precision of our instruments and upon our ability to measure the phenomena concerned with the science in question. If the student will examine the history of any of the sciences, he will find that development of better tools is almost invariably followed by important gains in scientific knowledge, disproof of some theories, and confirmation of others. The relatively late emergence of education, psychology, sociology, and the other behavioral sciences is due largely to the complexity of the phenomena they attempt to measure and the consequent slow progress in developing measurement tools. Because science is closely tied to measurement, little progress in educational research was possible until some of the early measurement tools were developed. The publication of J. M. Cattell's *Mental Tests and Measurements* in 1890, the development of the intelligence scale by Binet and Simon in 1905, and the development of the handwriting scale by Thorndike in 1910 were among the significant early steps in developing objective tools for educational research.

After an initial negative reaction to early research, such as Rice's study of spelling, most educators embraced the new science and sat back to await the solution to all of their educational problems. Of course, a new science with little theoretical foundation and few satisfactory tools and techniques failed to meet these great expectations. Ralph Tyler recalls for us the disillusionment of educators of the post World War I period:

When I was an instructor at the University of Nebraska nearly forty years ago, there was a great interest in educational research and even in that state, which had previously spent money only on agricultural research, there was established in that university a bureau of educational research with some state support. This was done with the optimistic view following World War I that educational research would give answers to pressing and immediate questions such as: What do you do to get everybody to read in the elementary school? What can you do to get every pupil to spell correctly? What can you do to achieve 100 per cent accuracy in arithmetic? Because of the success of psychological tests in selecting candidates for officer training in World War I and in the use of job analysis for building a short and effective curriculum for bricklayers and carpenters needed in the war effort, many people concluded that a bureau of educational research would quickly solve the immediate, practical problems of the Nebraska schools. But this was an expectation which was not warranted by the later results. The problems of education are not going to be answered in this way.[1]

Because of the pressure of educators in the public schools to get immediate solutions to practical classroom problems, educational research has been slow in developing the theoretical foundations upon which every science must be built. The real value of research is rarely found in its ability to provide quick answers to practical problems. Rather, its value lies in developing theory and advancing knowledge so that the answers it does provide are sound and lead to real gains. Educators, in their impatience to solve their problems, have often adopted new and unproven ideas that later research proved valueless or even detrimental to the educational process. The direct attack on practical problems is not necessarily the best way to arrive at a solution to these problems. Agricultural research provides an interesting illustration of the futility of concentrating too heavily upon direct solutions:

In a certain sense, agricultural researchers reached a kind of impasse when they sought to deal too directly with immediate, practical problems. Agriculture research gained new vitality when different sorts of questions were studied. For example, consider the case of hybrid corn. That hybrid corn existed and many hybrids could be produced was known for many years. But agricultural researchers were not greatly interested in this field because they had a different model to guide their thinking. This model was: We have good corn. How can it best be raised? They were conscious of the amount of water, the quality of seed, the physical and chemical characteristics of the soil, the use of fertilizer, the varying lengths of growing seasons, and these were the variables that were manipulated. When they reached a point where corn production was up to above sixty bushels an acre, this was considered tops; maximum production had been reached. The men working on hybrid corn

[1] F. W. Banghart (ed.), *First Annual Phi Delta Kappa Symposium on Educational Research* (Bloomington, Ind.: Phi Delta Kappa, 1960), p. 91. Reprinted by permission of Mr. F. W. Banghart.

spent nearly twenty years before they could even get attention by agronomists, because they were geneticists. They were not working on immediate practical problems but on more theoretical ones. When, finally, they got a hearing and corn production jumped, agricultural researchers in large numbers began to study more basic and theoretical problems in order to understand the more immediate ones.[2]

The science of education remains weak in theoretical foundation, but a sufficient body of theory has now been developed or borrowed from the other behavioral sciences to permit sound approaches to some of the practical problems of education. The public school administrator is still wanting in an appreciation for basic and theoretical research in education, but today his expectations are much more realistic than those of educators forty years ago. He knows research can provide answers to his problems, because many answers have already been provided. He has gained much insight into the complexities of the educational process, and is resigned to the fact that research moves slowly.

A COMPLEX SCIENCE

Few persons outside of the behavioral sciences have a clear insight into the tremendous problems faced by the research worker in education and the other behavioral sciences. Perhaps the greatest obstacle to progress in these sciences is the extreme complexity of the problems. Most laymen think of a science such as nuclear physics as being far more complex than such sciences as education, psychology, and sociology. Actually, the reverse is true. The forces and matter dealt with in physics and chemistry are far easier to understand than the structure of a strange society, the development of the personality, or the processes involved in human thought and problem solving. Living organisms are generally far more complex than the forces and inert matter that make up the content of the physical sciences. The human being—the subject of most educational research —is by far the most complex of the living organisms. In the physical sciences, formal laboratory techniques permit rigid control of the experimental conditions. Such control is generally impossible with human subjects, so the behavioral scientist must deal with many variables simultaneously and must work under conditions that are

[2] *Ibid.*, pp. 91–92.

much less precise. Despite these handicaps, education and the other behavioral sciences have made impressive contributions to our understanding of human behavior.

A VITALLY IMPORTANT SCIENCE

The impact of the behavioral sciences on our society is far greater than most people realize. At one level they are providing technical solutions for important human problems. But at a deeper level they are changing the conception of human nature—our fundamental ideas about human desires and human possibilities. When such conceptions change, society changes.

In the past few generations, many beliefs about such diverse matters as intelligence, child rearing, delinquency, sex, public opinion, and the management of organizations have been greatly modified by the results of filtering scientific fact and theory through numerous layers of popularizing translation.[3]

Nuclear weapons and their threat to humanity are the principal concern of most educated men in our time. Few realize that education and the other behavioral sciences offer us the best hope of controlling this power. Even fewer are aware that knowledge is quickly building up in the behavioral sciences that, if misused, may create a scientific monster potentially more destructive to civilized man than the H-bomb. One of our greatest physicists recently observed:

In the last ten years the physicists have been extraordinarily noisy about the immense powers which, largely through their efforts, but through other efforts as well, have come into the possession of man, powers notably and strikingly for very large-scale and dreadful destruction. We have spoken of our responsibilities and of our obligations to society in terms that sound to me very provincial, because the psychologist can hardly do anything without realizing that for him the acquisition of knowledge opens up the most terrifying prospects of controlling what people do and how they think and how they behave and how they feel. This is true for all of you who are engaged in practice, and as the corpus of psychology gains in certitude and subtlety and skill, I can see that the physicist's pleas that what he discovers be used with humanity and be used wisely will seem rather trivial compared to those

---

[3] Behavioral Sciences Subpanel of the President's Science Advisory Committee, "Strengthening the Behavioral Sciences," *Science*, CXXXVI, No. 3512 (April, 1962), 233. Reprinted by permission of *Science*.

pleas which you will have to make and for which you will have to be responsible.[4]

Thus, the thoughtful student may see that education and the related sciences are vitally important to the future of man. These sciences are in many ways analogous to the states of the physical sciences at the beginning of the nineteenth century. We are on the threshold of great new advances in knowledge that can contribute either to the elevation of mankind to new heights of dignity or to its degradation.

THE SCIENTIFIC METHOD IN EDUCATION

Perhaps a major reason for the slow and unsure progress in education has been the inefficient and unscientific methods used by educators in acquiring knowledge and solving their problems. An uncritical acceptance of authority opinion that is not supported by objective evidence and an overdependence upon personal experience have been characteristic of the educator's problem solving techniques.

Both of these techniques have led to many blunders in education. The opinions of authorities should be critically evaluated and checked for supporting evidence before being accepted. Uncritical acceptance of Aristotle's pronouncements greatly retarded the growth of knowledge in the Middle Ages. Uncritical application of Freudian concepts to elementary school education led to amazing blunders in some of the "progressive schools" of the 1920's. Uncritical acceptance of the "sales pitch" of producers of teaching machines and programmed learning materials by today's educators may well lead to another educational fiasco because these techniques, though promising, are far from the level of perfection suggested by the salesmen. A tragic feature of the uncritical acceptance of authority opinion is that it is usually followed by disillusionment and reaction. Thus, many of the useful concepts given to us by men like John Dewey and Sigmund Freud are rejected by educators after the fad of blind acceptance has passed.

Reliance upon personal experience is equally faulty as a means

[4] Robert Oppenheimer, "Analogy in Science," *The American Psychologist,* XI, No. 3 (March, 1956), 128. Reprinted by permission of the American Psychological Assoc.

for arriving at solutions to our educational problems. Personal experience almost always constitutes insufficient evidence upon which to make decisions, even if the individual were able to remember and objectively evaluate his experience. We know from psychological research that the individual tends to remember evidence that supports his opinion and to forget or distort evidence that does not. Personal experience often leads the individual to draw conclusions or assume relationships that are false. Yet, personal experience still plays a major role in decision making in the public schools. In recent years the author, in the course of a research project, has discussed ability grouping with a great many teachers and administrators in the public schools. Although nearly everyone in the public schools has strong feelings on this subject, very few have any knowledge of the research evidence concerning it. Education will mature greatly as a science when the majority of educators put aside personal experience and bias and seek scientific evidence as a basis for making decisions.

The scientific method offers the best approach that man has thus far developed for the solution of problems. The steps of the scientific method may be applied not only to the problems of the scientific laboratory but are equally applicable to the problems faced by the school teacher in his classroom. The basic steps of the scientific method are as follows:

1. Recognition of the problem.
2. Definition of the problem in clear, specific terms.
3. Development of hypotheses.
4. Development of techniques and measuring instruments that will provide objective data pertinent to the hypotheses.
5. Collection of data.
6. Analysis of data.
7. Drawing conclusions relative to the hypotheses based upon the data.

As important as these steps are, however, they are less important than the habits of objective and critical thinking that they help the scientist to develop. Few mature scientists follow these steps rigidly in the conduct of their research. This does not mean they are not using the scientific method but merely demonstrates that this method has become so closely bound up with the values and perceptions of the scientist that direct, conscious reference to its steps is no longer necessary.

he Long Beach Public Schools. Two groups of potential failures
e equated. One of the groups was required to repeat the grade
le the other was promoted on trial. When educational tests were
ninistered to both groups, it was found that children of normal
ity gained more from trial promotion than children of equal
lity who had repeated the grade. Children of less than average
lity gained slightly more by repeating the grade than they did by
al promotion.[6]

A study by McKinney found that 53 per cent of elementary school
peaters did not improve from repeating a grade. Thirty-five per
nt showed better work the second time through the grade and 12
r cent did poorer work.[7]

Some educators clung to nonpromotion as a device to "get lazy
ipils to work," but later studies indicated that the threat of failure
ad little or no effect as a method of motivation.[8]

The weight of this research caused public schools to move away
rom rigid promotion standards and the widespread practice of nonpromotion. As is often the case, many schools reacted strongly
gainst their previous practices and established 100 per cent promotion programs. At the present time, although few schools subscribe
rigidly to a 100 per cent promotion policy, the number of failures has
been drastically reduced. Exact figures on the percentage of failure
are difficult to determine and vary considerably, but all studies concerned with this topic have reported a trend toward a small number
of failures.

In all likelihood, the overall promotion rate at the present time in
the United States exceeds 95 per cent. Teachers, being well aware of
the dangers of nonpromotion that have been brought out by research
in this area, consider each case very carefully and tend to employ
nonpromotion only when considerable evidence seems to indicate
that this course of action is desirable in the particular case.[9]

[6] Vivian Klene and E. P. Branson, "Trial-Promotion vs. Failure," *Educational Research Bulletin,* VIII (January, 1929), 6–11.

[7] D. T. McKinney, "The Promotion of Pupils—A Problem of Educational Admin-istration" (Doctoral dissertation; Urbana, Ill.: University of Illinois, 1928).

[8] J. Henry Otto and Ernest O. Melby, "An Attempt to Evaluate the Threat of Failure as a Factor in Achievement," *Elementary School Journal,* XXXV (April, 1935), 588–96.

[9] Ironically, the recent clamor for higher standards has led some public school systems to reinstitute policies leading to nonpromotion of many pupils. Progress in

SOME CONTRIBUTIONS OF EDUCA

Although educational research is still in
short span already produced much useful kn
about great changes in educational practice
educators.

The following examples are not the most
of educational research but may serve to ill
few areas in which gains have been made.

Promotion

Up until the 1920's when extensive research v
devoted to the relative merits of promotion an
vast majority of public schools in the United S
rigid promotion standards. These standards w
pupil failed to attain the level of achievement th
every one of the subjects taught at a particular
retained in the grade until this level of achievemen
The success of teachers was judged largely by the
they succeeded in raising to the level required fo.
policy resulted in many children of low ability re
grade several times. These rigid promotion policies
"common sense" notion that, if a person failed to
grade material satisfactorily, the best way for him t
repeat the third grade until he did. The student shou
ful in his acceptance of "common sense" solutions. 1
with instances in which common sense has been pr
science. In the late 1920's and early '30's, however,
studies were conducted on some of the effects of prom
promotion. Among these were Arthur's study of sixty
peaters, which showed that the average repeater did n
in two years than the average nonrepeater of the sam
learned in one year.[5]

Another noteworthy study bearing on this question wa

[5] Grace Arthur, "A Study of the Achievement of 60 Grade-One
Compared with That of Nonrepeaters of the Same Mental Age," *Jour*
mental Education, V (December, 1930), 203–5.

The gifted child

One of the most significant pieces of educational research has been the longitudinal study of gifted children started by L. M. Terman in 1921. This study initially selected some 1,500 superior boys and girls and followed a large proportion of them through school, college, adulthood, and to middle life. Five volumes have been published based on three major field studies, and several mailed follow-ups carried out over a thirty-five-year period. The findings have given us much greater insights into the nature and development of superior individuals and have exploded the once widely held belief that precocious children usually grow up to be inferior adults. Among the results of the latest follow-up, we find that more than 70 per cent of Terman's group graduated from college or about ten times as many as would be found in the average population. The requirements for the Ph.D. degree were completed by 14 per cent of the men in the study, and these men had produced nearly 2,000 scientific papers, over 60 books and monographs, and at least 230 patents at the time of the thirty-five-year follow-up. The children of the subjects in the original sample have been tested and 30 per cent of these children are also gifted.[10] This classic study in educational psychology demonstrates the tremendous amount of knowledge pertinent to education that may be generated through a single research project.

Foreign language teaching

A more recent example of a major improvement in education that has been largely brought about through educational research is found in the teaching of foreign languages. Up until World War II, most foreign language instruction was conducted along the following lines: The teacher, who often had a limited command of the language being taught, carried out the class instruction in English. The usual lesson

---

education is not easily gained nor easily maintained. The willingness of some educators to reject scientific evidence in order to gain public approval reflects the immaturity of education as a science. In contrast one is reminded of the many astronomers in the sixteenth century who endured persecution rather than state falsely that the earth was the center of the universe.

[10] L. M. Terman and M. H. Oden, *The Gifted Group at Mid-Life: Thirty-five Years' Follow-up of the Superior Child* (Stanford, Calif.: Stanford Univ. Press, 1959).

consisted of a discussion of some grammatical point in the language, an exercise translating a selection from English into the foreign language being studied, another exercise involving translating a selection from the foreign language into English, and a daily vocabulary list to be memorized. Although many educators were dissatisfied with this method of language instruction, little real gains were made until World War II when the need for persons trained in foreign languages was very great and the methods then in use were found to be inadequate. Methods emphasizing conversation and the elimination of grammar and vocabulary lists were developed and tested by research. Many of the changes involved in these new methods were firmly based on principles of linguistics and educational psychology that had been known for many years. The language laboratory, with its use of tape recorders and other electronic equipment and its emphasis upon the oral-aural methods of language instruction, has been the result of this research and development.

Among the significant early studies comparing traditional and oral-aural methods of language instruction is the work of Hohlfeld who compared college students in two experimental Spanish classes—one emphasizing oral-aural skills and using a series of phonograph records as the chief teaching material, the other emphasizing use of a textbook, grammatical analysis, rapid silent reading, and translation. This study, although involving small samples, was very carefully controlled, subjects being matched with respect to seventeen variables. Hohlfeld's results indicated that in tests aimed primarily at measuring gains made by the traditional method, the oral-aural method was either equal or superior; and in areas such as phonics accuracy and reading, the results were overwhelmingly in favor of the newer method.[11]

A more extensive series of experiments were carried out at the University of Texas by Hamilton and Haden. This work extended over a three-year period and involved a total of 2,700 students. Results generally reflected a small difference in achievement, using the usual standard tests that are aimed at measuring the skills stressed in the formal program but revealed many features in the oral-aural methods that brought about favorable outcomes not obtained by the

[11] John M. Hohlfeld, *An Experiment Employing Two Methods of Teaching Spanish to College Freshmen* (Doctoral dissertation; Philadelphia: University of Pennsylvania, 1950).

formal methods. Among the most interesting results of these studies was the finding that it makes essentially no difference in grammar achievement whether grammar is emphasized in the traditional former manner or whether it is de-emphasized and taught inductively as is the case in the newer methods. Later research has supported this finding, and the body of evidence now available indicates that teaching of traditional grammar is essentially a waste of time.[12]

Such early studies, though often weak from a research standpoint, still contained enough significant evidence to indicate strongly the potential of the new methods. Since that time, more carefully controlled studies have generally supported the findings of this earlier work. The efficiency of the oral-aural method has greatly increased since 1950, when the earlier studies had generally established its superiority over traditional methods. Tremendous impetus was given for further research and development on the teaching of modern foreign languages by the National Defense Education Act (NDEA) of 1958. By 1962, the total funds allocated to research dealing with modern language instruction and the development of tests and specialized materials in this field under Title VI and Title VII of the NDEA approached ten million dollars. Much of the significant research concerning modern language instruction supported by this program has not yet been completed and published. It seems almost a certainty that the new knowledge, methods, and materials now developing in modern language instruction will bring about further great gains in teaching effectiveness in this vital field over the next few years.[13]

Important research now under way

Because much of the increase in funds for educational research has occurred since 1958, a great many studies of great significance, started since that date, are still under way. Many of these studies will be completed before 1965. Because there is usually several years lag between research findings and their application to problems in the public schools, the major impact of this new knowledge upon

[12] D. E. Hamilton and E. F. Haden, "Three Years of Experimentation at the University of Texas," *Modern Language Journal,* XXXIV (February, 1950), 85–102.

[13] M. C. Johnston, "Foreign Language Instruction," *Review of Educational Research,* XXXI, No. 2 (April, 1961), 188–96.

education will probably be in the 1970's. This will be an exciting and challenging decade for the teaching profession and a time when great opportunities for leadership will exist in all areas of education. Let us preview a few of the changes to come by looking at some of the important research now under way.

Project talent

This is a highly significant project being sponsored jointly by the University of Pittsburgh and the American Institute for Research. The study is aimed at obtaining an accurate inventory of the abilities and potentialities of American youth. After tryout and development of measuring instruments on 10,000 high school students, a total of approximately 500,000 students were tested in the spring of 1960. All students in about 1,200 secondary schools including grades 9 to 12 were tested, using a wide range of educational and psychological measures including aptitude and ability tests, measures of educational achievement, interest, and personality characteristics. A follow-up study will be carried out for a number of years in order to determine how closely the potentials of these students match their future accomplishments. The information that has been collected will also be compared with their behavior in a number of areas in later life. All of the high school students included in the study will be followed up approximately one year after their graduation from high school and will be contacted at later intervals to obtain information on their occupations, training they have undertaken, success and satisfaction in the activity they have chosen, and many other facts related to their education, career, and adjustment. These data will then be compared with the original measures, using electronic computing equipment. Dr. John T. Dailey is director of this project, and Dr. John C. Flanagan is the national administrative head of the project. Ninety regional coordinators were employed to arrange for the testing and guide schools in administration of the measures.

Some of the important results of this National Aptitude and Ability Census should be:

"A comprehensive counseling guide indicating the patterns of aptitude and ability which are predictive of success in various careers. In the follow-ups after the national examinations and analysis, students who took the test will be located and asked to report on educational and vocational experiences. A young girl may have become a secretary, or a housewife, or she may have

gone to college. By studying thousands of student aptitude, interest, and ability patterns and finding out the person's later activities and occupations, we will learn a great deal. This will help students by predicting more precisely what kinds of aptitudes and abilities, what kinds of courses, and what kinds of interests constitute the best basis for various kinds of careers. An artist needs good color sense, a scientist needs mathematical ability, but counselors know that many other factors enter into the qualifications for success in a career. Motivation is a necessary ingredient, but the best use of a student's special talents requires that he identify this talent early and obtain the education essential for the full development and effective use of his powers.

A better understanding of how young people choose their life work. Many people follow their family trade or profession. They tend to think that people know quite early what their life work will be. Other people drift into an occupation, and they tend to think that everyone more or less drifts into a particular trade, business, or profession. Many people feel that they have little choice.

However, many people today do have a choice, and the diversity of occupations and the need for special training continue to increase. We have begun to learn something about the process by which a young person decides that he would like to be a teacher, a lawyer, or an apprentice for a trade. This study and others can help us understand at what ages certain lifetime careers tend to be chosen.

A better understanding of the educational experiences which prepare students for their life work. American education is noted for its diversity. Only through the analysis of detailed information about students, their educational experiences, and their subsequent successes or failures can we hope to make our educational system as flexible and responsible to the individual needs of its students as it must be if our nation is to continue to develop and prosper.

Project TALENT has been carefully designed to fill an important national need for facts regarding the identification, development, and utilization of our human resources. This information is intended as a basis for manpower policies and as a basic resource for the many individuals responsible for the education of our children." [14]

Greater Cleveland mathematics program

Another research project of major significance is the Greater Cleveland Mathematics Program. The materials for this program were developed by the staff of the Educational Research Council of

[14] John C. Flanagan and John T. Dailey, "Project Talent—the Identification, Development, and Utilization of Human Talents," *Personnel and Guidance Journal,* XXXVIII (February, 1960), 504–5. Reprinted by permission of the *Personnel and Guidance Journal.*

Greater-Cleveland, six of the nation's leading mathematicians, and teachers in twenty-four school districts in suburban Cleveland. The curriculum developed for this program aims at introducing a new mathematics curriculum that systematically presents all the elements of basic mathematical skills. The program emphasizes inductive learning and the mastery of basic concepts rather than giving students specific mathematical tools designed to handle specific skills and problem situations without developing a full understanding of the underlying principles. In a rapidly changing society, the schools have often placed too much emphasis upon specific operations that are appropriate at the time taught but outdated by the time the pupil is called upon to use his knowledge. This amounts to educating the pupil for yesterday's society instead of tomorrow's. Educating for tomorrow is a difficult task. The Greater Cleveland Mathematics Program appears to be meeting this challenge in one subject area.

Actually, the psychological and educational principles upon which this program is being built are not new and have generally been recognized as superior for a number of years. Taking these principles and combining them with the most advanced educational concepts in a particular subject field such as mathematics, and then preparing materials and actually putting such a program into effect, however, is new and represents a giant step in closing the gap between research knowledge and educational practice. The first two years of the program have been devoted largely to the development and improvement of the curricular materials and rendering assistance to teachers in the use of these materials. Preliminary experimental materials are now in use in grades four through six, and work is progressing toward the development of suitable materials for the junior and senior high school level. Objective evaluation of pupil progress in classes using these materials was carried out in the spring of 1961, and the results showed the groups using the new materials to be significantly superior to control groups on standardized achievement tests. In addition to their superiority on standardized tests that reflect for the most part a knowledge of operations rather than an understanding of principles (and are thus biased in favor of the older curriculum), the pupils in the experimental groups were also found to be far superior in special tests aimed at dealing with more difficult mathematical concepts and understanding of mathematical principles. In all instances, where comparisons have been made, the mean scores for those children who were taught with the materials developed by the Greater Cleveland Mathematics Program were significantly higher than the scores for those children who did not have this material.

A very significant concept introduced in Cleveland is the Educational Research Council of Greater Cleveland that supervised the development of this mathematics program and is carrying out the research. The council was created in 1958 specifically to employ a dynamic approach to research in education and make possible immediate implementation of research findings. Dr. Baird, Executive Director of the Educational Research Council of Greater Cleveland, considers the following elements necessary in order to carry out and implement research findings in the manner done by the council:

1. Full financial backing to avoid the pitfalls of expediency and fiscal shortcoming of amateur, part-time, or ivory-tower research.

2. A willingness among regional groups of schools to support immediate active programs of experimentation and implementation.[15]

The Cleveland Council is being sponsored by a group of civic leaders from commerce and industry. Many prominent business men from the Greater Cleveland area are actively engaged in raising funds needed for the support of the council. At their instigation, the Cleveland Foundation granted $100,000 on a matching basis for the first two years of the program, and a group of leading superintendents from the Greater Cleveland area have enthusiastically supported the council's work.

Because the methods and curricular materials developed in the Cleveland project can be applied to any school system, it is very likely that this study will have a major impact upon mathematics teaching in American public schools. The method established in Cleveland of combining the talents of business leaders, professional educators, subject matter specialists, and educational research workers to make an effective team for conducting research and implementing research results sets a pattern that could lead to great improvements in education and may well solve the nagging problem of closing the gap between research findings and classroom practices. If every greater metropolitan area in the United States of over one

[15] George Baird, "Children 'Discover' Own Math," *SRA Insight,* II, No. 1 (1962), 7.

million population would develop a council and concentrate upon the improvement of the curriculum in one area or on the solution of one important educational problem, tremendous gains could be made in the next decade.

TYPES OF EDUCATIONAL RESEARCH

Control vs. reality

Educational research may be described under three broad classifications: basic research, applied research, and action research. One feature differentiating these types of research is the degree to which each type emphasizes precision and control as contrasted with reality. The research worker in education is faced with a difficult dilemma. If he attempts to maintain close control on the research situation in order to obtain scientific precision, he usually must alter the conditions so greatly that there is very little similarity between the research situation and the related situation in the public schools. On the other hand, if he strives for reality in his research so that his findings may have direct application to the public schools, he must usually sacrifice much of his scientific control. Even at its most precise level, research in education cannot match the precision and control possible in the physical science laboratory. Studies in psychology and sociology have demonstrated that the behavior of human subjects can be changed or affected by very subtle factors. The Hawthorne effect, well known among psychologists, is a term used to describe the tendency for subjects to react more favorably in a situation in which they realize they are part of an experiment or in a situation where they obtain special treatment or special attention. Many of our positive findings in education are due to lack of satisfactory control of the Hawthorne effect. Market research studies have demonstrated that many subtle factors relating to the interaction between an interviewer and an interviewee can affect the interviewee's responses. For example, if the interviewee perceives the interviewer as being of a higher social status than himself, his responses will be different than if he perceives the interviewer to be of a lower status. It has only been in recent years that we have developed an appreciation of some of the complexities and subtle biases that can effect data collection procedures when human subjects are involved.

Basic research

Basic research that is sometimes called "pure research" or "fundamental research" is aimed at the discovery of basic truths or principles. It is usually oriented strongly towards the testing and development of theory and is not immediately concerned with direct field application. Thus, in basic research, control and precision are emphasized while less attention is given to direct application of the results in a field situation. Such research is usually carried out in the laboratory, and many such studies, because they are concerned with fundamental principles of behavior, use animal subjects rather than human subjects. Research with animals, of course, permits a much higher level of control than is possible with human subjects although reducing considerably the degree to which the findings may be directly applied to human problems. Much of the basic research having implications for education has been carried out by workers in the other behavioral sciences such as psychology and sociology.

Harlow's research concerning the behavior of infant monkeys reared under different conditions in the laboratory provides an impressive example of basic research that has broad implications related to the education and development of humans. The controls required in Harlow's work would have made these studies impossible to carry out with human subjects. Now that certain principles concerning the behavior of the Macaque monkeys in Harlow's research have been established, however, this knowledge will be of value in providing a theoretical basis for establishing and testing hypotheses concerning similar behavior in human subjects. The following gives a brief review of some of Harlow's work.

For some years we have been attempting to establish experimental neuroses in infant monkeys by having them live on unfriendly and inconsistent mother surrogates. One preparation was a rejecting mother that on schedule or demand separated her baby when a wire frame embedded in her spun-nylon covering was displaced violently upward and backward. The baby was disturbed, but as soon as the frame was returned to its resting position, the baby returned to cling to its surrogate mother as tightly as ever. Next we developed an air-blast mother with a series of nozzles down the entire center of her body which released compressed air under high pressure—an extremely noxious stimulus to monkeys. The blasted baby never even left the mother, but in its moments of agony and duress, clung more and more tightly to the unworthy mother. Where else can a baby get protection? . . .

During the time that we were producing these evil mothers, we observed the monkeys which we had separated from their mothers at birth and raised under various mothered and nonmothered conditions. The first 47 baby monkeys were raised during the first year of life in wire cages so arranged that the infants could see and hear and call to other infants but not contact them. Now they are five to seven years old and sexually mature. As month after month and year after year have passed, these monkeys have appeared to be less and less normal. We have seen them sitting in their cages strangely mute, staring fixedly into space, relatively indifferent to people and other monkeys. Some clutch their heads in both hands and rock back and forth— the autistic behavior pattern that we have seen in babies raised on wire surrogates. Others, when approached or even left alone, go into violent frenzies of rage, grasping and tearing at their legs with such fury that they sometimes require medical care.

Eventually we realized that we had a laboratory full of neurotic monkeys. We had failed to produce neurotic monkeys by thoughtful planning and creative research, but we had succeeded in producing neurotic monkeys through misadventure. To err is human.

Because of housing pressures some of these monkeys and many of our surrogate-raised monkeys lived in pairs for several years while growing to sexual maturity, but we have seldom seen normal sex behavior, and we certainly have not had the validating criterion of newborn baby monkeys. Instead, these monkeys treat each other like brother and sister, proving that two can live in complete propinquity with perfect propriety as long as no one cares.

Their reason for being, as we saw it, was to produce babies for our researchers, and so at this point we deliberately initiated a breeding program which was frighteningly unsuccessful. When the older, wire-cage-raised males were paired with the females at the peak of estrus, the introduction led only to fighting, so violent and vicious that separation was essential to survival. In no case was there any indication of normal sex behavior. . . .

Two years later we had more than theoretical reasons to be disturbed because Mason tested a group of these isolation-raised monkeys, then between 2.5 and 3.5 years of age, and found evidence of severe social abnormalities, which might be described as a sociopathic syndrome. He matched the laboratory-raised monkeys on the basis of weight and dentition patterns with monkeys that had been born and raised in the wild for the first 12 to 18 months, then captured and subjected to various kinds of housing and caging treatments for the next year or two. In the test situations the laboratory-raised monkeys, as compared with feral monkeys, showed infantile sexual behavior, absence of grooming, exaggerated aggression, and absence of affectional interaction as measured by cooperation. . . . We have, however, had better success with some of the females, particularly the females raised on cloth surrogates.

Even so, one of the wire-cage-raised females is a mother and another is pregnant. Three cloth-surrogate female are mothers and four or five are expectant. . . .

Combining our human and male-monkey talents, we are winning the good fight and imparting to naive and even resistant female monkeys the priceless gift of motherhood. Possibly it is a Pyrrhic victory. As every scientist knows, the solution of one scientific problem inevitably leads to another, and this is our fate. Month after month female monkeys that never knew a real mother, themselves become mothers—helpless, hopeless, heartless mothers devoid, or almost devoid, of any maternal feeling.[16]

A great many other basic research projects have been carried out that have important implications for education, such as Cattell's research on factors in the human personality and the extensive research on the nature of creative behavior being conducted by Taylor at the University of Utah, Torrance at the University of Minnesota, and others.

Applied research

Applied research, or field research as it is often called, is concerned primarily with establishing relationships and testing theories in the field setting. Because transfer of the research results directly to field practice is usually a goal of applied research, control and precision must be sacrificed to some extent in order to carry out the research in a setting similar to that in which the results will be applied. Applied research may be aimed at the testing of theoretical constructs. There is a trend among educational researchers toward giving greater attention to the development and testing of theories in applied research, but many field studies are still conducted in education in which little or no attention is paid to theoretical considerations. Much research on teaching methods, for example, is

[16] H. F. Harlow, "The Heterosexual Affectional System in Monkeys," *The American Psychologist*, XVII (January, 1962), 6–9. Reprinted by permission of the American Psychological Assoc.

aimed at discovering *which* of two methods leads to a higher level of achievement and gives little attention to the question of *why* one method works better than the other. A knowledge of *why* is usually much more important both to the scientist and the practitioner in the field than the knowledge of *which* method works best. In seeking out the *why*, the scientist isolates the essential elements in the method that are leading to superior results. These essential elements, once identified, may be applied to many different situations.

Applied research aims at establishing generalizations that may be applied to other samples of the population from which the research subjects were taken. For example, a study of the friendship patterns of a sample of ninth grade public school pupils is most valuable if the sample has been chosen in such a way that the results may be expected to apply reasonably well to other samples of the same population. In other words, in order to be effective applied research must produce results that may be generally applied to the population studied. This means that the method of obtaining samples in applied research is of great importance. The Greater Cleveland Mathematics Project discussed earlier in this chapter is a good example of applied research. Although founded on psychological principles of learning, the project was not concerned primarily with the development or testing of learning theories but with the development and testing of specific methods and materials for teaching mathematics. The emphasis in this study is upon direct application of the research results to public school classrooms. The findings will have their greatest direct application in Cleveland and similar communities, but the research design is sufficiently controlled so as to have important implications for the teaching of mathematics in all American public schools.

Action research

Action research involves the application of the steps of the scientific method to classroom problems. Action research usually employs the highest level of reality and the least amount of control and precision of the three types. Action research is similar in many ways to applied research but differs from applied research principally in those aspects of research design that permit the generalizability of applied research results. Applied research usually involves a large number of cases in order to cancel out some of the random errors that occur in small samples; it involves establishing as much control as possible, consistent with the research goals, over such variables as teaching ability and, perhaps most important, involves more precise sampling techniques than are found in action research. Many action research projects are carried out in a single classroom by a single teacher, while others are carried on by all teachers in a school or even a school district. As action research projects become more extensive they become more similar to applied research. The emphasis in action research, however, is not on obtaining generalizable scientific knowledge about educational problems, but on obtaining specific knowledge concerning the subjects involved in the study. The results of an action research project by a single teacher have important implications for this teacher, but because of the few cases, lack of control and absence of sampling techniques are not generalizable to other similar classrooms. The principal advantage of action research is that it provides the teacher or administrator in the field with objective, systematic techniques of problem solving that are far superior to an appeal to authority or reliance on personal experience, which so often guides decisions in education.

Research may be subdivided not only into the three types discussed previously but also in terms of the specific research techniques, such as descriptive research, causal-comparative research, and experimental research. Although some of these techniques are more frequently used in one type of research than another, any of the three types of research may employ any of the research methods available. Both applied research and action research are often carried out using what are basically experimental techniques, while laboratory research often employs nonexperimental techniques such as those involved in the descriptive method.

The student should also realize that there are no clear-cut lines that differentiate the three types of research described. Although most projects can be easily classified as either basic, applied, or action research, as we approach the boundaries between two types, such differentiation becomes difficult.

ANNOTATED REFERENCES

1. AMERICAN EDUCATIONAL RESEARCH ASSOCIATION. "Educational Research in Countries Other than the U.S.A.," *Review of Educational Research,*

1957, 27 (1). This issue of the *Review* covers educational research in some of the western European countries, Latin American countries, and countries of the United Kingdom. Although relatively few countries are covered, this source still provides the student with useful information on research programs in other countries and helps him to gain a better orientation to the field of educational research. If the student wishes to enlarge his survey beyond the countries covered in this volume, he will find articles concerned with educational research in the Soviet Union and some other countries listed in the *Education Index*.

2. AMERICAN EDUCATIONAL RESEARCH ASSOCIATION. "Twenty-Five Years of Educational Research," *Review of Educational Research*, 1956, 26 (3). This entire issue of the *Review* is devoted to tracing some of the major trends in educational research between 1931 and 1956. Many significant developments occurring during that period are briefly discussed, and an assessment is made of gains we have made in present knowledge concerning many basic questions in education in such areas as school administration, curriculum research, educational psychology, educational measurement, counseling and adjustment, history and philosophy of education, and research methods. Reading this issue will give the student a brief and useful orientation to the field of educational research.

3. BANGHART, FRANK W. (ed.). *First Annual Phi Delta Kappa Symposium on Educational Research*. Bloomington, Ind.: Phi Delta Kappa, 1960. This symposium, involving several eminent educational researchers, provides the student with further background in educational research. Among the topics discussed are included "A Survey of Educational Research at Selected Universities, Contributions of the Federal Government to Educational Research Methodology, The Impact of Applied Problems on Educational Research, the Contributions of the Behavioral Sciences to Educational Research, and Philosophy of Educational Research."

4. BEHAVIORAL SCIENCES SUBPANEL OF THE PRESIDENT'S SCIENCE ADVISORY COMMITTEE. "Strengthening the Behavioral Sciences," *Science*, 1962, 136, 233–41. This is a report of the Behavioral Sciences Subpanel of the President's Science Advisory Committee. It contains a number of penetrating observations concerning the development of the behavioral sciences and their present state and probable future role in our society. It discusses some of the difficulties in these sciences in the past and makes a number of recommendations aimed at meeting the requirements for a continuing development of scientific study of human behavior. This article is of importance, not only because it expresses the views of one of the most influential scientific groups in the federal government, but also because it

contains a number of important ideas and insights pertaining to the behavioral sciences.

5. MELTON, ARTHUR W. "The Science of Learning and the Technology of Educational Methods," *Harvard Educational Review*, 1959, 29, 96–106. This article gives the student a penetrating insight into the relationship between basic and applied research and points out the fundamental similarities. This article points out that basic and applied research lie on a single continuum with the main difference being the freedom of the investigator to manipulate the independent variable. Because many educators draw erroneous distinctions between basic and applied research, this article will do much to help the graduate student gain a better understanding of these terms.

6. STILES, LINDLEY J. "The Cooperative Research Program Contributions and Next Steps," *Phi Delta Kappan*, 1962, 43 (6), 231–36. Discusses ten investigations being carried out under support from the Cooperative Research Program, U.S. Office of Education, to illustrate the wide range of questions being studied, the kind of knowledge emerging, and the potential impact of the program on education. Outlines some further steps that should be taken to improve the quality of our schools.

7. VAN DALEN, DEOBOLD D. *Understanding Educational Research.* New York: McGraw-Hill Book Co., Inc., 1962. The first three chapters in this text provide the student with a further introduction to research as it relates to social progress. The scientific method is introduced and compared with other methods of acquiring knowledge.

CHAPTER 2

Locating a Problem and Formulating a Tentative Research Plan

SELECTING A PROBLEM

The selection of a research problem for the Master's thesis is a very important step for the graduate student. Often, in his eagerness to get started on his research work, the student seizes upon the first research idea that comes along. If the student commits himself to a research problem before giving his choice much careful study and thought, he is likely to lose many of the important advantages that he can receive from carrying out his research. The very process of seeking a research problem is an important step in the professional maturation of the student. At the outset of his search, the student usually sees no problems or from his first explorations into the research literature concludes that research has already solved all of the problems in education. His first ideas for research are often naïve and, upon checking, he finds that they have already been thoroughly explored. As the student continues his search, however, his insight into the literature becomes sufficiently broad so that he can see research problems in everything he reads. This point is not reached without a considerable amount of scholarly work in the research literature, but once achieved, the student has made a significant step in his education.

One reason that students seize upon the first idea they encounter is that very often they go too far in their graduate program before starting to search for a suitable research problem. The student has had years of experience in taking courses and thus the classwork involved in his graduate program is a familiar experience and one that he is reasonably confident he can complete successfully. In contrast, the research aspect of his graduate program is new and different and something that he is strongly tempted to put off. Every university has a lengthy list of "allbuts" among its graduate students—those who have completed *all* work for an advanced degree *but* the thesis or dissertation. A great many such students never obtain their advanced degrees. It is usually desirable for the graduate student to obtain some insight into research and to commence his search for a suitable problem as soon as possible after entering graduate work, even if he does not plan to carry out his project until he nears the end of his work.

In looking for a research problem, the student should bear in mind some of the possible outcomes of his research effort in preparing him for his profession. The review of the literature provides the student with an understanding of the work that has already taken place relating to his problem area and prepares him to carry out a project that will add to the facts and information that have been accumulated by previous research workers. Because of the extensive reading the student must do in his problem area, he will usually build up a sizable fund of knowledge. Thus, in order that this knowledge may be of significant future value, the student should attempt to develop a research problem in an area that is closely related to his professional goals. For example, a student who plans to teach elementary school will profit much more from a research project in some area such as child development or the learning of elementary school subjects than in an area involving secondary education, adolescent development, or school administration.

Another reason for the selection of a topic closely allied to the student's interest is that the research project gives him an opportunity to do significant independent work in his problem area that will better prepare him for his professional work and will incidentally make him a more desirable prospect for employment. Although most Master's theses do not produce research findings of major significance, many of them do produce worthwhile information that makes a small but definite contribution to the field of knowledge. Because there are many significant problems in education for which we require further knowledge, the student should resist the temptation to do research that is essentially trivial or that can contribute nothing to educational knowledge. Students often rationalize carrying out a trivial study by saying that the real purpose of the Master's thesis is to provide practice in independent work and the results cannot be expected to be of any scientific value. Generally, once a significant project has been identified, it requires no more time and effort to carry out than a trivial project or one that repeats work that has already been adequately done. The difference between the trivial project and the significant project is not the amount of work required to carry it out but the amount of thought that the student applies in the selection and definition of his problem.

Another factor that should be considered by the student in selecting his problem is that he will not only gain valuable knowledge and experience in the problem area he selects, but if he carries out a worthwhile piece of research, it will be possible for him to publish the results in a professional journal. If a student publishes an article based on his thesis, this publication adds significantly to his professional status.

Working on a team project

Twenty years ago there was almost no money available for the support of educational research. Most research projects were small-scale studies carried out by university faculty members, and in many instances the faculty member himself did all of the work of the research including such tasks as administering and scoring tests used in the project. Since that time, however, money available for educational research has increased tremendously. Now, most universities are receiving financial support for educational research in the form of contracts and grants from federal agencies and private foundations, and the projects being carried out are much wider in scope and often involve a team of research workers rather than a single scientist. The graduate student often has an opportunity to participate in one of these extensive research projects as a member of the team. As a rule, such projects are developed by faculty members, and portions of the project are given to graduate students to complete. Completion of the allotted portion of the project then constitutes the research for the Master's thesis or doctoral dissertation.

Working on team projects has both advantages and disadvantages for the graduate student. Perhaps the most important advantage for most students is that financial support is usually available for the student working on such a project. This support may cover as little as paying for test administration or providing the graduate student with needed materials or clerical assistance, but in many cases also involves a scholarship or research assistantship that is sufficient to meet the student's expenses while he is completing his graduate work. The team project also offers the graduate student an opportunity to participate in a bigger and more sophisticated study than would be the case if he were working independently. These studies usually involve more complex research design and more advanced statistical procedures, and the student thus learns more about these procedures than he would otherwise. The student also has a chance to learn something about the workings of team research, and because most major projects are now carried out by research teams, this insight will be valuable in his future work. He also can learn a great deal from other members of the research team. Each team member in the project brings a different background of training and experience to bear upon the research problem, and therefore the team can usually produce a more polished research effort than is the case with a single investigator.

Participation in a team research project also has disadvantages for the graduate student. Perhaps the most important of these is that he loses the opportunity to find and develop his own project. In the team research, the project is usually created and designed by the faculty member who is directing it. At worst, the graduate student involved in a team project is little more than a clerk who carries out various tasks involved in the research without fully understanding what he is doing or why he is doing it. Even in team projects where the student does significant independent work—and this is usually the case—he does not get firsthand experience in all aspects of developing and carrying out a research plan. Another disadvantage of taking part in a team project is that very often the problem being studied is not closely allied with the student's interest nor does it contribute as directly to his future professional work as would be the case if he designed and carried out an independent project.

Whether the student carries out a small independent project or participates in a larger team project, the experience he gains through independent scholarship and research is perhaps the most important aspect of his graduate program. A significant piece of work done at this level can add materially to the student's professional maturity, improve his employment opportunities, and start him on the path to recognition and high professional status.

Finding a tentative problem

The first step in locating a specific problem for the Master's thesis is for the student to identify the broad problem areas that are most closely related to his interests and professional goals. The student will find it a profitable experience to write down in as much detail as possible the type of work he wishes to do upon completion of his graduate training and the specific aspects of this work that most interest him. The process of writing down this information will help the student clarify his goals and interests. Very often he will find that these goals are somewhat less clear in his own mind than he may have supposed. Typical broad areas of interest that might be listed are: high school counseling, teaching art to children in the primary grades, social problems of adolescents, remedial reading in the elementary school, relationships between teachers and principals, and intramural programs in physical education.

After one or more such areas of professional interest have been identified, the student is ready to seek out specific problems in these areas that could form the basis for his thesis.[1]

A reading program

Perhaps the most satisfactory method of locating specific problems within the scope of the student's broad interests is through a systematic program of reading. Let us say, for example, that the student plans to teach in the elementary schools and is particularly interested in problems related to working with bright children at the elementary school level. His first step would be to check the library card catalog in order to locate current textbooks in this field. If he has selected a field in which no complete textbooks have been written, he can usually find chapters dealing with his interest area in some of the introductory textbooks used in general courses in education and psychology. He should select two or three textbooks from those available and review pertinent chapters in each. This gives the student some background of basic information about his area of interest and also gives him insight into various subtopics in the field, a knowledge of current practices, and a brief summary

---

[1] The student will find a checklist in Appendix A that will help him evaluate his research idea.

of recent research. This preliminary reading will help the student narrow his attention to one or more specific subtopics. For example, the student whose broad interest is in working with bright children in the elementary school may decide to develop a research problem dealing with the creative abilities of bright children or perhaps to study the social development of bright children in the primary grades. These topics are, of course, still much too broad for a specific research plan, but this narrowing permits the student to explore the selected areas in somewhat greater depth by reading additional material that deals specifically with the more narrow subject. He will also obtain valuable information by checking these topics in the *Encyclopedia of Educational Research* and the *Review of Educational Research*.

This additional reading will usually result in the student identifying a number of tentative research problems that are sufficiently limited and specific to form a possible basis for his research. In the example given, the student interested in studying the social development of bright children in the elementary schools might develop specific research topics such as the following: (1) relationships between intelligence and sociometric choice among sixth grade children, (2) development of interest in the opposite sex in elementary school children between grades four and six, (3) social activities of bright children as compared with those of average children in ten fifth grade classrooms, and (4) social adjustment problems of extremely bright children in the intermediate grades.

Other methods of identifying tentative research problems

If, after carrying out a reading program such as described, the student still has not located a problem that he wishes to study, a number of other approaches may be tried. One of these is to observe carefully the existing practices in his area of interest. For example, a student interested in human relations problems in the public schools may observe faculty meetings, committee activities, and other situations where such problems may arise. These observations will often provide the student with ideas and insights that can lead to a worthwhile research project. The student may observe that in faculty meetings some principals are much more effective than others in enlisting cooperation and developing enthusiasm among teachers.

This observation might lead the student to a comparison of the methods of principals who are successful with those who are unsuccessful in obtaining teacher cooperation.

Another valuable source of research ideas is found in the advanced courses that the student takes in his graduate program. In class discussions as well as textbooks, questions are often brought up for which we have no answers. Some textbooks even go so far as to list problems that require additional research. The brief reviews of research in specific educational fields that are published in *The Review of Educational Research* almost always list specific areas in which further study is needed.

The graduate student in education has the advantage of working in an area where he has gained much experience during his years as a student. Very often, the graduate student can recall problems that he encountered in his own educational experience and from one of these problems develop a worthwhile research plan. The newspapers and popular magazines are sometimes valuable sources of research ideas. These periodicals often report at length on educational problems that are currently considered of major importance and usually report the opinions of educators and other persons in public life concerning these problems. These reports usually contain assertions, suggestions, and criticisms, the merits of which can be checked by research. For example, public debate in recent years concerning the need for changes in the methods of teaching reading has stimulated many research projects aimed at trying and evaluating some of the ideas and proposals that have been put forth.

A final source of research ideas is replication of previous work. The student may sometimes make a valuable research contribution through repeating a significant research project that someone else has carried out. The student must be very cautious about selecting a project for replication, however, if he decides upon this approach. In considering replication of a research project, he should ask the following three questions before going ahead with his work:

1. Does the project to be repeated make a significant contribution?

2. Will replication clear up doubtful points in the original study?

3. Are there reasons to doubt the accuracy or validity of the results of the original study?

The usual basis for replication is that the research reports significant findings that are in conflict with the results of previous work or theory. In such a case, repeating of the project can be extremely valuable. Some persons concerned with graduate education advocate wide use of replications for Master's theses on the grounds that repeating a good study is a better experience for the student than carrying out an original study of poor quality.[2] As replications follow very closely (if not exactly) the procedures of the original study in order that findings between the studies may be directly compared, the graduate student doing a replication has little opportunity for original work. If he is fortunate enough to have a faculty advisor who requires him to think through the procedures of the original study independently and critically, this deficiency is partially overcome. Alas, few advisors can afford to devote enough time to the student to make the replication a creative experience. Thus, in doing a replication, the student loses much of the valuable experience and insight that can be gained only by discovering, planning, and carrying out his own project.

OUTLINE OF YOUR TENTATIVE RESEARCH PROJECT

After having identified a specific project that appears to be satisfactory, the student should outline a research plan in as much detail as is possible. The project is still tentative at this point because the student's review of the literature has yet to be carried out and this review almost always leads to some changes in the research plan. The tentative outline, however, can do much to clarify the student's thinking and will also give focus and direction to his review of the literature. The tentative research plan should contain the following sections: general introduction, statement of objectives or hypotheses, listing of possible tests or measures to be used in the study, description of the proposed sample, procedure to be used in carrying out the project, and plans for carrying out analysis of data to be collected.

The general introduction should identify the student's area of interest and discuss how the planned research project will contribute to future knowledge in this area. It should also state the student's research problem in general terms.

[2] E. Gloye, E. Craig, and F. Carp, "On Replication," *Psychological Reports*, III (1957), 299.

Objectives or hypotheses

Hypotheses reflect the research worker's guess as to the probable outcomes of his experiment. The principal advantage of a well-thought-out set of hypotheses is that they place clear and specific goals before the research worker and provide him with a basis for selecting samples and research procedures to meet these goals. Many studies carried out in education fail to provide usable knowledge largely because of the lack of specific and well-thought-out hypotheses.

Hypotheses can be stated in a number of different forms. The declarative form usually states a relationship between the variables that the experimenter expects will emerge. For example, the following hypothesis is stated in declarative form: "There will be a significant difference between the scores on a measure of inferiority feelings of low ability pupils in ability grouped classrooms as compared with low ability pupils in random grouped classrooms." Another form in which hypotheses may be stated is the null form. A null hypothesis states that no relationship exists between the variables concerned. For example, in null form, the aforementioned hypothesis could be stated "There will be no significant difference between the scores on a measure of inferiority feelings of low ability pupils in ability grouped classrooms and low ability pupils in random grouped classrooms." The null hypothesis does not necessarily reflect the scientist's expectations but is used principally because it is better fitted to our statistical techniques, many of which are aimed at measuring the likelihood that a difference found is truly greater than zero. Stated another way—the null hypothesis, in the form usually used in education, states that no difference exists, and the statistical tools test this hypothesis by determining the probability that whatever difference is found in the research subjects is a true difference that also is present in the population from which the research samples have been drawn. The student is sometimes confused by the null hypothesis because it appears to him senseless to hypothesize the exact opposite of his expectations. This is a disadvantage of the null form, because the researcher's expectations, based as they are upon considerable insight into other research and theory, often make the study clearer to the person reading the research report. Some researchers overcome this problem by using both a research hypothesis that reflects their expectations based on theory or previous research and a statistical hypothesis that is usually in the null form and is set up to make evaluations of the research hypothesis statistically more precise.[3]

Hypotheses may also be stated in question form. The aforementioned hypothesis in question form might read "Is there a significant difference between the scores on a measure of inferiority feelings of a group of low ability pupils in ability grouped classrooms as compared with low ability pupils in random grouped classrooms?" The question form is often the easiest for the inexperienced research worker to use because it states specifically the question that the research will attempt to answer. In writing the research results, the student may organize his report so as to answer the questions posed in the hypotheses.

In cases where the experimenter has strong reasons to expect a difference to occur in a specific direction, he may state the aforementioned hypothesis as follows: "Pupils of low ability in an ability grouped classroom will receive significantly higher scores on a measure of inferiority feelings than pupils of low ability in a random grouped classroom." This hypothesis states a specific expected direction for the finding, and should only be used when there is little or no possibility that the findings will yield a difference in the opposite direction. These two different forms of declarative hypotheses call for different statistical treatment; the first requiring what is called the two-tailed test of significance and the second requiring a one-tailed test. The two-tailed test assumes that the difference could occur in either direction—that is, either the ability-grouped or random-grouped children could have significantly greater inferiority feelings. The one-tailed test on the other hand assumes that, if a difference occurs, it can occur in only one direction. The student is referred to Chapter 5 for a discussion of one-tailed and two-tailed tests.

Preparing hypotheses

If hypotheses are to be useful, they must meet the following criteria:

1. *The experimenter should have definite reasons based on either*

[3] Quinn McNemar, *Psychological Statistics* (3rd ed.; New York: John Wiley & Sons, 1962).

theory or fact for considering the hypothesis worthy of testing. After completing the review of the literature, the research worker will have detailed knowledge of previous work relating to his research project. In many cases, he will find conflicting research results so that his hypothesis cannot agree with all available information. In general, however, his hypothesis should not conflict with the preponderence of previously reported information.

In addition to being in agreement with knowledge already established within the field, hypotheses should be formulated in accordance with theories in education or psychology. When this is possible, the results of the research will contribute to the testing of the theory in question. In many areas of education so little research has been done that reasonably conclusive information is not available. In this case, educational theory may form the only basis for developing the hypothesis. The student must always have some basis in theory and/or fact for his hypotheses. Occasionally, we find a study in education that has used the "shotgun approach." In this approach, the research worker tries all the measures he can, in the hope that something he tries will yield useful results. This approach should be avoided because it uses measures for which no hypotheses have been developed. Many dangers are involved in applying such research results to educational practice. When we do not have some understanding of why a particular relationship exists, there is always a danger that factors are operating that may be detrimental to the educational program.[4]

2. A hypothesis should be testable. Hypotheses are generally stated so as to indicate an expected difference or an expected relationship between the measures used in the research. The relationships or differences that are stated in the hypotheses should be such that measurement of the variables involved can be made and necessary statistical comparisons carried out in order to determine whether the hypothesis as stated is or is not supported by the research. The student should not state any hypothesis that he does not have reason to believe can be tested or evaluated by some objective means. For example, the author recalls a hypothesis prepared by a teacher who wished to evaluate a high school course in civics. It was "to determine whether this course will make the student a better adult citi-

[4] A discussion of the "shotgun approach" will be found in Chapter 12.

zen." Such an objective would be very difficult to test as it would require: (1) waiting until pupils taking the course had become adult citizens, (2) setting up criteria to determine how good a citizen each pupil had become, (3) evaluating each adult in terms of the criteria established, and then, perhaps most difficult of all, (4) determining what aspects of the adult citizenship of the former pupils could be directly attributed to the civics course. It may be seen from the above example that such hypotheses are much easier to state than they are to evaluate by objective means. The hypotheses of inexperienced research workers in education often fail to meet the criterion of testability because relationships are stated that cannot be measured using today's tests. A similar mistake often made by the graduate student is to state his hypotheses in terms that would require many years to test.

3. *The hypothesis should be as brief as possible consistent with clarity.* In stating hypotheses, the simplest and most concise statement of the relationship expected is generally the best. Brief, clear hypotheses are easier for the reader to understand and also easier for the research worker to test. The hypothesis "Is a student counseling program desirable and economically feasible at the elementary school level?" reflects the sort of fuzzy thinking often found in the work of graduate students in education. A program can be "desirable" or "undesirable" from a very large number of different viewpoints. No specific guides are given by the hypothesis as to what aspect of the guidance program is to be studied. The second part of the hypothesis dealing with the economic feasibility is determined largely by the individual school district's financial resources. In order to make the aforementioned hypothesis meaningful, it would be necessary to determine first the specific aspects of the elementary school counseling program that the research worker plans to study. Let us say he wished to provide counseling for three classes of sixth grade pupils and not provide counseling for three other classes in a large elementary school and then compare his two groups on such variables as the number of behavior problems reported by the classroom teachers, the incidence of truancy, and the pupils' stated attitudes toward school. In this case, perhaps three specific hypotheses would be the best approach. Stated in the null form these might be:

1. Sixth grade pupils receiving counseling will not be significantly different in the number of behavior problems reported by the teacher from sixth grade pupils not receiving counseling.

2. Sixth grade pupils receiving counseling will not be significantly different in incidence of truancy from sixth grade pupils not receiving counseling.

3. Sixth grade pupils receiving counseling will not be significantly different in their stated attitudes toward school from sixth grade pupils not receiving counseling.

It will be noted in the aforementioned example that the broad general hypothesis has been changed to three specific hypotheses, each stating a specific relationship between two variables. It is usually desirable for the student to state his hypothesis in this more precise form. The advantage of stating a hypothesis for each relationship to be studied is that this procedure is simple and clear. The testing of multiple hypotheses involving several relationships leads to some confusion because portions of the hypothesis may be supported by the research evidence and other portions may not be supported. In writing the results of the experiment, the graduate student will find it possible to present a more easily understood picture of his findings if each hypothesis has stated only a single relationship.

Objectives

In some research carried out in education, especially descriptive studies, it is more appropriate for the research worker to list objectives rather than hypotheses. A survey, for example, aimed at determining the extent of differences in the salaries of university professors in different fields of learning, could list a hypothesis such as "There will be no significant differences between the mean salaries of faculty members of comparable ranks in different areas of learning." In a study of this sort, however, it is probably more desirable merely to state the objectives of the study as follows: "The objectives of this research are: (1) to study the salaries paid professors of comparable academic ranks in different fields of learning and (2) if differences are found to exist, to attempt to identify the factors that appear to contribute to the observed differences."

Possible measures

The next step in preparing the tentative research plan is to make a listing of possible measures. Most graduate students have had courses in educational measurement that give them some background in the types of measures available and sources of information about educational measures. This topic is covered briefly in Chapter 4. Very often, the process of identifying possible measures will require the student to clarify further his objectives and eliminate hypotheses for which no measures are available or can be developed.

Research subjects

The student should then describe the subjects that will be required for his study. At this point, he should carefully consider the chance of obtaining the type and number of subjects that he needs. If his study is concerned with a type of individual who occurs only rarely in the general population, he must be particularly careful to determine whether subjects are available to do the work he has planned. For example, studies of highly gifted children, let us say those with IQ's above 160, are difficult to carry out unless the student has a very large population to draw from because children at this IQ level occur very rarely in the general population. The student's method of selecting his sample should also be considered and tentatively decided upon. Careless selection of cases is an error often found in educational studies.

Procedure

A tentative research design should be described. The student will become familiar with the various types of research designs in Chapters 8 to 13. The student should be sure that the design he plans to use will permit testing his hypotheses. Students often give little thought to the design of their projects until too late.

Analysis

A tentative plan for analysis of the research results is very important because this plan may have a considerable bearing upon the number of subjects needed, the measures and scoring procedures used, and the methods of recording the data. Yet, many students give no thought to analysis until the data are collected. Then, they find that no analysis procedures fit their data very well, and often they discover that the only procedures that can be used to salvage the study are complex ones that they must then learn to use.

In no area is lack of foresight so costly and disastrous as in doing research. Careful planning saves time in the long run and results in much better research. It is emphasized that the student should complete his course in research methods prior to starting the work on his research problem because much of the knowledge he needs to carry out even the first steps in his research problem requires an understanding of the overall field of educational research.

MISTAKES OFTEN MADE BY GRADUATE STUDENTS

1. Puts off selection of a problem until he has finished all or most of his courses.
2. Uncritically accepts the first research idea that he thinks of or that is suggested to him.
3. Prepares fuzzy or untestable hypotheses.
4. Fails to consider methods or analysis procedures in developing his tentative research plan.

ANNOTATED REFERENCES

1. CHAMBERS, M. M. "Selection, Definition, and Delimitation of a Doctoral Research Problem," *Phi Delta Kappan*, 1960, 42 (2), 71–73. Offers sound advice to the student starting graduate work and alerts him to many important questions concerning his research plans.

2. LAMKE, T. A. "A Primer in Research: Lesson I. Defining the Problem," *Phi Delta Kappan*, 1957, 38, 127–29. This paper emphasizes the importance of translating research ideas to specifics. The author points out that many persons fail in research because they are unable to translate a general research problem into a plan "based on specific operations at specific times in specific places with specific materials." The ideas expressed are particularly pertinent for beginners in educational research.

3. ROBERTSON, MALCOLM H. "The Student's Need for an Issue," *Journal of Psychology*, 1960, 49, 349–52. This article is concerned mainly with the desirability of the graduate student embracing a particular theory or school of thought and staying with it. Provides some useful concepts for the student starting in educational research.

4. VAN DALEN, D. B. "The Role of Hypotheses in Educational Research," *Educational Administration and Supervision,* 1956, 17, 457–60. This article emphasizes the importance of hypotheses in educational research. The functions of hypotheses as a means of stating assumptions, as a basis for explanations, and as an aid in determining the relevancy of facts are discussed. Hypotheses, if well constructed, also help the researcher in determining research design, in presenting the research conclusions, and in formulating new hypotheses.

5. The following articles contain many ideas and suggestions for research in various educational areas. They may be checked by the student who is seeking an idea for his thesis:

(*a*) AMERICAN ASSOCIATION OF COLLEGES FOR TEACHER EDUCATION. *Needed Research in Teacher Education.* Oneonta, N.Y., 1954.

(*b*) ANGELINO, H. R. "Needed Research," *Review of Educational Research,* 1960, 30, 86–88.

(*c*) BROWNELL, S. M. "Unsolved Problems in American Education," *School Review,* 1954, 62, 519–26.

(*d*) CASWELL, HOLLIS T. "Great Challenges for Education," *Teachers College Record,* 1957, 59, 69–75.

(*e*) COCKING, WALTER. "Need for School Plan Research," *School Executive,* 1956, 76, 7.

(*f*) GAGNE, ROBERT M. "Training Devices and Stimulators: Some Research Issues," *American Psychologist,* 1954, 9, 95–107.

(*g*) GRAY, W. S. "Needed Research in Reading," *Elementary English,* 1952, 29, 100–108.

(*h*) HALL, ROY M. "Research Needed in Education," *School Life,* 1960, 42, 6–8.

(*i*) HENDRICKSON, GORDON. "Some Needed Research in Elementary Education," *Elementary School Journal,* 1950, 51, 127–35.

(*j*) O'SHEA, H. E., *et al.* "Needed Research on Gifted Children," *American Psychologist,* 1954, 9, 77–78.

(*k*) PASSOW, H. "Curriculum Research: Status, Needs, and Prospects," *Educational Research Bulletin,* 1960, 39, 197–205, 224.

(*l*) ROESCH, W. "Selected Areas for Research in School District Reorganization," *Phi Delta Kappan,* 1959, 40, 328–30.

(*m*) SMITH, G. K. (ed.). *Current Issues in Higher Education.* Washington, D.C.: National Education Association, 1960.

(*n*) ZIRBES, L. "Needed Research in Education," *Educational Leadership,* 1952, 10, 129–31.

CHAPTER 3

Reviewing the Literature

INTRODUCTION

The review of the literature involves locating, reading, and evaluating reports of research as well as reports of casual observation and opinion that are related to the individual's planned research project. This review differs in a number of ways from the reading program often used to locate a tentative research project. First, such a review is much more extensive and thorough because it is aimed at obtaining a detailed knowledge of the topic being studied, while the reading program is aimed at obtaining enough general knowledge and insight to recognize problems in the selected area.

Secondary sources

The reading program generally uses textbooks, encyclopedias, and other secondary source materials. Secondary source materials in education include any publications written by an author who was not a direct observer or participant in the events described. For example, most of the material found in textbooks of Roman history are secondary source materials because the author has merely compiled the reports of others and rearranged these reports into a textbook. Most of the content of textbooks in education and psychology is also secondary source material. Let us suppose that an individual wishes to write a textbook on methods of teaching remedial reading. The prospective author does an exhaustive review of the literature in this field, noting the results of all experiments and weighing and evaluating these results in terms of various approaches to remedial reading instruction. Then, based on his interpretation of the various research reports and articles he has read, he prepares his textbook. If, in the textbook, the author also reports the results of experiments that he himself has carried out, then this portion of the textbook would be considered a primary source. That portion, however, that is based on his interpretations of the work of others would be classified as a secondary source. Secondary sources are useful because they combine knowledge from many primary sources into a single publication. A good textbook, for example, combines the work of many other persons and simplifies or eliminates much of the technical material that is not of interest to the general reader, thus providing a quick and relatively easy method of obtaining a good overall understanding of the field.

Primary sources

The primary source differs from the secondary source in that it is a direct description of an occurrence by an individual who actually observed or witnessed the occurrence. In educational research, this generally means the description of the study by the individual who carried it out.

The principal disadvantage to the research scholar of using secondary sources is that it is never possible to be sure what changes have been made by the secondary source author. In the process of simplifying and combining the results of many studies, the author of a textbook or other secondary source report may slant his interpretation of the primary source to agree with his own views and often leaves out material that the person reviewing the literature needs to know. Thus, a review of the literature should be based, whenever possible, upon primary sources. Most secondary sources such as textbooks contain a bibliography listing the sources from which the material was obtained so that the student can generally locate the primary source.

The importance of the review

The review of the literature is an important part of the scientific approach and is carried out in all areas of scientific research whether in the physical sciences, natural sciences, or social sciences. Such reviews are also the basis of most research in the humanities. In fields such as history, the review of literature not only gives the scholar an understanding of previous work that has been done, but the results of the review actually provide the data used in his research. Historical studies in education, which we will discuss in a later chapter, are based almost entirely upon a careful study of existing printed knowledge in the field.

The review of the literature in educational research provides you with the means of getting to the frontier in your particular field of knowledge. Until you have learned what others have done and what remains still to be done in your area, you cannot develop a research project that will contribute to furthering knowledge in your field. Thus, the literature in any field forms the foundation upon which all future work must be built. If you fail to build this foundation of knowledge provided by the review of the literature, your work is likely to be shallow and naïve, and will often duplicate work that has already been done better by someone else. Although the importance of a thorough review of the literature is obvious to everyone, this task is more frequently slighted than any other phase of research. The research worker is always tempted to let a sketchy review of the literature suffice so that he can get started sooner on his own research project. The student, however, should make every effort to complete a thorough review before starting his research because the insights and knowledge gained by the review almost inevitably lead to a better designed project and greatly improve the chances of obtaining important and significant results. Often the insights gained through the review will save the research worker as much time in conducting his project as the review itself required.

PURPOSES OF THE REVIEW

Although the general purpose of the review is to help the research worker develop a thorough understanding and insight into previous work and the trends that have emerged, the review can also help in reaching a number of important specific goals.

Delimiting the research problem

The review of the literature can help in limiting the individual's research problem and in defining it better. Many studies attempted by graduate students are doomed to failure before the student starts because of his failure to limit his problem to an area small enough and sufficiently specific for him to work with satisfactorily. It is far better in research to select a limited problem and treat it well than to attempt the study of a broad general problem and do it poorly. Many graduate students also commit themselves to a research problem before they have thought it out adequately. A fuzzy or poorly defined problem can sometimes result in the student collecting data and then learning that his data cannot be applied to the problem he wishes to attack. Before the student starts his review of the literature, he should do sufficient background reading from secondary sources to permit a tentative outline of his research problem. The review of the literature will give the student the knowledge he needs to convert his tentative research problem to a detailed and concise plan of action.

Seeking new approaches

In the process of reviewing the literature, the student should not only learn what work has been done but should also be alert to research possibilities that have been overlooked. The unique experience and background of an individual may make it possible for him to see a facet of the problem that other research workers have not seen. Such new viewpoints are likely to occur most frequently in areas where little research has been done, but even in well researched areas, someone occasionally thinks of an approach that is unique and creative. A good example is Thompson's study of administration of the *Thematic Apperception Test* (*T.A.T.*) to Negro subjects.[1] Prior to this study, many clinicians were administering the standard *T.A.T.* cards to clients regardless of racial background. The persons pictured on the standard *T.A.T.* cards were white, and Thompson saw that the use of these cards with Negro subjects might well lead to different responses because of racial differences. In his research, he developed a comparable set of cards in which Negroes were substituted for the whites in the *T.A.T.* pictures and found that his hypothesis was correct. Although hundreds of research projects had been carried out prior to Thompson's work using the *T.A.T.*, his special insight led to a unique and valuable contribution to our knowledge of this important instrument.

Avoiding sterile approaches

In doing the review of literature, the student should also be on the lookout for research approaches in his area that have proved to be sterile. It is not uncommon in doing a review of the literature to encounter several very similar studies done over a period of years, all of which employ approximately the same approach and all of

---

[1] C. E. Thompson, "The Thompson Modification of the Thematic Apperception Test," *Rorschach Research Exchange and Journal of Projective Techniques,* XIII (1949), 469–78.

which fail to produce significant results. One or two repetitions of an unproductive approach can be justified on the grounds that these confirm the previous finding that the area is unproductive. Repetitions beyond this, however, serve no useful purpose and generally suggest that the persons repeating the study have not done an adequate review of the literature. In an excellent review of the literature on instructor effectiveness, Morsh and Wilder list eleven studies carried out between 1934 and 1948 in which an attempt was made to relate personality as measured by the Bernreuter Personality Inventory to instructor effectiveness.[2] None of these studies produced correlations sufficiently high to be of any value in predicting instructor effectiveness. In all likelihood, additional studies following the same futile approach have been carried out since 1952, the date at which Morsh's review terminated.

Insight into methods

The review of the literature can also give the student a great deal of insight into the methods, measures, subjects, and approaches used by other research workers and can thus lead to significant improvement of his design. A mistake made by many graduate students when reading research reports is to give little attention to anything but the results reported. Very often, a study that has little to contribute by way of results can help the student a great deal by suggesting methods and useful approaches. For example, discussion of the various measures used can help the student decide which of these measures would be best suited for his own research. A sampling problem discussed by one research worker can help other research workers in the field avoid the same difficulties. In a study relating the degree of pupil homogeneity in the classroom to achievement, Goldberg *et al.* set up fifteen different classroom patterns, each having a different level of homogeneity and a different range of ability.[3] Pattern 1, which was to include classes in which all pupils were above 130 IQ, appeared the easiest to obtain because the

---

[2] Joseph E. Morsh and Elinore W. Wilder, "Identifying the Effective Instructor: A Review of the Quantitative Studies, 1900–1952," *AFPTRC Research Bulletin TR-54-44* (Lackland Air Force Base, Tex.: October, 1954).

[3] M. L. Goldberg, Joseph Justman, A. H. Passow, and Gerald Hage, *The Effects of Ability Grouping* (New York: Teachers College, Columbia University, Horace-Mann-Lincoln Institute, Interim Report, 1961).

school system had already set up classes for children at this level. Thus, the research workers organized classes that were appropriate for other patterns but assumed that sufficient classes of Pattern 1 would be available. On checking, however, it was found that the IQ limit had not been adhered to by schools in setting up these classes and that only one of the ten thought to be available actually met the requirements for Pattern 1. Thus, in a research project involving 2,219 children, only twenty-nine were included in one of the most important groups to be studied. Goldberg's study, although making many valuable contributions to our knowledge of ability grouping, would have been much stronger if the research workers had had available a larger number of Pattern 1 classes. If the student looks carefully at such methodological problems, he can learn much that will help him improve his own research plan.

Recommendations for further research

The authors of research articles often include specific suggestions and recommendations for persons planning further research in the field. These suggestions should be considered very carefully because they represent the insights gained by the research worker after experience in the problem area. Specific research topics are often suggested that are particularly useful in helping the student delimit his research problem.

Sampling current opinions

Although research reports make up the most important source of information that the student covers in his review, he should also study newspaper accounts, nontechnical articles, and opinion articles related to his topic. Such articles occasionally contain unique ideas that can be tested through research and also help the research worker gain insight into those aspects of the problem area that are considered critical or controversial by educators. For example, a study of opinion articles in the field of ability grouping shows that most of the disputes between educators in this field center around the possible effects of ability grouping on the child's *personality* and *social development*. On the other hand, nearly all of the research reported in the field of ability grouping is concerned with the *achievement* of children in the ability grouped situation. These studies contribute valuable knowledge but have had little effect upon the judgments of most educators. Only research that presents objective data concerning the variables that educators consider critical is likely to have any effect upon their decisions concerning whether or not they should establish or support an ability grouping program.

SCOPE OF THE REVIEW

Perhaps the greatest frustration encountered by the graduate student in carrying out his first review of the literature centers around his attempt to determine what he should read and what he should not read. Unfortunately, there are no pat formulas that can be given the student to help him make this decision. Obviously the student should read all studies that are closely related to his research problem. The decisions that cause him difficulty involve those studies that are only partially related to his research problem or perhaps only related to one phase of the problem.

Relatively new research areas usually lack an organized body of secondary source information to provide general background and thus require a fairly broad review in which even those studies that are only peripheral to the main area should be read in order to give the student the foundation of knowledge he requires. For example, let us say the student wishes to do research on the use of teaching machines in the training of mentally retarded children. Because widespread interest in teaching machines is fairly new in education, the student should probably read most of the studies that have been done in this field, even if they are not closely related to his topic. For example, a study on the use of teaching machines for in-service training of business executives is quite remote from the student's problem but should probably be scanned in order to check for methods, programming techniques, and so forth that could be applied to his research. The student might also wish to review methods of teaching mentally retarded children other than those employing teaching machines. In such new research areas, the student often finds no more than two or three studies that are reasonably close to his topic—in this example studies that involve the use of teaching machines in the training of mentally retarded individuals.

In more thoroughly explored areas where research activity has extended over a longer period of time and much of the early work is covered in secondary sources such as textbooks, the student can usually develop adequate insight into the field by reading only those studies that are reasonably close to his research topic. In these more thoroughly explored areas, much greater depth is available and the student can cover a narrower topic range to a greater depth. In new areas little depth is available, and a broad review is therefore necessary to get sufficient insight. A study in a more thoroughly explored area might be concerned with the effectiveness of high school counseling in bringing about certain personality changes as measured by the *Thematic Apperception Test*. In this area, the student would find some studies that relate personality changes to counseling and involve the use of various personality instruments. These should all be covered. In addition, some studies using the *T.A.T.* in other related research areas should be read. For example, if studies were available involving changes in personality during psychotherapy, these studies should be read. As the *T.A.T.* is a well-established instrument that has been used in a great many research projects, it would not be advisable for the student to attempt to read all research involving the use of this instrument. A total of seventy articles dealing with the *T.A.T.* are abstracted in the 1959 *Psychological Abstracts* alone. Most of these studies would be of little value to the student carrying out the research described previously. Considerable background reading on the *T.A.T.* in secondary sources, however, would be desirable.

INITIAL STEPS IN REVIEWING THE LITERATURE

Although the review of the literature is a preliminary step in all scientific research, the methods of conducting the review differ to some extent from field to field. The method that will be described in detail in this section is one that works well in the field of education. This method has been developed over a number of years, and the student is advised to follow it closely until he has built up sufficient experience to make intelligent adaptations.

Step one—listing key words

In most sciences, basic reference books are available that cover most material published in the science in question. In education, the most useful source is *Education Index*.* *Education Index*, along with

* See annotated references for complete bibliographic data.

the indexes and abstracts published in other sciences, is organized by subject. It is necessary, therefore, that the research worker identify key words related to his topic so that he may look up these key words in the index to locate sources of information related to his topic. For example, let us say that you wish to do a study of the changes in racial attitudes that have occurred in three recently desegregated public schools. Your first step in reviewing the literature would be to make a list of key words that relate to this study. Your first list might include the following: attitudes, civil rights, desegregation, integration, prejudice, race relations, racial prejudice, segregation, and tolerance. This preliminary list of key words will almost certainly be incomplete and will be changed when the actual search of *Education Index* begins. It does, however, provide a starting point, and as many possible key words as the student can think of should be listed in order to reduce the likelihood of important studies being overlooked.

Step two—checking preliminary sources

We will define *preliminary sources* as references, such as indexes and abstracts, which help us find research articles and other primary sources of information. Until recently, *Education Index* was both an author and subject index—that is, each article was listed once under its subject and again under the name of the author. In using *Education Index*, the subject index is generally the most useful, and recent issues have dropped the author entries. *Education Index* is published monthly (except in July and August). It lists only the bibliographical data concerning each article or book references. The year for *Education Index* runs from July to the following June. For the current year, each of the monthly issues must be searched; but these monthly issues are combined quarterly, then into a yearly volume for the immediate past year, and subsequently into volumes containing two or three years.

Most reviews of the literature in education cover a minimum of ten years. A systematic method of searching *Education Index* for the period of the review should be developed and followed. The author has found that preparing a checklist of key words, such as is shown in Figure 1, is an effective method for insuring a systematic search. After this checklist has been prepared, the student may start with

Key words	Education Index volume							
	10/62	7/62	7/61 to 6/62	Vol. 12	Vol. 11	Vol. 10	Vol. 9	Vol. 8
attitudes (change of)	✓*	✓						
Civil rights	N†	N						
desegregation								
integration								
prejudice	✓	✓						
race attitudes	✓	✓						
race relations	✓	✓						
race social prejudice	✓	✓						
segregation	✓	✓						
school integration								
tolerance								
Negroes in U.S., segregation	✓	N						
Public schools, desegregation	✓	✓						

FIG. 1. Sample of checklist used in searching the *Education Index*.

* Indicated volume checked and bibliography cards made.
† Indicated volume contained no usable references under the key word.

the most recent issue of the *Education Index* and look up each of his key words. In looking up the key words, he should be alert for other possible key words that may be added to his list to provide more complete coverage.

To check each of these key words in a volume of *Education Index,* the student looks up the word and reads the titles of articles listed under the word. If titles are found that indicate the article deals with some phase of the student's topic, he copies the bibliographical data (author, title, and source of publication) onto a 3×5-inch card. A separate card should be used for each article or reference found. It is often difficult to judge the contents of an article from the title, and many of the articles for which a student prepares bibliography cards will later be found to contain nothing pertinent to the topic being studied. In deciding whether to prepare a bibliography card and check a particular article, the student should generally follow the rule that it is better to check an article that proves of no use than to overlook an article that may be important. Thus, whenever the student is in doubt, he should prepare a bibliography card and check the article in question. After the student checks the title under a key word, he should place a check on his checklist. If, after checking several volumes of the *Education Index,* nothing pertinent to the student's topic has been found under a given key word, this key word can be dropped and not checked in the remaining volumes.

In the aforementioned example, after checking several volumes of *Education Index,* it would be found that some of the original key words are satisfactory and some are unproductive and could be eliminated; and some new ones would be discovered and added. "Attitudes" would become "attitudes, change of"; "Desegregation" would be changed to "public schools, desegregation"; and "tolerance" would be dropped because no usable references are found. "Integration" and "school integration" would be dropped because they are not listed at all. "Civil rights" is listed but was found to contain no usable references. "Racial prejudice" would be changed to "race prejudice." New key words added would include: "race attitudes," "Negroes in the United States—segregation," and "race prejudice." It will be noted that the revised list of key words is given in Figure 1.

Psychological abstracts

Another valuable preliminary source for research workers in education is *Psychological Abstracts*.* This reference is published bimonthly by the American Psychological Association and contains abstracts of articles appearing in over five hundred journals in psychology and related areas. Every issue of *Psychological Abstracts* has twelve sections, each covering a different area of psychology. The section on developmental psychology, which includes abstracts on child development and adolescence, and the section on educational psychology, which includes abstracts in areas such as school learning, interest, attitudes and habits, special education, educational guidance, educational measurement, and educational staff personnel are most pertinent to the research worker in education. The coverage of these areas of psychology is very thorough. For example, many journals such as *Educational Administration and Supervision, Elementary School Journal,* and *Journal of Experimental Education,* which are predominantly educational journals, are covered in *Psychological Abstracts*. In searching *Psychological Abstracts,* the same key words can be used that you have developed in your search of *Education Index*. Sometimes an additional key word or two will have to be added because of the differences in indexing systems in the two periodicals.

The key word "bibliographies" should always be looked up in *Psychological Abstracts*. Under this heading, the student will find a listing of bibliographies on a wide variety of subjects. If he can locate a recent bibliography in his area of interest, it will, of course, be of great help to him in carrying out his review of the literature. We will discuss other sources of bibliographies later in this chapter. The December number of *Psychological Abstracts* contains both an author index and subject index of all articles abstracted in the previous five numbers for the year. In using *Psychological Abstracts,* the student turns first to this index number to check his key words. The index number of *Psychological Abstracts* does not contain complete bibliographical data such as are found in *Education Index,* but lists only the subject of the article in the briefest possible terms —usually a word or two. After the subject, the student will find one

* See annotated references for complete bibliographic data.

Achievement (*See also* Academic achievement; Failure)
   academic (*See* Academic achieve-
    ment)
   Anxiety Test, 5357
   in chemistry, age &, 5180
   & CMAS scores, 4722
   & ego-ideal, 2300(a)
   factors in, in high school & college,
    3980
   vs. failure, & children's behavior, 660
   fear of failure vs. hope of success,
    6477
   in high school, & temperament, 2005
   mathematical, & attitudes, 2733(a)
   measured by daydream question-
    naire, 6387
   in Naval Air Training, factor anal-
    ysis of tests of, 5393
   & neuroticism, 6477
   occupational, of farm reared youth
    in city, 6482
   physiological response, 3549
   prediction of USAF Cadet, 7204
   productive, students, 7024
   of psychotics, 5264
   reliability of Test of Insight meas-
    ure of, 3431
   self-scoring projective measurement
    of, 4908
   & social class, 4865
    & intelligence, 779
   social expectancy &, 1994
   under, correction of popular views
    of, 7076
   vocational courses, DAT &, 2775
Achievement/lack of (*See* Failure)
Achievement need (*See also* Aspiration
level; Expectation; Motivation)
   Adlerian approach to, 4969
   in computing experiment, 3504
   individual differences, 6471

   in Maori, 2065
   & parental attitudes, 2264(a)
   submarine school performance &,
    800
   in thematic apperception, 2228(a)
Achievement test, mentally retarded on,
   with anxiety, 1055
   psychology, specificity, 3984
   textbook, 2801
Achromatopsia (*See* Color blindness)
Acid reflexes, in dog, 578
ACOE (Automatic Check-Out Equipment), 7217
Acoustic reflex, protective effect of, 5662
Acquiescence, & F-Scale, 4986
   influence on CPI, 2218
   as a response tendency, & person-
    ality test scores, 6420
   & r of conformity and F-Scale, 2093
   in test responses, & authoritarianism,
    2305
    & parental attitudes, 2305
Acquired drive, shock intensity, 1951(a)
   & acquisition trials, 4659
ACTH (*See* Corticotropin)
Acting out (*See also* Play)
   of disturbed adolescents, 6892
Action, administrative, determining effective, 4121
Activation, nonspecific stimulation as,
   learning &, 4443
Activation theory of emotion (*See* Emotion)
Activity, & age, in rats, 3186
   chair stabilometer for measuring,
    3075
   & coenzymes, in mice, 1792
   deprivation, & activity incentive,
    6053
   & external stimulation in the rat,
    1911
   & food deprivation, in rats, 3199

FIG. 2. Sample from the subject index of *Psychological Abstracts*.*

* Taken from *Psychological Abstracts*, XXXV, No. 6 (1961), 781. Reprinted by permission of the American Psychological Assoc.

or more numbers. These numbers refer to the numbers of abstracts in the first five issues. Figure 2 shows a sample of an index number. The student may then check these numbers to obtain the bibliographical data for articles that may be appropriate to his review of the literature. For example in the index number for December, 1959, under "prejudice" we find "and desegregation, psychological aspects, 6032." As this article seems pertinent to our study, we look up abstract number 6032, which is in the June, 1959, issue. Under this number we find the reference:

Lief, Harold I., and Stevenson, Ian P. (Tulane U. School Medicine) "Psychological aspects of prejudice with special reference to desegregation." *Amer. J. Psychiat.*, 1958, 114, 816–823.

Following the bibliographical data is a brief abstract of the article. These brief abstracts contained in *Psychological Abstracts* are very useful to the research worker because they help him to make a decision as to whether or not a given article actually pertains to his problem. This decision is much easier to make on the basis of an abstract than solely on the basis of the bibliographical data as is found in *Education Index*. After reading the abstract, the research worker decides whether the article is pertinent and if it is, he records the bibliographical data on a 3 × 5-inch bibliography card so that he may read the entire article later. When the research is on a topic that is exclusively education, such as the school lunch program, little is to be gained by checking *Psychological Abstracts*. On the other hand, in areas relating to educational psychology, it is usually desirable to check both *Psychological Abstracts* and *Education Index* in order to be assured of getting a full coverage of the field. When both of these preliminary sources are to be checked, the student should check *Psychological Abstracts* first because of the advantage of an abstract over bibliographical data only. A checklist such as is shown in Figure 1 can also be used in searching *Psychological Abstracts*.

A number of other publications are available, which, while less important than *Education Index* or *Psychological Abstracts,* can still be very valuable in locating research articles in the student's field of interest. Some of these sources are valuable because of the bibliographies they contain, some because they help locate information related to education that has not been published in professional journals. We will discuss a few of the most useful of these sources in the following pages. Many such sources that have only limited application to education or that largely duplicate other references will not be covered. The student should seek the help of the reference librarian in his college library if he wishes to learn more about reference materials.

Perhaps the most useful educational source after *Education Index* is the *Review of Educational Research,** which is published five times a year by the American Educational Research Association. Each number of the *Review of Educational Research* covers an important educational topic and usually contains several articles dealing with different phases of the topic covered. Each of these articles in turn contains an extensive bibliography that a research worker can check for references pertinent to his project. At present, the *Review of Educational Research* summarizes the research literature in twenty-three major topics. Most of these topics are covered every three years, and the majority of the research discussed will have been done since the previous review of the topic. Some topics are covered only once every six years, and a few topics have been treated at irregular intervals. Among the topics covered by *Review of Educational Research* are such areas as: adult education, curriculum planning and development, educational and psychological testing, and guidance and counseling. In order to use the *Review of Educational Research* as a preliminary source, the student must check the topic list that can be found on the back inside cover to determine when reviews pertinent to his subject have been published. He should then obtain these issues and read the articles that provide a very brief discussion and evaluation of the research. Finally, he should check carefully the bibliographies contained in each issue against the bibliography cards he has previously prepared from his search of *Education Index* and/or *Psychological Abstracts* and make up cards for any pertinent sources he has overlooked.

The *Encyclopedia of Educational Research* (3rd edition)* is primarily of value as a secondary source that gives the student a brief coverage of the status of research in most educational topics. Most of the articles in the *Encyclopedia,* however, have extensive lists of references that the student may check while doing his review of the literature. Occasionally articles will be found in these reference lists that the student has overlooked in his previous search.

* See annotated references for complete bibliographic data.

PRELIMINARY SOURCES FOR BIBLIOGRAPHIES

The research worker's review of the literature is greatly simplified if someone else has previously prepared a bibliography on his research topic. In addition to those sources already mentioned, the following sources of bibliographies should be checked:

Bibliographic Index, New York: H. W. Wilson Co. (1938 to date). A subject index that lists bibliographical material in about 1,500 periodicals. The format is very similar to the *Education Index* except that only references containing a bibliography are listed. If the bibliography is annotated, the abbreviation "annot" is given.

The School Review, Chicago: Univ. of Chicago Press (1893 to date). Each issue of this quarterly journal contains a review of some educational topic. Listings of new books, pamphlets, and annual reports on secondary education, and publications for high school teachers and students are also included in each issue.

The Elementary School Journal, Chicago: Univ. of Chicago Press (1900 to date). This journal is published monthly October through May. Each issue contains an annotated list of selected reference on some topic in elementary education. The student whose research topic relates to some aspect of elementary education should check this section of the *Elementary School Journal* as an early step in his review of the literature. Each issue also contains a list of new books, pamphlets, and so forth relating to elementary education.

PRELIMINARY SOURCES COVERING THESES AND DISSERTATIONS

Because many theses and dissertations are never published, a check of the following sources is necessary for a thorough coverage of the research literature:

Dissertation Abstracts, Ann Arbor, Mich.: University Microfilms, Inc. (1955 to date). A monthly compilation of abstracts of doctoral dissertations submitted by over one hundred cooperating institutions. Abstracts in education vary in length up to a full page and usually give a good coverage of the essentials of the dissertation. Any dissertation covered in *Dissertation Abstracts* may be purchased from University Microfilms on either microfilm or Xerox, the price being given at the end of the abstract.

Research Studies in Education, Bloomington, Ind.: Phi Delta Kappa (1953 to date). A yearly compilation of doctoral dissertations completed and underway in education. Contains a subject index of dissertations underway, a subject index of dissertations completed, an author index, and a bibliography on research methods. The coverage of dissertations underway is especially useful in helping the student locate current work and avoid duplicating research someone else is doing. The research methods bibliography gives a good coverage of current trends and problems in education, a listing of library guides, bibliographies, and summaries, as well as many useful references dealing with the collection, analysis, and interpretation of research data. *Dissertation Abstracts* is a more useful source for completed dissertations because of the abstract provided.

Master's Theses in Education, H. M. Silvey (ed.), Cedar Falls, Iowa: Recent Publication (1952 to date). Master's theses are listed under about forty major educational topics covered in the table of contents such as Achievement and Progress, Adult Education, Delinquency, and Higher Education. Each volume also contains an author index, a subject index, and an institutional index where theses written at a given institution may be located.

PRELIMINARY SOURCES COVERING POPULAR PERIODICALS AND NEWSPAPERS

Education is a topic of wide general interest, and as a result much is written about it in popular magazines and newspapers. If your research topic is in an area that has received public attention, the following sources should be checked:

Reader's Guide to Periodical Literature, New York: H. W. Wilson Co. (1900 to date). An author and subject index similar in format to *Education Index* but covering general and nontechnical periodicals published in the United States. The magazines indexed change from time to time because the aim is to maintain a good subject balance and overlook no major field rather than provide exhaustive coverage. At present, about 130 magazines are being indexed. *Reader's Guide* is an excellent source for studying the layman's views on education. Because many of the magazines covered have wide circulation, their influence upon public opinion can be significant.

International Index, New York: H. W. Wilson Co. (1907 to date).

An author and subject index that covers about 170 periodicals in the social sciences and humanities, including many foreign publications. A good source of views and reports of other social scientists concerning education. There is very little overlapping between the journals covered in *International Index* and *Education Index*.

The New York Times Index, New York: The New York Times Co. (1913 to date). Provides an index of news printed in the *New York Times*. This is primarily a subject index but is extensively cross-referenced and also references by the names of persons covered in news stories. Brief summaries of most articles are given along with date, page, and column of the issue where the story may be found. This index is an excellent source of current information about education and permits the studying of the development of educational issues and events that could not be traced as accurately through any other source. It is recommended that the student look up some current topic that interests him, such as federal aid to education, school building programs, or racial integration in order to get some insight into the value of this index as a source of educational information.

Facts on File, New York: Facts on File, Inc. (1941 to date). A weekly digest of world news that is indexed yearly and published as a yearbook. Material from newspapers, magazines, broadcasts, government reports, and so forth are processed daily to produce the weekly digest. Material is indexed by subject and names of persons appearing in the news. Date of the event, page, and location on page in the digest section of the yearbook are given. Because the yearly index and weekly digests are bound together in one volume, *Facts on File* permits the student to locate and read summaries of important educational news stories without going to another source. It is much easier to use, but coverage is less thorough than *The New York Times Index.*

THE BIBLIOGRAPHY CARD

During his search of the preliminary sources, the student should prepare a bibliography card for each book or article that he believes might contain material pertinent to his review. Although the bibliographical data for a publication is always about the same, these data can be recorded in many different formats. Before starting his review of the literature, the graduate student should check the rules in effect at his college concerning acceptable format for the bibliography section of the thesis or dissertation. Some schools permit the student to use any format that is generally acceptable in his field of study. Other schools have a specific format that must be followed by all graduate students. If your school permits the use of any form that is acceptable in your field, the easiest approach will be for you to use the format of the preliminary source from which you expect to obtain most of your references. *Education Index* is the most productive source for most students working in education, and therefore its format is advantageous to use when permitted. Most of your references will come from the subject index of the *Education Index,* and articles listed by subject give the title of the book or article before the author's name. For your bibliography card, the author's name (last name first), should be listed before the title. This change is necessary because it is much more convenient for you to maintain your note-card file in alphabetical order by author, and the bibliography as prepared for your thesis normally will be listed in this order. Figure 3.*a*. shows a bibliography card in the *Education Index* format. If this format is chosen, the bibliographic data from articles found

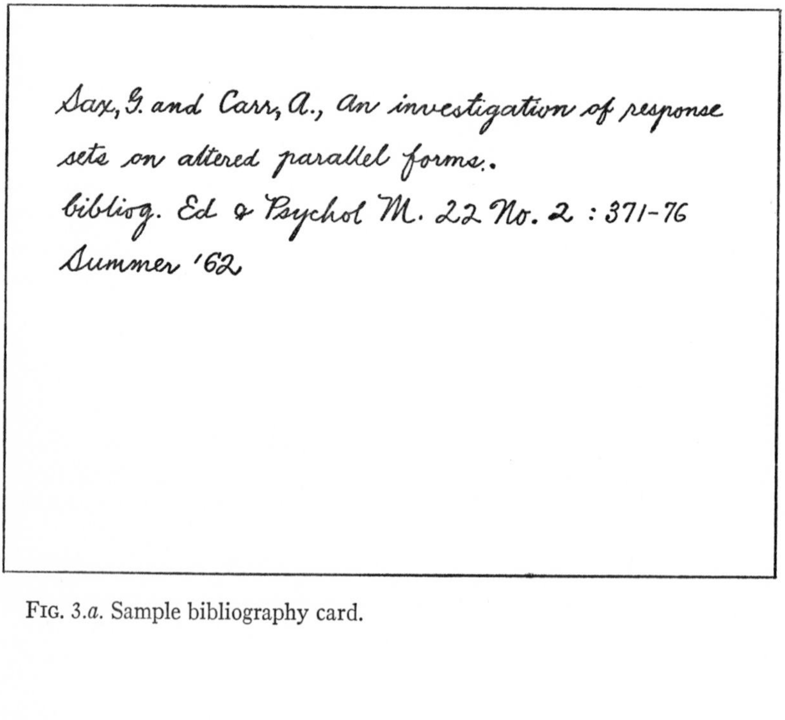
Sax, G. and Carr, A., an investigation of response sets on altered parallel forms.
bibliog. Ed & Psychol M. 22 No. 2 : 371-76
Summer '62

FIG. 3.*a*. Sample bibliography card.

in other sources such as *Psychological Abstracts* should be converted to the *Education Index* format. Let us compare bibliographical data for an article as it appears in *Education Index* and *Psychological Abstracts*:

Education Index
Walters, J. and Fisher, C., Changes in the attitudes of young women toward child guidance over a two-year period. bibliog *J Ed Res* 52: 115–18 N'58

Psychological Abstracts
Walters, James & Fisher, Clara (Florida State U.) Changes in the attitudes of young women toward child guidance over a two-year period. *J. educ. Res.,* 1958, 52, 115–118.

Although these forms are similar, it will be noted that the *Journal of Educational Research* is abbreviated differently in the two forms, the volume number, pages, and year are given in different order; the *Education Index* gives month of publication and indicates that the article contains a bibliography, while the *Psychological Abstracts* form does not. Students reviewing the literature in one of the areas of educational psychology will normally obtain the majority of their references from *Psychological Abstracts,* and, in this case, the *Psychological Abstracts* format may be preferred.

If your college has specified a format for the thesis bibliography that differs from the one used by your preliminary sources, the easiest procedure to follow is to copy the bibliographic data from the preliminary sources in whatever form it is found. Then, when checking the reference in order to determine whether it contains anything pertinent to your review of the literature, you may recopy the bibliographic data in the required school format at the bottom of your bibliography card. You need copy this only for studies that contain pertinent information. Usually, only one out of every three or four references for which the student has prepared bibliography cards will contain material that he wishes to use in his review of the literature.

In preparing bibliography cards, accuracy is extremely important. A mistake made in copying the bibliographic data can often cause the student a great deal of extra work. For example, if the student incorrectly copies the name of the journal, date, volume number, or pages he will fail to find the article when he checks out the source. On failing to find the article, he is faced with the problem of trying to determine which portion of his bibliographic material is incorrect. Unless the student takes special care, it is easy to make any of the above mistakes. After such a mistake has been made, the student must usually go back to the preliminary sources in order to find his mistake. As he may well have covered a number of preliminary sources, this search can take much longer than it would have taken to use more care initially. Even if the student makes an error in some portion of the bibliographic data that will not interfere with his finding the material, such as misspelling the author's name, this mistake is still serious because it will probably be repeated in his thesis. Nothing reflects more unfavorably upon the scholarship of the research worker than frequent errors in his bibliographic data.

USING THE LIBRARY

Now that you have completed your search of the preliminary sources in your field and have assembled a set of bibliography cards, it is time to start checking these references in the library. The majority of your references will probably be in professional journals because this is the principal outlet for primary source research articles.

Checking out references

In using the library to obtain these materials, a great deal of time may be wasted. The student, therefore, is advised to obtain a stack permit and examine the layout of the library to determine what method of obtaining his materials will require the least amount of time. In a library where periodicals in a given field are all shelved in a central location and where study space is available in the stacks, it is usually desirable for the student to work in the stacks. Some libraries, however, do not permit students to enter the stacks and some, because of space limitations, have journals shelved in such a way that they are difficult to find and cannot be used in the immediate area in which they are shelved. In this case, the student can usually save time by making out call slips for about ten periodicals. While waiting for the library clerk to return with these periodicals, the student can make out call slips for his next ten references. The clerk can then look for the second ten references while the student is scanning and making notes on whatever he has received from the first ten call slips. Because a certain percentage of the references that the student wants will be lost, checked out, or in the bindery, it is always advisable to submit call slips for ten or more at a time. Spending a few minutes to determine the most efficient way of obtaining references in his college library will, in the long run, save the student a great deal of time and effort.

Obtaining materials not locally available

The student will almost certainly find that some of the materials he wishes to examine are not available in his college library. There are several ways to obtain these materials, and the student should not give up merely because a source is not available locally. With respect to articles published in professional journals, the quickest and easiest way to obtain those not locally available is to write directly to the author and ask for a reprint of the article. Authors usually receive reprints of their articles and usually are willing to send a reprint to anyone requesting it. Reprints thus received are the student's personal property and should be kept in his file so that he may recheck the article if necessary. The main problem encountered by students in writing for reprints is obtaining the address of the author. If the source has been located in *Psychological Abstracts,* the address is usually given. This information, however, is not available in *Education Index.* A great many authors, however, may be located by checking the various professional directories that are available such as *Who's Who In American Education, American Psychological Association Directory,* and *American Educational Research Association Directory of Members.* The reference librarian can usually suggest other directories if an individual is not listed in any of the aforementioned.

If the student is unable to obtain a reprint of the article from the uthor, the next step is to see if the needed journal is available in ther libraries in the student's vicinity. In large population centers, here several colleges or universities are located within a small geographical area, the student can usually find the materials he needs at one of the libraries available. In areas where other libraries are not locally available, the student may obtain materials he needs through interlibrary loan. The student should check the policies of his local library regarding interlibrary loan. Many libraries place restrictions upon graduate students in the use of this service because it is rather expensive.

Very often the student wishes to examine several theses and dissertations that are available only in the school library where the work was done. These may be obtained through interlibrary loan, or microfilmed copies of most dissertations may be obtained from University Microfilms, Inc., Ann Arbor, Michigan. Microfilm copies of a dissertation often can be obtained at less expense than borrowing the dissertation through interlibrary loan. Even when more expensive, the microfilm copy is often preferable as it need not be returned and is available for future reference.

The student may usually obtain microfilm or photostatic copies of any reference not locally available. The librarian in his local library will locate needed materials and arrange for their reproduction, but the cost of reproduction and shipping must usually be borne by the student. This cost varies considerably, usually from 15 cents to 35 cents per page. This method is often practical for short articles but expensive for books or lengthy documents. If, however, the needed reference appears to be of major importance, the student should obtain it by some means. The satisfaction of knowing you have done a thorough and scholarly review of the literature will more than compensate for the expense.

Taking notes on research articles

It is advisable for the student to check through his bibliography cards and identify those covering studies that appear most important to his review of the literature. The student should then start his review by checking the most recent of these important studies. The reason for starting with the most recent studies is that these, having the earlier research as a foundation, are likely to be more valuable. By reading the most important articles first, the student quickly builds up a reasonably deep understanding of his problem, and this makes it possible for him to profit more from the subsequent study of articles that are only peripherally related to his topic. After gaining this insight, it is much easier for him to fit these less important studies into the overall picture that he builds of his field through his review of the literature.

When the student finally opens the journal to an article he wishes to check, he should first turn to the summary. The research article almost always contains a short summary, and by reading this the student can usually determine whether the article contains any information that would justify reading the entire article. After reading the summary, if the student decides the article is sufficiently pertinent, he should first check the accuracy of the data on his bibliography card, because the source where he obtained these data could have been in error. He should then record the same bibliographic data on the top of a 5×8-inch note card and take notes on the article as he reads it.

In a research article, the writer attempts to present the essential materials in as brief a form as possible. The student will find that the average research article is only five or six pages in length and thus takes little time to read. The student will also find that the majority of research articles follow a standard pattern that further reduces the time needed to review them. This format usually includes (1) a brief introduction, (2) the hypotheses to be tested, (3) a statement of the procedure including a description of subjects, measures used, and research design, (4) a section giving the findings, and (5) a summary and conclusions. In taking notes, the student should be as brief as possible but should not omit anything that he feels he will later use in the design of his study or in the preparation of his research report. A brief outline of the reference using short sentences or phrases with headings for the problem or hypotheses, procedure, findings, and conclusions will usually be sufficient. It is also desirable for the student to record his own evaluation of the study and to note how it may relate to his research while the article is still fresh in his mind. In addition to his outline of the study, it is often profitable to record promising or unusual techniques employed in the study, new measures that may be of use, interesting theoretical points, and a critical evaluation including apparent weaknesses that make the results questionable. This critical evaluation of the research is important because the student will often find several research reports that test similar hypotheses but yield different results. Unless the student can make a critical evaluation of the research, it is difficult for him to determine which of the conflicting results is more likely to be correct. Chapter 15 presents a detailed discussion of methods for critically evaluating research articles. (See Figure 3.*b*. for a sample note card.)

+M

Sax, G. and Carr, A., An investigation of response sets on altered parallel forms, bibliog. Ed & Psychol M 22 no 2: 371-76 Summer '62

Problem: (a) Does response set in subtest format lower reliability? (b) How do subj. responses differ on same test in spiral-omnibus & subtest form?

Procedure: (a) Subj. 335 U. Hawaii freshman, (b) One form Henmon-Nelson Test of mental ability for Col. students adm. in spiral-omnibus form, other converted to subtest form. All subj. two both forms, order of adm. reversed for ½.

Findings a) Subj. attempted sig. more items on spiral-omnibus form (p >.001), and also got higher scores (p >.001). b) Manual rel. spiral omnibus .89 vs .62 for subtest form (alt. form), c) K-R rel. spiral omnibus .81 vs.85 for subtest form.

Conclusions: Response sets reduce rel. This supporting Cronbach's hyp.

Implications: a) Increasingly complex items on subtest form discourages students from responding to difficult items. Special-omnibus form provides partial reinforcement.

Comments: a) Pupil rigidity should have been considered as other studies show rigid pupils may do better on subtest form that requires fewer changes in set. b) K-R doubtful choice for rel. due to speed factor in H-N test. c) study generally well-designed.

Fig. 3.b. Sample note card.

Taking notes on opinion articles

In education, many of the articles that the student encounters will not be reports of research projects but will state the experiences or opinions of the author concerning some educational topic. Opinion articles do not follow the research article format and usually do not contain a summary. When checking the opinion article, the student should first scan the article to get some idea of its content. One method of scanning is to read only the first sentence in each paragraph. After scanning, the student should decide whether the article contains material of importance, in which case he should read the entire article. An abstract of the opinion article can usually be prepared most quickly using a sentence outline approach.

Quotations

When reading articles, the student should be alert for quotations that might be useful in preparing the review of the literature for his thesis or dissertation. If the student finds material he may wish to quote, the material to be quoted should be copied very carefully on the note card, enclosed in quotation marks, and the page from which the quote was taken noted. Most systems of referencing require that the page be given for direct quotations, and this also facilitates checking the quotation if necessary.

Students often use far too many quotations in their reviews. A good rule to follow is to copy for possible quotation only materials that are stated very skillfully, or in very concise terms, or are typical and clear reflections of a particular point of view the student wishes to illustrate in his thesis. After copying a quotation, the student should recheck to be sure that he has copied it exactly. Inaccurate quotations are a serious reflection on the scholarship of the writer, and it is almost certain that some of the quotations will be checked for accuracy by the faculty members who read the thesis.

Classifying articles you read

In reading articles for your review of the literature, you should keep constantly in mind the objective of your research and should attempt to relate the material you read to your research plan. Do not restrict yourself to the narrow study of only that research that is closely related to the work you are planning. Very often studies that are only partially related to your work will give you new theoretical viewpoints and acquaint you with new tools and methods that can be profitably applied to your research plan.

In doing his review of the literature, the student usually finds that the articles he reads can be classified into several categories. For example, in doing a review of literature in the field of ability grouping, the author found some articles that compare the achievement of students in ability grouping and random grouping systems, some articles that make comparisons of sociometric scores and social status measures between the two systems, some that measure personality differences of pupils under the two systems, some that discuss methods of grouping, and so on. In carrying out his review, the student should be alert for such natural subdivisions because they form a basis for classifying his note cards.

A coding system

As some such pattern for his review emerges, the student should develop a system of coding that will permit him to indicate what type of material is contained on a given note card. The coding system adopted by the research worker will be different for each review of the literature. An example of a coding system used by the author in a recent review of the literature in ability grouping may be helpful to the student in developing his own coding. These codes are generally placed in the upper right hand corner of the note card.

+ – Indicates an important study.
S – Studies dealing with social interaction.
A – Studies dealing with achievement of pupils in different grouping systems.
G – Studies describing grouping systems and studies discussing problems involved in grouping, such as individual variability, and so forth.
B – Studies relating grouping to behavior problems.
P – Studies relating grouping to personality adjustment, personality variables, and self concept.

Using such a code is helpful to the student in several ways. It makes him actively aware of the major areas of concentration in his topic. It makes it possible for him to check quickly his notes on a specific portion of the literature, and it makes the job of writing up his review of the literature much easier. The more extensive studies, of course, may contain material relating to two or three subtopics. These are recorded by indicating all of the codes for subtopics covered.

MISTAKES OFTEN MADE BY GRADUATE STUDENTS

1. Carries out a hurried review of the literature in order to get started on the research project. This usually results in overlooking previous studies containing ideas that would have improved the student's project.

2. Relies too heavily upon secondary sources.

3. Concentrates on research findings when reading research articles, thus overlooking valuable information on methods, measures, and so forth.

4. Overlooks sources other than education journals, such as newspapers and popular magazines, which often contain articles on educational topics.

5. Fails to define satisfactorily the topic limits of his review of the literature. Searching too broad an area often leads to the student becoming discouraged or doing a slipshod job. Searching too narrow an area causes him to overlook many articles that are peripheral to his research topic but contain information that would help him design a better study.

6. Copies bibliographic data incorrectly and is then unable to locate the reference needed.

7. Copies far too much material onto note cards. This often indicates that the student does not have a clear understanding of his project and thus cannot separate important from unimportant information.

ANNOTATED REFERENCES

1. ALEXANDER, CARTER, and BURKE, ARVID J. *How to Locate Educational Information and Data* (4th ed. revised). New York: Teachers College, Columbia University, 1958. A very valuable reference book for any student in education who plans to carry out a review of the literature. Deals with such topics as library searching, making a bibliography, and note-taking. Familiarizes the student with many sources that are widely used and are often difficult to find, such as institutional publications, publications of regional educational associations, educational directories, government documents, news items, and others.

2. The following sources are helpful to the student in gaining a quick overview of research in education or psychology.
   (a) FARNSWORTH, P. R. (ed.). *Annual Review of Psychology*. Palo Alto, Calif.: Annual Reviews, Inc., 1950 to date (published each year).
   (b) HARRIS, CHESTER W. (ed.). *Encyclopedia of Educational Research* (3rd ed.). New York: The Macmillan Co., 1960 (published at ten year intervals).
   (c) *Review of Educational Research*. Washington, D.C.: American Educational Research Association, 1931 to date (published five times each year).
   (d) *What Research Says to the Teacher*. Washington, D.C.: Department of Classroom Teachers and American Educational Research Association (published at irregular intervals). A series of pamphlets, each discussing research in an area of interest to teachers. Back cover of latest issue lists topics covered in all previous issues.

3. The following preliminary sources will be most useful in locating research articles that have been published in the professional journals in psychology and education:
   (a) *Education Abstracts*. Paris: Educational Clearing House, UNESCO, 1949 to date.
   (b) *Education Index*. New York: H. W. Wilson Co., 1929 to date.
   (c) *Psychological Abstracts*. Washington, D.C.: American Psychological Association, 1927 to date.

4. The following directories will help the student locate the addresses of professional workers in education and psychology. This information is needed in order to obtain reprints of articles not available in the local library. If the following directories do not produce the needed information, check under "Directories" in recent issues of *Education Index,* for other sources, or the *Guide to American Directories*. If your library does not have a directory you need, check with faculty members or local educators who may be members of the association publishing the directory.
   (a) AMERICAN EDUCATIONAL RESEARCH ASSOCIATION. *Directory of Members as of January, 1962*. Washington, D.C.: American Educational Research Association, 1962.
   (b) *American School Curriculum*. Washington, D.C.: American Association of School Administrators (published each year). Lists names and addresses of over 12,000 members.
   (c) CATTELL, JAQUES (ed.). *American Men of Science* (9th ed., Vol. III) *The Social and Behavioral Sciences*. New York: R. R. Bowker Co., 1956 (new edition in press). Lists most educational and psychological researchers who had done significant work at time of publication.

(*d*) Cook, Robert C. *Who's Who in American Education* (20th ed., 1961–62). Nashville, Tenn.: Who's Who in American Education, 1962 (published every two years). Coverage spotty but will occasionally contain a needed address. A random check of twenty eminent educational researchers in the 20th edition showed only one to be listed.

(*e*) Holsopple, James Q. (ed.). *1962 Directory American Psychological Association.* Washington, D.C.: American Psychological Association, 1962.

(*f*) *Membership Directory and Annual Report.* Washington, D.C.: Department of Elementary School Principals (published each year). Lists names and addresses of over 18,000 elementary school principals, supervisors, and superintendents.

CHAPTER 4

Gathering Research Data

INTRODUCTION

This chapter is concerned with the techniques of gathering research data and with the selection and development of measuring devices to be used for this purpose. The major concern of the chapter is the application of measurement devices to research, and it emphasizes ways to evaluate measures used in research related to the student's problem and the selection of measures by the student for his own research project. If the student has not taken a course in educational measurement or evaluation, it is strongly recommended that such a course be taken prior to the design of his research project.

HUMAN RELATIONS IN DATA GATHERING

In most educational research projects, the subjects used by the researcher are human beings. The human subject is, without a doubt, the most complex subject used in any field of research, and the research worker can avoid many difficulties and pitfalls if he never loses sight of the special requirements and problems involved in working with humans. Many educational research projects select subjects from the public schools. When using school children as subjects in research, it is necessary to obtain the understanding and cooperation of school administrators, teachers, parents, interested community groups, and the subjects themselves. Inadequate attention to any of these groups can lead to problems that may make it impossible to complete the research satisfactorily.

Questions about your research

There are several rules that the research worker should observe if he plans to select his subjects from the public schools. First, he must have a thorough and detailed research design that he can explain in terms that administrators, teachers, and parents can understand.

Many school administrators are doubtful of the value of educational research and are likely to be critical in their appraisal of the research design. If the student has failed to think through his design carefully, he may find himself unable to answer the questions put to him by educators, and this failure will almost certainly lead to a decision by school administrators not to participate in the study.

Before approaching parents or school administrators, the student should have thorough and convincing answers to the following questions that are likely to arise. Questions he must be prepared to answer include: What is the purpose of the study, what does it hope to find out? Are the findings likely to be worthwhile? Is the study important to education? If the student cannot convince school personnel that the work is worthwhile and likely to produce useful results, it is doubtful whether cooperation can be obtained. Schools generally cooperate in research projects because of a feeling of professional responsibility that exists among educators. Research projects almost always cause school personnel a certain amount of inconvenience and extra work, and unless the research worker can convince these persons that the research to be done is worth this extra effort and inconvenience, cooperation will not be obtained.

Another question that school personnel usually bring up in discussing research is: "Will the results of this research apply directly to our school?" In other words, the schools are interested in the direct returns that they may obtain from the research project. One of the direct returns, of course, will be that the research data will have greater application to the schools in which the research is done than it will to other schools. To be of significant value, of course, the research must be designed to obtain findings that can be applied beyond the situation in which the work was carried out. If research could only be applied to the isolated situation and to the specific subjects upon which the experiment were carried out, there would be little value in doing such work. However, the fact remains that a research project will be more applicable to the specific situation in which the experiment is carried out than to similar situations in other schools.

Very often the schools are interested in other possible advantages that they may obtain from the research. These advantages differ depending upon the project but can include such things as test scores that can be used by the school in guidance and in other of its regular activities, new curricular materials, visual aids, and improved administrative procedures. Some studies also involve the use of special measures that the school cannot afford to administer but that can be useful if administered by the research worker. These include such things as individual intelligence tests, individually administered projective measures, and depth interviews. For example, the author recently carried out a research project that included administering the *T.A.T.*[1] to a sample of low achieving children. Because this measure was given on an individual basis and required a clinical psychologist for administration and scoring, the cost would have been too great for most school districts. This test identified a number of children who appeared to have serious emotional disturbances. Once identified, the school district was able to arrange for help for these children. Any such possibilities of direct advantage to the schools should be pointed out by the research worker as this is often a major consideration of school administrators in deciding whether to cooperate with the research.

Administrators will wish to know in considerable detail just what the school's role and responsibility will be in the research project. How much time will be required of the subjects? At what part of the school year must this time be scheduled? Will adjustments to the testing schedule be possible if other school activities interfere. Can subjects be tested in their classroom or will it be necessary to take subjects from their classes to another room? Will teachers be required to administer any of the tests or measures? Will it be necessary for the schools to provide pencils, answer sheets, lap boards, or other materials? Such questions should be thought through carefully by the research worker before approaching the school administrator. The price that the school generally must pay to participate in educational research is measured in the aforementioned terms, and the administrator must weigh the possible advantages to his school and to the profession against the losses in time, extra adjustments that must be made, and possible expenses to the school district. At this point, the student should be cautioned against making compromises with the administrator that weaken the research design. For example, if a random sampling of subjects within the school is required for a research project and the school administrator

[1] Thematic Apperception Test—a projective personality measure in which the subject is shown pictures and makes up a story around each picture.

suggests that volunteers be taken instead, the research worker should explain in detail the disadvantages of using volunteers and attempt to win the administrator over to paying the additional price in inconvenience that is required to obtain the random sample. If the administrator insists upon changes that seriously weaken the research design, it is wiser for the research worker to attempt to carry out the study elsewhere than to carry it out with disabling restrictions. In general the research worker should follow the rule that *all* concessions should be made that do not seriously weaken the scientific value of the study and *no* concessions should be made that do so compromise the research.

Another question that the administrator often will not mention but that may concern him greatly: "Will the results of this research reflect unfavorably upon my school?" The research worker should bring this question up and discuss it objectively. As most educational research is aimed at the establishing of general principles and insights rather than the yielding of specific information about the schools or subjects participating, results can usually be prepared in such a way that they will not reflect unfavorably upon the schools used in the study. These results are generally reported in professional research journals, and it is customary to describe the study without identifying the specific schools involved. Such reassurance to the school administrator is especially needed when the study is such that he may have some anxiety concerning the performance of his pupils. Even if research findings reflect unfavorably upon participating schools, the research worker should in all of his public statements emphasize that by cooperating in the research, school personnel have shown themselves to be interested in improving their service. It should be pointed out that educators who admit that their schools are not perfect and who are seeking ways to improve are more to be commended than those who are blind to their own shortcomings or those who try to hide deficiencies rather than correct them.

The school administrator will also be concerned with the specific measuring instruments that are to be used in the research. Samples of these measures should be shown to teachers and administrators in order that they may examine them carefully. The research worker should answer any questions concerning the measures and explain the specific purpose of each measure in the research. An exception to this rule occurs in some studies in which a knowledge of the measures can result in teachers biasing or contaminating the research results. For example, it is sometimes undesirable to allow teachers more than a brief examination of the achievement test to be used in a research project, because some teachers will coach their pupils on the correct answers if they have a copy of the test available. This is usually done by teachers who are insecure and who feel that poor performance of their pupils will reflect unfavorably upon themselves.

Many psychological measures used in educational research projects are difficult for the school administrators to understand. If such measures are to be used, the research worker must be prepared to explain very thoroughly the purpose of these measures and to provide evidence that the measure is a valid and useful one. In examining such measures, the administrators will often have in mind the possible response made by parents to such a measure. If the measure contains items that may cause unfavorable reactions from parents or other community groups, the research worker must have very strong justification for the use of these devices. He should also carry out careful public relations work with the groups concerned prior to the use of these devices. The research worker should avoid the use of measures that he can not defend on the basis of appropriateness to the study and psychological significance. Prior approval for all measures to be used should be obtained from school authorities before the research is started.

Following channels

It is very important when working with any administrative hierarchy such as a school district to follow appropriate channels of authority. If the student plans to use subjects from more than one school, it is generally necessary for him first to obtain approval from the district superintendent or from the assistant superintendent in charge of research. After obtaining such approval, the student must visit each school concerned and present his ideas to the principal. Even though the superintendent has given tentative approval for the project, if the principal objects strongly to testing pupils in his school, the superintendent will usually support the principal. Even if the superintendent were inclined to force the principal to cooperate, such an arrangement would create a situation in which it would be very difficult to carry out effective research. The interest and cooperation of all persons concerned with the research is necessary if it is to be carried through to a successful conclusion.

After the principal and superintendent have been briefed concerning the purposes of the research and the procedures to be followed, it usually will be necessary for the research worker to meet with teachers in the schools and obtain their interest and cooperation. Often, a faculty meeting can be devoted to the research topic, and the research worker can present his plans and get the responses of the teachers at this time. Teachers and school administrators frequently will see problems or difficulties in the research plans that the research worker has not recognized. The suggestions of school personnel should be solicited and followed whenever this may be done without compromising some scientific aspect of the research.

In many studies, it is also desirable that parents be informed concerning the nature of the study and given an opportunity to express their opinions. This may often be done by having the research worker present his plans at P.T.A. meetings in the schools involved. The purposes of the study and the procedures should be discussed as frankly as possible omitting only information that could lead to compromising the study in some way. In addition to such a presentation, it is often wise for the research worker to prepare a letter explaining the study. This letter is sent home to parents of all children who will participate as subjects and usually provides a place where the parent may sign to signify his approval of his child's participation in the research.

The degree of rapport that must be built up between the research worker and other community groups is dependent to a great extent upon the nature of the study. Studies dealing with areas such as achievement, which are generally regarded as a major aspect of the school's business, need a less extensive public relations program than studies involving such areas as personality and social adjustment where the role of the school is less clear and where some of the measures to be employed might be resented or misunderstood by the parent.

Finally, it is necessary to obtain some level of cooperation from the students who will be involved in the research as subjects. It is often not possible to explain to the student in detail the purposes of the project because this explanation may influence the student's performance on the measures and therefore compromise the research. The student should receive some explanation, however, of why he is taking certain tests. This explanation must satisfy the student that his participation is important and desirable and it is to his advantage to cooperate.

Dealing with public relations problems

Public relations problems arise occasionally in educational field studies, in spite of the efforts of the research worker to establish good public relations with concerned groups. The most frequent problem involves a protest to measures used in the research. Such protests are usually made by small but vocal groups of citizens who are primarily interested in obtaining publicity. Often, local newspapers, in the quest for more sensational news stories will encourage such groups by giving their protests wide and sometimes biased coverage. Most of these protests can be traced back to the fact that items occur in many psychological tests, the purpose of which cannot be easily explained to the layman. Many psychological tests in such areas as personality, mental health, social adjustment, attitudes, and interests are still in the early stages of development, and not even their strongest advocates would claim them to be highly valid measures. In many cases, however, such measures are the best available and must be used if research in a particular area is to be carried forward. In one unfortunate episode in Houston, Texas, the answer sheets to six sociometric and psychological measures that had been administered to some 5,000 ninth grade students were ordered burned by the school board. In this instance, accounts indicated that parents objected to having their children respond to such items as: "I enjoy soaking in the bathtub." "Sometimes I tell dirty jokes when I would rather not." "Dad always seems too busy to pal around with me."[2]

In a more recent episode, in spite of a thorough and well planned public relations program, a similar problem arose. In this case, the research program dealt with mental health and was being carried out by a foundation that was well established and had good rapport in the community. An extensive public relations program was carried out including meetings and discussions with school boards,

[2] Gwynn Nettler, "Test Burning in Texas," *The American Psychologist,* XIV (1959), 682–83.

superintendents, administrative personnel, school nurses and teachers, religious leaders, P.T.A. groups, the Lions Club, and other civic groups. In this case, the research worker's difficulty started because a local right-wing group was currently involved in a campaign opposing the "mental health movement."

The man who spearheaded this opposition was also a member of the American Legion and later read a statement along the same lines at a P.T.A. panel on which members of the research team appeared. He accused us of implanting "Red" ideas in children's minds and said our "Guess-Who" technique was a way of "fingering" certain children (designating them at an early age so they would be marked for life for our own ulterior motives).[3]

The author has had some experience with a similar protest movement, and when this experience is compared with the previously described situations, it appears that all three have a number of things in common. First, individual test items are generally attacked without reference to their context or psychological foundations. Second, such attacks are usually led by small extreme groups of one sort or another. In the author's experience, the protest group was made up almost entirely of a close-knit group of health food faddists. Another characteristic of all three of these situations is that although the protesting group was vigorous and noisy, it did not represent any significant parent group. In the Houston episode, tests were returned to a number of small school districts—the Spring Branch Board of Education decided to destroy the answer sheets only of pupils whose parents objected to the testing. Six weeks after that decision, only eleven parents out of the possible 750 requested that the answer sheets be destroyed. In the second episode discussed, a similar offer was made and only three parents, those who started the original protest, requested that their children's records be destroyed. In the author's experience, approximately 5,000 children were tested and in spite of the considerable bedlam raised by the small protesting group, only one parent came forward to request that her child's test papers be destroyed.

In dealing with such problems, a number of points might be worth mentioning. First, remember that in many instances these protests are led by demagogues who are not truly concerned about the test-

[3] L. D. Eron and L. O. Walter, "Test Burning II," *The American Psychologist,* XVI (May, 1961), 239.

ing but wish to use it merely as a vehicle to gain publicity or gratify some personal need. Second, it is impossible to explain adequately to a lay group the function of many items used on psychological tests. It is doubtful whether the research worker should ever attempt to debate the merits of specific test items. Instead, he should explain how the test was developed and attempt to demonstrate that the test, as a whole, is valid and useful. Third, it is important to take all action that seems appropriate at the very outset of any such protest. If the research is well designed and the measures are justified, those parents who are truly concerned can generally be convinced of the value of the study, thus depriving the extreme group of their support. The researcher should work closely with the newspapers and do everything possible to acquaint them with his side of the question. Finally, it is wise to offer to withdraw children from the study if the parents examine the tests and make a written request that their children be withdrawn.

CHARACTERISTICS OF MEASURING INSTRUMENTS

To a considerable degree, the maturity of a science can be estimated by the characteristics of its measurement tools. Education, being a relatively new and immature science, employs tools that are often far less objective and accurate than those used in the physical sciences. There are certain general characteristics, however, that may be applied to nearly all the measurement devices used in education and psychology, and, if understood, are very helpful to the student in evaluating measures that he is considering for use in his research projects.

OBJECTIVITY

Objectivity, as it refers to measurement devices in education, is determined largely by the degree to which the measure is uninfluenced or undistorted by the beliefs or prejudices of the individual using the instrument. Objectivity is an extremely important factor in evaluating the effectiveness of measuring instruments in education. Prescientific measures and the measures used in the less mature sciences tend to have relatively little objectivity. In other words, many of these measures are influenced to a considerable degree by the biases of the individual using the tool. However, as a science becomes more exact, we find personal errors being ruled out to a greater and greater degree until the measuring devices employed leave very little room for personal error or bias. In evaluating educational measures, the degree of objectivity can usually be determined by analyzing the testing and scoring procedures and considering the places in which the administration or scoring permits the use of personal judgment or makes possible the entrance of bias. Although a high level of objectivity in scientific measurements is always desirable, attempts to increase the objectivity of some educational and psychological measures can result in weakening other characteristics of the measurement device. Thus, in educational research, the level of objectivity required must be weighed against other important test characteristics such as validity. Obtaining information through interviewing usually permits much less objectivity than obtaining information by having the subjects complete a checklist. If, however, the information needed cannot be validly obtained through the use of a checklist, the interview approach is superior even though it is less objective. For example, it has been found that in order to obtain information concerning socially taboo topics such as sexual behavior, it is necessary to establish a high level of rapport with the subjects. If this rapport is not established, the subjects will often refuse to answer or will not answer truthfully. Under these conditions, the loss of objectivity that occurs through the personal interview is far outweighed by the gain of validity when compared with attempting to collect these data through printed questionnaires that do not permit establishment of the necessary rapport. Sometimes in our quest for objectivity, we throw away critical elements of the situation we are attempting to measure because these elements cannot be measured objectively. In a research project on leadership behavior carried out by the author, an attempt was made to break down the behavior patterns of the subjects into highly specific and objectively observable acts. This, of course, was done to reduce the number of judgments and simplify the decisions that had to be made by the persons observing and evaluating the behavior, thus increasing objectivity. It was found, however, that, in the process of breaking down the complex patterns of behavior related to leadership, most of the apparently important elements of successful leadership behavior were lost. The observational data obtained, although highly objective, were of little value in pursuing the study of leadership.

VALIDITY

Validity is generally defined as the degree to which a test measures what it claims to measure. This general concept of validity, however, is not sufficient in present day educational testing. Four specific types of validity are generally recognized. These are: content validity, predictive validity, concurrent validity, and construct validity.[4]

Content validity

Content validity is the degree to which the sample of test items represents the content that the test is designed to measure. Items on a test generally represent only a sampling of the material available to measure the skill, knowledge, or characteristic concerned with the topic. For example, in measuring achievement, if the items covered on the test are closely representative of the content of the course of study, the test has high content validity. If test items cover topics not covered in the course of study, ignore certain important concepts, and unduly emphasize others as compared with emphasis in the course of study, the content validity is lower. Content validity is important primarily in achievement testing and various tests of skills and proficiency such as trade tests. Content validity is usually established by the test producer at the time the test is developed. For example, let us say that a test producer wishes to develop a standardized test of achievement in ninth grade general science. He would assemble course outlines and widely used textbooks in the field, and would then analyze these sources in order to determine what concepts are usually covered in ninth grade general science and how much emphasis is placed on the various concepts. After obtaining a composite picture from these various sources, he could construct test items that would sample the student's understanding of these concepts. Often the sampling of test items will be representative in that the emphasis given in the test through the

[4] *Technical Recommendations for Psychological Tests and Diagnostic Techniques* (New York: American Psychological Assoc., 1954).

number of items devoted to a concept will be proportional to the emphasis of this concept in the content sources. To establish the content validity of his test, the test producer usually describes in the manual the techniques used to arrive at the test content. Content validity is usually not expressed in numerical terms as are some other types. Actually, the content validity of a general science test will be different for students taking science in different classes. In some classes, one of the textbooks used in developing the test will be used in teaching the class, and the content emphasis of the test may be very similar to the content emphasis in the course. In another class, however, a different textbook not employed by the test producer and varying considerably from those employed might be used to teach the class. For this class, the content validity of the test will be lower. Whether a test has satisfactory content validity for the sample that you plan to test is determined largely by comparing the content of the course taken by your subjects with the content of the test. It is usually possible to develop local achievement tests that will have higher content validity for a particular school system than the standardized tests used nationally. The standardized tests, however, offer a number of other advantages, such as more elaborate norms and more professional development, which often makes them preferable to locally developed measures.

Predictive validity

Predictive validity is the degree to which the predictions made by a test are confirmed by the later behavior of the subjects tested. The usual method of determining predictive validity is to administer the test, then wait until the events that the test attempts to predict have occurred, and then correlate the occurrence of the event with the scores of the subjects on the test. Let us take an algebra aptitude test as an example. Such tests are designed to predict success in ninth grade algebra and are usually administered near the end of the eighth grade. In order to determine the predictive validity of such a test, it would be administered to a large random sampling of eighth grade pupils. The scores of these pupils would then be held until the pupils had completed ninth grade algebra. At the end of ninth grade algebra, the predictions of the test could be correlated with a measure of algebra achievement, such as grades in the algebra class or an algebra achievement test. In this case, the algebra grades or the achievement test scores would be called the criterion measure—that is, the measure against which the predictive measure is compared to establish its validity. The correlation between the algebra aptitude test and the algebra achievement test would give us a measure of the predictive validity of the aptitude test—that is, the degree to which its prediction of the student's success in algebra was borne out by his performance. Much educational research is concerned with the prediction of success in various courses of study.

Concurrent validity

The concurrent validity of a test is determined by relating the test scores of a group of subjects to some concurrent criterion measure. Concurrent validity is very similar to predictive validity except that the criterion measure is taken concurrently with the predictive measure instead of being taken somewhat later, as is the case with predictive validity. The principal advantage of concurrent validity is realized in studies where predictive validity could only be established after waiting a long period of time to obtain a criterion measure. Vocational interest tests have often employed concurrent validity. Let us say, for example, that we wish to measure the interests of high school students and from these measured interests attempt to determine vocations for which the student's interests might suit him. If we wished to establish predictive validities on a measure of this nature, it would be necessary to administer the interest measure to a high school group and then wait until these students had become successful in various occupations. After this, it would be possible to correlate the interest patterns obtained in high school with the later success or failure of these students in various occupations. Obtaining these predictive validities would, of course, require many years. For example, for a profession such as medicine, it would be necessary to wait until the student had completed college, medical school, and internship before a satisfactory criterion for success or failure would be available. In establishing concurrent validity, however, the interest patterns of successful physicians might be compared with interest patterns of other professions to determine whether the test could reliably identify the physicians from their interest patterns. Once these interest patterns had been established for different vocational groups, they could be used to determine if the vocational interests of a high school student fit the profiles of any of the occupational groups. Concurrent validity, although frequently used in this way, is not nearly so dependable as predictive validity. It is very possible, for example, that the interest patterns of high school students who are destined to become successful physicians are not the same as these interest patterns will be after the students have completed their medical training and become successful physicians. Computing concurrent validity is justified because it provides some immediate evidence of the usefulness of the test. Whenever possible, however, predictive validity should be established on tests that are to be used in prediction.

Like predictive validity, concurrent validity can be established by correlating the test score with the criterion measure. The correlation is referred to as a validity coefficient.

Construct validity

Construct validity is the degree to which a test is based upon a particular theory or theoretical construct. Although tests may be developed that have no theoretical basis in psychology or education, interpretation of such tests is difficult and can often lead to serious errors. For example, it would be possible to collect a large quantity of miscellaneous test items, administer them to large numbers of high school students, and then develop a test made up only of those items related to student success in extracurricular activities. Such a test might appear to have high concurrent validity, but it is doubtful whether this high validity would be found if the test were then tried on a different sample; and it is also possible that some of these items, although valid, are based on factors the test developer does not wish to consider. An example of the latter might be found in items that are related indirectly to racial background and therefore, in effect, merely demonstrate that certain racial groups are discriminated against in the extracurricular activities program. Thus, the establishment of construct validity in educational and psychological tests is important. This is particularly important in the measurement of highly complex behavior patterns and variables such as attitudes, personality characteristics, or leadership.

The construct validity of some tests is established by correlating the scores of these tests with scores on other measures already accepted as having construct validity. For example, group intelligence test scores are often correlated with scores on the Stanford-Binet Intelligence Test. The Stanford-Binet test is based on a number of theoretical concepts developed by Binet and Simon on the nature of intelligence. Thus, if the group test correlates highly with the Stanford-Binet, it may be concluded that this test follows similar theoretical concepts and has similar construct validity.

Often the establishment of construct validity amounts to a simultaneous validation of both a test and a theory. In many studies concerned with construct validity, both the theoretical construct and the measure are being validated. In this case, the investigator first hypothesises that, based on his theory, certain predictions can be made concerning the scores of individuals on a measure he has developed. He then collects data to determine the degree to which his predictions are confirmed. If the predictions are confirmed to a high degree, he is provided with tentative evidence to support the validity of his theory and also to support the validity of the test for measuring the variables pertinent to the theory.

RELIABILITY

Reliability, as applied to educational measurements, may be defined as the level of consistency of the measuring device. In general, this consistency reflects the degree to which the test may be considered stable or may be depended upon to yield similar test results under similar circumstances. Reliability is expressed as a coefficient, reliability coefficients usually being correlation coefficients. Each type of reliability obtains this coefficient by using a different approach, and the coefficients obtained therefore have somewhat different meaning. In spite of the differences, however, when more than one type of reliability is computed for a given test, the results of the different types computed are usually in fairly close agreement. Reliability is an extremely important characteristic of measurement devices and must be considered carefully in selecting measures for research purposes. The lower the reliability of the measuring instrument, the greater will be the chance fluctuations we can expect in the scores of our subjects. In other words, with a test of low reliability, the score obtained by the average subject may differ considerably from his true score in the variable being measured, some obtained scores being too high and some too low. Let us say, for example, that we have set up a research project aimed at comparing the level of aggression of juvenile delinquent boys from "broken homes" with the level of aggression of juvenile delinquent boys from "complete homes." If our measure of aggression has a low reliability coefficient, it is possible that even though differences in the aggression levels of the two groups might be present, the wide chance fluctuations of the individual scores permitted by the lower reliability of the measure could hide this difference or render it insignificant. For example, let us say that if some precise measure were available, we would find that the delinquent boys from "broken homes" were more aggressive than those from "complete homes." Because of the low reliability of the obtained score, however, it would be possible for a number of these delinquents from "broken homes" to obtain scores indicating less than their true level of aggression. Conversely, it would be possible for a number of boys in the "complete home" group to obtain higher than their true scores. In certain samples it is possible that, although in terms of true scores the delinquent boys from "broken homes" are more aggressive, the obtained scores could show just the opposite effect because of the obtained score fluctuations that occurred in that particular sample. Thus, the use of a test of low reliability in your research can result in negative or insignificant findings even though your hypothesis is valid and true differences are present.

TYPES OF RELIABILITY

Coefficient of internal consistency

This type of reliability is based upon estimates of the internal consistency of the test. The most widely used method of estimating internal consistency is through the split-half correlation. In this method, the test for which reliability is to be calculated is administered to an appropriate sample. It is then split into two subtests, usually by placing all odd-numbered items in one subtest and all even-numbered items in another subtest.[5] The scores of the two subtests are then computed for each individual, and these two sets of scores are correlated. The correlation obtained, however, represents

[5] Other methods of splitting the test are sometimes used such as a logical division of the test into two sets of comparable items.

the reliability coefficient of only half of the test, so that a correction must be applied in order to obtain the reliability of the entire test. The Spearman-Brown Prophesy Formula is used to make this correction.[6]

The method of rational equivalence

The method of rational equivalence is the only widely used technique for calculating reliability that does not require the calculation of a correlation coefficient. This method gets at the internal consistency of the test through an analysis of the individual test items. A number of formulas have been developed to calculate reliability using this method. These are generally referred to as the Kuder-Richardson formulas (after the authors of an article in which these formulas were first discussed).[7] The formulas in this article are numbered, and the two most widely used are numbers 20 and 21. Formula 20 is considered by many specialists in educational and psychological measurement to be the most satisfactory method of determining reliability. This formula is being used to an increasing degree to determine the reliability of standardized tests.

Formula 21 is a simplified approximation of Formula 20, and it is of value primarily in that it provides a very easy method of determining a reliability coefficient. The use of Formula 21 requires so much less time than other methods for estimating test reliability that it is highly appropriate for use in teacher-made tests and short experimental tests being developed by a research worker. One desirable aspect of the Kuder-Richardson formulas is that they generally yield a lower reliability coefficient than would be obtained by using the other methods described. Thus, they can be thought of as providing a minimum estimate of reliability and, if used, tend to eliminate the danger of making an overestimate.

Coefficient of equivalence

This method of calculating reliability may be used whenever two or more parallel forms of a test are available. This method is often

[6] See Henry Garrett, *Statistics in Psychology and Education* (5th ed.; New York: David McKay Co., 1958), chap. 13.

[7] M. W. Richardson and G. F. Kuder, "The Calculation of Test Reliability Coefficients Based upon the Method of Rational Equivalence," *Journal of Educational Psychology*, XXX (1939), 681–87.

called "alternate form reliability" and is computed by administering two parallel forms of the test to the same group of individuals, and then correlating the scores obtained on the two forms in order to yield a reliability coefficient. Some interval between the administration of the forms is usually desirable, especially if the alternate forms are nearly identical as is the case with some achievement measures. This interval tends to reduce practice effects that may be an important factor if the two forms of the test are administered at the same sitting. At the present time, the coefficient of equivalence is the most commonly used estimate of reliability for standardized tests. It is very widely used with standardized achievement and intelligence tests.

Coefficient of stability

This form of reliability is useful when alternate forms of the test are not available or not possible to construct. To calculate the co-efficient of stability, sometimes called "test-retest reliability," the measure is administered to a sample of individuals, and then after a delay the same measure is again administered to the same sample. Scores obtained from the two administrations are then correlated in order to determine the coefficient of stability. The most critical problem in calculating this form of reliability is to determine the correct delay between the two administrations of the measure. If the retest is administered too quickly after the initial test, students will recall their responses to many of the items and this will tend to produce a spuriously high reliability coefficient. On the other hand, if the retesting is delayed for too long a period, there is a good possibility that the student's ability to answer some items will change. For example, he may pass through a period of development or learning and thus be better prepared to answer questions on the retest.

EVALUATION OF STANDARD MEASURES

The student must be able to evaluate standard educational and psychological tests for two reasons. First, this evaluation is necessary if he is to understand the significance of research done by others. Without the ability to evaluate the measures used in other research projects, the student cannot make a sound judgment concerning the results of these projects. Secondly, he must be able to evaluate such measures in order to select the most suitable tests for his own research work. There are a number of sources of material that the student may use in evaluating a standard test. The most useful include the test itself, the test manual, the various editions of the *Mental Measurements Yearbook,* and research reports and articles concerned with specific tests.

The test manual

The test manual provides the student with much that he needs to evaluate the standardized test. Among the questions that the manual usually answers are the following:

1. *What validity data are available? What type of validity is reported? Is the evidence of validity sufficient for use in the planned research?* Validity must be a major consideration in evaluating any standard measure. Perhaps the most important type of validity in research measures is construct validity. If the test contains reasonable evidence with regard to construct validity, it may well be useful in research even though the evidence may be meager with respect to other types of validity. Many psychological measures, particularly those dealing with some of the more complex human characteristics such as personality, often present very limited validity data. This limitation need not rule out the test from consideration, but interpretation of the results of such tests is difficult. Certainly, if other aspects of two tests are equal, the test with more substantial evidence of validity would be preferred. Because most persons who work in education are aware of the importance of test validity, a section on this topic will usually be found in the test manual even if little or no evidence concerning the validity of the measure is available. In some cases, the manual gives a general treatment of validity without providing the reader with any specific information concerning the type of validity referred to or the validity coefficients that have been obtained. Such general statements are probably included to influence the noncritical reader or the person who has not been trained to evaluate standardized tests.

Occasionally, the material discussed under the heading of validity in the test manual will be rather misleading. For example, some test manuals give data on item validity.[8] Although item validity data are sometimes useful, they tell us little about the validity of the total test.

[8] The degree to which individual test items correlate with the total test score.

Other test manuals report reliability coefficients in the section headed validity. Although the validity of a test is limited by its reliability, a test can be highly reliable and yet be invalid for its stated purpose. Reliability data are to some degree related to validity but reliability coefficients do not give us a sufficient basis for assessing the validity of the measure.

Often no validity data are given in the test manual. This does not necessarily mean that the test is invalid but usually indicates that no evidence concerning its validity has been gathered. In the case of new tests and tests still limited to experimental use, this lack of validity data may be expected. In the case of tests that have been available for a number of years, however, such a lack must be regarded with suspicion as it may well indicate that attempts have been made to establish the validity of the measure and these attempts have failed. In some cases, validity data are given for an earlier edition of the measure. These data of course, can only be applied to a limited degree to a new edition.

2. *What reliability data are available? Is the measure sufficiently reliable to meet the needs of the planned research?* It is much easier to establish the reliability of a test than to establish its validity. Therefore, reliability data are almost always reported in the test manual. The level of reliability the research worker can expect is determined largely by the nature of the research in which he plans to use the measure. If the research project is such that the research worker can expect only small differences between his experimental and control groups on a variable measured by the test, it is necessary that a test of high reliability be used. Conversely, if large samples are to be used and if the test scores are expected to differ materially for the experimental and control groups, the research worker may select a measure of relatively low reliability if this measure is superior to others available in other respects, such as construct validity. The reason a test of high reliability is required in the first situation and not the second is that when only small differences are likely to be found, a test of low reliability may be too crude to reveal these differences. For example, let us say we wished to measure the height of two samples of adult men, but had only a crude measuring device such as the span.[9] Even such an unreliable measure would reveal

[9] The space from the tip of the thumb to the tip of the little finger when extended.

differences of several inches but would not reliably differentiate men who differed only an inch or less in height.

A point that must be watched for in evaluating test reliability is that many tests yield a number of subscores in addition to a total score. Often reliability is reported only for the total score. This is the case for some intelligence and achievement tests that provide subscores in order to give a profile of the student's performance in the various areas making up the test. Such subscores, however, must be used cautiously unless reliability data are available for them. When such data are not available, the research worker will have difficulty making an intelligent appraisal of the worth of the subscores. He may be sure that all or most of these subscores will have lower reliabilities than the total test reliability. The reliability coefficients of the subscores, however, may differ considerably with some that are as reliable as the total test and some that are of such low reliability that they cannot be used in the planned research.

If no specific information on reliability is provided in the test manual, the research worker may safely assume that the reliability of the test is low. While validity data are often very difficult to obtain and may not be available at the time the manual is published, it is a simple matter to obtain reliability data for most tests and its absence should be viewed with suspicion.

3. *Is the test appropriate for the level of subjects to be used in the planned research?* Each test is designed to work most efficiently at a particular level. Some tests claim to be usable over a fairly wide age or grade range, but such measures are generally more accurate at the center of their range than at the extremes. In using a test for research, it is necessary that the test is appropriate for the level of subjects to be tested. If not appropriate, it will not discriminate, that is it will fail to reflect differences that exist among some of the subjects tested. A test that is too easy discriminates poorly because subjects who are superior in the area being measured will all receive perfect or near perfect scores. For example, if we administer a third grade arithmetic test to ninth grade pupils, all but the very poorest ninth grade pupils will obtain nearly perfect scores. Therefore, from this test it is impossible to determine how much arithmetic a ninth grade pupil knows. Average students, above average students, and highly superior students will all receive about the same score on the test. The same, of course, is true of a test that is much too difficult or ad-

vanced for the subjects. In this case, all but a few students will receive very low scores.

Another point to regard in determining the appropriate test level is to check the reading level of the test. Occasionally, one finds a test that the manual describes as usable at a particular grade level but that includes many words not generally known by students at that level. Such a test would be invalid as it will be measuring to some degree the person's vocabulary and reading ability rather than his ability in the characteristic the test purports to measure.

In many research projects, the test norms provided by the publisher are used in some phase of the research. If these norms are to be used, they must be based on subjects who are reasonably comparable to the research subjects in order to be appropriate.

4. *Can the test be administered satisfactorily in the planned research situation?* Some tests require special administration requirements that can not be met in the public school situation. In some cases, only small groups can be tested successfully because of the necessity of checking the child's responses while the test is being administered. Some tests require special training in order to be administered satisfactorily, and if the research worker or the persons who are to administer this test lack this training, the training must be given or the test not used.

5. *Does the test require special training for interpretation?* Some tests that can be administered without difficulty by the research worker require considerable special training to score and interpret. Many of the projective personality tests such as the *Rorschach Test* and *Thematic Apperception Test* fall into this category. If the research worker is to use such tests, he must first obtain the training necessary to do a satisfactory job of scoring and interpretation. Very often courses are provided to train the graduate student in the use of these measures, but these courses must usually be followed by considerable practice before the student can carry out effective interpretation. Therefore, the selection of such a measure may well require a great deal of preliminary work by the student before he may begin to score the test that he has administered as a portion of his research project.

6. *Is a shorter test available that will yield substantially equal results?* Because the research worker usually has only a limited amount of time available to test the subjects in his research, each

test must be evaluated in the terms of the results it will yield as compared with the time it requires. Sometimes, a test having lower reliability will be a better choice if the saving of time more than compensates for the loss of reliability. For example, the total test reliability of the *California Short Form Test of Mental Maturity* (*Junior High Level*) using Kuder-Richardson Formula 21 is .87, while the reliability of the long form of the same test is .92.[10] The short form requires 51 minutes to administer, while the long form requires 88 minutes. In view of the relatively small difference in reliability, in most cases it would be advisable to use the short form, thus giving the research worker 37 minutes that will permit him either to reduce his testing time requirements or add some other measure that might make a significant contribution to his study.

The Mental Measurements Yearbooks

A very important source of information on standard tests are the *Mental Measurements Yearbooks*. Over the past thirty years, Oscar K. Buros has edited this series of very useful references to standard tests in psychology and education. The most recent of the series is the *Fifth Mental Measurements Yearbook,* published in 1959. This is a complete new work that supplements the earlier editions. Thus, the earlier editions are often valuable sources of information for tests on the market at the time of their publication. On many of the more important tests, the current edition contains new reviews that supplement reviews of the tests published earlier. The current edition lists 957 tests. There are 698 original test reviews and 6,468 references on the construction, use, and limitations of the specific tests in this edition. Another section of this reference lists and reviews books and monographs on measurement and related fields. The current edition lists 485 books, and many of the more important ones have several reviews.

The *Mental Measurements Yearbooks* can be used to obtain information on specific tests that the student has located elsewhere or can help the student locate tests that are available in a particular field. In the process of evaluating the research of others and in

---

[10] See *Manual, California Short-Form Test of Mental Maturity, Junior High Level, 1957 S-Form,* p. 4; and *Manual, California Test of Mental Maturity, Junior High Level, 1957 Edition,* p. 5.

locating measures for possible use in his project, the *Mental Measurements Yearbooks* are very valuable tools for the student.

In using this reference, the student first refers to the Classified Index of Tests. Here he will find the tests classified under a number of broad categories such as "achievement batteries," "character and personality," "foreign language," and "intelligence." Under each category he will find the pertinent tests listed alphabetically by title. Thus, he may quickly check the tests available in his area of interest. Upon locating tests that interest him in the classified index, he may note the number of the test and check each number in the Tests and Reviews section of the book. Under the test number, he will find first a brief listing of practical information such as the level of subjects that may be tested, the scores yielded by the test, the administration time, cost, and publisher. Following these data, he will usually find a number of references containing information about the test. For the more widely used tests, several hundred references may be available. A quick examination of these references will often reveal several, dealing with a particular aspect of the test, that interest the student. Reviews are available for many of the tests listed. These are perhaps the most valuable feature of the *Mental Measurements Yearbooks* because they give the student an evaluation of the test by one or more authorities in the field. These reviews are generally written by persons who have worked extensively in the field with which the test is concerned and are written specifically to provide test users with appraisals that can help them in evaluating the test. The reviews are generally critical and treat most of the essential elements important in test evaluation, thus providing the student with a sounder evaluation than he could make for himself.

Other sources of information on tests

Psychological Abstracts. Psychological Abstracts provides perhaps the best source of information on newly developed tests. Each number of the *Abstracts* contains a section on new tests, which the student may check rather quickly. Articles and other information concerning tests can also be found in the index number of each year's *Abstracts* under the title of the test. These articles provide the student with information on new tests not covered in the *Mental Measurements Yearbooks* and also give the most up-to-date information on the older tests. For example, the index number of the 1961 volume of *Psychological Abstracts* lists 29 references dealing with the Wechsler-Adult Intelligence Scale and over 100 references on the Rorschach Test. There are, of course, many research projects using these tests that are not indexed under the name of the test in *Psychological Abstracts*. References listed are generally those that supply information on the application or interpretation of the test itself, such as validity data, scores of special groups, and comparisons with other measures.

Review of Educational Research. An issue of the *Review of Educational Research* dealing with education measurement is published every three years. The latest in this series was the February 1962 issue entitled *Educational and Psychological Testing* (Vol. 32, No. 1). This source does not present an exhaustive coverage of new measurement devices in education and psychology but usually contains several articles dealing with different aspects of measurement, each of which is followed by an extensive bibliography. This review is particularly useful in acquainting the student with new trends in measurement.

MISTAKES OFTEN MADE BY GRADUATE STUDENTS

1. Pays insufficient attention to establishing and maintaining rapport with his subjects. This often leads to refusals to cooperate or to a negative attitude that can reduce the validity of tests and other measures.

2. Weakens his research design by making changes for the administrative convenience of the schools from which he is drawing his subjects.

3. Fails to explain the purposes of measures used in the research to teachers and administrators. If a teacher thinks a test or measure is silly or worthless, her attitude is quickly sensed by pupils and leads to poor cooperation.

4. Fails to evaluate available measures thoroughly before selecting those to be used in his research. This often leads to the use of invalid or inappropriate measures.

5. Selects measures to use in his research of such low reliability that true differences are hidden by the errors of the measure.

6. Selects measures to use in his research that he is not qualified to administer and score.

ANNOTATED REFERENCES

1. AMERICAN PSYCHOLOGICAL ASSOCIATION, *Technical Recommendations for Psychological Tests and Diagnostic Techniques.* Washington, D.C.: American Psychological Association, 1954. This booklet was prepared to assist test producers in developing useful measures, and it also attempts to provide information necessary for qualified users of psychological tests to evaluate these measures. Although many of the recommendations and standards established by this booklet are of a technical nature, most will be meaningful to students who have had one course in tests and measurements. This manual provides the reader with a great deal of information concerning the validity, reliability, administration, and scoring of tests, the establishing of norms, and other pertinent topics.

2. COMMITTEE ON TEST STANDARDS, AMERICAN EDUCATIONAL RESEARCH ASSOCIATION, *Technical Recommendations for Achievement Tests,* Washington, D.C.: National Education Association, January, 1955. This booklet was prepared to establish professional standards for the development of achievement measures. Students will find the recommendations helpful in evaluating achievement measures. The booklet also contains a treatment of validity and reliability as these concepts apply to achievement testing.

3. CRONBACH, LEE J. *Essentials of Psychological Testing,* 2nd ed. New York: Harper & Row, Pub., 1960. This text is written with a strong psychological orientation and is more useful than most educational measurement texts for the student concerned primarily with psychological measures. The basic concepts of psychological measurement are well treated and provide the student with an excellent background. Coverage of ability measurement and personality measurement is excellent.

4. HINES, V. A., and GROVMAN, H. "Rapport in Field Research," *Educational Administration and Supervision,* November, 1956, 42 (7), 403–11. This article discusses methods of obtaining cooperation and maintaining rapport between research personnel and teachers and administrators in the public schools. Many factors relating to rapport are discussed. This article will give the student a great deal of valuable insight into methods of building and maintaining good working relationships with public school personnel.

5. KRAUSE, M. S. "The Validity of Ratings," *Psychological Reports,* 1960, 7, 71–79. This article discusses some of the problems and difficulties in assessing the validity of ratings. Methods of dealing with these problems are suggested. Should be read by students anticipating the use of rating devices in their research.

6. THORNDIKE, R. L., and HAGEN, E. *Measurements and Evaluation in Psychology and Education*, 2nd ed., New York: John Wiley & Sons, Inc., 1961. This textbook is highly recommended for the graduate student who has not had a course in educational measurement recently and who wishes to review this important subject. It provides a thorough, up-to-date, and easy-to-read coverage of the essentials of educational and psychological measurement.

CHAPTER 5

Standard Measures

ACHIEVEMENT TESTS

Inasmuch as achievement is one of the major goals of education, measures of achievement are often used in educational research. Many standardized achievement tests are available to the research worker. Some of these are essentially aimed at measuring the student's knowledge of specific facts, while some of the more recent tests attempt also to measure the student's understanding and mastery of basic principles related to the subject. Administration time for different achievement tests varies greatly; some test batteries take as little as fifty minutes, while others require two days of testing to administer the entire battery. Achievement test batteries also differ in the subject matter areas covered. The *California Achievement Test Battery,** for example, contains tests in the areas of reading, language, and arithmetic, and requires only an hour and a half for the primary battery. The *Sequential Tests of Educational Progress (STEP) Battery,* on the other hand, includes tests on essay writing, listening comprehension, reading comprehension, writing, science, mathematics, and social studies, and requires over nine hours to administer.

In selecting an achievement test or battery for his research project, the student should first decide what areas of achievement he wishes to measure, and then evaluate the tests that purport to measure achievement in these areas. Because he usually has a limited time available for testing in the public schools, it is often necessary for the student to administer single achievement tests rather than an entire test battery. As a rule, the research worker will administer only tests measuring achievement in the specific areas concerned with the research. In addition to studying the evaluations available in the *Mental Measurements Yearbooks* and evaluating the test manual, the

---

* Further information on tests referred to in this chapter may be found in Oscar K. Buros, *Fifth Mental Measurement Yearbook* (Highland Park, N.J.: Gryphon Press, 1959).

student should also administer the test to himself (even if it is at the elementary school level) in order to check the instructions and gain an insight into the specific content covered. A major problem in developing achievement tests is to select content sufficiently common to the curriculums of most school systems so that the test will have a satisfactory level of content validity. It is much more difficult to achieve content validity in areas such as social studies than in areas such as arithmetic where the sequence and content is reasonably standard. A test may be very well constructed and receive good reviews in the *Mental Measurements Yearbooks* and still be inappropriate if it does not fit the content covered in the schools to be used in the research. In selecting an achievement test or battery to be used in more than one school district, the problem of content validity is increasingly acute because tests may fit the curriculum of one district better than the other. In this case, obtained differences in achievement may be due to differences in content validity rather than actual differences brought about by the research conditions. Very often, some of the newer achievement batteries, which place more emphasis upon principles and less upon specific facts, are more appropriate for use in studies involving more than one district. Another aspect of content validity that the student should check when examining the test is the degree to which the test is up-to-date. Some achievement tests that were excellent several years ago are considerably less valid today. A common weakness found in the older tests is that illustrations of devices that have changed in physical appearance, such as the airplane, the automobile, and the telephone may be so outdated that many students in today's schools would not even recognize them.

Another factor to be considered in selecting achievement measures for research is the test battery already being used by the schools from which the research sample will be drawn. Nearly all school districts now administer achievement tests on a regular basis as part of their program of self-evaluation and improvement. It is generally undesirable to use the same battery for research that is being used for other purposes in the public schools unless a very close control of the testing situation is possible. Achievement testing is psychologically threatening to many teachers because they fear that unless their students do well on the tests, it will be a reflection on the teacher's ability. Thus, it is not uncommon, if teachers have copies of the test at their disposal, for them to give their pupils special preparation in areas and sometimes even on specific items covered by the test. If the research worker selects his own measures, there is much less likelihood of the teacher being able to give this sort of special assistance to his pupils.

When the research conditions call for measures of very specific knowledge, it is often necessary for the research worker to develop an achievement test for use in the research project. The principal advantage of the locally developed achievement test is that it can be tailored to the precise content area with which the research worker is concerned. The disadvantages are the additional time required to construct such a test and the fact that most research workers cannot bring a locally developed test to the high technical level attained by standardized tests.

APTITUDE TESTS

Aptitude tests are aimed at predicting the student's later performance in a specific type of behavior. Tests are available to measure aptitudes for many specific school subjects such as foreign language, art, music, and the various areas of mathematics. Test batteries that measure a wide range of aptitudes that are related to success in different occupations are also available. These tests usually yield a set of scores that can be charted to provide a profile of the student's aptitudes. The student's profile can then be compared with profiles of persons who are successful in various occupations in order to locate types of work for which the student has the aptitude required for success. The *General Aptitude Test Battery* (*GATB*) used by the United States Employment Service is such a battery and measures aptitude in ten areas such as verbal aptitude, numerical aptitude, clerical perception, motor speed, and eye-hand coordination. In many research projects, only one or two subtests from the general aptitude battery are used. Single tests purporting to measure specific skills such as clerical aptitude, mechanical aptitude, and aptitude for selling are also available, and are appropriate for some research projects.

The usual evaluation procedures should be followed by the research worker in the selection of aptitude tests for research purposes. Predictive validity is especially important in aptitude tests because they are primarily concerned with prediction of future behavior. Aptitude tests are often used in educational research initially to equate groups that are to receive two different experimental treatments. For example, let us say we wish to compare the effectiveness of two methods of teaching ninth grade algebra. If the students to be used in the experiment are initially different in terms of algebraic aptitude, the group with the higher aptitude might learn more regardless of the method. Therefore, in order to evaluate the effectiveness of the two methods, it would be desirable either to equate the two groups being studied by matching students on algebraic aptitude or to make statistical adjustments for initial differences found by the aptitude test. If either of these methods were employed, the experimenter could be more confident that achievement differences measured at the end of the study were due to differences in method than he could if he had no knowledge of the initial aptitude of the two groups.

Aptitude tests are also used in research to identify students of a particular aptitude level for special study. For example, the research worker may wish to identify students who have very low aptitude for learning a foreign language in order to determine whether a method could be developed to teach foreign language effectively to students at this level.

INTELLIGENCE TESTS

Educational psychologists now believe that most of our intelligence tests measure only a limited aspect of human intelligence. These tests are often called scholastic aptitude tests instead of intelligence tests because the majority of them measure those aspects of intelligence that appear to be required for success in school learning. Intelligence tests may be identified as either group or individual group tests administerable simultaneously to large groups of students, while individual tests must be administered to one person at a time. The group intelligence tests have the advantage of low cost, and these tests provide a measure of scholastic aptitude that is satisfactory for most research purposes. Perhaps the most serious weakness of the group intelligence test is its inability to identify pupils in the group who are ill, negative toward the test, or suffer from some handicap that will cause them to make spuriously low scores. The individual tests overcome this difficulty because the examiner can usually determine by the student's answers and his general behavior whether extraneous factors are entering the testing situation that would tend to lower the student's score. Another disadvantage of the group test that can seriously distort research results in studies involving young children or children of below average achievement is that most of these tests depend to a considerable degree on the student's ability to read, and students whose reading ability is low will generally receive a spuriously low score on the test.

The disadvantage of the individual test, of course, is its expense. A trained examiner requires about an hour to administer the usual individual intelligence test to a single pupil. The individual tests also require considerable training to score and take much longer to score than the group tests, most of which are machine scoreable. In spite of these disadvantages, however, the research worker should use an individual intelligence test whenever his subjects are such that he has reason to doubt the accuracy of results obtained from group tests. It is better for the research worker to reduce the size of his sample to permit individual testing than to test a large sample with a group measure of questionable validity.

Most intelligence tests yield an IQ score. Some tests also yield subscores in verbal and nonverbal IQ, and, on a number of others, subscores may be obtained in specific intelligence subareas such as spacial relationships, verbal ability, numerical reasoning, and logical reasoning.

In selecting an intelligence test for use in research, after determining whether a group test or individual test is required, the student may apply the usual procedure for test evaluation. If he plans to use any of the subscores in his research analysis, he should carefully check to determine if these scores are supported by sufficient evidence of construct validity and reliability. Occasionally, the student encounters a research situation in which his subjects already have been tested with one of several intelligence measures. This is often the case when subjects have been selected for the public schools. Unfortunately, IQ scores obtained from different tests are not directly comparable. Different intelligence tests have different standard deviations, and although scores close to 100 IQ might be closely comparable, those at the high and low extremes may differ considerably because of this difference in standard deviation.

The student is often under pressure in carrying out his research for the Master's thesis to use test data already collected by the schools. This is usually not advisable for several reasons. First, the measures available are often not those that are most appropriate for the research project. Second, there will probably be some subjects whom the student wishes to include in his sample who will not have taken the test. Third, the research worker does not know the conditions under which the test was administered and, of course, had no control over these conditions. The student is therefore urged to select and administer the measures that seem most appropriate for his research whenever this is possible and avoid using data not collected under his control.

INTEREST INVENTORIES

A number of inventories are available that aim at determining the vocational interest of the individual tested. These are self-reporting devices in which the student indicates activities that he likes or dislikes. His responses are combined to provide a set of scores. Like all measures that depend on self-reporting, the results tell us how the subject perceives himself and what he is willing to reveal about himself. This may differ considerably from the objective facts concerning the individual. In spite of this limitation, vocational interest inventories have been proven useful in vocational counseling and have been used widely in educational research. These measures are usually developed by determining the interest patterns of individuals successful in different occupations or occupational areas. They are interpreted by comparing the patterns of the individual tested with the patterns of the norm groups. The various forms of the *Kuder Preference Record* and the *Strong Vocational Interest Blank* are the most widely used of these inventories. The *Preference Record* (vocational) yields scores in ten interest areas: outdoor, mechanical, computational, scientific, persuasive, artistic, literary, musical, social service, and clerical. The *Vocational Interest Blank,* in contrast, yields interest scores for specific occupations rather than broad occupational areas. At the present time, scores may be obtained on this test for over forty occupations. The research worker must determine which of the above approaches is more appropriate, in view of his research goals.

PERSONALITY MEASURES

Personality measures can be classified into three types : inventories, projective techniques, and rating scales.

General inventories

These usually aim at measuring a group of personality or adjustment variables. Like most self-reporting devices, they are subject to the basic weakness that they are only accurate to the degree that the individual's self-perceptions are accurate and to the degree that he is willing to express these honestly. This weakness is generally more serious in the personality inventories than in other self-report measures, such as vocational interest tests. Most persons are somewhat more reluctant to reply honestly to questions concerning personality than to questions dealing with interests or opinions. The inventory obtains information about the individual's personality by asking him questions or requiring him to respond to statements. Because many of the questions used on these inventories are direct, the subject can often guess the areas that the inventory is attempting to measure. The early personality inventories were generally little more than a collection of items the test author thought might be useful in measuring a certain trait. Often these so-called traits were not distinct and independent personality factors. For example, Flanagan found that scores on introversion and neurotic tendency obtained on the *Bernreuter Personality Inventory* correlated .87, indicating that both scores measure essentially the same thing.[1] Although some of these essentially empirical tests such as the *Minnesota Multiphasic Personality Inventory* have been used widely and provide valuable data, the lack of precision in developing many of these early instruments has made interpretation difficult and has led to more rigorous statistical approaches in constructing recent instruments. Many of the instruments published since 1945 are based upon factor analytical studies. The use of factor analysis makes possible the development of tests that provide scores on reasonably independent characteristics—that is, characteristics that do not correlate highly with one another. Perhaps the best known early examples of factor

---

[1] John C. Flanagan, *Factor Analysis in the Study of Personality* (Stanford, Calif.: Stanford University Press, 1935).

analyzed inventories are Guilford's *Inventory of Factors STDCR* and Cattell and Saunder's *Sixteen Personality Factor Questionnaire*. The most interesting of the recent inventories employing the factor analytical approach is the *Objective Analytical Test Battery*. This battery, developed under the leadership of R. B. Cattell, is based on a number of factor analytical studies by Cattell, Eysenck, and other personality theorists. The battery is built around eighteen personality factors that Cattell considers to have reoccurred often enough in the research of various investigators so that they may be considered stable personality characteristics. This battery contains a large number of both individual and group administerable measures. Different forms of the battery are available for adults and children. Although some of these tests contain items similar to those found in other personality inventories, the majority of the tests are considerably less direct and therefore more appropriate for research and other applications in which the disadvantages of direct testing (such as susceptibility to faking) are important. This battery is particularly well adapted for research purposes because a number of tests are available to measure each factor; and it is therefore possible to obtain a rough measure of the factor in a relatively short period of time or, if desired, to administer more tests related to the factor in order to obtain a more complete measure. It is not necessary to administer the entire battery, so the research worker may select only those personality factors with which he is directly concerned in his research.

Advantages and disadvantages of the personality inventory

The principal advantages of the personality inventory are its low cost and ease of administration and scoring. A few of these measures, however, require considerable training in order to interpret. A serious weakness of many of these inventories has been the lack of attention to construct validity, although some present evidence of concurrent validity. Many of the questions contained in personality inventories are direct and, therefore, subject to faking by the person taking the test. This limits the use of such inventories to situations where the subject has no motive to make a favorable score in certain areas. For example, such inventories are not usable in selection programs. If the individual strongly desires to be selected for a job opening, his answers will almost certainly be slanted to some extent. Even when nothing is at stake, many subjects will distort their answers in order to make a better appearance on the test.[2] Inventories, of course, vary considerably in the degree to which they can be faked, but the majority of them are fakeable to some extent.

Research application

Personality inventories are used frequently in educational and psychological research. Perhaps their most widespread use is to provide trait descriptions of groups being studied such as underachievers, members of minority groups, children from broken homes, or members of a particular vocational group (such as nurses). Other uses include identification of individuals with deviant personalities for special study or counseling and use in studies concerned with interrelationships between personality characteristics and other variables such as intelligence, racial attitude, or popularity. In selecting a personality inventory for research use, the student should apply the usual evaluation criteria, paying particular attention to evidences of construct validity and concurrent validity. It is also wise to check the reliability coefficient of subtest scores because some of these are too low for some research applications. For example, reliability coefficients of the subtests on the *Sixteen Personality Factor Questionnaire* range from .88 down to .50.[3] Another problem that must be considered in the selection of a personality inventory for research is to determine whether a measure using direct questions can be expected to yield valid results in the planned research. If the subjects have any reason for faking their answers, the direct question inventory will not yield accurate information.

Another problem faced by the research worker is to determine the variables that he wishes to measure in his project. There is a great deal of confusion in psychology concerning personality trait names. Different tests may measure substantially the same variable but give the variable different names. Therefore, it is necessary for the research worker to make a careful study of the test content and the descriptive data in the manual and other sources in order to obtain

[2] Allen L. Edwards, *The Social Desirability Variable in Personality Assessment and Research* (New York: Holt, Rinehart & Winston, 1957).

[3] R. B. Cattell, D. R. Saunders, and G. Stice, *The Sixteen Personality Factor Questionnaire Handbook Supplement A—Tabular Supplement* (Champaign, Ill.: Institute for Personality and Ability Testing), p. 1.

a clear picture of the variables that the test measures. There is certainly strong need for a standardization of terminology in this field. Cattell has developed such a terminology in his factor analytical studies of personality that may eventually lead to a clarification of this problem.

Frequently, the research worker has no need for scores on all of the variables covered in the personality inventory that he chooses. Under these conditions, if testing time available to the research worker is limited, he may select only those items that are weighted on the particular trait or factor scores he wishes to obtain. It is usually possible for the research worker to make arrangements with the publisher to reproduce for research purposes only those items that he needs. When it is necessary to do this, however, the test norms should be used cautiously because the omission of certain items from the test can result in different patterns of answers.

In selecting a measure, the research worker must also be sure that he has adequate training to interpret the results. Some personality inventories require little training for interpretation, while others require a special college course and considerable experience if they are to be used effectively.[4]

Finally, the research worker should realize that the use of personality measures is considered by many individuals as an invasion of privacy. Although this is a more serious problem in clinical and guidance situations than in research, public relations problems can exist if the research worker is not careful in his selection and use of personality inventories. He should carefully study the items in the inventory he is considering to see if items are present that might cause public relations difficulties with parents or community groups. For example, administering an inventory that contained questions dealing with sexual intercourse to junior high school students might cause serious repercussions in the community and make it impossible to complete the research. If such items are essential to the research objectives, very extensive public relations work must be carried out before and during the study.

Most research workers consider it their responsibility to treat research data as highly confidential. It is especially important that this

---

[4] See Lee J. Cronbach, *Essentials of Psychological Testing* (2nd ed.; New York: Harper & Row, Pub., 1960), pp. 498–99, for a classification of self-report inventories in terms of training needed for interpretation.

rule be observed with regard to scores on personality inventories. Most research reports deal with quantitative results, and it is generally not necessary to single out individual cases for discussion. If individual cases must be cited, the report should conceal the identity of the individual.

Special inventories

In addition to the rather general personality inventories that measure a number of characteristics or factors, a group of more limited inventories measuring a single personality variable or oriented towards a particular theory of personality are available. Perhaps the best known of these measures is the *Study of Values,* which attempts to determine the predominant value system of the person tested. This inventory yields scores indicating the dominant values that shape the individual's personality. Six value scores are provided: theoretical, economic, aesthetic, social, political, and religious.[5]

The *California F Scale* is an example of an inventory designed to measure a single variable—authoritarianism. Other recent personality inventories oriented around a single dimension are the *Index of Adjustment and Values* by Bills, which attempts to measure various aspects of self-concept and the *A.S.O. Scale* by Fiedler.

Rating scales

Personality Inventories also take the form of rating scales in which an inventory of the individual is made by someone other than himself. These scales are subject to observer bias, just as the self-report is subject to errors due to lack of insight. Examples of the rating devices available include (1) the *Vineland Social Maturity Scale* that has been used primarily by clinical psychologists and counselors working with children, and (2) *The Child Personality Scale* that is designed for ratings by classmates and teachers, as well as self-rating from kindergarten through the ninth grade.

Finally, a number of problem checklists might be classified as self-report personality inventories. The most well-known of these is the *Mooney Problem Check List.* Because normative data are not available on the problem checklist, the *S.R.A. Junior Inventory* and the

---

[5] Gordon W. Allport, Philip E. Vernon, and Gardner Lindzey, *The Study of Values: A Scale for Measuring the Dominant Interest in Personality* (Rev. ed.; Boston: Houghton Mifflin Co., 1951).

S.R.A. Youth Inventory are sometimes more useful for research. Both of these are problem checklists similar to the *Mooney*. On the *Junior Inventory*, pupils check problems in five areas: school, home, myself, people, and health.[6] The latest revision of this instrument (form *S*) also provides for an indication of the seriousness of the problem. The *Youth Inventory* is constructed similarly for grades 7 to 12 but yields nine scores: school, future, myself, people, home, dates and sex, health, general, and a basic difficulty score.[7] These measures, with their focus upon adjustment problems, are basically similar to the other self-reports inventories in spite of differences in organization and format.

Projective measures

Based upon the idea that the personality of the individual is projected into his perception, the subject is usually shown a series of pictures that can be described or interpreted in different ways. The subject's perceptions or descriptions can then be interpreted in terms of the emotional and personality patterns that he has projected. In some of these measures, the pictures are unstructured to a degree that the subject can see almost anything. The *Rorschach Test*, with its ten irregular inkblots, is the best known example of the unstructured type of projective measure.[8]

Other projective measures use pictures that are designed to bring out responses in a particular area that interests the clinician. These are often referred to as thematic projective measures. *The Thematic Apperception Test (T.A.T.)* is the most widely used technique of this type. In this test the subject is shown a picture and asked to tell a story describing what is happening, what led up to the scene, and what will be the outcome. In the full test the individual is shown ten cards, although fewer are often used to save time.

Although the *Rorschach* and *T.A.T.* are the most widely used projective techniques, many others are available—the *Fifth Mental*

---

[6] H. H. Remmers and R. H. Bauernfeind, *Examiner Manual for the SRA Junior Inventory, Form S* (2nd ed.; Chicago: Science Research Associates, 1957).

[7] H. H. Remmers, B. Shimberg, and A. J. Drucker, *Examiner Manual for the SRA Youth Inventory, Form A* (2nd ed.; Chicago: Science Research Associates, 1953).

[8] The *Holtzman Inkblot Test* is a promising new variation of this approach.

Measurements Yearbook lists 48. These techniques have been used mainly by clinical psychologists for the study and diagnosis of persons with emotional problems. They have usually been interpreted subjectively and have been combined with other techniques to aid the clinical psychologist in obtaining insight into the subject's personality and emotional problems.

Projective techniques as research tools

These techniques are being used to an increasing degree as research tools in education and psychology. Perhaps their greatest advantage over the personality inventory is that they are much less direct, and thus less subject to faking and faulty insight. On the *T.A.T.*, the subject is usually told that his imagination is being tested—thus providing a plausible and nonthreatening explanation for the test.

The disadvantages of projective techniques are the subjective nature of the scoring, the high level of training required for interpretation, and the cost, which is always high for individually administered measures. These disadvantages are being overcome, thus making the projective techniques increasingly appropriate for research use. A number of reasonably objective scoring systems have been developed for the more widely used measures. These systems, although not permitting full clinical interpretations, do provide reliable data and generally can be used by persons who have less training than is required for clinical use of the instruments.

Forms of some of these measures that permit group administration have been developed. These forms overcome the last serious drawback of the projective technique for educational research—the expense of individual administration.

ATTITUDE SCALES

Attitude scales are usually developed by collecting a large number of statements about the attitude object.[9] These statements range from very favorable to very unfavorable and are usually obtained from essays dealing with the attitude object. Several techniques are

[9] The attitude object is the group or institution toward which the attitude is directed.

available to select items to be included in the final form of the scale, with those developed by Thurstone and Likert being most widely used.

Attitude scales have been developed to measure attitudes toward many institutions, issues, and groups of people (such as communism, Negroes, capital punishment, war, and the Church).

In many cases, however, the research worker wishes to measure an attitude for which no scale is available. The author, for example, recently found it necessary to develop a scale to measure teachers' attitudes toward ability grouping. Satisfactory attitude scales can be developed by the research worker if he follows closely the procedures outlined in textbooks on psychological testing. The Likert technique is usually the easiest method of developing scales needed in research projects.

Unfortunately, these scales are direct self-report measures and suffer from the usual deficiencies of this type of instrument. Thus, we can never be sure of the degree to which the subject's responses reflect his true attitudes. Under certain conditions, for example, when the individual's attitude is in conflict with the social norm, he may go to considerable lengths to hide his true attitude. Less direct attitude measures are needed to overcome this difficulty, but, to date, few such measures have been developed. In spite of this weakness, attitude scales are used frequently in educational research.

The attitudes of subjects often must be considered in the research design because this variable can have a significant effect upon the subject's performance on other measures. For example, the poor achievement of juvenile delinquents might be due to unfavorable attitudes toward school rather than low academic ability.

SOCIOMETRIC MEASURES

Sociometric techniques are designed to measure the social structure of a group and to appraise the social status of each individual with respect to other members of his group. A number of different techniques are used to collect these data. In the usual approach, each group member is asked to select persons in the group most preferred by him on the basis of a specific criterion. For example, he may be asked to indicate the three persons with whom he would most like to work on a committee assignment. In studies involving classroom groups, pupils are often asked to indicate persons with whom they would most like to study an assignment, near whom they would prefer to have their desks, and so on. Moreno, in the earliest development of sociometric measurement, used such methods as a means of rearranging groups of school children so that they could study together more harmoniously.[10] Occasionally selections of least preferred individuals are also made. In another version of the sociometric measure, the individual is also asked to identify persons whom he believes have chosen him. The choices that he believes were made can then be compared with actual choices in order to obtain an indication of his insight into his social position.

Another form of sociometric measure is the "Guess Who Test." Measures following this pattern contain descriptions of various social roles, and subjects are asked to indicate the group member who best fits each role.

These techniques can give the educational research worker insights into the classroom social structure that are difficult to obtain by other means.

PERFORMANCE TESTS

Performance tests can be used to measure a wide variety of behavior ranging from very simple problems such as assembling the bodily parts of a manikin to highly complex behavior patterns such as the emergence of leadership behavior in a group of business executives. Performance tests are useful in measuring many work skills in which the manipulation of concrete materials and tools are involved. Many clerical and mechanical skills lend themselves to performance testing. It is much more realistic to test a group of typists by having them type under standard conditions than to ask them questions about typing on a multiple choice test.

Perhaps the major advantage of the performance test for such tasks is its obvious validity. The main disadvantage is that most performance tests must be administered individually and thus are time consuming and expensive.

In recent years, situational testing has been employed to measure complex performance. In this technique, the individual to be tested is placed in a situation and is required to play a role that can be

[10] J. L. Moreno, *Who Shall Survive?* (New York: Beacon House, Inc., 1953).

evaluated. For example, situational tests aimed at measuring leadership ability may require the individual to assume leadership of a group of men and lead them out of a difficult situation. Situational tests may involve verbal interaction between several individuals such as in the Leaderless Group Discussion situation, may involve discovering and acting out the solution to leadership or human relations problems such as planning and carrying out an escape from a prison camp, or may require the individual to solve administrative problems that do not require the participation of other persons, such as are found in "inbasket tests." [11]

ADMINISTERING RESEARCH MEASURES

After the research worker has selected the measures that he will use in his research, it is necessary that he make careful preparations prior to administering these measures. In the process of selecting his measures, he should administer each measure to himself in order to become familiar with its contents. Before administering the measure, he should rehearse the instructions several times and make tentative decisions on such routine matters as how the tests will be passed out and collected, whether hand scoreable or machine scoreable answer sheets will be used, and so on. He should also make up a brief introductory statement to be read to his subjects prior to testing to provide them with some explanation of why they are taking the test and to develop a favorable attitude toward the testing.

It is essential that the research worker pretest all of his measures on subjects not to be included in the research, unless he has previously used the measure. The pretest should be administered to a group similar in size and other characteristics to the groups that he will test in order to obtain his research data. Often, groups in the same schools from which the research sample is to be taken can be used for the pretest. During the pretest, the research worker should follow very closely the instructions, time limits, and other testing procedures outlined in the test manual. For most of the widely used standard measures, the administration procedures will be well thought out and adequate. In some experimental measures, however,

[11] In these tests, the subject finds material in his "inbasket" that requires administrative decisions. He is evaluated on his decisions and the action he takes.

or in cases in which the subjects being tested are somewhat different from the test norm group, it will be necessary to check carefully the adequacy of the instructions and procedures. The research worker should take careful note of any questions that are asked before or during the pretest. Many standard measures do not permit questions to be answered during the test period, but because the pretest data are to be used only in gaining insight into the applicability of the test, questions should be permitted as they often give insight into inadequacies in the test or the administration procedure. During the pretest, the research worker should also check the best methods of handling the routines of test administration, such as distributing and collecting pencils, answer sheets, and test booklets; seating arrangements; need for extra materials; need for proctors; and others. After the pretest has been administered, the research worker should also check carefully his scoring procedures. In scoring the answer sheets, he should be alert for omitted questions and incorrectly completed answer sheets that may reflect deficiencies in the test instructions, the motivation of the subjects, or some other problem. If it is necessary to change the test instructions, the research worker must realize that the test norms will no longer be appropriate when new instructions are used. It is often more desirable to change the instructions, however, and obtain a better testing situation than to retain inadequate instructions in order to be able to use the test norms. Often, little is lost because inadequate instructions are most likely to be found in new or experimental tests, and such tests frequently have very little normative data.

After the pretest has been administered and scored, the research worker should have enough insight into the testing procedures, time required to distribute and collect material, questions likely to occur, and other factors relating to the test situation so that he can schedule his research testing program. If all data are to be collected in one school, scheduling is usually arranged through the principal. If data are to be collected in several schools, the principal of each school and the district psychologist or pupil personnel officer usually must be contacted in order to prepare the schedule.

In setting up the schedule, a number of points should be remembered. First, do not schedule excessively long testing sessions. The nature of the test and the motivation of the students must be considered in setting up the length of the testing session, but it is doubtful whether children in the upper elementary grades should be tested more than ninety minutes in a single session and whether single sessions should extend beyond three hours for students at the secondary level. The ideal testing times for most materials are probably about one half of the above limits. If testing is to be scheduled for more than one school period, it is usually necessary and desirable to schedule breaks. These breaks may be scheduled between tests or even during a nontimed test. It is usually sufficient to permit the students to stand at their chairs, stretch, and talk for two or three minutes.

In setting up the schedule, the research worker should attempt to complete all testing within a reasonably short period. If the testing program is stretched out over a period of several weeks, as is sometimes the case when large samples must be tested, there is some danger that the testing situation will be somewhat different for those persons tested last as compared to those persons tested first. In the case of achievement measures, for example, students tested last will have had additional time in which to achieve, and may therefore earn higher scores than pupils tested early in the program. The research worker should avoid testing near holidays or too close to the end of the school year. The excitement attending the holiday can make a significant difference in the attitude of students concerning the testing. Testing during the last month of the school year often causes problems because students are less likely to be attentive to the test, and it may be difficult to arrange makeup tests prior to the end of the term. Also, because numerous special programs and extracurricular activities are scheduled at this time, many students will be absent from the testing.

Whenever possible, students should be tested in small groups. The regular classroom unit is probably the most desirable group to test because the students are in a familiar environment and the group is small enough so that the test administrator can maintain good control over the situation. Testing in large groups, on the other hand, makes it difficult for the administrator to answer questions, passing and collecting materials is somewhat slower, and a single giggle can result in the test situation degenerating into chaos and confusion.

Although the research worker will often be unable to achieve an ideal testing situation, he should attempt to set up the most favorable situation possible. If experimental and control groups are to be tested separately, as is often the case, he should also attempt to equalize as much as possible the situation faced by the two groups. For example, it would be undesirable to test all experimental subjects in the morning and all control subjects in the afternoon because students are often less alert and less highly motivated during the afternoon session. It would be similarly undesirable to test all experimental subjects during the first week of the testing program and all control groups during the second week. To whatever extent such scheduling variables can be equalized between the experimental and control groups, this should be done.

During the scheduling session, the research worker should also come to an agreement with the school principal involving such questions as: What help will the schools provide for the testing program? How will makeup tests be scheduled and who will administer them? What role will the classroom teacher play in the testing program? How will disciplinary problems that occur during the testing period be handled? This latter question is especially important because a prompt and efficient means of handling disciplinary problems often makes the difference between maintaining control of the testing situation or losing this control to the students. If the testing is to be carried out in the classroom, the research worker should also visit each teacher who will be involved and discuss the teacher's role during the testing. Under certain conditions it would be more desirable for the teacher not to be present during the testing session, while in others the teacher might assist as a proctor and be responsible for disciplinary problems. The role of the teacher must be decided on the basis of the needs of the specific study, but should always be fully understood prior to the start of the session.

If the research worker has done a thorough job of pretesting and preparing for the testing program in which he will collect his research data, he has little to do during the actual session except follow closely the procedure he has developed and tried. In the event that some unusual or some unforeseen situation arises during a testing period, the research worker should make careful notes of what occurred in order to determine later whether the occurrence has introduced factors or biases into the data that will reduce its value.

USING EXPERIMENTAL MEASURES

If the research worker has chosen new or experimental measures for inclusion in his battery, it is usually necessary to carry out a more extensive pretesting. It is also necessary to do somewhat more preliminary work if the measures to be used by the research worker require extensive practice or training to administer effectively. For example, if the student plans to use a projective measure that requires such training, he should administer the measure to a sufficient number of subjects so that he is confident that he is fully qualified before he tests any of the subjects in his research sample. Often, in using projective tests, the research worker must also develop scoring procedures or must familiarize himself with scoring procedures that are complex and sometimes subjective. Such procedures should be fully developed and tried prior to the administration of the test to the research sample. Occasionally, scoring procedures developed by others will not meet the requirements of the student's research project. For example, the author is familiar with a doctoral research project recently completed in which the system for scoring the *T.A.T.* that was adopted by the graduate student was found to be entirely unsatisfactory in his pretest of the measure. In this case, the failure of the scoring system was due to the fact that the graduate student's subjects were less mature than those for whom the scoring system had been developed, and as a result, all of the responses were scored zero.

Of course, if it is necessary for the research worker to develop a measure specifically for his study, very extensive preparation is required. It is usually necessary to pretest the instrument several times, carry out item analysis, compute reliabilities, and collect at least preliminary cross validation data. Therefore, it is recommended that the student carefully study appropriate textbooks in educational and psychological measurement before attempting to develop a test or measurement tool.

MISTAKES OFTEN MADE BY GRADUATE STUDENTS

1. Fails to check the content validity of achievement measures in the situation in which the research is to be carried out.

2. Fails to standardize or control the teacher's role in the data collection situation therefore introducing bias resulting from nonstandard instructions, coaching of some of the pupils involved in the study, and variations in degree of assistance given pupils during test.

3. Checks overall validity and reliability of measures selected but fails to check validity and reliability data on subtest scores even though these scores are to be employed in the research analysis.

4. Uses personality inventories and other self-reporting devices in situations in which the subject might be expected to fake his replies in order to create a desired impression.

5. Assumes that standard tests measure what they claim to measure without making a thorough evaluation of validity data available.

6. Attempts to use measures that he is not sufficiently trained to administer, analyze, or interpret.

7. Fails to make optimum use of the testing time he has available by administering long tests when shorter ones are available that meet the requirements of the research project equally well.

8. Does not carry out a pretrial of his measuring instruments and as a result makes blunders in the administration procedures during the collection of his first data, thus introducing bias.

9. Fails to establish rapport with research subjects before administering tests.

ANNOTATED REFERENCES

1. AMERICAN EDUCATIONAL RESEARCH ASSOCIATION, "Educational and Psychological Testing," *Review of Educational Research,* February, 1962, 32 (1). This issue of the *Review* gives the student a brief coverage of most of the recent developments in educational and psychological testing. The literature in this topic is reviewed in three year intervals, and the student may wish to refer to the February, 1959, issue of the *Review* for additional information.

2. CRISWELL, JOAN D. "Sociometric Measures: Some Practical Advantages and New Developments," *Sociometry*, 1955, 18, 639–47. This article discusses a number of recent developments in sociometric measures that will be of interest to the student planning to collect this type of information in his research.

3. EDWARDS, ALLEN L. *Techniques of Attitude Scale Construction*, New York: Appleton-Century-Crofts, Inc., 1957. This text provides the student with a thorough coverage of the different methods available for the construction of attitude scales. Each method is discussed in detail along with the statistical techniques necessary for its development. Frequent examples are given to help the student to understand the procedures described.

4. FURST, EDWARD J. *Constructing Evaluation Instruments*. New York: David McKay Co., Inc., 1958. This textbook presents the fundamental problems involved in developing any evaluation technique, and then goes on to acquaint the reader with specific procedures that may be applied to the development, analysis, and improvement of measuring devices. This reference will be of particular value to the graduate student who must develop one or more research tools in conjunction with his thesis or dissertation project.

5. GRONLUND, NORMAN E. *Sociometry in the Classroom*. New York: Harper & Row, Pub., 1959. This text presents a brief straightforward coverage of sociometric techniques. Construction and administration of sociometric tests, analysis of results, reliability and validity of sociometric data, and application to educational problems are covered. This text is useful to both the teacher and educational research worker who plan to use sociometric techniques.

6. MASLING, JOSEPH. "The Influence of Situation and Interpersonal Variables on Projective Testing," *Psychological Bulletin*, 1960, 57, 65–85. Students contemplating the use of projective measures in their research should study this article carefully. Masling examines the evidence concerned with the method of test administration, testing situation, examiner influence, and subject influence on the responses made to projective tests and demonstrates that these variables are important determiners of subject response.

7. TRAXLER, ARTHUR E. "Ten Essential Steps in a Testing Program," *Education*, 1959, 71, 357–62. This article discusses the wide use of tests in the public schools in recent years and presents ten steps essential to any effective testing program for the schools. These steps apply primarily to public school testing programs, but have implications for research use

of tests. Areas covered include administration, interpretation of results, and others.

8. The following articles are recommended for students interested in the problem of faking in personality and attitude measurements:

(a) GREEN, R. F. "Does a Selection Situation Induce Testees to Bias Their Answers on Interest and Temperament Tests?," *Educational and Psychological Measurement*, 1951, 11, 503–16.

(b) NOLL, V. H. "Simulation by College Students of a Prescribed Pattern on a Personality Scale," *Educational and Psychological Measurement*, 1951, 11, 478–88.

(c) POLMANTIER, PAUL C., and FERGUSON, JOHN L. "Faking the Minnesota Teacher Attitude Inventory," *Educational and Psychological Measurement*, 1960, 20, 79–82.

(d) WESMAN, A. G. "Faking Personality Test Scores in a Simulated Employment Situation," *Journal of Applied Psychology*, 1952, 36, 112–13.

CHAPTER 6

Statistical Tools

INTRODUCTION

Statistics, along with tests and other measurement techniques, provide the basic tools used by the educational research worker. Without an understanding of the tools available, it is impossible for the student to design and carry through a sound educational research project.

Most statistical tools used in educational research serve one of three functions. Descriptive statistics involve tools that tell us about the nature of the groups we are studying. The mean, median, and standard deviation are examples of devices that describe groups. Inferential statistics provide us with the means of measuring differences and relationships. Such tools as the t-test, analysis of variance, and chi-square are employed to determine the significance of differences that we obtain in educational experiments. The various correlational techniques, on the other hand, are used for measuring the degree of relationship between educational variables and are employed in research where relationships are sought out and applied. Studies involving educational prediction and selection commonly employ correlational techniques.

Statistical tools are used primarily during the analysis of research data, but these tools are also important in other aspects of the total research picture. If the individual does not understand how these tools are used and what the statistical results mean, he is unable to understand the research reports of other workers in the field. He cannot relate their findings to his problem, nor critically evaluate the quality of their work. A shallow review of the literature will in turn prevent him from obtaining the broad and accurate picture of previous work that he needs as a foundation upon which to build his own research design.

There are four kinds of information about statistics that the student should have. This information can be summarized in the following four questions: (1) What statistical tools are available? (2)

120

Under what conditions is each tool used? (3) What do the statistical results mean? and (4) How are the statistical calculations made?

What statistical tools are available?

One of the most serious weaknesses of Master's theses and other research reports written by inexperienced research workers is that they often fail to make maximum use of the data collected. It is not uncommon for the student to limit his analysis to two or three comparisons between his experimental and control groups. In many instances, a more thorough analysis would produce valuable results that the student loses through his lack of ability to make use of statistical tools. Often the student compares final mean scores for his experimental and control groups and finds no significant results but overlooks the possibility that significant differences in variability, as measured by the standard deviation, may have occurred as a result of the experiment. For example, one teaching method emphasizing drill and the mastery of basic operations may result in a reduction of variability in student performance from the beginning to the end of the experiment. This reduction might occur because the teaching method, with its thorough coverage of concrete materials, is well within the grasp of the less able students in the class. These students may consequently gain more than would normally be expected. The bright students might have little opportunity in this teaching situation to take full advantage of their superior ability and thus may gain little more than the less able students. The relatively large gain by slow students and small gain by bright students would make the group less variable. On the other hand, a teaching method that emphasized the understanding of abstract principles and attempted to cover a large content area in a short time might result in an increase in the variability between the initial and final testing. In this case, the bright students would probably learn much more than they would under the first method described, while the slow students would learn very little because they could not master the complex content in the time available. If we were to conduct a learning experiment using these two teaching methods, we may find no significant difference between the mean achievement gains of groups of pupils taught by the different methods, but marked differences might occur in standard deviation. The statistical significance of these variability changes can be calculated and often provides valuable insights.

Many useful research tools are not covered in the elementary statistics course usually required for Master's degree candidates. This chapter will discuss some of these tools. The calculations required to apply these statistical techniques do not usually involve complex or difficult mathematics and can easily be mastered by the graduate student if necessary for the treatment of his research data. Mastering the mathematics involved is much less important than knowing what tools exist and how to apply them to research problems.

Under what conditions are statistical tools appropriate?

To develop a sound research plan, the student must be able to examine his hypotheses and procedures and decide what statistical tools will be most appropriate for carrying out his analysis. This decision should always be made prior to the collection of data because different statistical tools often require that the data be collected in different forms. A common error made by graduate students in educational research is to fail to recognize which statistical tools would do the best job of analysis in their projects. This often results in the student using tools that do not provide a satisfactory analysis of the data. On many occasions, students use a tool that is completely inappropriate for the data they are attempting to analyze. A common mistake, for example, is to use the incorrect formula to calculate the standard error of the difference between means. If the final mean scores of the experimental and control groups are correlated, as they usually are if matched groups have been used, a special form of this formula must be used. On many occasions, however, the simpler formula for uncorrelated means is used instead. This error lowers the apparent significance of the results and often leads the student to report his results as not significant, when he would have found them to be significant if the correct formula had been used.

Another common error is to use a statistical tool when the data to be analyzed do not meet the conditions required for the tool in question. For example, most of our tests of statistical significance are based on the assumption that the characteristics we have measured are normally distributed in the population. This assumption of normality is justified for most of the variables we use in education, but when not justified, nonparametric or "distribution free" methods should be used, because these techniques make no assumptions about the shape of the distribution.

What do the statistical results mean?

After the student has decided what statistical tools are most appropriate for the analysis of his research data and has applied these tools, he is faced with the problem of interpreting the research results. On many occasions research results are misinterpreted, even though the student has selected the correct statistical tool and made his calculations without error. A common misinterpretation made by inexperienced research workers in education is to confuse statistical significance with practical significance. For example, let us say that a student is interested in the relationship between physical strength and intelligence. If he calculated a product-moment correlation between a composite physical strength score and the score on a group intelligence test for his sample of 1,000 elementary school pupils, he would probably obtain a correlation of about .20. With 1,000 cases, this correlation is statistically significant, because a correlation coefficient of only .081 would be significant at the 1 per cent level with this number of cases. In terms of indicating a practical relationship between strength and intelligence that could be used for prediction purposes, however, the .20 correlation in this particular study would indicate that a slight, but statistically significant, relationship exists between the two variables, but that this relationship is so small as to be of no value for most practical applications.

How are calculations made?

This is the question that demands the majority of time in most statistics courses and is not within the scope of this book. It is concerned with the mathematical procedures involved in the use of statistical formulas. In this chapter, as few references as possible will be made to statistical calculations. Most of the calculations are not difficult, and it is generally a more practical procedure for the student to direct his attention to learning what statistical tools are available, when they are used, and what the results mean after they are used. With this knowledge, he can make most of the decisions he will be called on to make during his review of the research literature and the development of his own research plan. Inasmuch as most of us rapidly forget formulas and calculation techniques, it is doubtful whether much time should ever be spent on this aspect of statistics until the research worker is ready to use specific statistical tools. Then, with a reasonable foundation in elementary statistics and the help of a statistics text, he can learn how to make the calculations required for his analysis.[1]

Let us now examine those statistical tools that are most commonly used in educational research, with emphasis upon the first three questions already discussed. Try to fit each of the statistical tools discussed into your "mental tool box." Carefully consider each tool available and think of the conditions under which you might use this tool and the points you must remember to interpret accurately the findings provided by the tool.

DESCRIPTIVE STATISTICS

Measures of central tendency

Though a number of measures of central tendency can be found in most elementary statistics books, the only ones used to any extent in educational research are the mean and the median. These measures are sometimes called descriptive statistics because they give a very brief description of the sample that has been measured. For example, if one has the scores of one hundred pupils on a test of algebraic ability, it is hard to get even a crude picture of the level of the group by examining these individual scores. Calculating the mean or median, however, gives a rough description of the group in terms of the average score attained. The mean is generally considered the best measure of central tendency.

Computing the mean is one of the initial steps in applying many of the more advanced statistical tools such as standard deviation, analysis of variance, and correlation. One advantage of the mean over the median is that it is more stable. This means that if one or two of your subjects are lost, as often occurs in educational research, this change in your sample would have a more predictable effect on the mean than on the median. For example, in Table 1 the mean

[1] The author recommends Henry Garrett, *Statistics in Psychology and Education* (5th ed.; New York: David McKay Co., 1958). This text employs a step-by-step technique that students find easy to follow.

IQ is 102.7 and the median IQ is 99. If cases L, P, and Q were eliminated from the group, the mean would become 104.7 and the median would become 105. On the other hand, if cases D, F, and H had been eliminated, the mean would become 100.6 and the median would remain 99. It may be seen that in the first case the median was much affected by the sampling changes, while in the second case it was not changed at all. These fluctuations of the median are most likely to occur when small samples are involved.

The mean, calculated by dividing the sum of the scores by the number of scores, emphasizes each score in direct proportion to its distance from the mean. In other words, scores that are extreme are weighted more heavily in calculating the mean than scores that are less extreme. The median, by comparison, is merely the middle score in the distribution and is not affected by the magnitude of scores at either end of the distribution. When a distribution of scores is symmetrical, the mean and the median are located at the same point. When the distribution has more extreme scores at one end than the other, that is, when it is skewed, the mean will always be in the direction of the greater number of extreme scores (see Figure 4). Let us say that you have collected data on the reading rates of 1,000 college students. Such a distribution will generally be skewed with most students reading at rates between 200 and 500 words a minute. Relatively few will be found reading at less than 200 words a minute, but a few will read at much higher rates, ranging to over 2,000 words a minute. If the purpose of your study is to reflect the amount of reading one might expect from the average college student, the median would probably be a more accurate measure than the mean. In this case, the mean score would be raised several words a minute merely because of the presence of the few extreme cases of students reading over 1,000 words a minute. Because of the difference between the mean and median in skewed distributions, the two measures can have considerably different implications. Have you ever noticed when reading about labor disputes in the newspaper that the average wage reported by the labor union is usually somewhat different than the average wage reported by management? This difference is sometimes due to the fact that the management representatives are more likely to calculate the *mean* wage of all persons employed by the company, including high level executive personnel, thus giving a skewed distribution. The union, on the other hand, is more likely to use only union members (thus excluding highly paid executives), and then to calculate the *median*. This would usually result in a figure considerably lower than that calculated by the company. The motive of the persons calculating

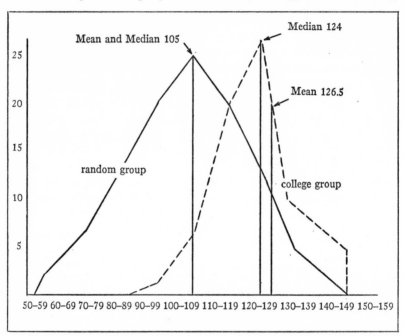

FIG. 4. The position of mean and median in symmetrical and skewed distributions. IQ distributions of 100 randomly selected adult males and 100 graduate students.

such figures is, of course, to support their own cause. In research, the purpose of statistics is to provide the most accurate picture of the data being studied. In most cases, the median gives a more accurate description of the group when the distribution is considerably skewed.

Measures of variability

Most statistics texts deal with several measures of variability, including the quartile deviation, average deviation, and standard deviation. In educational research at the present time, very little use is made of any measure of variability except the standard de-

TABLE 1

CONTINUOUS SCORES AND RANKS OF TWENTY SUBJECTS
ON AN INTELLIGENCE TEST

STUDENT	IQ SCORE	RANK
A	150	1
B	135	2
C	121	3
D	120	4
E	118	5
F	115	6
G	108	7½
H	108	7½
I	105	9
J	99	11
K	99	11
L	99	11
M	92	13
N	90	14
O	89	15½
P	89	15½
Q	86	17
R	82	18
S	80	19
T	69	20

viation. Standard deviation is generally considered to be the most useful and stable measure of variability, and because the calculation of standard deviation is a necessary step for applying many of the more advanced statistical tools, it has become the only measure of variability enjoying wide use. The standard deviation, like the mean, provides a way of describing the scores of the group on the basis of a single measure. Like the mean, the standard deviation gives a rather rough picture of the composition of the group. The mean and standard deviation taken together, however, give us a reasonably good description of the nature of the group being studied. Variability is important in educational research because the significance of many of our findings is dependent to a degree upon the variability of the groups being studied. For example, the more variable the group being studied, the higher will be correlations between related test scores obtained from the group. It may be easier to understand why this is the case if we consider the following illustration. Research correlating success in school with IQ generally yields correlations around .55 to .70 at the elementary school level.[2] At the high school level, however, the correlations reported between intelligence and school success are usually .40 to .60, and at the college level, correlations between these variables are usually under .40.[3] This lowering of the correlation reflects the fact that as we move up into the higher school grades, students become less and less variable in terms of intelligence. Students of low intelligence start dropping out of school during the elementary years, and as the scholarship demands become greater through the high school and college years, an increasing proportion of the less intelligent students are unable to remain in school. Thus, a sample of one hundred first grade pupils will be much more variable in intelligence than a sample of college seniors. As the students become more similar in intelligence, other variables such as motivation and study habits become more important in determining success in school.

In selecting samples for your research, it should be remembered that if you select from a population [4] that is somewhat homogeneous in terms of one or more of the measures you plan to use, this low variability will reduce your chances of finding significant differences or significant relationships.

Standard deviation and the normal curve

Many characteristics of human behavior, including most of those measured by educational tests, have been found to be distributed along a bell-shaped curve similar to that shown in Figure 5. This curve is a frequency polygon—that is, the height of the curve at a given point indicates the proportion of cases at that point. This

[2] A. N. Frandsen and J. W. Grimes, "Age Discrimination in Intelligence Tests," *Journal of Educational Research,* LI (1957), 229–33.

[3] H. L. Henderson, "Predictors of Freshmen Grades in a Long Island College," *Educational and Psychological Measurement,* XVII (1957), 623–27.

[4] The population is the entire group from which your sample will be drawn, such as male college graduates under thirty years of age, elementary school principals, teachers of junior high school Spanish, and so forth.

curve shows that the majority of individuals whom we have measured are clustered close to the mean, and as we move further and further from the mean we find fewer and fewer cases. Take, for example, a characteristic such as the height of adult men. The

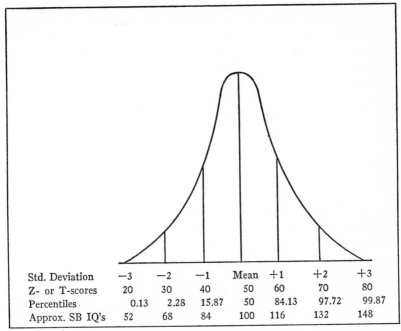

Std. Deviation	−3	−2	−1	Mean	+1	+2	+3
Z- or T-scores	20	30	40	50	60	70	80
Percentiles		0.13	2.28	15.87	50	84.13	97.72	99.87
Approx. SB IQ's	52	68	84	100	116	132	148

FIG. 5. The normal probability curve.

average height of American adult men is approximately 5 ft. 9 in., and the vast majority of adult men are of heights between 5 ft. 6 in. and 6 feet. As we move further from the mean we find fewer and fewer individuals until we reach a point in the vicinity of 7 feet where cases are extremely rare. On the other side of the distribution, we find very few adult men of heights under 5 feet. The curve that we obtain when we plot such things as height of adult males, intelligence test scores, time required to swim 100 yards, and, for that matter, most measures of complex human characteristics and behavior usually has a shape similar to that shown in Figure 5. This bell-shaped curve is known as the normal curve or normal probability curve. The exact normal curve has a mathematical formula, just as is the case for other geometrical curves such as the parabola and the circle. This normal curve can be developed by any technique that involves chance occurrences. If you would like to develop a normal curve, flip ten pennies and record how many heads and how many tails occur. Then flip the ten pennies again and record again how many heads and tails occur. Continue to repeat this procedure for one hundred sequences of ten flips. Then make a distribution showing the number of sequences of ten in which all the coins were heads, the number in which there were nine heads and one tail, eight heads and two tails, and so on. This distribution will roughly approximate the normal probability curve. If the coins were perfectly balanced so that the chances of flipping a head or tail were exactly equal and if the ten coins were flipped 10,000 times, the distribution plotted would very closely approximate the normal curve. Most of the measures that we use in educational research are such that their distributions approximate the normal curve. Because our measures are not precise and the number of cases we work with is usually small, the distributions we obtain sometimes deviate considerably from the normal curve formula.

If we divide the base line of the normal curve into a number of equal intervals such as are shown in Figure 5, we find that the percentage of cases that occur between two points on the base line is always the same if the interval we are concerned with is at the same distance from the mean and of the same length. The standard deviation divides the normal curve into a number of equal units. Because most of our data in educational research only approximates the normal curve, these percentages are also only approximate but are still of great value in statistics. The standard deviation of the *Stanford-Binet Intelligence Scale* is about 16 IQ points (see Figure 5).[5] Thus, a person with an IQ of 116 would be at approximately the 84th percentile. This percentile is easily arrived at if we remember that 50 per cent of the cases would occur up to the mean and that the interval between the mean and a point one standard deviation above the mean (116 IQ) contains approximately 34 per cent of the cases.

In analysis of research data, the standard deviation is an intermediate step that is computed as part of other statistical calculations. The standard error, product-moment correlation, and many other statistical tools are based partially on the standard deviation.

[5] Lewis N. Terman and Maud A. Merrill, *Measuring Intelligence* (Boston: Houghton Mifflin Co., 1937), p. 40.

The standard deviation also forms the basis for various types of standard scores such as Z-scores, T-scores, and Stanine Scores.

INFERENTIAL STATISTICS—MEASURING DIFFERENCES

Much educational experimentation is concerned with measuring the different results that occur under different experimental conditions and determining the level of significance of these differences. Studies of different types of classroom organization, different teaching methods, different study techniques, and many other typical educational problems involve this type of measurement.

Standard error of measurement

Every measure used by man is subject to error. The measures used in the more mature sciences, such as physics, often are accurate within very small tolerances. The latest atomic clock, for example, recently developed by physicists, is capable of measuring time intervals to the nearest billionth part of a second.[6] You will note, however, that even though this device is highly accurate, it is only accurate to a certain fraction of a second. This indicates that errors in its measurements, though very small, do occur. The measurement devices that we use in education are subject to much larger errors than those that we find in the physical sciences.

If it were possible to administer the same test to the same student on one hundred occasions without his gaining any knowledge from practice, we would still not obtain the same score for each of the one hundred administrations of the test. Many of the student's scores would be considerably higher or lower than this mean. If we were to construct a frequency polygon showing the distribution of these one hundred different scores, its shape would approximate the normal curve. Measurement errors are normally distributed. Relatively small errors occur with considerable frequency, but, as the size of the error increases, the fequency decreases. If we were to calculate the standard deviation of the curve showing the errors in measurement based on repeating the same test one hundred times, this standard deviation would give us an estimate of how frequently an error of a given magnitude might be expected to occur in using this

[6] Leonard A. Stevens, "They're Slicing the Second into Billionths," *Think*, XXVI, No. 8 (1960), 12–16.

particular test. This standard deviation of the error curve is called the standard error of measurement. Fortunately, we need not employ the procedure described previously in order to obtain the standard error of measurement. A simple formula for estimating standard error of measurement may be found in most textbooks in elementary statistics.

Many published tests in education report the standard error of measurement. This information can be of value in interpreting test scores. For example, the standard error of measurement on the *Stanford-Binet Intelligence Scale* is reported by Terman to be 4.5 IQ points for persons whose scores range between 90 and 109 IQ.[7] The standard error, being the standard deviation of the error curve, includes the same per cent of cases between standard deviation intervals as any other normal curve (see Figure 5). Thus, if a pupil receives a score of 100 on the *Stanford-Binet Intelligence Scale,* we can estimate that there are about two chances out of three ($\pm$ 1 SD = 68 per cent) that his true score will be 100 $\pm$ 4.5 or will be between 95.5 and 104.5. Similarly there are about 95 chances out of 100 that his true score will be within two standard errors of his obtained score of 100. Two standard errors would equal 9 IQ points, so we could assume that his true score would very likely be between 91 and 109 IQ (100 $\pm$ 9).

Standard error of measurement helps us to understand that the scores we obtain on educational tests are only estimates and can be considerably different from the individual's "true score." With this in mind we can avoid the blind faith in test scores that many teachers seem to have. We can see, for example, that there may be no real intelligence difference between two pupils who receive scores of 97 and 102 IQ. Standard error of measurement can also be regarded as a means of indicating to us how much a test score may be relied upon. It is, in fact, closely related to the reliability coefficient although expressed in different form.

Standard error of the mean

Statistical measures such as the mean are also subject to error and the errors of statistical measures are also normally distributed. Let us say that instead of repeating the measurement of a single

[7] Terman and Merrill, *op. cit.*, p. 46.

individual 100 times, we randomly selected 100 individuals from a large population such as American sixth grade children, administered a test to those 100 children, and calculated their mean score. If we repeated this procedure 100 times, each time selecting a new random sample of 100 cases from the defined population, we would find that the 100 means we had calculated would not all be the same. If we calculated the average of these, we would again find that most of the means clustered close to this average, but an occasional mean would differ considerably from the average. That is, an occasional group of 100 randomly selected children would score considerably higher or considerably lower on the test than most of the other groups. If we were to plot these 100 group averages on a frequency polygon, we would obtain again a figure that approximated in shape the normal probability curve. The standard deviation of this curve would give us the standard error of the mean. The standard error of the mean tells us the amount we might expect our group mean to fluctuate if we repeated our study with other random samples.

Standard error in testing significance

Standard error of the mean is an important concept in educational research because it forms one basis for determining whether the groups we compare in our research are significantly different. The comparison most frequently made is between mean scores of the same measure administered to two or more groups. Suppose that we had taken a random sampling of 100 sixth grade girls and another random sampling of 100 sixth grade boys and had administered an intelligence test to both groups to determine whether the average girl scored higher on the test than the average boy. After calculating the mean scores for the two groups and finding them to be different, we are faced with the question of whether this difference is statistically significant—is it a true difference or is it due to chance fluctuations in sampling? To determine whether the difference between the two means is significant, we compute a critical ratio or t-test. This is a ratio comparing the difference that we have found between the two means in our experiment and the difference, based on the standard errors of the two means, that might be expected due to chance. If the difference between the means obtained in the experiment is larger than the difference we could expect to occur by chance, we report that the difference is statistically significant.[8] This indication of significance tells the reader that our differences are large enough so that there is only a slight possibility that the difference we have obtained between the two mean scores in our experiment is due to chance fluctuations.

"One-tailed" and "two-tailed" tests of significance

The ends of a normal curve where it approaches the base line are called the tails of the distribution. In effect, when we compare two means to determine whether they are significantly different, we are checking the degree of overlap between the tails of the standard error curves of these two means. In Part 1 of Figure 6, for example, Mean A is significantly higher than Mean B because there is almost no overlap between the two error curves. In Part 2, however, there is some overlap. If the experiment were repeated, there is a good chance that Mean C would be higher than Mean D in some repetitions. For example, on repetition of the experiment, Mean C may move to C-1 and Mean D to D-1, thus reversing the relationship between C and D. This is the situation that exists when two means are not significantly different.

In most educational research, such as a study comparing two teaching methods, we may expect Method B to produce greater achievement gains than Method A, but we must not ignore the possibility that the reverse will be true. In Figure 6, Part 1, we are comparing the overlap between Tail B-2 of Error Curve B and Tail A-1 of Error Curve A to determine if the means are significantly different. If Mean A had been higher, however, we would compare the overlap between Tail B-1 and Tail A-2. Under these conditions, a "two-tailed" test of significance is used in which both tails of the error curve are considered. In a few studies, however, we can be almost positive that if any change is to take place, it will be in the hypothesized direction. For example, suppose we did a study of the effect upon school achievement of administering vitamins and dietary supplements to undernourished school children. In such a study, we would randomly divide a sample of undernourished chil-

---

[8] A critical ratio of at least 1.96 is necessary for a difference to be significant at the 5 per cent level. A statistics text should be consulted to learn the exact critical ratio required for a given number of cases.

dren into two groups, give one group dietary supplements and the other group placebos. In this study, it seems extremely unlikely that these nutritional aids would lead to *lower* achievement as compared to a control group. In such cases a "one-tailed test" can be used that, in effect, makes the assumption that if any difference is found it will be in favor of the children who received the dietary

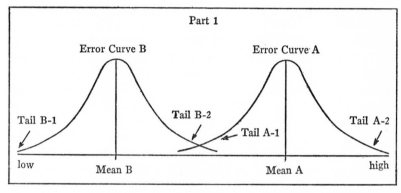

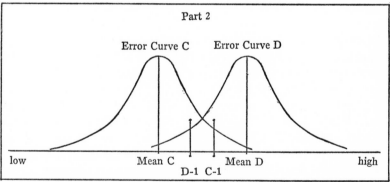

Fig. 6. Error curves and statistical significance.

supplement rather than the children who received a nutritionally worthless placebo. In this case, we need consider only one tail of the error curve because the difference can occur in only one direction. The main advantage of the "one-tailed test" of significance is that a smaller critical ratio (t-test) is needed to be statistically significant. Inexperienced researchers often use the "one-tailed test" under circumstances where it is not justified in order to make their results appear more significant. The graduate student should avoid the "one-tailed test" unless he is absolutely sure that its use is justified in his study.

Standard error of other statistical measures

In addition to the standard error of the mean, standard errors can be calculated for the standard deviation, correlation coefficients, and other statistical tools. These standard errors can then be employed to determine whether the two statistics being compared are significantly different from one another. For example, it is possible to determine whether two correlations are significantly different or whether the standard deviation obtained for one of our experimental groups is significantly different from the standard deviation obtained for the other group.

The critical ratio based on the t-test is the most generally used device for determining the level of significance of differences.[9] Let us now discuss the meaning of statistical significance and some of its applications to educational research.

The meaning of significance

A fundamental purpose of research is to make inferences about the characteristics of populations by studying the characteristics of samples of these populations. Our findings, based upon samples, are subject to error, and if we had no way of estimating this error, we could not make any inferences about the characteristics of the population group. Statistical procedures, such as standard error, provide us with a means of estimating the accuracy of our findings. Measures of statistical significance tell us the likelihood that our findings, based upon a sample, also apply to the population concerned.

Statistical significance is usually reported at one of the several "levels of confidence." For example, if we were to report that the mean height of American born men of English descent is significantly greater at the 1 per cent level than the height of American born men of Japanese descent, we would be saying, in effect, that if we selected new random samples of American men of English descent and new random samples of American men of Japanese

---

[9] See Henry Garrett, *op. cit.*, chaps. 8 and 9, for a more detailed discussion of the topic.

descent and again calculated the means and repeated this procedure one hundred times, the American men of English descent would be taller on the average in 99 of 100 repetitions.

In education, the two levels of significance usually employed are the 5 per cent level and the 1 per cent level. Significance at the 5 per cent level means that differences found between our samples would occur in 95 of 100 repetitions of the experiment. Occasionally findings are reported as significant at the 2 per cent level, and in exploratory studies, findings significant at the 10 per cent level are sometimes reported. The 10 per cent level is considered too low to be reported by many researchers. In exploratory studies that deal with new or little known variables, however, it is desirable to report findings at this level to provide clues for further research. Confidence levels are reported in several different forms. The 1 per cent level is also reported as the .01 level and sometimes as the 99 per cent level. All of these forms are acceptable, but the research worker should consistently use whichever form he selects.

Because statistical significance is influenced to a considerable degree by the number of individuals tested in the research project, we find that with very large samples, even a very small difference may be statistically significant. Thus, in interpreting statistically significant findings, the student must keep in mind the measures used, the size of his group, and the level of significance obtained, in order to make an intelligent interpretation. Correlation coefficients are reported as significant if they are significantly greater than zero. With 1,000 subjects, a correlation coefficient of .081 is significant at the 1 per cent level. This means that this correlation is significantly greater than zero, and if the experiment were repeated, would be greater than zero in 99 out of 100 instances. This finding would indicate that the experimenter can be reasonably confident that some relationship does exist between the variables he is correlating. The relationship in this case, however, is extremely slight and would be of little or no practical value in working with the types of educational problems we attempt to solve with correlational studies. A correlation of .081 means that the variables being correlated actually have very, very little in common. In this case, approximately ⅔ of 1 per cent of what is being measured is common to both variables.

In determining whether or not two mean scores are significantly different, another factor that enters into the calculation is whether or not the means that we are comparing are correlated. Different formulas are required for calculating the standard error of the difference between means depending upon the method used in obtaining the data. Means may be correlated in one of several ways. If two independent groups are measured with the same test as in the previously mentioned example, the means are considered uncorrelated. However, if the same group is administered the same test on two different occasions, such as would be the case if we were studying the effect of practice upon learning a particular skill, the two means involved would be correlated and a different formula would be required to calculate the standard error of the difference between these means. In some studies, different individuals are tested but are matched at the start of the experiment on the basis of some variable such as intelligence. Under these conditions, a different application of the same formula would be required to calculate accurately the standard error of the difference between the means. Sometimes, instead of person-to-person matching in educational research projects, a matching of the total groups is attempted on the basis of some pertinent variable. This is usually done by arranging the groups so that both have about the same mean score and standard deviation on the matching variable. If group matching is used in your research project, still another formula is required for calculating the standard error of the difference between means. All of these standard error formulas are essentially similar, but use of one formula where another is called for will give misleading results. Before the research worker employs the critical ratio or t-test method of determining statistical significance, he should review this topic in a statistics text to be sure that he has selected the correct formulas.

The chi-square test

The chi-square test provides the educational research worker with a simple and useful technique for comparing results obtained in his experiment to those results that would be expected on the basis of his hypothesis. For example, let us assume that the research problem is to determine whether bright students, average students, and slow students who have been placed in "homogeneous" classroom groups on the basis of intelligence have developed significantly favorable or unfavorable attitudes toward ability grouping. In other words, are their responses on an attitude scale different from the distribution of responses that could be expected by chance?

In Table 2, the first three chi-square tables are designed to test whether the distribution of attitude responses of 100 above-average pupils, 100 below-average pupils, and 100 average pupils differ from frequencies expected on the basis of the null hypothesis.[10] After the

TABLE 2

DISTRIBUTIONS OF ATTITUDES TOWARD ABILITY GROUPING
OF BRIGHT, AVERAGE, AND SLOW PUPILS

| | Bright pupils | | | | |
	Very favorable	Favorable	Indifferent	Unfavorable	Very unfavorable
Observed attitude	32	39	14	12	3
Expected attitude	20	20	20	20	20
	Average pupils				
Observed attitude	19	21	30	23	7
Expected attitude	20	20	20	20	20
	Slow pupils				
Observed attitude	10	21	27	34	—
Expected attitude	20	20	20	20	20
	Contingency table				
Bright pupils	32	39	14	12	3
Average pupils	19	21	30	23	7
Slow pupils	10	21	27	31	11

[10] The null hypothesis assumes that each of the five answers is equally probable if the 100 members of the group have no real preference.

chi-square tables have been constructed in the form shown on Table 2, differences between the expected frequency and the observed frequency for each of the five responses are calculated, squared, and divided by the expected number in each case. The sum of these quotients is the chi-square value.[11] The greater the difference between the expected and observed frequencies, the larger the chi-square value will be. After the chi-square value has been calculated, the research worker can determine its level of significance by checking in a chi-square table such as is found in the appendixes of most textbooks in educational statistics.

One might argue that the null hypothesis that states that the frequency of each response in this example would be expected to be equal is not the correct expectation because attitude responses are more likely to be normally distributed. If the student wished to hypothesize that the distribution of responses for each group would be expected to follow a normal curve rather than be equally divided among the five choices, it is a simple matter to calculate the number of responses that would be expected in each of the five categories from a table giving percentages of cases in the normal curve. These numbers would then be placed in the expected frequency column, and the chi-square between the expected and observed frequencies would tell us whether each of the groups of 100 pupils had showed an attitude toward ability grouping that was significantly different from the expected normal distribution.

Chi-square contingency table

Another objective of the aforementioned research could be to determine whether there is a relationship between attitudes toward ability grouping and the individual's status as a student. In other words, do bright students, average students, and slow students differ significantly in their attitudes toward ability grouping? In this case, a chi-square contingency table is used (see Table 2). The expected frequencies or "independence values" are calculated. Comparisons are made between the expected and observed frequencies in each box. The chi-square values for all of the boxes are totaled and the total chi-square checked in the chi-square table to determine whether a significant trend or relationship exists.

[11] For detailed information on the calculation of chi-square, see Henry Garrett, *op. cit.*, chap. 10.

In the previous example, it would have been possible for the research worker, by collecting his data in somewhat different forms, to have used other techniques for attacking the same problem. Chi-square, however, is often the only technique available to the research worker. This is true in cases where the categories into which the groups fall are discrete rather than continuous variables. For example, let us assume we want to determine whether large families contribute more or fewer than the expected proportion of children appearing before juvenile courts. The number of children is a discrete variable (because a family can have 3 or 4 children but never $3\frac{1}{2}$). Appearance before juvenile court is similarly a situation that has either occurred or not occurred and is also discrete. Under conditions such as these, chi-square is often the only analysis technique available to the graduate student with a limited statistical background.

Chi-square, however, is equally useful when the traits or characteristics being considered are actually continuous variables that have been categorized. The school system, for example, may provide the researcher with categories by the placement of children into ability-grouped classrooms. In some instances the research worker has data in the form of a continuous score but divides it into categories in order to permit the use of chi-square or because chi-square analysis seems to be most likely to yield meaningful results in terms of the hypotheses being tested. For example, in sociometric measurement the popularity score of a child is a continuous variable. In practice, the child's popularity score is usually taken as the sum of favorable choices given him by other members of the class. Research workers using sociometric data, however, often categorize pupils into several groups, such as "stars," "isolates," and "neglectees," based upon the number of choices each pupil receives. The sociometric category into which the individual is classified sometimes provides a more meaningful basis for analyzing the data than his popularity score, and in this case analysis using chi-square would be appropriate.

Analysis of variance

Analysis of variance is a statistical technique that makes it possible to divide the differences (variance) that we obtain in our experimental data into parts and assign each part to its correct source.

Let us take a situation in which we are comparing the final scores of five groups of retarded readers on a reading test after exposing the groups to five different types of remedial reading instruction. Part of the variation that we would observe in comparing the groups would be due to differences that occur between the children within each group and part would be due to differences that occur among the groups as a result of the different instructional methods.

In educational research the most common application of analysis of variance is to determine the significance of differences among group means. For example, let us say we wished to learn the effects of different types of rewards on the performance of random groups of nursery school children. Different types of rewards (independent variable) tried on different groups in the research might include: (1) praise given immediately after successful behavior, (2) praise given immediately after both successful and unsuccessful behavior, (3) praise given the day following successful behavior, (4) blame or criticism given immediately after unsuccessful behavior, and (5) praise after successful behavior coupled with blame after unsuccessful behavior. The dependent variable could be the scores made by pupils in each group on the memorization of nonsense syllables.[12] Analysis of this research could be attacked by the traditional approach in which the mean score, the standard deviation, and the standard error of the mean of each group would be calculated followed by determining the significance of difference between the mean scores of each pair of groups using the t-test.

Analysis of variance could be used to accomplish the same purpose, however, and has some advantages over the t-test approach. In using analysis of variance, a preliminary test is possible (the F-test) that will tell us whether there are significant differences existing among the mean scores of any of the five groups. If no significant differences exist among any of the means, it is not necessary to calculate the many t-tests required to compare each pair of mean scores. If the F-test shows there are significant differences present among the mean scores, however, the t-test is usually employed as the second step to determine which means are signifi-

---

[12] The independent variable or experimental treatment is the variable that is manipulated in an experiment, while the dependent variable is the variable that is measured to determine the effects of changing or manipulating the independent variable. See Chap. 13 for more details.

cantly different. T-tests calculated with analysis of variance have the advantage of using a more accurate standard deviation than is available when analysis of variance is not used.

In some studies it is desirable to employ two independent variables and to identify the variations in our experimental results that are attributable to each and also the variation due to interaction between the two. For example, let us say that we are interested in the achievement gains made by subjects receiving pupil-centered vs. teacher-centered instruction from teachers who are authoritarian in their personality as compared with teachers who are egalitarian in terms of personality structure. We now have two independent variables—teacher personality and instructional approach. There is a strong likelihood that the interaction between the two variables will cause variation in achievement that cannot be attributed to either variable acting alone. For example, the combination of the autocratic teacher and the teacher-centered learning situation might result in learning differences partially due to the type of learning situation, partially due to the type of teacher, and partially due to the interaction between this type of teacher in this learning situation. This research problem calls for a two-way classification analysis of variance. The problem could also be dealt with by using several groups so that each group represents a different possible combination of the two independent variables, and then using the t-test to evaluate mean differences. This approach, however, would not provide us with a direct measure of the effect of interaction such as we have when analysis of variance is employed, and would require more subjects.

Analysis of covariance

The analysis of covariance technique is especially well suited to research in education. This technique is an extension of analysis of variance and has one very useful additional feature—it enables us to compensate for initial differences in the groups we are studying. In analysis of variance, the groups compared are usually random samples, and it is assumed that these groups are initially equal in terms of the dependent variable. Let us refer again to the example concerned with the effect of five different techniques for teaching remedial reading upon the reading rate of retarded readers. If analysis of variance were used, we would randomly select groups of retarded readers to be exposed to each of the various remedial reading techniques. The dependent variable (reading rate) would then be compared at the end of the experiment by administering a reading test to all of the participating groups. The problem in using analysis of variance technique in studies of this sort is that it is often difficult to select randomly the groups that are to be exposed to the various experimental techniques. Many Master's theses are started after the children to be studied have already been assigned to a classroom, and school authorities are generally unwilling to rearrange classes in order to accommodate the research worker. It is not possible under these circumstances for the pupils in these classes to be assigned randomly to the different experimental conditions. This limitation rules out analysis of variance. In this case, initial differences between the groups are likely to occur, and these initial differences will, of course, have an effect on the final measurement of the dependent variable. Covariance analysis permits the experimenter to adjust the mean scores obtained on the final measure to compensate for differences between groups that have been discovered in the initial testing.

Because much educational research must be done on groups that are already in existence, covariance analysis is an extremely valuable tool for use by educational research workers. As a further example of this technique, let us say that we wish to compare the effectiveness of three different techniques for teaching algebra. Upon visiting the local junior high school, we find several algebra teachers who are willing to cooperate to the extent of using the three techniques in different sections they teach. However, the pupils have already been assigned to algebra sections and these sections are probably not equal in terms of average algebra aptitude. In this case covariance analysis would be employed. A preliminary test such as the Iowa Algebra Aptitude Test would be administered to each section to determine initial group differences in algebra aptitude. Then, the different teaching methods would be applied to different sections, and at the end of the period of the experiment, an algebra achievement test would be administered. The mean achievement scores for each group could then be adjusted for initial group differences in aptitude before making final comparisons of achievement between groups learning under the different teaching methods.

MISTAKES OFTEN MADE BY GRADUATE STUDENTS

1. Selects statistical tool that is not appropriate or correct for proposed analysis.

2. Collects research data, and then tries to find a statistical technique that can be used in analysis.

3. Uses only one statistical procedure when several can be applied to the data. This often leads to overlooking results that could have made a significant contribution to the thesis.

4. Uses statistical tools in situations in which the data grossly fail to meet the assumptions upon which the tools are based. Most statistical tools will give reasonably accurate results unless assumptions are seriously violated.

5. Overstates the importance of small differences that are statistically significant.

ANNOTATED REFERENCES

1. BONEAU, C. ALAN. "The Effects of Violations on Assumptions Underlying the t-test," *Psychological Bulletin,* 1960, 57, 49–64. This article demonstrates by means of empirical analysis that the probability values for t and F are not influenced greatly by data that do not meet the assumptions on which these tools are based. This study, along with a number of others that have been carried out in recent years, seems to indicate that unless the assumptions underlying parametric statistics are violated in the extreme, these techniques are still preferable to the less powerful nonparametric statistical techniques.

2. EDWARDS, ALLEN L. *Statistical Methods in the Behavioral Sciences.* New York: Holt, Rinehart & Winston, Inc., 1954. This is an excellent text for research workers in the behavioral sciences. In addition to covering all of the usual statistical information, a number of refinements and special techniques not treated in most other textbooks are covered by Edwards. An excellent treatment of two and three condition analysis of variance is given.

3. GARRETT, HENRY E. *Statistics in Psychology and Education* (5th ed.). New York: David McKay Co., Inc., 1958. This text provides an excellent coverage of most of the statistical tools used in the behavioral sciences and is especially recommended to students having a weak back-

ground in mathematics. Garrett employs very simple statistical terminology and provides clear and detailed explanations of every step involved in carrying out each statistical operation. These explanations are usually given in conjunction with an example, which is worked out for the student in step-by-step fashion. This book places statistics within the reach of any student who has mastered the basic operations of arithmetic.

4. MAYO, SAMUEL T. "Toward Strengthening the Contingency Table as a Statistical Method," *Psychological Bulletin,* 1959, 56, 461–70. This article examines the contingency table in terms of such pertinent issues as small samples, indexes of relationships, and computational procedures. Techniques are discussed for improving the methods of interpreting contingency data and providing methods of quantifying qualitative data.

5. PETERS, CHARLES C., and VAN VOORHIS, WALTER R. *Statistical Procedures and Their Mathematical Bases.* New York: McGraw-Hill Book Co., Inc., 1940. This text provides much material concerning the derivation of statistical procedures that will be of special interest to the student with some background in mathematics. It also contains many formulas not generally found in other books in the field such as the formula for the widespread biserial correlation, formulas for estimating the standard error of the biserial correlation, and others.

CHAPTER 7

Statistical Tools (Concluded)

MEASURING RELATIONSHIPS

One of the major objectives of educational research is to seek out relationships between different educational and psychological variables. These relationships are generally aimed at either gaining a better understanding of the variables being related or developing techniques for predicting performance on one variable on the basis of its relationship to other variables we can measure. Correlation is the principal statistical tool employed in studies of relationships. There are several correlational techniques that are commonly used in educational research. All of these techniques are similar in that they generally yield correlation coefficients ranging from +1, which is indicative of a perfect positive relationship, through zero to −1, which indicates a perfect negative relationship. Perfect relationships are almost nonexistent in educational research, but certain correlations, such as reliability coefficients of standardized achievement test batteries, often yield coefficients around .95, indicating a very high level of relationship.

In this chapter we will discuss nine simple correlational methods in addition to partial correlation and multiple correlation. There are other techniques that are used very rarely in educational research that will not be discussed. The reason that several approaches are required in educational research is that different correlational techniques must be used depending upon the form of the variables to be correlated. Educational information to be correlated is usually expressed in one of five forms: the continuous score, the rank, the artificial dichotomy, the true dichotomy, and the category.

The continuous score

The continuous score is the type of score that we obtain from intelligence tests, achievement tests, and most other standardized

147

tests employed in educational research. When we say a variable is in continuous form, it means that scores on the variable could theoretically occur at any point along a continuum. For example, in measurement of IQ, it is possible, theoretically, for a person to obtain a score at any IQ point within the broad range of IQ's possessed by human beings. This not only means it is possible for a person to obtain a score of 101 while another person obtains a score of 102, it also means that theoretically it would be possible to find a person who would perform slightly better than a person at 101 and slightly lower than a person at 102 IQ, thus earning a score between the two. In practice, scores on continuous variables are usually limited to whole numbers, but the continuous variable, in theory, must be such that it would be possible to construct tests that would measure at any fractional point along the continuum.

The rank score

We also find educational data in the form of ranks. In some instances, it is simpler to rank individuals than to assign quantitative scores to them. For example, ranking procedures are used very commonly in the evaluation of teachers. Some forms of educational data are available only as ranks, such as the student's high school graduation rank, which is often used in educational studies. The ranks used in education are usually another form of continuous variable, because it may be assumed that, if a greater number of persons were studied, cases would fall between the ranks already assigned. Continuous scores, such as IQ, can be converted to ranks, and this is often done in order to simplify analysis of research results.

The artificial dichotomy

Sometimes educational information that at least theoretically could be expressed in terms of continuous scores is available in two categories only. For example, a common division of a continuous variable into two categories is found in what is called the "pass-fail dichotomy." Taking any group of students who complete a given course of study, it is possible to divide these students into those who passed and those who failed. The term "dichotomy" refers to any division into two distinct groups. In the case of a "pass-fail dichotomy," the criterion for dividing the individuals into two groups is artificial or arbitrary. In other words, someone must specify the point we will use to divide passing from failing pupils. In some schools, this point is 70 per cent, in others 60 per cent, and in others no specific criterion such as a percentage point is employed. The division of individuals into two categories on the basis of performance on a continuous variable is called an artificial dichotomy. It is easy to see that the "pass-fail dichotomy" is artificial because we know that if we very carefully tested the individuals who complete a given course of study, we would find that their test scores, reflecting the amount learned, would make a continuous distribution ranging from those persons who learned a great deal to those persons who learned little or nothing. The point at which we divide this continuous variable into pass-fail groups is based upon an arbitrary cutting point or criterion. If we compare the person who barely passes and the person who barely fails, we find that these individuals are very similar and do not have any characteristic except their score or grade in the course of study to indicate that one person belongs in the failing group and the other person in the passing group.

The true dichotomy

Occasionally in education, we encounter groups that are different because of some distinct and recognizable trait. When individuals are divided into two groups on the basis of a true difference, the dichotomy resulting is referred to as a true dichotomy. The true dichotomy differs from the artificial dichotomy in that it is not necessary to establish any arbitrary cutting point for dividing the cases into two groups. Members of each group have some distinct characteristic that makes it possible to differentiate them from members of the other group. Perhaps the true dichotomy most frequently used in educational research is sex. Many studies are concerned with differences between the performance of boys and girls in learning patterns, verbal fluency, personality, and other measurable characteristics. In these studies, one of the variables studied is usually of a continuous nature such as scores on a verbal fluency test. The other variable is sex, which is a true dichotomy.

Variables expressed in categories

Variables in education occasionally are expressed in two or more categories. Student participation in high school athletics, for example, could be recorded in such categories as (1) earned letter in varsity sports, (2) participated but did not earn letter, (3) participated in intramural sports, (4) participated in physical education classes, or (5) did not participate in any athletics. Classification into two categories, of course, constitutes a dichotomy, but classification into several categories such as in the aforementioned example presents a different situation and calls for a different correlational technique.

Occasionally, data we wish to use in correlational studies are available only in categories. For example, studies in eye-hand dominance usually classify individuals in such categories as left-left, left-right, right-left, and right-right. Such data cannot usually be obtained in any of the other score forms.

Thus, we find that most educational data that we want to correlate is expressed in one of five forms: continuous scores, ranks, artificial dichotomies, true dichotomies, and categories. If we know the form in which our information is available on each of the two variables to be correlated, it is possible to select the correct correlational technique.

TYPES OF CORRELATION

Product-moment correlation (r)

The product-moment correlation (r) is used when both variables that we wish to correlate are expressed as continuous scores. For example, if we administer an intelligence test such as the *California Test of Mental Maturity* and an achievement test such as the *STEP Social Studies Test* to the same group of individuals, we will have two sets of continuous scores, each individual having a score on each of the two tests. Because most educational data are expressed in continuous scores, this is the most frequently used correlational technique. The product-moment correlation is subject to a smaller standard error than the other techniques we will discuss in this chapter and is generally preferred when its use is possible.

Rank difference correlation (ρ)

The rank difference correlation (Rho), developed by Spearman, is a special form of the product-moment correlation. The rank difference correlation is used to correlate two continuous variables under the special condition that the data for one or both of these variables is available only in rank form. For example, studies comparing various measures of intelligence with graduation standing in high school would generally employ the rank difference correlation because the individual's graduation standing is expressed as a rank. To use this correlational technique, however, both variables must be expressed as a rank, so in this case the scores of the subjects on the other variable (intelligence test), which is available in the form of a continuous score, would have to be converted to ranks before the correlation could be calculated. Converting continuous scores to rank scores involves the simple procedure of listing the continuous scores in order of magnitude and then assigning ranks on that basis.

As a rule, one would expect the product-moment correlation to be slightly more precise than the rank difference correlation. Let us refer back to Table 1 in Chapter 6. Students A and B, who have consecutive ranks, differ 15 IQ points when their scores are expressed in intelligence quotients. On the other hand, Students N and O in the same group also have consecutive ranks but differ by only one IQ point. Thus, it may be seen that rank scores do not reflect the differences between subjects nearly as accurately as do continuous scores. Although the rank difference correlation reduces the precision of the data, this reduction is usually slight. For example, if we calculated a product-moment correlation between scores made by a group of pupils on two continuous variables, then converted these continuous scores to rank scores and calculated a rank difference correlation with the same data, we would find that the two correlations obtained would be very close to the same.

Although the rank difference correlation is valuable when data are available only in ranks, its main use is in studies where the experimenter must calculate a large number of correlations on moderately small samples of individuals. With fewer than thirty subjects, the rank difference correlation is far quicker and easier to calculate than the product-moment correlation and yields results that are very similar. When the number of cases becomes large, however, the ranking procedure becomes laborious, and *Rho* cannot be calculated as quickly as *r*.

Kendall's Tau (T)

Tau is another form of rank correlation that has some theoretical advantage over the better known Spearman's *Rho*. Like *Rho,* it is used to correlate two sets of ranks. Data not in rank form can be converted to ranks if it is desired to use *Tau.* Its principal advantage is that it has a more normal sampling distribution than *Rho* for numbers under 10. It is somewhat more difficult to calculate than *Rho,* and yields lower correlation coefficients when computed from the same data. As *Rho* very closely approximates the Pearson *r* calculated from the same data, it is less likely than *Tau* to be misinterpreted by the educator.

The biserial correlation (r_{bis})

The biserial correlation (r_{bis}) is used when one of the variables we wish to correlate is in the form of continuous scores and the other variable is in the form of an artificial dichotomy. For example, if we wish to determine the relationship between success and failure in algebra and scores on an algebra aptitude test, we would use the biserial correlation. In this case, the aptitude test yields continuous scores, while the record of each subject as having passed or failed algebra takes the form of an artificial dichotomy. Unlike the rank difference correlation, the biserial correlation is not a form of the product-moment correlation. The results of the two techniques are roughly comparable, but as a rule, the correlations obtained using the biserial technique are somewhat higher than those obtained for comparable data using the product-moment technique.

Although the theoretical limits of any correlation are $+1$ to -1, it is mathematically possible to obtain biserial correlations greater than 1 if the variables are not normally distributed. This fact should be kept in mind by the research worker when employing the biserial technique. If he is unaware of this characteristic of the biserial correlation greater than 1, he will spend a great deal of time looking for an error that does not exist. In addition to yielding higher correlations, the biserial technique is somewhat less precise than the product-moment correlation and has a larger standard error reflecting this lesser degree of accuracy. Therefore, if we wished to conduct a study relating success in school to IQ, it would be better to employ a continuous variable as a measure of school success such as grade-point average rather than use the pass-fail dichotomy. With this approach, we would have two continuous variables and could use the product-moment correlation. In many instances, however, information cannot be obtained in continuous form for one of the variables. Under these circumstances, the research worker should not hesitate to use the biserial correlation if data for one of the variables are available only in the form of an artificial dichotomy.

The point biserial correlation (r_{pbis})

The point biserial correlation (r_{pbis}) is used when one of the variables we wish to correlate is in the form of a continuous score and the other variable is in the form of a true dichotomy. This type of correlation is used very widely in studies relating sex to different continuous variables such as intelligence, verbal fluency, reading ability, and achievement. In such studies, sex provides the true dichotomy, and the other measure provides the continuous variable. The point biserial correlation is a form of the product moment correlation and therefore differs from the biserial and the widespread biserial. As a rule, the correlation coefficients obtained when using the point biserial will be somewhat lower than if the same data were analyzed using the biserial correlation. This technique has several advantages over the biserial correlation. It does not yield correlations greater than 1.0. Its standard error is easier to calculate, and, being a product moment correlation, its statistical significance can be determined using the significance tables for the regular Pearson correlation that are found in most elementary statistics texts. The point biserial may also be used in regression equations and is a better tool than the biserial for item analysis. In situations in which an artificial dichotomy is not based upon a normally distributed continuous variable, the point biserial is often used in preference to the biserial.

The widespread biserial correlation (r_{wbis})

There are many instances in educational research where it is desirable to correlate scores on a continuous variable such as intelligence with extreme scores on some other characteristic. Let us say, for example, that we wished to determine whether teaching success was correlated with certain personality traits. The measurement of teaching success is a difficult task for which satisfactory measures are not easily obtained. Evaluations of teaching ability are usually based on a composite evaluation made by two or more raters. In making ratings, raters usually find it relatively easy to pick out the extremes—that is, the better and poorer teachers in the group. The real difficulty in making such ratings arises when we attempt to discriminate between teachers who are within the average range of teaching ability. For example, if five raters were used to evaluate one hundred teachers, we would find that the raters would agree much more closely in their identification of the ten best teachers and the ten poorest teachers than they would agree on the relative ability of teachers close to the average. This situation occurs in many studies where ratings are used as a basis for evaluation.

In addition to those research situations where it is difficult to obtain reliable scores except for persons at the extremes, there are also many situations in educational research where, even though it is possible to obtain a continuous score, the nature of the variable studied is such that a more meaningful interpretation can be made by studying extreme cases. For example, in studying personality traits related to overachievement and underachievement in school children, it is possible to classify all students as being either over-achievers, underachievers, or normal achievers. A correlational tech-nique that left out the normal achievers and used overachievers and underachievers as the two ends of a dichotomy would be more useful than one that divided all individuals into either overachievers or underachievers, including those whose achievement was actually not sufficiently extreme to be considered other than as normal. When only those individuals whose scores are at the two extreme ends on a dichotomized variable are used, we have a widespread dichotomy. In research situations where we wish to correlate a continuous score with a widespread dichotomy, we use the widespread biserial cor-relation.[1]

The widespread biserial is closely related to the biserial correla-tion and always involves artificial dichotomies. In most situations in which the widespread biserial correlaton is used in educational research, the cutoff points for identifying extreme cases are defined in such a way that the two extreme groups are equal. For example, let us assume that we wish to determine whether popularity in high schools is related to certain personality characteristics such as in-troversion, ascendency, inferiority feelings, and cooperativeness. In

[1] See Charles C. Peters and Walter R. Van Voorhis, *Statistical Procedures and Their Mathematical Bases* (New York: McGraw-Hill Book Co., 1940), pp. 384–91.

this case, the various personality traits probably would be measured with a personality inventory that would yield continuous scores. A study of very popular and very unpopular persons (perhaps the top and bottom 10 per cent) on these personality characteristics using the widespread biserial correlation would probably give us better insights into student popularity than an approach using the product-moment correlation in which all students would be included. If we used the latter technique, the scores of the preponderance of students who are neither very popular nor very unpopular might obscure personality differences that existed between the extreme groups.

It is not necessary, however, that these extreme groups be equal in order to calculate a widespread biserial correlation. One way of establishing each individual's popularity would be to obtain friendship nominations for each person in the sample on a sociometric measure. This would give us a popularity score for each individual equal to the number of nominations he had received from his peers. In establishing the widespread dichotomy in the above example, we could either select a percentage of cases from each extreme that would give us equal groups or we could define our popular and unpopular groups in terms of specific criteria that would give us unequal groups. Some research workers define individuals who receive more than a certain number of the possible sociometric choices as "stars," while those receiving a somewhat smaller number are defined as "neglectees." [2] It would be possible to use these two defined terms as the limits for our widespread groups, and if this were done, the size of the two groups would usually be different.

The tetrachoric correlation (r_t)

Occasionally we encounter a situation in educational research where both variables that we wish to correlate are in the form of artificial dichotomies. Under these conditions, the tetrachoric correlation is used. It is assumed that, if continuous scores could be obtained, the variables underlying the dichotomies in the tetrachoric correlation would be continuous and normally distributed. The tetrachoric correlation is sometimes employed, however, even though continuous scores are available on one of the variables. For certain variables, such as aptitude test scores, the research worker

[2] U. Bronfenbrenner, "The Measurement of Sociometric Status, Structure, and Development," *Sociometry Monographs,* No. 6 (New York: Beacon House, 1945).

may be more interested in whether or not the student reaches a critical cutoff point on the test than he is with the precise score earned by the student. If this is the case, the continuous scores are converted into an artificial dichotomy using the critical point of the test as the basis for dichotomizing the scores. An example of this approach is found in validation studies of the *General Aptitude Test Battery (GATB)* currently used by the U.S. Employment Service.

This test measures a number of aptitudes related to different occupations. Cutoff points have been established for each aptitude. In using the test, the principal concern is to determine whether the counselee obtains scores above or below the cutoff point in those aptitudes required for a given occupation. If the person is above the cutoff he is considered to have sufficient aptitude; and if below, insufficient aptitude. Thus, the cutoff point constitutes a critical score and is the only point that is considered in advising the counselee. In validating the *GATB*, there is another critical point to consider—the point separating success or failure in the occupation in question. Thus, in validating this test, two artificial dichotomies are used, the cutoff point on the aptitude test and success or failure in the occupation. This situation makes the tetrachoric correlation ideally suited for validation of the *GATB,* and it has been used extensively for this purpose.[3]

In any situation where a critical score point exists for a continuous variable, conversion to an artificial dichotomy often provides a more useful basis for analysis than use of the variable in continuous form. This is because the dichotomy ignores all differences except the critical point of difference. If the research worker has continuous data available on the variables he wishes to correlate, however, he should not use the tetrachoric correlation unless he has a well defined reason for doing so. The tetrachoric correlation is considerably less stable than is the Pearson product-moment correlation, having a standard error that is 50 to 100 per cent larger than the standard error for the product-moment correlation under similar conditions. The standard error of the tetrachoric correlation

[3] United States Department of Labor, *Guide to the Use of General Aptitude Test Battery, Section III: Development* (Washington, D.C.: Bureau of Employment Security, 1952).

is also quite difficult to compute, which means that considerable effort is required to determine whether the correlation obtained is

TABLE 3

APPROPRIATE CORRELATIONAL TECHNIQUES FOR DIFFERENT FORMS OF VARIABLES

TECHNIQUE	SYMBOL	VARIABLE 1	VARIABLE 2	REMARKS
Product-moment correlation	r	Continuous	Continuous	The most stable technique
Rank-difference correlation	ρ	Ranks	Ranks	Often used instead of product-moment when no. of cases is under 30
Kendall's Tau	τ	Ranks	Ranks	Preferable to Rho for nos. under 10
Biserial correlation	r_{bis}	Artificial dichotomy	Continuous	Sometimes exceeds 1—has a larger standard error than r—commonly used in item analysis
Widespread biserial correlation	r_{wbis}	Widespread artificial dichotomy	Continuous	Used when you are especially interested in persons at the extremes on the dichotomized variable
Point-biserial correlation	r_{pbis}	True dichotomy	Continuous	Yields a lower correlation than r and much lower than r_{bis}
Tetrachoric correlation	r_t	Artificial dichotomy	Artificial dichotomy	Used when both variables can be split at critical points
Phi coefficient	ϕ	True dichotomy	True dichotomy	Used in calculating inter-item correlations
Contingency coefficient	C	2 or more categories	2 or more categories	Comparable to r_t under certain conditions—closely related to chi-square

significant. The tetrachoric correlation is most stable when a large number of cases are used and when the dichotomies divide the sample into approximately equal groups.

The Phi coefficient (ϕ)

The *Phi* coefficient is employed in the case where both variables that we wish to correlate are true dichotomies. Because we deal with relatively few true dichotomies in education, *Phi* coefficients are used rarely in educational research. Perhaps the widest use of this technique is to determine the correlation between two items on a test during item analysis. Each subject's response to each item can be classified as either correct or incorrect, thus giving us two true dichotomies. In general, when we are dealing with fairly large numbers of cases and when we are confident that the variables underlying our dichotomies are continuous and normally distributed, the tetrachoric correlation is preferred. When the aforementioned conditions cannot be met to a reasonable degree, the *Phi* coefficient is preferable. The *Phi* coefficient yields a somewhat lower correlation coefficient than does the tetrachoric correlation but is somewhat more stable, and its level of significance is easily determined.

The contingency coefficient (C)

The contingency coefficient may be used when the variables to be correlated are in the form of categories. Although C can be used when the variables are divided into dichotomies, the *Phi* coefficient or tetrachoric correlation are preferable under these conditions. When either or both variables are classified into more than two categories, however, ϕ or r_t cannot be applied, and C should be used if a measure of relationship is required. C is closely related to chi-square and is computed using a contingency table. If chi-square has been computed, C can easily be derived from chi-square. Conversely, chi-square can be computed from C, and this is usually done when C is computed because chi-square provides the easiest method of determining the statistical significance of C.

The contingency coefficient yields correlations closely comparable to the Pearson r if each variable is split into at least five categories and if the sample is large.

C should not be used unless the data are available only in categories or unless converting the scores to categories presents the data in a more logical or understandable form. For example, sociometric data obtained as continuous scores are often divided into categories such as stars, above average, below average, neglectees, and isolates because these classifications have meaning among persons using sociometric techniques.

CORRECTIONS TO THE CORRELATION COEFFICIENT

A number of corrections may be applied to correlation coefficients. The most important of these are correction for attenuation and correction for restriction in range. When we correlate two test scores, the correlation coefficient obtained is lowered to some extent by the fact that the tests or other measures we have correlated are not perfectly reliable. This lowering of the correlation coefficient due to reliability of the measures employed is called attenuation. Correction for attenuation provides us with an estimate of what the correlation between the variables would be if the tests employed had perfect reliability. In prediction studies, correction for attenuation is not usually applied because we must make predictions on the basis of the measures we have; and the reliability of these measures, even if low, must be accepted as a limitation. This correction is used, however, in exploratory studies. In these studies, crude measures of low reliability are often used, and the correction for attenuation helps us determine whether usable relationships would exist if we improved the reliability of these exploratory measures. Correction for attenuation also is used to give us some inkling of the possible relationship between traits. Because correction for attenuation is only an estimate, it sometimes yields corrected correlations above 1. These are spurious and are usually dropped to .99 in research reports. Finally, one should remember that a correlation corrected for attenuation tells us "what might have been" rather than "what is."

Correction for restriction in range is applied to correlation coefficients when we know that the range of scores for our sample is restricted on one of the variables being correlated. Restriction in range leads to a lowering of the correlation coefficient. For example, if we study the correlation between IQ and college achievement, it is sometimes appropriate to correct the correlation we obtain for restriction in range. A group of college students represent a restricted range of intelligence that includes very few persons with

IQ's below 100. By knowing the variability of the group we are studying and the variability of an unrestricted group on the measure in question, it is possible to make a correction for restriction in range that will give us a more accurate picture of the true relationship between the variables we have correlated.

PARTIAL CORRELATION

In many research problems it is desirable to determine the relationship between two variables when a third variable is held constant. A partial correlation is employed under these conditions. This type of correlation is particularly useful under conditions in which a third variable is known to exercise an important influence over the behavior being studied. If the influence of this variable were not removed, it would be difficult to ascertain the relationship between the other two variables. For example, let us say that we are concerned with the relationship between motivation and achievement in high school students. We know that intelligence is an important factor in the level of achievement at the secondary school level, and, unless this variable is controlled, any correlations we compute between motivation and achievement will be influenced to such a great extent by intelligence that it will be difficult for the effect of motivation to be determined. In this case a partial correlation would be employed in which the correlation between motivation and achievement would be calculated, while holding constant the influence of intelligence on achievement. In effect the partial correlation would give us the same outcome we would obtain if we controlled intelligence by studying the relationship between motivation and achievement for groups of students all of whom have the same IQ. When we control for only one variable such as intelligence, we use what is called a first order partial correlation. It is possible to control statistically any number of variables with this technique. For example, if four variables are to be controlled we would use a technique called the fourth order partial correlation. It is rare in educational research, however, to control for more than two or three variables. The procedures for calculating the higher order partial correlations are complex and time-consuming. In most studies, it is sufficient to control for the one or two variables that are most likely to influence the results.

MULTIPLE CORRELATION (R)

In certain educational research problems, particularly those involving prediction, it is desirable to determine the correlation between the behavior we wish to predict (such as success in school) and a combination of preliminary tests or measures, each of which correlates to some extent with the predicted behavior. For example, we may find that grade point average in college is correlated with general intelligence, study skills, motivation, and reading rate. Because we can obtain scores on these four prediction measures prior to the student's entry into college, it would be possible to make a prediction based on the combination of these four measures that will estimate the student's college grade-point average before he enters college. This sort of prediction is often used by colleges that accept only a small number of those applying for admission. Inasmuch as each of the prediction measures correlates with college grade-point average, it follows that a prediction based on all four of these measures will be more accurate than a prediction based upon only one measure. In order to determine the correlation between the combined variables and grade-point average in college, a multiple correlation would be employed. Closely related to multiple correlation is the multiple-regression equation. The multiple-regression equation combines the predictive value of several tests or measures into a single formula in order to make an improved prediction. Several predictive instruments, each having 15 per cent or more variance in common with the behavior being predicted, can, when combined, yield a satisfactory prediction provided that they measure different aspects of the predicted behavior.[4] The multiple-regression equation weights each variable in terms of its importance in making the desired prediction. The scores of each applicant on the prediction measures can be placed in the formula, and those who have the highest weighted scores are most likely to succeed in the predicted behavior. A study by Webb illustrates a typical prediction study using the multiple-correlation and multiple-regression equation.[5] In

[4] By 15 per cent "common variance" we mean that the predictive test measures 15 per cent of whatever goes into the behavior we are trying to predict.

[5] Sam C. Webb, "The Prediction of Achievement for First Year Dental Students," *Educational and Psychological Measurement,* XVI, No. 4 (1957), 543–48.

this study, Webb wished to develop a battery to predict the success of applicants to a dental school. Webb correlated sixteen prediction measures with grade-point average using regular product-moment correlations. Then, based on these correlations, he selected five of his prediction measures, which he combined using multiple correlation. It may be seen in Table 4 that the multiple correlation with grades based on these five variables is .503 as compared with the product-moment correlation of .402 for predental grade average, the best single predictor. Although the R of .503 does not permit highly accurate prediction, it indicates that the combined predictor battery has about 25 per cent of common variance (R^2) with dental school grades, while the best single predictor has only 16 per cent common variance (r^2) with this criterion. Better gains are usually obtained with multiple correlation when individual predictors correlate .35 or more with the criterion and when these predictors are not closely related to each other.

TABLE 4

CORRELATIONS BETWEEN FIVE PREDICTORS AND FIRST YEAR GRADE POINTS IN DENTAL SCHOOL

	r	R
Predental grade average	.402	.402
Carving score	.27	.463
Biology score	.21	.493
Chemistry score	.28	.500
Object visualization score	.16	.503

DISTRIBUTION FREE STATISTICS

The statistical tools discussed up to this point, with the exception of chi-square, are known as parametric statistics. These are techniques that make certain assumptions concerning the shape of the distribution that must be met if the use of parametric statistics is to be fully justified. Because much of the data in educational research does not meet the assumptions required by a rigorous application of parametric statistics, various nonparametric or distribution free statistical techniques have been developed and used in recent years.[6]

These techniques have several advantages over parametric statistics when extremely large deviations from the assumptions of the parametric statistics are present in the research worker's data. The most pertinent advantage is that these techniques relieve the research worker of the necessity of making unjustified assumptions concerning the distribution of the variables with which he is concerned. A second advantage is that the nonparametric techniques are usually somewhat quicker and easier to use.

In spite of these advantages, however, in most studies in education it is still advisable to use the parametric methods we have discussed. Statisticians have found that even if research data do not meet the assumptions underlying parametric statistics, these techniques still provide information of satisfactory accuracy for almost all experimental data normally encountered. A number of studies have tested the effect on the results of using parametric statistics under the conditions where the assumptions are not met, and the general finding is that even with extreme departures from the theoretical assumptions, the results obtained are still reasonably accurate. Cockrin, in a review of studies dealing with theoretical assumptions for analysis of variance, concludes "the concensus from these investigations is that no serious error is introduced by nonnormality in the significance level of the F-test or the two-tailed t-test."[7] In using the F- and t-tests in situations where the theoretical assumptions are violated to a serious degree, it has been recommended that an allowance can be made for this effect by using a more rigorous significance level. For example, Cockrin recommends the use of the ½ and 2 per cent levels instead of the 1 and 5 per cent levels.

The main reasons for recommending the use of parametric statistics even in cases where the theoretical assumptions are not met are: (1) Studies have shown that moderate departure from the theoretical

---

[6] Treatments of nonparametric methods applicable to educational research can be found in A. L. Edwards, *Statistical Methods for the Behavioral Sciences* (New York: Rinehart and Co., 1954) and S. Siegel, *Nonparametric Statistics for the Behavioral Sciences* (New York: McGraw-Hill Book Co., 1956).

[7] W. G. Cockrin, "Some Consequences When the Assumptions for the Analysis of Variance are not Satisfied," *Biometrics,* III (1947), 22–38.

assumptions has very little effect upon the value of the parametric technique. (2) Nonparametric techniques are considerably less powerful—that is, they require larger samples in order to yield the same level of significance. (3) In many of the problems involved in educational research, suitable nonparametric tests are either not available or are complicated and difficult for the student to obtain. Gaito, in a discussion of nonparametric methods as contrasted with the t-test and analysis of variance, discusses other advantages and disadvantages of the nonparametric methods for the student who is interested in pursuing this topic further.[8]

MISTAKES OFTEN MADE BY GRADUATE STUDENTS

1. Student avoids correlational analysis if the standard product-moment correlation cannot be applied.

2. Uses the incorrect correlation technique—such as using the biserial correlation when the widespread biserial correlation is called for.

3. Uses the product-moment correlation significance tables to interpret non-Pearsonian correlations. Because most non-Pearsonian correlations have a larger standard error than the product-moment correlation, this mistake leads to overestimating the significance of coefficients so interpreted.

4. Uses correction for attenuation in situations where it is not appropriate in order to make the results appear more significant.

ANNOTATED REFERENCES

1. FISHER, R. A. *Statistical Methods for Research Workers* (13th ed.). New York: Hafner Publishing Co., Inc., 1958. This text book is one of the classics for research workers in the behavioral sciences. Fisher has made many significant contributions to statistics. The treatment is not highly technical and may be understood by a student with some background in college mathematics and is recommended for students particularly interested in application of statistics to research problems.

2. GAITO, JOHN. "Nonparametric Methods in Psychological Research," *Psychological Reports*, 1959, 5, 115–25. This paper is concerned with the effects of failure to meet the assumptions of the analysis of variance technique on the subsequent test of significance. The assumptions are dis-

[8] John Gaito, "Nonparametric Methods in Psychological Research," *Psychological Reports*, V (1959), 115–25.

cussed and examples are given of the results of failure to meet them. The article also discusses in considerable detail the advantages and disadvantages of nonparametric techniques as compared with parametric methods. This discussion is particularly useful to the graduate student who is faced with a research situation in which nonparametric methods appear appropriate.

3. RAY, WILLIAM F. *Statistics in Psychological Research.* New York: The Macmillan Co., 1962. In addition to covering the material usually treated in textbooks in educational and psychological statistics, this text provides the student with a brief review of arithmetic and algebra and also provides him with much information on the application of statistics to research problems that is not contained in most books of this type. Among the most valuable portions of the book are the sections on sampling theory and sampling techniques, statistical inference, experimental inference, and inference in empirical research.

4. SIEGEL, SIDNEY. *Nonparametric Statistics for the Behavioral Sciences.* New York: McGraw-Hill Book Co., Inc., 1956. Nonparametric techniques have a number of advantages that make them particularly well suited for certain data of the behavioral sciences. These techniques make no assumptions concerning the population distribution, are easy to compute, and are particularly useful with small samples such as are often used by the graduate student. This text presents nonparametric techniques in a form that can be understood by the average behavioral scientist who lacks advanced mathematical training. Siegel's emphasis is upon research application of these techniques, and he strengthens his presentation with many interesting examples taken from the behavioral sciences. Although some of the techniques presented such as chi-square and the Spearman's *Rho* are treated in most textbooks in educational and psychological statistics, many of the techniques covered in this text are not generally found in these sources.

CHAPTER 8

Fundamentals of Research Design

INTRODUCTION

In setting up his research plan, the graduate student must take certain steps and consider certain problems that are essentially the same regardless of the type of research design he proposes to use. It is often at this stage of planning that decisions are made that will make the difference between a sound study (producing knowledge with meaningful implications to education) and a faulty study (with mistakes and biases that render the findings valueless). The factor that most often differentiates between good and poor research is not the funds available, the size of the sample, or the sophistication of the statistics—it is the care and thought that goes into the research plan. In this chapter we will discuss some fundamentals that will help you develop a worthwhile research project.

REVISING THE TENTATIVE RESEARCH PLAN

In Chapter 2 we discussed the development of hypotheses and the tentative research outline. Now, having completed the review of the literature, it is time to reexamine our hypotheses and enlarge this tentative outline into a detailed plan of action.

The tentative hypotheses that represented the student's guess as to the probable outcomes of his research can now be developed into more precise "educated guesses" based upon the insight into theory and the knowledge of previous studies that he has gained through his review of the literature. These revised hypotheses should meet the previously discussed criteria of testability, brevity, clarity, and consistency with available knowledge. Similarly, the research worker now has the knowledge necessary to reduce the list of possible measures in his tentative research plan to the specific measurement tools that he will use. In developing a tentative research plan, the student makes estimates concerning the type and number of sub-

166

jects he will require, but he is not prepared at that point to define the specific population from which his sample will be drawn or the procedures by which the sample will be selected. These steps require some knowledge of sampling techniques that will be discussed later in this chapter.

The review of literature gives the research worker ideas for improving his procedures, and these ideas should be incorporated into his revised research plan. A review at this point of the note cards that have been coded as having important methodological data will assist in revising the tentatively planned procedures.

After completing this step-by-step revision, the student should reappraise the total plan for consistency. In a research plan, each part is tied closely to all other parts, and a change in one part of the plan, such as the hypotheses, requires adjustments in other parts of the plan. His final research plan will largely determine the success of the student's research and should be based upon the sum total of knowledge that he has gained through his research training and review of the literature.

SAMPLING TECHNIQUES

Introduction

Educational research involves the study of samples of a defined population. The purpose of this research is to make observations of the selected sample, the results of which can be applied to the population. If research data are not generalizable to some degree beyond the sample used in the research, then the research can not provide us with new knowledge, cannot advance education as a science, and is largely a waste of time. Perhaps the most important factor in determining the generalizability of research results is the selection of the sample used in collecting the research data.

Defining the population

The first step in selecting a sample for research is to define the population from which the sample is to be drawn. Typical populations from which educational research samples might be drawn include: school superintendents in the state of Utah, practice teaching supervisors in state supported teacher's colleges, bilingual children in the primary grades of the San Antonio City School District, pupils failing algebra in Hoover High School, and seniors graduating from American public high schools in June of 1963. It may be seen from the previously mentioned examples that the population to be sampled may represent a large group scattered over a wide geographical area or a rather small group concentrated in a single school. If the research worker defines his population narrowly, the results of his research on a sample of this population will be generalizable only to the narrow population, although the results may have implications for a broader population having similar characteristics. For example, let us say that we wish to study the reading ability of fifth grade pupils in American public elementary schools. This is a broadly defined population, and in order to obtain a satisfactory sample of this population, a complex method of identifying and selecting cases from different areas, different sized communities, and different types of schools would have to be developed. Obviously, the selection of such a sample and collection of data would involve a tremendous amount of work. Opinion polls such as those that attempt to predict the outcome of national elections must use such complex techniques in order to have some assurance that their samples are representative.[1] On the other hand, the aforementioned population could be defined as all fifth grade pupils in a selected state. Now, because the population is much smaller, the problem of obtaining a sample of this population would be easier. However, the research results based on this sample would be generalizable only to fifth grade students in the state from which the sample was selected. To the degree to which these fifth grade pupils were similar to the fifth grade pupils in other states, the findings of the research could have implications for a broader population. Often, the financial limitations or the nature of the research area limit us to sampling the student population of a single school district. Studies based upon this narrow population are, of course, less generalizable but may still have important implications for other educators.

---

[1] The student is referred to the National Education Assoc., Research Division, "Small Sampling Techniques," *NEA Research Bulletin*, XXXVIII, No. 4 (1960), 99–104, for description of a method of selecting small random samples from large populations.

Random samples

A random sample is one in which each individual in the defined population has an equal chance of being selected as a member of the sample to be studied. Random samples may be obtained in a number of ways. Let us say, for example, that the research director in a large city school system wishes to obtain a random sampling of 200 pupils currently enrolled in the ninth grade from a population of 10,000 cases. In this case, one method of selecting such a sample would be to obtain a copy of the district census for ninth grade pupils and select every fiftieth name.[2] Another method of selecting random samples is to assign numbers to individuals in the population and then select cases, using a table of random numbers. Such a table lists a series of numbers at random, and the experimenter selects cases numbered corresponding to the numbers in the table. Still another technique for obtaining a random sample that is often used when dealing with small populations is to place the name of each individual in the population in a container and draw the required number of names. The advantage of using random samples is that, although different random samples selected from a defined population will differ in terms of the variables involved in the study, these will be chance fluctuations, and statistical tools such as standard error are available to estimate the probable magnitude of these errors. The aforementioned methods apply to relatively small samples in which the members of the population can be specifically identified. In selecting samples from large populations for which no name lists are available, strictly random techniques cannot be applied. In this case "area" sampling methods are used. This method usually involves dividing the population into areas, randomly selecting areas to be included in the sample, and then randomly selecting cases from the chosen areas. For example, a city could be divided into areas containing sixteen square blocks. Each area would be numbered, and the areas to be sampled would be drawn at random. In each area selected, the adult occupants of every tenth house could be chosen as the subjects for the research.

[2] Divide the population by the number needed for the sample to get "n." Then select at random a number smaller than "n." Starting with that number, select every nth case from a list of the population.

Such techniques are complex and unless carried out with care can produce nonrepresentative samples. If the research worker wishes to select samples from large populations where the exact size or specific members are not known, he should consult sources covering such samples. Most educational studies can apply the methods for small populations previously cited.

Stratified samples

In many educational studies, it is desirable to select a sample in such a way that the research worker is assured that certain subgroups in the population will be represented in the sample in proportion to their numbers in the population itself. Such samples are usually referred to as stratified or representative samples. Let us say, for example, that we wish to conduct a study to see if there are significant differences on TAT aggression scores of pupils at different ability levels selected from ability grouped sixth grade classrooms. Under this grouping system, pupils are classified into three levels on the basis of general intelligence and placed in classrooms accordingly. In this case, if we were to define the population as all sixth grade pupils in the district being studied and select a random sample, our random sample may not include a sufficient number of cases from one of the three ability levels. In this research, we must also consider the possibility that girls will react differently in terms of aggression scores than boys. In order to avoid samples that do not include a sufficient number of pupils of each sex at each ability level, a stratified sample could be selected. In order to obtain a stratified sample in this case, all sixth grade pupils in the district would be divided into one of the following six groups: superior boys, superior girls, average boys, average girls, slow boys, and slow girls. Subsamples of the desired size would then be selected at random from each of the six groups. Using this technique, we would predetermine the number of cases that would be available in each of the subgroups, but would randomly select the cases that would be used in the sample. Stratified samples are particularly appropriate in studies where part of the research analysis is likely to be concerned with comparisons between various subgroups. In summary, stratified sampling procedure assures the research worker that his sample will be representative of the population in terms of certain critical factors that have been used by the research worker as a basis for stratification and also assures him of adequate cases for sub-group analysis.

Large or small sample?

A problem that must be faced in planning every research project is to determine the size of the sample necessary to attain the objectives of the planned research. We have learned from the study of statistical tools that, other things being equal, the larger the sample employed in the research, the smaller will be the standard error and the greater the likelihood of obtaining significant results. In every study, however, a point is reached where the statistical advantage of adding more cases is offset by the additional cost of collecting data on these cases. Under certain conditions, however, large samples are desirable and often essential. These include the following:

1. *When many uncontrolled variables are present.* In many educational research problems, it is impossible for the research worker to control some of the important variables that could have an effect upon the research findings. Under these conditions, the research worker can have more confidence in his findings if he employs large random samples. The large random sample insures to some extent that the uncontrolled variables will themselves be operating randomly for the different groups being studied and therefore will not have a systematic effect upon the results. Teaching ability, for example, is a difficult variable to control but is important in many educational studies. If a study of teaching methods involves only two teachers, one using method A and one method B, teaching ability differences may cause more change in achievement than method differences. On the other hand, if we have a dozen or more teachers using each method, teaching ability differences will probably "randomize out," thus permitting us to appraise method differences.

2. *When small differences are anticipated.* In research projects in which only small differences on the dependent variable are expected among the various groups being studied, it is desirable to use large samples. For example, a teacher may have developed a set of visual aids to help in teaching certain mathematical concepts. Such aids usually cannot be expected to make large differences in achievement. In order to evaluate these aids, large comparable samples of pupils using and not using the aids would have to be compared. In this

case, the reason for using large samples is that, if small samples were used, the larger standard errors attending such samples may obscure small but important relationships that would be found to be significant in a large sample study.

3. *When groups must be broken into subgroups.* Many educational research projects involve not only general comparisons between the major groups studied but can also contribute additional worthwhile knowledge if these major groups are divided into subgroups and further comparisons are made. For example, let us suppose that we were carrying out a study of the possible effects of an extracurricular program upon the attitudes of high school students toward school. Ten schools having no organized extracurricular programs could be selected, and in five of these schools such a program could be developed. A pretest of student attitudes could be administered before the extracurricular program was introduced, and after a period of one or two years final measures could be administered to determine what changes had taken place in student attitudes toward school. Attitude changes occurring in the schools that had adopted an organized program could then be compared with the changes that occurred in the schools in which no extracurricular program had been present. After an overall analysis of these results had been made, however, the research worker might wish to compare the effects of the extracurricular program upon different groups in order to develop some theoretical framework that fits his results. For example, he may hypothesize that girls' attitudes would be changed more markedly than boys' by the introduction of such a program because they value social activities more highly at the high school level. This would require dividing the groups studied by sex, and making further comparisons. It may then occur to him that students at different socioeconomic levels might respond differently to the organized program. Perhaps such a program would lead to favorable attitude changes on the part of middle-class children and unfavorable changes on the part of lower-class children. Again, it would be necessary to subdivide the original sample on the basis of social class in order to conduct this further analysis. Such analyses often provide us with worthwhile knowledge and interesting theoretical constructs but can only be carried out if the original groups are large enough so that, after such divisions are made, the subgroups still have sufficient numbers

of cases to permit a statistical analysis. In the above example, a group of 100 students might be adequate to make the overall comparisons of the effects of the extracurricular program. However, in dividing the 100 cases into groups on the basis of sex and socioeconomic status, it may be found that only seven of the subjects can be classified as lower-class girls. This would indicate that 100 cases would not be sufficient if such subgroup analysis were planned.

A mistake commonly made by inexperienced research workers is to select a random sample that would be large enough for division into the anticipated subgroups only if the subgroups are equally represented in the sample. The research worker then discovers that he has an unequal representation, such as is given in the previously mentioned example, which leaves him with an insufficient number of cases to carry out the analysis that he planned. This problem usually can be avoided by stratified sampling, but because the research worker cannot always predict all subgroups he may want to study, a large number of cases reduces the chances of disappointment.

4. *When the population is highly heterogeneous on the variables being studied.* If every person in the population were exactly alike in the variable studied, a sample of one would be sufficient. As the population becomes more variable, however, larger samples must be used in order that persons at different levels of skill or having different amounts of the characteristic in question will be satisfactorily represented.

In many educational research projects, small samples are more appropriate than large samples. This is often the case in studies in which role playing, depth interviews, projective measures, and other such time-consuming measurement techniques are employed. Such techniques cannot be used in large sample studies unless considerable financial support is available and would be inefficient even if support were available if a small sample can satisfactorily test the hypotheses.[3] A study that probes deeply into the characteristics of a small sample often provides more knowledge than a study that attacks the same problem by collecting only shallow information on a large sample. For example, a number of studies have attempted

---

[3] The most efficient research project is the one that tests the hypotheses at the required level of confidence with a minimum effort.

to learn the reasons why many superior college students drop out of college. Most of these studies have consisted of little more than classifying the one-sentence responses made by students on the dropout cards they completed for the registrar. Our knowledge of related studies in sociology and social psychology would lead us to doubt whether the student will give his true reasons for dropping out of college on such a card. Many students will write down a convenient or socially acceptable reason regardless of their true reason for withdrawal. Other students will not themselves be aware of the true reasons why they are dropping out. The author recently participated in a research project in which superior students dropping out of Utah State University were given a carefully planned depth interview. These interviews, carried out by a trained psychologist, revealed that the student's true reasons for dropping out of college were almost always different from the reasons stated on the registrar's dropout card. Although this study involved less than fifty superior dropouts, it produced insights into the reasons for withdrawal from college that probably could never be obtained by the shallower approach employed by other studies.[4]

In other studies, very close matching of subjects on the critical variables concerned in the study is possible, and under these conditions, small sampling studies often yield the information sought more efficiently than large sampling studies. The research by Newman, Freeman, and Holzinger on the intelligence of identical twins is a good example of such a study.[5] One phase of this study, although concerned with only nineteen pairs of separated identical twins, provided information on the relative influences of heredity and environment upon intelligence that would have been difficult to obtain with large samples of less closely matched subjects.

Sampling errors

In selecting random samples, some degree of difference may be expected to occur between groups even though statistically acceptable methods of selection are used. For example, one group may contain subjects that are more intelligent, more highly motivated, or in other ways different from the subjects in other groups in the

[4] This study was conducted by Luna Brite.
[5] H. H. Newman, F. N. Freeman, and K. J. Holzinger, *Twins: A Study of Heredity and Environment* (Chicago: Univ. of Chicago Press, 1937).

experiment. Such errors may be large in groups made up of few cases but may be expected to decrease as the number of subjects increases. Let us say, for example, that we wish to compare the achievement of a group of ninth grade pupils taught algebra using an inductive method with the achievement of another group taught algebra using a deductive method. We could randomly assign seventy pupils who wish to take algebra to two classes at the start of the term and assign algebra teachers of comparable experience to teach the classes. In this experiment, errors due to sampling may be expected to be large because only one class of thirty-five pupils is involved in each group. If, among the seventy subjects, there were two very brilliant students and if these two students were both assigned to the same group (as could easily occur in the random process), the achievement of these students could be high enough to raise the mean achievement of their entire group by several points. If, however, we could repeat our study ten times and if ten classes of thirty-five subjects were to be included in each group instead of one class, the chances of the twenty brightest students all being assigned to groups being taught by the same method would be very remote.

Even if groups are made up by random selection from the available subjects, a further problem arises from the fact that the available sample may not be representative of the population studied. In the example given, the schools from which ninth grade algebra classes are selected may differ in certain important ways when compared to all schools that offer ninth grade algebra. For example, the schools may be located in predominantly middle-class neighborhoods, may be in college towns where academic work receives greater emphasis, or may be located in an area where the dominant religious group has certain values that are reflected in pupil attitude. Such a difference can lead to findings that are valid for the schools studied but not generally valid in other schools where ninth grade algebra is taught. In most educational studies, this type of error cannot be entirely avoided. The research worker can do his best to select his sample from representative schools and can describe the source of his sample in detail so that other educators can compare his research subjects with the pupils in their schools to decide whether the research findings may be applied. In a few major projects, samples have been studied that represent a large number of schools selected from different sized communities of different socioeconomic levels in different geographical areas. Unfortunately, few research projects have sufficient financial support to permit obtaining samples of this type.

Sampling bias

The problems involved in obtaining random or stratified random samplings of human subjects, even for a narrowly defined population, are often considerable. Because of these difficulties, many research workers fall into one or another of several pitfalls when selecting their sample that result in sampling biases that invalidate the results of their research.

Perhaps the most common sampling mistake made in educational research is to use volunteers as research subjects. Volunteers can rarely be used as a research sample because the very fact that they volunteer makes them different from persons in the population who did not volunteer. Therefore, samples of volunteers can be assumed to be biased, and the results of studies employing volunteers must usually be discounted because of this bias. The author is familiar with a study, for example, in which an attempt was made to determine the success of college football players in later life as compared with other college graduates. In this study, questionnaires requesting such information as the person's occupation and income were sent to football players who had graduated from a particular college. Only a small per cent of these questionnaires were returned. The results were most encouraging when compared with the income of large samples of unselected college graduates taken from other surveys. Before accepting these data, however, let us look at the possible biases of this study. The small percentage of persons returning the questionnaire were, in effect, volunteers. Who is most likely to volunteer information concerning his financial status? In most cases, this information is most freely volunteered by persons who are financially successful. Thus, the results of such a questionnaire can tell us little about the population—in this case all football players graduating from the university in question. In studies involving achievement, volunteers are equally inappropriate because they generally represent a group that is somewhat more highly motivated than those members of the population not volunteering.

Still another problem encountered in studies using volunteer samples is that individuals who are participating in a research project on a voluntary basis usually feel free to withdraw from the study before all data are gathered if they lose interest or find further participation inconvenient. The author is familiar with a study that clearly illustrates the problems that can be encountered under the aforementioned circumstances. The purpose of this research was to determine whether college freshmen who were very poor spellers could be helped significantly by special spelling instruction using teaching machines. Volunteers from the poor spelling group were called for and these were randomly divided into a control group that received no special instruction and an experimental group that received weekly instruction on the teaching machine. As the study progressed, students in the experimental group began dropping out because they became bored with the teaching machine or found the study schedule inconvenient. No withdrawals occurred in the control group because no demands were made on this group. By the end of the study, more than half of the experimental group had dropped out. A final spelling test was then administered to the experimental and control groups, and the results showed significantly greater spelling gains for the experimental group. The question, of course, arises as to whether this gain was due to the special instruction using the teaching machines or whether it was due to the fact that only the more highly motivated students in the experimental group remained until the end of the study. Studies with sampling biases of this type generally produce results that are meaningless and, in many cases, can lead the naïve reader into drawing faulty or unjustified conclusions from the data.

A procedure that, though usually not as serious as using volunteers, often leads to a biased sample is the use of subjects, merely because they happen to be available, who are not appropriate for the research. College sophomores have been the subjects for so much research in education and psychology that the use of sophomores in research projects finds its way into many of the jokes about research workers in these fields. Some studies suffer relatively little from using available subjects. For example, exploratory studies on the effects of drugs upon learning and other forms of behavior are not seriously damaged by the use of such subjects. Whenever the research worker wishes to generalize his results to specifically defined populations, however, the use of subjects merely because they are available is inappropriate.

Many educational field studies are biased because the research worker chose his experimental and control groups from different populations. For example, some of the early studies on the effectiveness of TV instruction used high school students receiving conventional instruction as a control group, but used adults who wanted to complete their high school education in home study as an experimental or "TV-instruction" group. The age, interests, motivation, and dropout rates for the two groups are much different, thus making the results of such studies meaningless.

Occasionally, the methods the research worker must use to identify the subjects he wants are sufficiently time-consuming and expensive to warrant the use of shortcuts. Terman's famous study of "gifted children" provides us with an example of a sampling shortcut.[6] In this study, Terman wished to locate 1,000 children with IQ's over 140 on the *Stanford-Binet* test. Because the *Stanford-Binet* is expensive and time-consuming to administer, he decided that rather than test many pupils who had little chance of obtaining a score of 140, he would ask teachers to suggest the names of students whom they considered to be superior, and would test only these. The difficulty with this procedure was that teachers tend to underestimate the intelligence of pupils who create disturbances and are not cooperative in the classroom. Thus, Terman's sample does not include this type of individual, and, as a result of this apparently small blunder in selecting his original sample, all of the findings of this important study must be qualified. This means that a preponderance of the children Terman selected came from middle-class families where education is valued, and conformity to the school situation and respect for the teacher are expected. Thus, Terman's results, rather than being applicable to gifted children in general, refer primarily to a particular type of gifted child.

Often, the research worker is under considerable pressure to alter his sampling techniques in order to fit administrative convenience.

[6] Lewis M. Terman (ed.), *Genetic Studies of Genius, Volume I, Mental and Physical Traits of a Thousand Gifted Children* (Stanford, Calif.: Stanford University Press, 1926), p. 21.

This problem is particularly common when working with the public school populations. In selecting a sample of fifth grade students in a given school district, for example, it is much easier administratively to test all of the fifth grade children in one school than to test a few cases from each of several schools in the district. This process, however, significantly weakens the sample because there is little reason to believe that the pupils in one school are representative of the district as a whole. The degree to which such changes can damage the research design depends on the nature of the research problem. It should again be emphasized that if the student feels that certain changes cannot be made in the sampling procedures without seriously weakening the study, it is better for him to attempt to obtain his sample elsewhere or give up the study altogether than to devote his time, effort, and money to a study with serious sampling flaws.

PRACTICAL CONSIDERATIONS IN RESEARCH PLANNING

In revising the tentative research plan, the student must consider many practical problems and questions. Few research workers ever have an opportunity to design and carry out a research project exactly as they would like. Limitations in time and money, scheduling and administrative problems in the schools, and difficulties in obtaining the full cooperation of subjects are often factors placing a practical limit on the goals of the educational research worker. These limitations are usually more severe for the graduate student than for the experienced research worker. The unwillingness of many students to recognize and accept these limitations often leads to serious weaknesses in their research and even more often places the student in a position where it is impossible for him to complete his thesis or dissertation. Attention to the following practical considerations may save the student much difficulty.

Be sure appropriate subjects are available. A question that should be answered early in the student's research planning is, "Are the kinds of subjects that are required for this research available?" The subjects needed for certain types of educational research are quite rare and may require a large base population or a great deal of effort to obtain an adequate sample. For example, studies involving children of very high IQ's can present serious problems unless the research worker is located near a large urban center, because individuals with very high IQ's are rare in the general population.

Some graduate students develop research plans that require a level of cooperation that is hard to obtain unless subjects are strongly motivated or receive compensation for their participation. Often, it is easy enough to obtain the initial cooperation of the needed subjects, but as the experiment goes on, unless the research worker has some means of motivating the subjects or requiring their participation, many will not complete their part in the study, thus leaving the research worker with a biased sample. It is difficult for the graduate student to obtain cooperation from certain types of individuals. For example, mentally retarded children are often incapable of the level of cooperation expected of them by inexperienced research workers. Antisocial individuals such as juvenile delinquents often refuse to cooperate or deliberately provide the research worker with false information. Persons in important administrative positions such as school superintendents often refuse to cooperate because they cannot spare the time required. The graduate student who attempts research requiring extensive cooperation from such groups often finds it necessary to drop his project after he has done much work because he cannot obtain needed information.

Check time requirements. The graduate student should make careful estimates of the time requirements of his study if he hopes to complete his work within a reasonable length of time. Those studies in which the experimental group requires a long exposure to the variable being studied must usually be avoided. For example, a study on the effects of vitamins on the learning efficiency of college students probably would require a minimum of a year of administering vitamin supplements to the experimental group. If attempts were made to carry out the study in a short time, the student would almost certainly obtain negative results because it is not reasonable to expect such variables to have any immediate effect upon behavior.

In some studies, the measures planned by the research worker can be administered quickly and easily, but criteria needed may take considerable time to develop. For example, a study relating study habits and attitudes of freshmen to later academic success would require a minimum of one year to carry out. This is because the usual criterion for college success is college grades, and a full year of college grades would probably be the minimum usable as a criterion.

A problem occasionally encountered by graduate students is that their data must be collected in a very short period of time to be usable. For example, the author is familiar with a study of the attitudes of farmers toward hunters in which such time limitations operated. In this case, the graduate student wished to carry out structured interviews with a sampling of about two hundred farmers concerning their attitudes toward hunters. The difficulty in this study, however, is that the attitudes of farmers may be expected to be different immediately prior, during, or immediately after hunting season than during the remainder of the year. The attitude could also be expected to change rather markedly if some serious act of hunter vandalism occurred such as shooting one of the farmer's cows. Thus, in a study of this nature, it is often necessary to collect the data over a reasonably short period of time or considerable danger exists that the attitudes of the first farmer interviewed will have changed by the time the last farmer in the sample has been interviewed. This type of problem is present in many attitude and opinion studies. Collection of data within the necessary time limits is often not possible for the graduate student.

Are special skills required? Some data gathering procedures such as those used in observational studies, interview studies, and projective testing require considerable experience to be used effectively. It is usually inadvisable for the graduate student who does not have the necessary experience to plan a study requiring such procedures because the acquisition of these skills to a point where the research data will be reliable can require a long period of preparation that might better be devoted to a more extensive study using other techniques. College courses are often available that assist the student in gaining skill in these procedures, but such courses rarely bring the person to a level of proficiency required to make effective use of the skills in research.

Will assistance be needed? The graduate student should look very carefully at his experiment to determine whether he will need assistance in carrying out the project. For example, some equipment used in educational and psychological research requires more than one operator. In some studies, although one person can collect the data, if certain data are collected by the experimenter, his knowledge of these data will tend to influence his judgment in the collection of other data needed in the research. This situation in which one phase of the research data is unduly or inappropriately influenced by some other phase of the research data is known as contamination.[7] Contamination is a serious problem in many thesis research problems because of the fact that the graduate student is usually the only one involved in data collection, and in many research designs, his knowledge of one phase of the research can have this contaminating influence on another phase. For example, let us say you were doing a research project in which you were studying antisocial attitudes of delinquent and nondelinquent junior high school boys. In such a study, antisocial attitudes might be estimated from the subjects' responses in a depth interview situation. If, however, the graduate student knew at the time of the interviews which students were delinquents and which were not delinquents, this knowledge could influence his interpretation of the individual's responses in the interview, and thus lead to results that would strongly support the interviewer's biases and preconceived notions.

In some studies, more than one individual must be involved in the data collection in order to obtain estimates of reliability. Such is the case, for example, in studies in which the data are collected through observations. Under these circumstances, it is generally necessary for at least two independent observers to evaluate the behavior being observed. If only a single observer is used, the observations may be slanted in the direction of this individual's biases, and it will not be possible to uncover the biases or make any estimate of how reliable his observations are.

Can you bear the cost of the research? An inexperienced research worker usually underestimates the cost of his research in terms of both time and money. This is probably because he assumes that his research will go off essentially as he has planned it, in other words "without a hitch." This is almost never the case. Schedules will generally have to be changed, subjects will fail to appear when scheduled and will have to be rescheduled, clerical errors will be made that require repeating much work, statistical errors will occur

[7] See Chap. 15 for a discussion of other types of contamination.

that necessitate additional calculations, and unexpected results will call for different analysis procedures. The author was once in a position in which he evaluated research proposals being submitted for financial support. Even research workers with extensive experience in small studies were found to underestimate grossly the cost of the more elaborate projects they were proposing. Cost estimates often turn out to be less than half of the actual cost of carrying out the project. Another factor increasing cost is that in many projects the research worker develops new insights and wishes to follow up interesting new leads during the course of the project itself. New ideas or clues often provide the most valuable data in the research project and should be pursued. Such new leads, however, are impossible to predict and often add considerably to the cost of the study.

What analysis facilities will be needed? Some research projects require analysis procedures and facilities that are beyond the reach of most graduate students. Certain kinds of data, for example, are so difficult and time-consuming to analyze manually that IBM analysis is almost indispensable. Factor analytical studies, for example, that require the calculation of large intercorrelational matrixes are of this type. Sociometric studies in which large numbers of interactions between individual students must be appraised are also difficult to evaluate adequately without IBM facilities.

Some of the statistical procedures that might be called for in complex data analyses are beyond the abilities of the graduate student. The student should always plan in detail his analysis and determine what statistics he will use before starting his research project. Students often collect their data, and then attempt to determine what kind of analysis should be used. Under these conditions, the student often finds he must use analysis procedures that he does not know and that he may find difficult to learn. Other students with strong backgrounds in mathematics, in contrast, become fascinated with some of the new and highly complex analysis procedures and in designing their study, are more concerned with the procedures than with the purposes of their research. Most studies in educational research can be analyzed using the relatively simple statistical tools discussed in Chapters 5 and 6. Some authorities in the behavioral sciences deplore the current preoccupation with complex analysis techniques that are often used as a substitute for a sound research design and a worthwhile research problem.[8]

What treatment errors can be avoided? Anticipating and avoiding treatment errors is a major consideration for the educational research worker. In the process of carrying out an experiment, we aim at giving all of our groups the same treatment except for the independent variable. In educational research, however, it is not possible to maintain identical conditions for our different groups. Differences in the experiences of different groups are called treatment errors. Such errors are most serious in studies involving few groups, because in this case such errors have no chance to "randomize out." Treatment errors often found in educational studies include the following: one class among those in the research sample may be taught by a more able teacher, one class may have fewer meetings because of special assemblies scheduled during this class hour, one class may be scheduled immediately after lunch when pupils are less alert, or one class may have been diverted while taking the achievement test by a band practicing in the next room. Some of the above treatment differences can be avoided by the research worker, but, because he cannot predict many of them and could not control others even if they were anticipated, some such errors will inevitably occur. The best safeguard against treatment errors is to have a sufficient number of repetitions so that treatment differences might be expected to cancel themselves out by occurring about equally in classes containing experimental and control subjects. Even when large samples and many classes are involved, however, the research worker should control for or avoid treatment differences that can be handled without excessive effort or expense.

THE PILOT STUDY

A preliminary trial of research measures and techniques is essential to the development of a sound research plan. Whenever possible, this preliminary trial should be enlarged into a pilot study. In a pilot study the entire research procedure is carried out including analysis of the data collected. In addition to serving all of the pur-

---

[8] Quinn McNemar, "At Random: Sense and Nonsense," *The American Psychologist*, XV (1960), 295–300.

poses of the usual tryout procedures, such as improving data collecting routines, trying scoring techniques, revising locally developed measures, and checking the appropriateness of standard measures, the pilot study provides additional knowledge that leads to improved research:

1. It permits a preliminary testing of the hypotheses that leads to testing more precise hypotheses in the main study. It may lead to changing some hypotheses, dropping some, and developing new hypotheses when called for.

2. It often provides the research worker with ideas, approaches, and clues not foreseen prior to the pilot study. Such ideas and clues greatly increase the chances of obtaining clear-cut findings in the main study.

3. It permits a thorough check of the planned statistical and analytical procedures, thus allowing an appraisal of their adequacy in treating the data. Needed alterations also may be made in the data-collecting methods, so that data in the main study may be analyzed more efficiently.

4. It greatly reduces the number of treatment errors, because unforeseen problems revealed in the pilot study may be overcome in redesigning the main study.

5. It may save the research worker a major expenditure of time and money on a research project that will yield nothing. Unfortunately, many research ideas that seem to show great promise are unproductive when carried out in the field or laboratory. The pilot study almost always provides enough data for the research worker to make a sound decision on the advisability of going ahead with the main study.

6. In the pilot study, the research worker may try out a number of alternative measures, and then select those that produce the best results for the main study without some tentative evidence that they would be productive. If the student plans to continue beyond the Master's degree, his Master's research may sometimes serve as a pilot study for later research to be carried out as part of his doctoral program. The less research experience the student has, the more he is likely to profit from the pilot study. Because of this, the student should attempt a pilot study whenever possible, even if it must be limited to only a dozen or so cases.

MISTAKES OFTEN MADE BY GRADUATE STUDENTS

1. Student fails to define his research population.

2. Uses a sample too small to permit analysis of the performance of interesting subgroups.

3. Attempts to conduct his research using volunteer subjects.

4. Changes his design in ways that weaken the research in order to make data collection more convenient for the schools involved.

5. In an attempt to collect as much data as possible, he makes excessive demands upon his subjects that lead to their refusal to cooperate.

6. Attempts to carry out a study in one semester that would require two or three years to do satisfactorily.

7. Fails to plan his data collection in sufficient detail to avoid excessive treatment errors.

8. Starts collecting his research data without carrying out a pilot study or adequately testing his measures and procedures.

ANNOTATED REFERENCES

1. COLADARCI, ARTHUR P. "Towards More Rigorous Educational Research," *Harvard Educational Review*, 1960, 30, 3–11. This article explores some of the deficiencies in educational research and suggests ways of correcting them. Among the difficulties cited are the nonresearch orientation of educators in the field and in teacher-training institutions, the lack of research sophistication among many educational research workers, and the tendency to study relationships in the field without integrating them into a theoretical network.

2. KERLINGER, F. N. "Practicality and Educational Research," *School Review*, 1959, 67 (3), 281–91. This article discusses the dearth of educational theory and the tendency for graduate students in education to receive training primarily in the "practical" problems in education. The author points out the inability of many educators to differentiate between fact and opinion, and demonstrates that most educational opinions, if carried to a logical conclusion, have theoretical implications that their proponents are often unaware of. He suggests that the practical emphasis in education is tending to convert the field into something more similar to a

religion than to a science. This thought-provoking article should be read by every graduate student in education.

3. McCORMICK, THOMAS C., and FRANCIS, ROY G. *Methods of Research in the Behavioral Sciences*. New York: Harper & Bros., 1958. This text is written primarily for the graduate student in sociology and anthropology. The chapters on basic ideas underlying research and research design provide useful background reading for the graduate student in education.

4. McHUGH, RICHARD B. "Determining Sample Size in Validation Research," *Educational and Psychological Measurement*, 1957, 17, 136–41. An equation is developed in this article to help the researcher determine the size of the sample required in validation research. Factors considered in the equation are the amount of precision required for the estimate and the permissible risk of failure.

5. McNEMAR, QUINN. "At Random: Sense and Nonsense," *The American Psychologist*, 1960, 15, 295–300. In this article, McNemar, an eminent psychologist and statistician, discusses the preoccupation of many behavioral scientists with complex research design and statistical tools. He questions the usefulness of mathematical models and to a certain extent the value of high-powered statistical techniques. This article is required reading for the graduate student with a strong mathematical background because such individuals are most likely to fall into the traps discussed.

6. NATIONAL EDUCATION ASSOCIATION, RESEARCH DIVISION. "Small-Sample Techniques," *NEA Research Bulletin*, 1960, 38, (4), 99–104. This article is concerned with the selection of a random sample from a large population. A formula is presented that permits the researcher to determine the size of a sample needed to attain a given degree of accuracy. The use of the formula is illustrated in the selection of a sample of male public school teachers who are to respond to a questionnaire. This article is extremely valuable to the research worker faced with the problem of selecting a sample from a large population.

7. SELVIN, HANAN C. "A Critique of Tests of Significance in Survey Research," *American Sociological Review*, 1957, 22, 519–27. This article discusses the difficulty involved in obtaining random samples in sociological research and points out that tests of significance are not appropriate with nonrandom groups. This article gives the student valuable insight into some important sampling problems.

CHAPTER 9

Historical Research

INTRODUCTION

Historical research is the systematic and objective location, evaluation, and synthesis of evidence in order to establish facts and draw conclusions concerning past events. Many students consider the pursuit of a historical study as being completely divorced from science and, therefore, not demanding the rigor and objectivity of scientific methods. Such studies are often selected as an "easy way out" by students who are afraid to attempt an experimental study.

A critical analysis of a large sample of historical studies in secondary education published between 1900 and 1948 revealed that fewer than one half met the requirements of historical research.[1] Actually, the demands for objectivity are as high in historical research as in other scientific methods, and these demands are much more difficult to meet because of the nature of historical data. Although historical research is perhaps the most difficult type of educational research to do well, it is important and necessary because it gives us an insight into some educational problems that could not be gained by any other technique. The historical study of an educational idea or institution gives us a perspective that can do much to help us understand our present educational system, and this understanding in turn can help to establish a sound basis for further progress and improvement. Historical research also can give us an insight into human behavior that can be very valuable in arriving at practical solutions for educational problems. For example, a careful historical study of the school bond elections in a given school district might give us broad insights into the human interactions involved in these elections, critical factors contributing to the success or failure of the issue, clues to obtaining support for future bond elections in the district, and finally a gen-

---

[1] Philip W. Perdew, *A Critical Analysis of Research in the History of Secondary Education in America* (Unpublished doctoral dissertation; Los Angeles: University of California, 1948).

eral understanding of variables operating in such elections that could be applied to other districts as well. In this chapter the student will find an introduction to the fundamentals of historical research. If he plans to carry out this type of project, he should take a course in historical research methods (usually offered by the history department) or should study one of the texts devoted to this topic.

DESIGNING THE HISTORICAL RESEARCH PROJECT

Appropriate problems for historical research in education may be identified using most of the same approaches suggested in Chapter 2 for locating other types of research problems. Perhaps the most fruitful problems, however, develop from a knowledge of current practices and an interest in how these practices developed. At the present time, for example, there is much dispute as to whether the age-grade form of grouping currently in effect in most of our public schools provides a desirable setting for learning. Certainly, a historical study that traced the development of the present system and weighed the various factors contributing to the establishment of this system would provide us with an understanding of age-grade grouping that could be of considerable value in evaluating the effectiveness of this system for present day instruction. Historical studies often reveal that current practices were originally developed to fit situations and meet needs that no longer exist.

The essential steps of historical research are defining the problem, gathering the data, and evaluating and synthesizing the data into an accurate account of the subject investigated. It will be noted that these steps are essentially the same as those involved in other types of research projects. There are, however, important differences in the way that these steps are carried out between the historical research project and other educational research methods. In historical research, it is especially important that the student carefully defines his problem and appraises its appropriateness before committing himself too fully. Many problems are not adaptable to historical research methods and cannot be adequately treated using this approach. Other problems have little or no chance of producing significant results either because of the lack of pertinent data or because the problem is a trivial one.

A fact that many students fail to realize is that historical research usually requires the setting up of specific, testable hypotheses. Without such hypotheses, historical research often becomes little more than an aimless gathering of facts. In searching the materials that make up the source of historical research data, unless the student's attention is aimed at information relating to specific questions or concerned with specific hypotheses, he has little chance of extracting a body of data from the available documents that can be synthesized to provide new knowledge or new understanding of the topic studied. Even after specific hypotheses have been established, the student must exercise strict self-control in his study of historical documents, or he will find himself collecting much information that is interesting but is not related to his area of inquiry. If the student's hypotheses are not sufficiently delimited and specific, it is an easy matter for him to become distracted and led astray by information that is not really related to his field of investigation.

GATHERING DATA

Perhaps the major difference between historical research and other forms of scientific research is that historical research must deal with data that are already in existence. Hockett points out that:

History is not a science of *direct* observation, like chemistry and physics. The historian like the geologist interprets past events by the traces they have left; he deals with the evidences of man's past acts and thoughts. *But the historian, no less than the scientist, must utilize evidence resting on reliable observation.* The difference in procedure is due to the fact that the historian usually does not make his own observations, and that those upon whose observations he must depend are, or were, often if not usually untrained observers. Historical method is, strictly speaking, a process *supplementary* to observations, a process by which the historian attempts to test the truthfulness of the reports of observations made by others. Like the scientist, he examines his data and formulates hypotheses, i.e., tentative conclusions. These conjectures he must test by seeking fresh evidence or reexamining the old, and this process he must continue until, in the light of all available evidence, the hypotheses are abandoned as untenable or modified until they are brought into conformity with the available evidence.[2]

[2] Homer C. Hockett, *The Critical Method in Historical Research and Writing* (New York: The Macmillan Co., 1955), pp. 7–8. Reprinted by permission of The Macmillan Co.

Sources of historical data

Historical sources may usually be classified as either documents or relics. Documents include a wide range of written and printed materials recorded for the purpose of transmitting information. Relics include physical objects related to the period or the institution being studied. In education these might include such materials as school furniture or various physical objects used in teaching, such as flash cards, multiplication tables, and so on. Textbooks, although printed, may be regarded as relics if they are studied as physical objects, and the printed content is not the source of the information being sought. For example, in a study of printing methods used in textbooks, the textbook could be classified as a relic. On the other hand, a study of the viewpoints concerning some phase of American history presented by textbooks of different periods would use the textbooks as documents. In historical research concerning education, there has been relatively little use made of relics.

Primary sources and secondary sources are defined in historical research in basically the same terms as in the appraisal of scientific research. In historical research, primary sources are generally defined as those documents in which the individual observing the event being described was present. Secondary sources are those in which the person describing the event was not present but has obtained his description from someone else who may or may not have directly observed the event. Occasionally, the number of times that the writing is removed from the observer is indicated, but generally all levels of removal are lumped together as secondary sources.

Search for historical data

In other forms of educational research, the review of the literature is considered a preliminary step to gathering data and is aimed at providing the student with a knowledge of previous research that he can apply to the improvement of his own research plan. In historical research, however, the review of the literature actually provides the research data. In reviewing research literature, most of the information the student seeks will be contained in research articles published in the professional journals. These articles describe in brief and concise terms the procedures and findings of a single research project. Many of the documents that will be studied by the student in a historical research project, in contrast, will be much longer, but only a small portion of each document may relate to the specific hypotheses of the historical research project. Because of these differences in the nature of the materials searched, the search and note-taking procedures required in historical research are somewhat different and more difficult than those carried out by a student who is concerned with a review of the literature in a limited research topic. A difference already stated is in the length and breadth of content of historical documents as compared with research articles. Another difference is that documents required in historical research often date back much further than those that must be searched in order to carry out a review of the literature in a specific research area. Still another difficulty arises because historical documents used in education are often unpublished materials such as school board reports, curriculum plans, records of physical examinations, and personal letters, and therefore are not classified in such source books as *Education Index*.

Note-taking

Effective note-taking procedures are extremely important in historical research. In fact, many of the inaccuracies found in histories produced up until recent times are considered to be largely the result of unwieldy or ineffective note-taking techniques. The system used by early historians of compiling notes in chronological order in a bound note ledger made it impossible to arrange these notes into logical sequence after they had been collected. Laborious indexes were often developed to make use of the bound volumes of notes, but such an approach was a great deal less effective than the use of a note-card system or looseleaf system in which notes may be arranged in any order desired (Hockett [3]). While the student whose review of the literature is limited to brief research articles may usually outline the entire article on a single card, authorities in historical research recommend placing only one item of information on each note card. The difference in procedure is necessary because of the fact that many small bits of information relating to the various hypotheses of the research worker may be obtained from one important document such as an autobiography or a diary. If

[3] *Op. cit.*

all notes from a single major document such as a diary were copied on a single card, the process of rearranging the information would be much more difficult and complicated. Each card may be coded to indicate the hypothesis or subtopic to which the note relates.

EVALUATION OF DATA

The historical research worker, while in the process of gathering research data, concurrently carries on an evaluation of these data. Inasmuch as the pertinent documents provide the sole source of information for historical research, the evaluation of these documents is of critical importance in helping the research worker to place each bit of information in its proper perspective and draw sound conclusions from the total picture obtained. The evaluation of historical evidence is usually referred to as historical criticism. It is in the process of historical criticism that the historical research worker leans most heavily upon scientific methods and frequently upon other sciences that can assist him in making a valid appraisal of the authenticity and accuracy of his data. Historical criticism is generally divided into two major categories—external criticism and internal criticism.

External criticism

The methods of external criticism are primarily aimed at determining whether the evidence being evaluated is authentic. External criticism is therefore aimed primarily at the document itself rather than the statements contained in the document. A careful study of a document can give us a great many clues concerning its authenticity. Analyses of the physical materials such as the paper used can often permit an approximate dating of the document. Other clues such as references to place-names can also be helpful in establishing dates. Since place-names frequently change over the years, many forgeries are uncovered because they contain incorrect place-names for the places referred to at the time the forged document was supposed to have been written. Forgeries are constantly being uncovered by historians through the use of techniques of internal and external criticism. Hockett [4] discusses the "False Decretals," religious documents that were allegedly written in the third and

[4] *Op. cit.*

fourth centuries but were actually forged in the ninth century. These forgeries, however, were accepted as genuine until subjected to historical criticism in the latter part of the nineteenth century. The student of educational history is less likely to encounter forged and spurious documents than would be the historical research worker studying in some political or religious area where stronger motivations usually exist for creating forgeries.

Internal criticism

After the authenticity of a document has been established, the task of evaluating the accuracy and worth of the data contained in the document must be undertaken. Internal criticism is usually much more difficult than external criticism because it involves evaluating the writer, his biases, and his possible motives for distortion. This evaluation requires an extensive knowledge of the individual concerned, as well as the training in psychology necessary to interpret this knowledge. In testing the competence of an observer, we also must attempt to determine what opportunities the individual had for knowing the facts. If he witnessed the events that he described, do we have evidence from these observations or others that he is a reliable observer? Many studies in psychology have demonstrated that eyewitnesses can be extremely unreliable, especially if they are emotionally aroused or under stress at the time of the event. Even under conditions where no emotional involvement occurs, some individuals are a great deal more competent as observers than others. The location of the individual, his ability to take notes, and his understanding of the events that he is observing are all factors that can affect the accuracy of his observation. If several observers have described the same situation differently, it is obvious that someone has recorded the event inaccurately.

The person who has an ax to grind or has strong motives for wanting a particular version of a described event to be accepted can usually be expected to produce biased information. For example, a school superintendent, when writing an account of a school-board meeting in which a dispute occurred between himself and members of the school board, will tend to present his own side of the argument in the most favorable light, may subconsciously alter his position to agree with facts that have become apparent since the meeting, and may forget or deliberately omit statements of his opponents that have been found to have merit since the meeting occurred. Many historical research projects in education are concerned with fairly recent events, and under these conditions the research worker may supplement the information available from documents with information he may obtain by interviewing some of the participants in the event in question. The evidence collected through such interviews, however, must be evaluated carefully and checked whenever possible against other witnesses or other documentary evidence. The individual's recollection of even fairly recent events may be considerably in error. If the events involve a dispute, differences in opinion, or argument, one may be sure that each witness' report of the event will be somewhat distorted to support his own views. This may not be a deliberate distortion but merely reflects the well-known tendency to remember best those things that agree with our own opinions and biases.

Historical research workers must put much of their documentary evidence to the test of truthfulness as well as competence. Even a competent observer, if sufficiently biased in the direction of a given point of view, may record an untruthful record of the occurrences in question. If the author of a document or maker of a statement has some interest to be promoted by the acceptance of a particular point of view, one may expect that this viewpoint will be put forth, whether truthful or not. Historians must often delve to a considerable degree into the race, political party, religious group, and social status of the observer in an effort to appraise the likelihood of prejudices or biases. The use of emotionally charged or intemperate language whether of a favorable or unfavorable nature usually suggests bias and should be watched for.

Persons often exaggerate their own roles in important affairs. This exaggeration frequently is not deliberate but merely reflects the occurrences from the point of view of the individual concerned. Much material that is basically untruthful can be traced to the tendency of many individuals to elaborate or color their description of events in order to make a more interesting story or to call more attention to their own role or importance in the events being described. Sometimes, on the other hand, the social or political position of the individual is such as to require him to make conventional statements rather than honest ones. For example, a school superintendent faced with internal difficulties with principals or other members of his organization might, upon being questioned, give the usual answers indicating the high morale and level of agreement of his staff, because he may feel that airing the internal difficulties of the school district can serve no useful purpose. People in public life frequently make conventional statements concerning political opponents or in eulogizing other individuals that may have little or no bearing upon the true feelings of the individual making the statement.

There are, of course, many documents in educational history that are essentially neutral in character and in which it is difficult to imagine anyone having a motive to distort the facts deliberately. Such documents may, of course, be in error because of the incompetence of the observer.

COMMON ERRORS IN HISTORICAL RESEARCH

Historical research projects carried out by graduate students in education often contain one or more of the following errors:

1. *A research area is selected in which sufficient evidence is not available to conduct a worthwhile study or test the hypotheses adequately.* The vast majority of documents available to the student carrying out historical research in education relate to events that are not of major importance and have usually been recorded by persons unaware that their observations might have any future historical significance. For example, let us say that we are conducting a historical study tracing the development of a student-teaching program in a particular university. The minutes of faculty meetings in which the program was discussed would be an important source of data for the research worker. In all likelihood, however, minutes would have been kept by only one person and, because such minutes are often kept by a secretary who is unable to recognize significant points in the discussion, the information available may be very sketchy. Furthermore, most historians follow the rule that the statement of one person should not be regarded as establishing the truth of details described in the document. Essential agreement in the statements of independent witnesses is considered to establish truth beyond a reasonable doubt, while identical statements are generally considered to prove that the various documents are not independent.

2. *Excessive use of secondary sources of information is frequently found in studies not dealing with recent events.* The student often discovers that the time and expense involved in locating and examining primary sources is so great that he has little or no chance of covering these sources thoroughly. Primary source documents are often located at distant libraries, and they are generally not available through interlibrary loan. Thus, students must either visit the libraries or obtain photostatic copies of the needed documents. Both of these procedures are expensive, and because the pertinence of a document cannot be determined accurately until it has been examined, the student often must pay for photostating much material that will be of little or no use to him. In selecting a problem, the availability of primary sources should be carefully considered, and if needed sources are not available, the study should not be attempted. Studies of recent, local history are most practical for the graduate student in education. If the student attempts a study beyond these limitations, he will almost surely be forced to rely too heavily on secondary sources. For example, an article dealing with "Teacher Education in the Fifteenth Century" was based entirely upon secondary sources, the earliest of which was published in 1841.[5]

3. *Attempts to work on a broad and poorly defined problem.* The failure to establish specific hypotheses and the failure to delimit the research problem often go hand-in-hand. Poorly defined hypotheses make it impossible for the student to decide what documents are pertinent to his problem. If the student persists in too broad a problem in historical research, the result is almost inevitably a cursory or slipshod treatment of the evidence available. It is much more satisfactory for a student to carry out a thorough study dealing with a small specific problem than attempt to work with a problem that is beyond the scope of his time, money, and ability.

4. *Fails to evaluate adequately his historical data.* Although the student doing historical research in education rarely encounters forged documents, he should be prepared to apply the principles of external criticism to documents where some doubt as to their authenticity exists. The more difficult application of internal criticism, however, is appropriate for most of the historical evidence the student in education will collect. Failure to apply the principles of

[5] Clara P. McMahon, "Teacher Education in the Fifteenth Century," *Journal of Educational Research*, XLIV (1950), 134–37.

internal criticism is perhaps the most serious weakness found in historical studies in the field of education.

5. *Allows personal bias to influence his research procedures.* Because many historical studies in education deal with recent events and with questions and procedures about which the research worker might have definite feelings and opinions, the possibilities for personal bias are great. It is inadvisable for the student to attempt to test hypotheses in historical research that are concerned with topics about which he already has strong feelings or convictions. Such convictions will almost surely influence his selection and interpretation of the evidence available. Historical research, like all other forms of research, must be aimed primarily at gaining new knowledge rather than proving a point. Important evidence is easily overlooked or ignored in the study of historical documents. Thus, bias has a greater opportunity to operate in historical research than in experimental studies.

6. *The student's report recites facts but does not synthesize or integrate these facts into meaningful generalizations.* Many students consider that the historical research study is complete when the facts related to the topic have been assembled. The mere recitation of facts is not historical research and without synthesis and interpretation cannot provide us with the better understanding and perspective that is the usual goal of historical research.

CRITERIA FOR RESEARCH IN EDUCATIONAL HISTORY

Perdew lists the following criteria for research in educational history. If the student follows these criteria and avoids the errors already stated, he is likely to produce worthwhile historical research.[6]

a. Purpose. One of the common concepts in the definitions of research is that research has the purpose of extending, correcting, or verifying knowledge. Some reports using historical data may merely restate knowledge already the common property of scholars in the field. This is usually true of textbooks, which commonly have the purpose of instructing students, and are not designed to add to the knowledge of scholars.

---

[6] Philip W. Perdew, "Criteria of Research in Educational History," *Journal of Educational Research,* XLIV (1950), 217–23. Reprinted by permission of the *Journal of Educational Research.*

b. Presentation of facts. It is difficult to conceive of a report of historical research which does not deal with facts. The second measure of a publication which uses historical data is the extent to which it presents facts.

c. Generalizations. History is dependent upon the synthesis of facts or small-scale generalizations and interpretations, and it does not lead to universal laws nor a philosophy of history. Reports which do not recognize the necessity for the proper balance between fact and interpretation do not qualify as historical research. Critical or philosophical articles which use historical data to illustrate and strengthen the argument, although good in themselves, are not historical research.

Except as an investigation meets in full the first three criteria listed above, it cannot be classified as historical research in education.

d. Demonstration of sources. Since, obviously, past events cannot be repeated or brought in for experimentation, the historian turns to sources contemporary with the events. A report of historical research, then, must show evidence of being based upon such sources. This evidence may be in the text of the publication, in footnotes, or in the bibliography. There is room for historical writing which is largely interpretative and done by men whose reputation justifies their recognition, but, in doing such writing, one hazards his reputation as an historian.

e. Selection of sources. The selection and evaluation of sources is a delicate task requiring training and judgment. Every subject has its own special sources. In general the student should attempt to locate sources as close in time and place as possible to the event, in other words, to use as extensively as possible the primary sources.

f. Statements of problems. The good research report shows evidence of delimitation in the problem studied. An occasional work sets for itself too large a problem for the space allotted to it, leading to generalization without supporting data. Sometimes a title with a large scope is given whereas the publication deals with only a small aspect of it. These tendencies weaken the quality of research publications.

g. Logical organization. Weaknesses in the logical organization of a report of historical research suggest weaknesses in the author's understanding and analysis of the problem.

h. Social forces. Since historians of education generally support the view that education is to be shown in its interrelation with other social institutions and forces, proper recognition of such relationships is a characteristic of a good research report.

i. Development and cause and effect relationships. History is not a listing of events. That is the area of the annalist or the chronicler. To be history, the events must be brought into causal relationships.

j. Language and style. Language and style are significant aspects of a report of historical research. A clear lucid style is imperative if communication between the writer and the reader is to be established. Beyond this is the style of the consummate artist with words, who charms and interests his audience to a greater extent than the subject and material alone justify. The historical geniuses have the gift of language in large measure. It must not be forgotten by even the humble monographer that history is a great subject and warrants the grand style.

ANNOTATED REFERENCES

1. GARRAGHAN, GILBERT J. *A Guide to Historical Method.* New York: Fordham University Press, 1946. This textbook provides the student planning a historical research project with a firm foundation in historical research method. A general orientation to history and the historical method, and its relationship to other sciences is presented. The section on locating sources gives the student an introduction to the types of historical sources, as well as information on note-taking systems and the use of libraries. Sections dealing with historical criticism and presentation of the results of historical research are very useful, the former borrowing heavily from Bernheim's *Lehrbuch der Historischen Methode,* which is generally recognized as the classic work in the field of historical research method.

2. GOOD, CARTER V. *Introduction to Educational Research.* New York: Appleton-Century-Crofts, Inc., 1959. The student is referred to Chapter 4, which describes the processes of historical research and the major steps in carrying it out, including collection of data, evaluation of data, and preparation of the report. Although this chapter provides a good coverage of basic principles, the student planning a historical research project should consult more complete sources, such as Hockett or Gottschalk (see References 3. and 5.). The student may find other references pertinent to his specific interest in historical research in the extensive reference list provided.

3. GOTTSCHALK, LOUIS. *Understanding History: A Primer of Historical Method.* New York: Alfred A. Knopf, Inc., 1951. This book is written primarily for the student who wishes to do historical research and writing in the college or university and is strongly oriented towards "how to do it." Treatment of internal and external criticism is somewhat less thorough than Hockett (see Reference 5.). Contains more emphasis on such practical subjects as choosing a subject, use of footnotes, note-taking, use of quotations, preparing a draft, and others.

4. HANDLIN, OSCAR; SCHLESINGER, ARTHUR; *et al. Harvard Guide to American History.* Cambridge, Mass.: Harvard University Press, 1954. This book is a comprehensive treatment of American history. The first five

chapters, however, provide the student with extensive information on research and historical writing, historical materials, aids to historical research, and historical sources. The student planning a historical research project can learn much from these chapters.

5. HOCKETT, HOMER C. *The Critical Method in Historical Research and Writing.* New York: The Macmillan Co., 1955. This textbook orients the student to the role of history, traces the development of the historical method, and presents a thorough coverage of historical criticism. Because it has been prepared primarily for the use of graduate students, emphasis is also given to the preparation of the Master's thesis and doctoral dissertation. It contains a very extensive bibliography on historical methodology, writing and teaching, and other topics important to the historical research worker. This text is highly recommended as basic reading for the student planning a historical research project in education.

6. PERDEW, PHILIP W. "Criteria of Research in Educational History," *Journal of Educational Research,* 1950, 44, 217–23. The author discusses criteria for research from various sources and develops ten criteria that can guide students in conducting historical research in education. He points out that, of over 900 historical writings published in the field of secondary education since 1900, less than half can rightfully be considered historical research. This article calls the attention of the graduate student interested in historical research to factors that he must consider in developing and carrying out his project.

7. WOODY, THOMAS. "Of History and Its Method," *Journal of Experimental Education,* 1947, 15, 175–201. Provides a brief but useful background in history and historical method, including philosophy of history, historical method, qualifications needed to carry out historical research, selection of a subject, internal and external criticism, documentation, note-taking, and other related topics. Contains a great deal of useful information in very brief form.

CHAPTER 10

The Methods and Tools of Descriptive Research

INTRODUCTION

The major purpose of descriptive research in education is to tell "what is." A glance at the titles of some recent descriptive studies gives some idea of the tremendous scope covered by this important phase of educational research: "The Financial Problems of Medical Students, Senior Class, May, 1959"; "Fellowships, Scholarships, and Assistantships for Guidance and Personnel Graduate Training. 1961–62"; "The Purpose of Physical Education in Higher Education"; "Evaluation of the AEC Equipment Grant Programs in Nuclear Engineering and Science"; "The Blind Person as a College Teacher"; "Follow-up Questionnaire on College Reading Improvement Program"; "Firearms and Hunting Instruction"; "Survey of Mathematics Programs in Institutions Granting Bachelor and Higher Degrees." [1]

Descriptive studies serve several very important functions in education. First, in new sciences the body of knowledge is relatively small, and we are often confused with conflicting claims and theories. Under these conditions, it is often of great value merely to know the current state of the science. Descriptive research provides us with a starting point and, therefore, is often carried out as a preliminary step to be followed by research using more rigorous control and more objective methods. For example, a questionnaire or interview study might be used to estimate the extent and types of personal counseling needed at the high school level. After these data have been obtained, a more rigorous design involving experimental

---

[1] These titles taken from Report on Questionnaires, Nos. 42–44, published by the Office of Statistical Information and Research, American Council on Education, January, February, and March, 1961.

and control groups might be employed to determine the effectiveness of different counseling approaches such as group counseling, nondirective counseling, and directive counseling coupled with teaching needed social skills.

We need not justify descriptive research, however, merely as a preliminary step to the use of more objective research techniques. A great many descriptive studies are the direct sources of valuable knowledge concerning human behavior. For example, an observational study of the interaction that takes place among a gang of juvenile delinquents can give us a sound insight into the needs and problems of these individuals, and of other similar groups.

In addition to providing us with a great deal of sound scientific information, descriptive studies are used widely by public school systems in their educational planning. Perhaps the most universal application of descriptive methods to educational planning is the school census, which permits the administrator to predict the educational needs his schools will be called upon to meet in future years. Descriptive studies also provide the school system with the means for internal evaluation and improvement. Follow-up studies of graduates help the school system to determine whether the curriculum has adequately prepared its former students for their adult roles in the community.

Although the major function of descriptive studies in education will probably always be directed to "what is," many surveys do go further than a description of the existing situation. Surveys dealing with curriculum, for example, can obtain information not only about the strengths and weaknesses of the current curriculum but can also elicit recommendations for change. Many of the more recent surveys give us both a description of current status and a source of ideas for change and improvement.

TYPES OF DESCRIPTIVE RESEARCH

There are many different types of descriptive research that are currently being used in education and the other behavioral sciences. The most extensive descriptive studies are generally those conducted in sociology and social psychology. The social survey, for example, usually involves the use of interview, observation, and questionnaire techniques to make a broad analysis of some social phenomenon or problem. Social surveys are usually conducted by a team of scientists with representatives from such disciplines as sociology, psychology, economics, and cultural anthropology.

The community survey is similar in scope to the social survey except that instead of focusing on a specific social phenomenon or problem, the focus is usually upon aspects of behavior and social interaction within a given community. Community surveys help give us insight into such matters as racial and intergroup relations, recreation, physical aspects of the area, housing, and industry. Such studies usually provide some historical perspective and often explore transitions such as population mobility, technological changes, and changes in status and values.

The comprehensive school survey usually explores and evaluates many aspects of the school system such as school plants, maintenance, administrative procedures, financial support and procedures, teaching staff, learning objectives, curriculum, and teaching methods. Such surveys are usually carried out by a team of visiting specialists from universities and other school systems.

Such surveys are conducted to help solve the problems of the community studied, as well as to gain basic scientific knowledge that can be applied generally. These extensive projects are beyond the resources of the graduate student in education. In this chapter we will emphasize those applications of descriptive research methods that can be employed in small-scale educational studies.

THE MAILED QUESTIONNAIRE IN DESCRIPTIVE RESEARCH

Among the various methods of descriptive research, the questionnaire survey is by far the most widely used in education. The questionnaire survey can be a very valuable technique in helping us to understand the current situation in some particular educational area. This technique is used very widely by the U.S. Office of Education, the National Education Association, and other state and national organizations. A recent research bulletin published by the National Educational Association provides an example of the type of information that may be obtained. This report covers a comprehensive survey of 24,193 urban school districts in the United States and presents detailed information on salaries paid in these districts to classroom teachers, principals, and other administrative personnel.[2] This study also compares median salaries paid in 1957 with those paid as early as 1930. Further comparisons are made between salaries paid in urban districts of different sizes ranging from small, urban districts of 2,500 to 5,000 population up to large urban districts of over 500,000 population. Extensive questionnaire surveys of this type can do much to help us understand certain aspects of our educational system. In spite of the fact that questionnaire surveys can be of great value, the technique is generally held in low esteem by research workers. Few graduate students embarking upon a questionnaire survey realize the difficulties involved in planning and carrying out a satisfactory study of this type. Poor planning and construction of the questionnaire usually leads to poorly defined results and a small percentage of responses from individuals receiving the questionnaire. The data obtained from a poorly designed questionnaire based on a small percentage of responses are often worse than no data at all because the results reported may lead the unsophisticated reader to draw inaccurate conclusions or take inappropriate action.

Defining the problem

The first step in carrying out a satisfactory questionnaire study is to list specific objectives to be achieved by the questionnaire. It is not uncommon for a graduate student to develop a questionnaire before he has a clear understanding of what he hopes to obtain from the results. Unless you are able to state specifically and in detail what information you need, what you will do with this information after you get it, and how each item on the questionnaire contributes to meeting your specific objectives, you have not thought through your problem sufficiently. In preparing your objectives, you need not limit yourself to determining the current situation or "what is." Many questionnaire studies go further and seek the ideas and recommendations of the persons responding. These recommendations may deal with changes that would be desirable to improve the situation covered by the questionnaire and may also include suggestions of ways that these improvements may be brought about. For example, one section of a questionnaire could be concerned with the

[2] "Salaries and Salary Schedules of Urban School Employees, 1956–57," *NEA Research Bulletin,* Vol. XXXV, No. 2 (1957).

specific amount and type of parental participation in the extra-curricular activities of elementary schools. Another section of this questionnaire may seek the ideas or recommendations of a sample of teachers and parents concerning the kind and amount of parental participation they think is desirable in extracurricular activities and how the desired participation can be encouraged by the school.

Constructing the questionnaire

Many of the questionnaires that are received by principals, super-intendents, and other educators appear to have been thrown together by the graduate student during the short break between lunch and his two o'clock class. This type of questionnaire has led many school administrators to develop negative attitudes about the questionnaire as a research approach. Some of the more harrassed administrators deposit the questionnaires they receive in the wastebasket with little more than a quick glance. This attitude, of course, presents an obstacle that the graduate student planning to use this technique must and can overcome by the careful construction and administration of his questionnaire. Each item on your questionnaire must be developed to measure a specific aspect of one of your objectives or hypotheses. You should be able to explain in detail *why* you are asking the question and *how* you will analyze the responses. Objectivity is an important requirement for questionnaire items. Questions may be of either the closed form in which the question permits only certain responses (such as a multiple choice question), or the open form in which the subject makes any response he wishes in his own words (such as an essay question). Which form will be used is determined by the objective of the particular question. Open-ended questions requiring lengthy replies, however, are usually un-desirable because it is very difficult to summarize such answers in quantitative terms. When constructing questionnaire items you must keep in mind that in most cases the individual responses must be reduced to some form that permits them to be counted or fitted into quantitative categories. Another disadvantage of long, subjective replies is that they require considerable time and effort on the part of the person responding. Finally, open-form questions yield many unusable replies because of inadequate information or mis-interpretation of the question by the subjects. Inasmuch as it is necessary to classify responses into a number of categories in order to present the results quantitatively, a sound alternative to the open-form question is to determine what categories the open-ended responses are likely to fall into, and then develop the question as a multiple-choice item. For example, let us suppose you are interested in provisions made for gifted pupils in elementary schools. An open-form question could be used: "What provisions are made for gifted pupils in your school? Please be specific and indicate the extent to which each technique was employed during the past school year." More complete and usable information could be obtained by using the following items:

1. Do you have a systematic program for identifying gifted children in your school? _____ _____ If yes, what means of identification do you use?
                                        yes   no

        _____ *a.* Group intelligence test
        _____ *b.* Individual intelligence test
        _____ *c.* Achievement battery
        _____ *d.* Aptitude battery
        _____ *e.* Teacher ratings
        _____ *f.* Other (specify) _____

2. What provisions were made for gifted pupils in your school during the school year 1960–61? (Check appropriate answers.)

        _____ *a.* Acceleration (grade skipping)
        _____ *b.* Ungraded program
        _____ *c.* Ability grouping
        _____ *d.* Enrichment
        _____ *e.* Special classes
        _____ *f.* Others (specify) _____

Depending on the specific objectives of the questionnaire, other questions could be added concerned with such matters as the number of pupils at each grade level who skipped a grade, the number of pupils in special classes, the criteria for establishing ability grouped sections, and others.

Perhaps the best method of determining the multiple choice categories to use in closed questions is to ask the question in essay form of a small sample of respondents, and then use their answers to develop the categories for the multiple-choice item that will be included in the final form of the questionnaire. In multiple-choice areas where a certain number of unexpected responses might occur, an "other" choice can be used along with a space for explanation. If your topic is such that it is not possible to get the information you want using closed-form items, you should consider using interviews rather than questionnaires because the interview approach is much more adaptable to the open-form question.

In addition to aiming at objectivity in the construction of questionnaire items, it is also desirable to design the questions in such a way that quantification and analysis of the results may be carried out efficiently. Let us suppose you wish to know the size of the teacher's hometown so that you can compare teachers from different sized towns in terms of interests and vocational goals. There are several ways that this question could be asked. Perhaps the poorest technique would be to ask "What is your home town?" This question requires that you be able to read the person's reply and look it up in an atlas to determine the population. A technique that would be somewhat better would be to ask "What is the population of your home town?" In this case you could classify the responses into population categories such as those used by the U.S. Census Bureau. A still better means of obtaining this information would be to ask: "What is the population of your home town?" (Check one.)

         _____ rural, unincorporated
         _____ incorporated, under 1,000
         _____ 1,000 to 2,500
         _____ 2,500 to 5,000
         _____ 5,000 to 10,000
         _____ 10,000 to 50,000
         _____ 50,000 to 250,000
         _____ over 250,000

This latter technique would provide you with the information you want in immediately usable form, thus requiring less effort on your part, while requiring no more effort by your subjects.

Another rule you should observe in constructing questionnaire items is to avoid questions that may in some way be psychologically threatening to the person answering. For example, a questionnaire sent to school principals concerning the morale of teachers at their schools would be threatening to some of the principals because low morale suggests that the principal is failing in part of his job. When a person receives a questionnaire containing threatening items, he usually does not return it. If he does return it, little confidence can be placed in the accuracy of his reply because of his ego-involvement in the situation.

In constructing the questionnaire, you must remember that you have a much more thorough understanding of your objectives and the specific purposes of each of your questions than any of your respondents. Your familiarity with the problem may result in your phrasing questions in such a way that the person who lacks your knowledge will find them ambiguous or even pointless or stupid. Even if you have the soundest reasons for asking a question, if the person responding feels that the question is pointless, his reaction may well be to throw away the questionnaire, leave the question blank, or insert a sarcastic or facetious remark. Thus, it is desirable to check each item personally with a number of people whose backgrounds are similar to those who will be included in your study in order to determine whether you have made serious blunders in item construction. The thorough pretesting of the questionnaire, which we will discuss later, will serve as a further check against ambiguous or apparently pointless items.

Most questionnaires deal with factual material, and in many cases each item is analyzed separately to provide a specific bit of information that contributes to the overall picture that you are attempting to obtain. Thus, it is possible to look upon the questionnaire as a collection of one-item tests. The use of a one-item test is quite satisfactory when one is seeking out a specific fact such as teacher salary, number of baseball bats owned by the physical education department, or number of students failing algebra. When questions get into the area of attitude and opinion, however, the one-item test approach is extremely unreliable. I recently encountered a study in which a student working in wildlife management was interested in constructing a questionnaire dealing with the attitudes of farmers toward hunters. In this case, the farmer's overall attitude is, in all likelihood, a rather complex combination of specific attitudes dealing with different aspects of the question. A questionnaire dealing with a topic of this type must generally be constructed as an attitude scale and must use a number of items (usually at least ten) in order to obtain a reasonable picture of the attitude concerned. A review of attitude measurement is therefore necessary before the student attempts to construct a questionnaire of this type.

Finally, it is very important that an effort be made to avoid leading questions. If the subject is given hints as to the type of answer you would most prefer, there is some tendency for him to give you what you wish. This tendency is especially strong when the letter of transmittal that accompanies the questionnaire has been signed by someone whom the subject is anxious to please.

Selecting subjects

The most obvious consideration involved in selection of subjects for a questionnaire study is to get people who will be able to supply the information you want. Very often the group who will have the data you want is immediately apparent. But in some cases, if you do not have a thorough knowledge of the situation involved, you may send your questionnaire to a group of persons who do not have the desired information. For example: A graduate student seeking data on school financial policies sent questionnaires to principals of a large number of elementary schools. Many of the questionnaires returned were incomplete, and few specific facts of the sort wanted were obtained. This study failed because the trend in recent years has been for the superintendent and his staff to handle most matters concerning school finance. Inasmuch as the principals who received the questionnaire had little specific knowledge concerning this topic, they were unable to supply the information requested on the questionnaire.

Most questionnaire studies conducted in education are aimed at specific professional groups. Once you have established that the professional group selected actually has access to the information you wish to obtain, the best method of selecting the subjects you want from the population involved is by some random technique such as taking names from a hat.[3] Many professional groups in education have special organizations or societies, and in some cases a random selection of names from the directory of organization members gives a satisfactory group. This type of selection, however, must be used cautiously as there may be a tendency for the more competent mem-

[3] A general discussion of sampling may be found in Chapter 7.

bers of the professional group to belong to the organization, thus leading the researcher to select a biased sample.

State public school directories are more satisfactory for selection of subjects because they list all persons involved in public education in the state and are usually up to date. When the population is very large, such as all elementary school teachers in the United States, and no complete name list is available, it is usually necessary to use a two-stage procedure to obtain a random sample. The first stage in obtaining a nationwide sample could be to select randomly a specified number of school districts. Since most districts print rosters of their teachers, the next step would be to request a copy of the rosters from districts selected in the first stage. A specified number of teachers could then be randomly selected by name from each roster.[4]

In some cases, it is desirable to obtain responses from several specific categories of persons within the professional group being sampled. For example, you may wish to compare responses dealing with the use of pupil-centered instruction gathered from teachers with different amounts of professional experience. Some surveys involve samples of teachers, principals, and superintendents in order to obtain a broader idea of the views of educators and also in some cases in order to contrast their responses. The process of selecting subsamples from different levels of the population is referred to as stratification. In general, when a stratified sample is used, that is, when certain numbers of subjects are to be selected from specific levels or on the basis of specific criteria, it is still desirable to select within each of the strata on a random basis. If subsamples of 100 inexperienced teachers, 100 with one-to-three years experience, and 100 with four or more years of experience were required it would be desirable to select each subsample randomly from a specified population of teachers available in each category.

Pretesting the questionnaire

In addition to the preliminary check that you make of your questions in order to locate ambiguities, it is very desirable to carry out a thorough pretest of your questionnaire before using it in your study. For the pretest of your questionnaire, you should select a

[4] See National Education Association, Research Division, "Small-Sample Techniques," *NEA Research Bulletin*, XXXVIII (1960), 99–104. This article gives a detailed plan for selecting a sample from a large population.

sample of individuals from a population similar to that from which you plan to draw your research subjects. For example, if you were concerned with mechanical aids used for teaching foreign languages in California high schools, you could pretest your questionnaire using a sample of foreign language teachers employed in another state. The pretest form of the questionnaire should provide space for the respondents to make comments about the questionnaire itself so they may indicate whether some questions seem ambiguous to them, whether provisions should be made for certain responses that are not included in the questionnaire, and other points that can lead to improving the instrument. The techniques for administering the questionnaire during the pretest should be essentially the same as planned for the main study; except when there is some doubt as to which of two questions or two approaches might be most useful, both can be tried on portions of the pretest sample. The number of cases in the pretest sample need not be large. If the subjects are taken from a well-defined professional group such as school superintendents, as few as twenty cases will often be sufficient. For more heterogeneous groups, such as persons paying property taxes or parents with one or more children in elementary school, a larger pretest group is advisable.

When the pretest results are in, first check the percentage of replies obtained. Educational studies generally can be expected to yield a higher percentage of replies than questionnaires sent to random samples of the general population because the educational questionnaire usually aims at a reasonably homogeneous group, and this makes it possible to prepare an appeal to the group for cooperation, which is more likely to be successful. If, in checking the percentage of replies, you have received less than 75 per cent of the pretest sample, it is probable that major changes will be needed in the questionnaire or in the procedures for administering it. The next step is to read the subjects' comments concerning the questionnaire. These comments often give specific information on how the questionnaire can be improved. Then, check the responses item by item. If you find items that are often left blank or answered in ways that you did not predict, it is very likely that the item was misinterpreted by some of the subjects.

It is now possible to do a brief analysis of the pretest results. This will give you a chance to determine whether the methods you have planned to use for summarizing and quantifying the data will work satisfactorily. Also, the pretest results may suggest additional questions to you. For example, if sharp disagreement is found in the responses to a particular item of the questionnaire, it may be desirable to construct additional items that will help you understand the reasons for this disagreement.

After the above procedure has been completed and all improvements made in the pretest questionnaire, you are ready to proceed with the administration of your questionnaire to the sample you have selected.

The letter of transmittal

The major problem of the student doing a questionnaire study is to get a sufficient percentage of responses to use as a basis for drawing general conclusions. Perhaps the most important single factor in determining the percentage of responses you will obtain is the letter of transmittal used with your questionnaire. This letter must be brief but yet must convey certain information and impressions to the subjects if you are to obtain a satisfactory percentage of responses. First, it is essential that you give the subjects good reasons for completing your questionnaire and sending it back to you. Whenever possible, the purposes of the study should be explained briefly and in such a way as to make the subject feel that the study is significant and important. If your questionnaire is aimed at a group with specific professional ties, such as mathematics teachers, it is usually desirable to make some reference to the person's professional status and his feelings of affiliation with this group. In some cases, a certain amount of subtle flattery is also useful in preparing the letter of transmittal. This is usually accomplished by stressing the importance of the subjects' professional group and the value of the information they can supply. An offer to send the respondent a copy of the results is often effective. If made, however, such a promise should be honored because neglect of such matters is not ethical and will weaken future studies involving persons in your sample.

If possible, it is also desirable to associate your study with some professional institution or organization with which individuals in your sample might be expected to value or identify. For example, superintendents within a particular state might be expected to respond favorably to a letter signed by the state superintendent, the

Sample Letter of Transmittal

Letterhead paper ——➤ OKLABAMA STATE UNIVERSITY

Collegetown, Oklabama

M. A. Brown, President

College of Education

I. B. Smith, Dean

February 1, 1963

Typed with same   Mr. A. B. Jones
machine used in ——➤ Superintendent of Schools
cutting offset stencil   Mediumtown, Oklabama

Dear Sir:

Duplicated using offset
process to look like ——➤ The attached questionnaire con-
individually typed cerned with procedures used in selec-
letter ting elementary school principals is
    part of a state-wide study being car-
Purpose of study ╱ ried on cooperatively by the State De-
    partment of Public Instruction and Okla-
    bama State University. This project
    is concerned specifically with deter-
    mining the present status of principal
Importance of ——➤ selection in our state. The results
study of this study will help to provide pre-
    liminary criteria to be used for develop-
    ing better selection procedures and for
    improving the administrator training pro-
    gram at Oklahoma University.

     We are particularly desirous of ob-
Importance of taining your responses because your ex-
respondent ——➤ perience in principal selection will con-
    tribute significantly toward solving some
    of the problems we face in this important
    area of education. The enclosed question-
    naire has been tested with a sampling of
    school administrators, and we have revised
    it in order to make it possible for us
    to obtain all necessary data while requir-
    ing a minimum of your time. The average
    time required for administrators trying
    out the questionnaire was $9\frac{1}{2}$ minutes.

Reasonable but specific
time limit ————————→ It will be appreciated if you will
complete the questionnaire prior to Feb-
ruary 10th and return it in the stamped,
Special delivery ⟋special delivery envelope enclosed. Other
further stresses—⟋ phases of this research cannot be carried
importance . out until we complete analysis of the questionnaire data. We would welcome any com-
ments that you may have concerning any aspect of principal selection not covered
in the questionnaire. We will be pleased
to send you a summary of questionnaire
Offer results ————————→results if you desire. Thank you for
your cooperation.

                                    Sincerely yours,

Printed different color to ————————————————→
appear personally signed   *I. B. Smith*

                                    ⟋I. B. Smith, Dean
Signed by important educator—⟋
rather than graduate student

                Enc.
                sjc

state or national president of a superintendent's association, or the Dean of Education at the state university. If your study is well-designed and deals with a significant problem, it is usually possible to have someone sign your letter of transmittal who will represent a favorable authority symbol to the persons responding.

If your questionnaire is not aimed at a specific professional group, it is much more difficult to obtain responses, because specific appeals cannot be made. Under these conditions, you might slant your appeal along lines in which you might expect even the members of a widely diversified group to have common views, such as patriotism, desire to improve the community, and so on. However, if your study is one where these general appeals are obviously inappropriate, the best approach is probably an appeal to the individual's sense of humor. For example, several years ago a national magazine wished to obtain information from its readers on the extent to which they used commercial flying in pursuing their sports activities. As the subscribers were a highly heterogeneous group having very little in common except subscription to this periodical and as the topic was not one where a general appeal could be expected to work, the magazine sent their very brief questionnaire along with a letter of transmittal on which was glued a dime. The letter of transmittal started out by asking the person to take a coffee break at the expense of the magazine and while drinking the coffee to check off answers on the attached postcard. This sort of approach is likely to get good response because it amuses the subject while making very modest demands upon his time. Inflation seems to have struck the questionnaire survey, however, because a recent study reported by Bressler indicated that pennies, nickles, and dimes had little effect on numbers of questionnaires returned, while quarters and special delivery stamps were found to be extremely effective as inducements to return the questionnaire.[5]

One of the items to be contained in the letter of transmittal is a request that the questionnaire be returned by a particular date. It is important to set this date so that the subject will have sufficient time to fill out and return the questionnaire without rushing or inconvenience, but on the other hand, will not be likely to put it aside to do later as is the tendency if too generous a time allowance is

[5] Marvin Bressler and William Kephart, "An Experience with the Use of the Mail Questionnaire," *Nursing Research*, V (1956), 35–39.

given. A satisfactory rule-of-thumb would be to calculate the probable mailing time and allow the individual an additional week or less to complete the questionnaire and return it. Included with the questionnaire and the letter of transmittal should be a stamped, self-addressed envelope so that the individual can respond with a minimum of inconvenience.

The follow-up letter

A few days after the time limit that you have set in your letter of transmittal it is usually desirable to send a follow-up letter along with another copy of the questionnaire and another self-addressed envelope to individuals who have not responded. The follow-up letter must generally assume the tone that you are certain the individual wished to fill out the questionnaire, but perhaps due to an error on your part or some oversight, it was overlooked. The follow-up letter should then go on to point out again the importance of the study and value of the individual's contribution to this important project.

As a rule, if careful attention is given to the design of the questionnaire, the letter of transmittal, and follow-up letter, a sufficient percentage of subjects will respond. In cases where a very high percentage of response is required, it may be necessary to conduct a further follow-up using a different approach. A second follow-up letter will generally produce little result, but if a new approach is used, it might bring in the additional cases needed. On some occasions as many as three follow-up letters are used. Figure 7 shows the pattern of responses to one questionnaire study in which three follow-ups were used. It will be noted that in this study the first follow-up brought in an additional 20 per cent of the sample, the second about 15 per cent, and the third about 2 per cent. The effectiveness of the second and third follow-ups in this study was greater than average, probably because these were sent as telegrams, which are more likely than letters to command attention. On some occasions, a telephone call is effective if the first follow-up letter does not yield sufficient returns.

The neatness and composition of your questionnaire and accompanying material is also an important factor in determining the number of replies. The more expensive methods of duplication are usually worth the extra cost. A letter of transmittal reproduced by the offset process on letterhead paper and signed with a different color of ink will command more attention than one poorly dittoed on cheap paper. A poorly reproduced questionnaire indicates to the respondent that the study is of little importance to you or anyone else in spite of your protestations to the contrary.

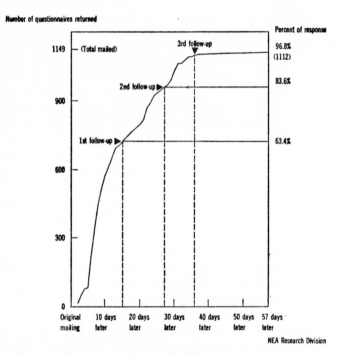

FIG. 7. Pattern of response to Opinion Poll No. 1.*

* Taken from National Education Assoc., Research Division, "Small-Sample Techniques," *NEA Research Bulletin*, XXXVIII (December, 1960), 102. Reprinted by permission of the NEA Research Division.

What to do about nonresponding subjects

After the responses have been obtained, the research worker faces the problem of analyzing his results. The question that usually arises at this point is "How would the results have been changed if all subjects had returned the questionnaire?" If only a small percentage of your subjects failed to respond, this question is not critical. If more than 20 per cent are missing, however, it is very likely that most of the findings of the study could have been altered considerably if the nonresponding group had returned the questionnaire and had answered in a markedly different manner than the responding group. This could be the case if the nonresponding group represents a biased sampling—that is, if those people who did not respond to the questionnaire are in some measurable way different from those who did respond. A common sampling bias of this type is that persons having a good program are more likely to respond than those having a poor program. For example, a questionnaire dealing with the physical education program at the elementary school level will get a higher percentage of responses from those schools having programs that the respondents believe to be above par. School administrators are often reluctant to admit the deficiencies of their schools and therefore fail to return questionnaires in which these deficiencies would be revealed.

Therefore, if more than 20 per cent of the questionnaires are not returned, it is desirable to check a portion of the nonresponding group even though this checking usually involves considerable effort. The ideal method of checking is to select a small number of cases randomly from the nonresponding group, and then interview these subjects in order to obtain the necessary information. If the questionnaire has been sent over a wide geographical area, interviewing a random selection of nonresponding cases is usually not possible. Under these circumstances the student can get some insight into the nature of the nonresponding group by checking those persons who are within a reasonable distance. In most educational studies of the sort conducted by graduate students, twenty cases are adequate to check the nonresponding group. After data have been obtained from these cases, the responses of this group to each item are compared with the responses of those who replied initially to determine whether the nonresponding sample is biased. If this sample of nonresponding subjects answers the questions in about the same manner as the responding group, it is probably safe to assume that the responding group is an unbiased sample of those to whom you mailed the questionnaire. If this sample, however, is considerably different in their responses, these differences should be noted and their significance discussed in reporting the results of the responding sample.

Effect of anonymity on questionnaire responses

In most educational studies the respondent is asked to identify himself. Anonymity is sometimes called for if data of a personal nature or data that may be threatening to the individual are requested. A questionnaire dealing with sexual behavior, for example, may receive more honest responses if anonymous.

The anonymous questionnaire poses many research problems. Follow-ups are difficult and inefficient because nonresponding individuals cannot be identified. Furthermore, it is usually not possible to make some of the statistical breakdowns of the group that may be desirable. For example, in a study of teacher-principal relationships, it may be desirable to divide the respondents into men and women teachers, married and unmarried teachers, and teachers with different amounts of experience, and then compare the responses of these different groups. In the anonymous questionnaire, breakdowns of this sort that were not anticipated and provided for in the questionnaire cannot be made. Often the desirability of analyzing certain subgroups separately is not apparent until the data are collected.

The essential question that must be answered, however, is whether anonymity is necessary to get accurate replies. In a study of 400 military officers one half were given a questionnaire requiring that they identify themselves by name, while the other half were given the same questionnaire but were not required to identify themselves by name. Significant differences in response were found in only 2 per cent of the 118 items with no trend favoring either subjects who identified themselves or subjects who remained anonymous. Persons who signed their names took a longer period to answer their questionnaire, which may indicate that they were more careful in their responses. No significant differences, however, were found between the groups in either the quality or the quantity of their responses as measured by "degree of careless thinking," "number of omitted questions," or "number of ideas represented in open-ended questions." [6] This study suggests that mature adult respondents tend to answer the questions whether they are asked to identify themselves or not. The factors to be considered in deciding whether identifica-

[6] Francis J. DiVesta, "Problems in the Use of Questionnaires for Studying the Effectiveness of Programs," *Educational and Psychological Measurement*, XIV (1954), 138–50.

tion is to be asked for are the importance of identification in the analysis of results, the level of maturity of the respondents, the degree to which questions involve answers that the respondent might be reluctant to give if he is identified, the probable effect of anonymity on the number of returns, and the procedures that can be used in the analysis of results.

THE RESEARCH INTERVIEW

Introduction

The interview as a research method in descriptive research is unique in that it involves the collection of data through direct verbal interaction between individuals. This direct interaction is the source of most of the advantages and disadvantages of the interview as a research technique. Perhaps its principal advantage is its adaptability. The well-trained interviewer can make full use of the responses of the subject to alter the interview situation. As contrasted with the questionnaire that provides no immediate feedback, the interview permits the research worker to follow-up leads, and thus obtain more data and greater clarity. The interview situation usually permits much greater depth than the other methods of collecting research data. A serious criticism of questionnaire studies is that they are often shallow—that is, they fail to dig deeply enough to provide a true picture of opinions and feelings. The skilled interviewer on the other hand can obtain information through the careful motivation of the subject and maintenance of rapport that the subject would probably not reveal under any other circumstances. Clinical psychologists, for example, frequently deal with information that can only be obtained through very skillful interview techniques.

On the other hand, the interview has definite limitations as a research tool. Most important, the very adaptability gained by the interpersonal situation leads to subjectivity and possible bias. The interactions between the respondent and the interviewer are subject to bias from many sources. Eagerness of the respondent to please the interviewer, a vague antagonism that sometimes arises between the interviewer and the respondent, and the tendency of the interviewer to seek out answers that support his preconceived notions are but a few of the factors that contribute to the possible biasing of data obtained from the interview. Another problem related to the interview method that seriously limits the graduate student in education is that considerable training is required before the individual can successfully carry out an interview study. The student must gain a thorough knowledge of interview procedures and must obtain practice in interviewing before he can expect to collect usable data through this technique. This chapter will acquaint the student with the basic information needed to plan an interview study, but he should carefully study some of the books dealing exclusively with interviewing before attempting to use this technique in research. The interview is also time-consuming and therefore limits the number of subjects from whom the graduate student can expect to obtain data. In research areas where depth is needed, the use of the interview is usually called for. It is not recommended, however, that the graduate student employ the interview technique when information to be collected is such that it can be obtained by other means.

Structure in research interviews

Interviews may be classified in a number of different ways. Perhaps the most important is the level of structure of the interview. Structure refers to the amount of direction and restriction imposed by the interview situation. Certain types of information such as the limited specific facts or opinions collected in public opinion polls call for a highly structured interview situation. In these studies, the interviewer usually asks each respondent a brief series of questions that can be answered either "yes" or "no," or by selecting one of a set of alternate choices. The respondent's answers are not followed up to obtain greater depth, and the level of structure in this case is such that the data could be collected quite satisfactorily with a mailed questionnaire. The only advantage of the interview over the mailed questionnaire for this type of data collection is that the interviewer is likely to get responses from more of the persons in the sample selected. The disadvantage of the interview, of course, is the greater expense of collecting data.

In the semistructured interview, some of the information required will be obtained by asking a series of structured questions. The interviewer will then probe more deeply, using open form questions in order to obtain more complete data. The semistructured interview, therefore, has the advantage of being reasonably objective while still permitting a more thorough understanding of the respondent's opinions and the reasons behind them than would be possible using the mailed questionnaire. The semistructured interview is generally most appropriate for interview studies in education. It provides a desirable combination of objectivity and depth, and often permits gathering valuable data that could not be successfully obtained by any other approach.

The unstructured interview is best illustrated by the client-centered approaches used in clinical psychology and psychiatry. In this type of interview, the interviewer generally has some specific objectives, but these objectives are such that they can be met better in a situation in which the individual freely expresses his feelings without restriction. In the unstructured interview, the interviewer does not employ a detailed interview plan but has a general plan and usually asks questions or makes comments intended to lead the respondent toward giving data to meet the interviewer's objectives. Unstructured interviews are generally called for in situations where the type of information sought is difficult for the subject to express or is psychologically distressing to the individual. Because of the threatening nature of topics usually covered by unstructured interviews, this procedure must constantly adapt to the respondent and is highly subjective and time-consuming. The graduate student can very seldom employ the unstructured interview in his research because skillful use of this technique requires a great deal of training and experience.

STEPS IN CONDUCTING AN INTERVIEW STUDY

Objectives

The first step in conducting an interview study is to develop a broad general statement of the purpose of the research. This statement should discuss the theoretical basis for the study, the general goals and possible application of the results, and the reasons for using the interview approach. The next and probably most important step in conducting the interview study is to translate this general statement of the problem into a series of detailed and specific objectives. It is at this point that many graduate studies fail. The usual result of failure to establish these detailed objectives is that the interviews do not produce the data needed to provide satisfactory answers to the problems under investigation. The importance of a careful thinking through of the problem and a detailed and specific statement of objectives cannot be overstated.

The interview guide

The next step in the interview procedure is to develop a tentative guide to be used during the interview that will make it possible to obtain the data required to meet the specific objectives. In preparing this tentative form, the following advantages of the interview technique should be kept in mind because there is little justification for using the interview unless these advantages can be exploited.

1. The interview permits greater depth.
2. The interview permits following up leads in order to obtain more complete data.
3. The interview makes it possible to establish and maintain rapport with the respondent or at least determine when rapport has not been established.
4. The interview provides a means of checking and assuring the effectiveness of communication between the respondent and the interviewer.

In developing the interview guide, the research worker should be able to explain the purpose for each question and tell how the data to be collected with the question will be applied to the specific objectives of the study. In educational research, it is usually necessary to use the open-form question to exploit the aforementioned advantages satisfactorily. Closed-form questions, such as the multiple choice questions often asked in public opinion surveys, are rarely included in interview studies in education because information adaptable to this form can be obtained more easily through a mailed questionnaire. A problem that usually arises in the use of open-form questions is the development of satisfactory methods of recording replies. One method is to write down a summary of the response during the interview situation. This has the disadvantage of breaking the continuity of the interview and can result in bias because the interviewer may unconsciously emphasize responses that agree with his expectations and fail to record responses that do not. In some interviews it is possible to record a summary of the individual's reply after the interview has been completed. This avoids the breaks in continuity but is even more subject to bias because the delay leads to the interviewer forgetting more details, and these forgotten details are most likely to be the ones that disagree with his expectations.

It is usually possible to use open-form questions but to record the majority of responses into a number of predetermined classifications. These classifications may be developed during a pilot study and permit the data to be recorded in quantitative terms, thus being more readily available for analysis. It is necessary, however, to make provisions to record additional comments or statements not fitting the classifications and to provide for additional data that would be lost if the open-form question were categorized without this provision.

The use of tape recorders has several advantages in recording interview data for research. Most important perhaps is that it reduces the tendency of the interviewer to make an unconscious selection of data favoring his biases. The tape recorded data can be played back more than once and can be studied much more thoroughly than would be the case if data were limited to notes taken during the interview. It is also possible to reanalyze the taped interview data to test hypotheses not set up in the original study. For example, interview data originally taped to study the interests of college freshmen could be reanalyzed to study their grammatical errors. Finally, it is possible with tape recorded data for a person other than the interviewer to evaluate and classify the responses. This permits calculation of a reliability coefficient for the interview data. Reliability estimates can be made by comparing interviewer evaluations with evaluations of another research worker using the tape only, or by comparing initial interviewer evaluations with evaluations made by the same interviewer at a later date based on playback of the taped interview. In well-designed interview studies, these reliability coefficients will be as high as .90.[7] The tape recorder also speeds up the interview process because there is no necessity for extensive note taking, although some minimal notes may be desirable. For example, some record of gestures might be appropriate in certain interview situations.

The principal disadvantage of the use of the tape recorder with

[7] Robert C. Anderson, "The Guided   Interview as an Evaluative Instrument," *Journal of Educational Research*, XLVIII (1954), 85.

the interview is that the presence of the tape recorder changes the interview situation to some degree. In interviews involving information of a highly personal nature, the respondent may be reluctant to express his feelings freely if he knows that his responses are being recorded. The interviewer should carefully explain the purpose of the recording and gain the confidence of the respondent, so as to minimize any undesirable effects of having the interview recorded. In interviews not aiming primarily at the collection of research data, it is seldom necessary to tape record the results. The opportunity to calculate reliability coefficients and the gain in objectivity provided by the taped record are very important factors, however, in research, and therefore the use of the tape recorder should be seriously considered for research interviews.

FRAMING QUESTIONS FOR THE INTERVIEW

In preparing the questions to be included in the interview guide, two major objectives should be kept in mind: each question must be aimed at one of the specific objectives of the research and must be presented in such a way that the respondent understands what is wanted and is motivated to give the information.

Effective communication

Questions must be framed in language that insures effective communication between the interviewer and the respondent. The respondent must fully understand the language in which the question is framed. In those educational research studies where the respondents are professional educators, the problem of phrasing questions in language common to both interviewer and respondent is not usually serious. But for studies involving interviews with laymen, the educational jargon we in the profession know and use can seriously block effective communication. For example, if a question such as "What is your opinion of homogeneous grouping in the public schools?" were asked, it is likely that many of the persons answering would not have a clear understanding of the term "homogeneous grouping." Often the respondent is reluctant to admit that he doesn't understand the meaning of the question. The fact that he has been asked the question implies that he should understand it, and rather than admit his ignorance, he may give an evasive or noncommital answer. The graduate student is better educated than the members of most groups he will interview, so he must not only avoid jargon but must also resist the temptation of using technical or uncommon words. The purpose of the interview is to get information, not to demonstrate the superiority of the interviewer. Finally, the respondent will usually resent being asked questions that he does not understand, and this resentment will carry over to his responses to later questions.

Another essential to complete communication between the interviewer and the respondent is that the respondent appreciates the purpose of each question that he is asked. With the help of the interviewer, the respondent develops an idea of the purpose of the interview, and if he can see no connection between his perception of the purpose and a question that is asked, he is likely to react negatively. He may become suspicious of the interviewer and wonder whether the interview actually has some purpose other than the one he has been told. Inasmuch as he cannot be sure of what this hidden purpose is, his suspicions are aroused, and he is immediately placed on his guard. Under these circumstances, his answers will be evasive, and his attitude guarded or hostile. On the other hand, he may consider such a question as indicative of a lack of ability or poor planning on the part of the interviewer. In this case, he is likely to feel that his participation is a waste of time. This loss of confidence in the interviewer is serious in that it is often followed by a refusal to cooperate. If the status of the respondent is higher than that of the interviewer, a special effort must be made to avoid questions that the respondent can interpret as wasting his time. The problem of questions that appear irrelevant arises often in studies involving psychological data, such as personality. Indirect questioning is often necessary in this area, and unless considerable groundwork is laid by the interviewer, resistance by the respondents will be encountered.

Accessibility of information

In addition to being sure that the question is in language that the respondent understands, it is also necessary to ascertain whether the population from which the respondents were selected actually have the information desired. This problem also occurs in questionnaire studies. The chances of making this error, however, are less in the interview study because the research worker can usually sense such deficiencies in the answers of the respondents he interviews in his pilot study. Occasionally a graduate student is carried away by his enthusiasm for a research idea and asks for information that no one could be reasonably expected to have. An example of this was an interview study proposed recently by a graduate student that would ask college students to recall conversations the students had during their childhood with teachers or other adults that exerted a major influence on the moral values and educational and vocational goals of the students. The graduate student believed that there are certain critical moments in everyone's childhood when the words of a parent or teacher become a major factor in determining the future goals and behavior of the child. Such a theory may be valid, but the line of questioning planned by the graduate student called for a level of recall as well as a level of insight that few persons could be expected to possess.

An error frequently made in educational studies is to ask parents to comment on technical aspects of education about which they have little or no knowledge. For example, an interview study carried out to learn the parents' opinions of different methods of teaching reading could produce very little useful information. Many of the parents would probably have opinions concerning the teaching of reading, but for the most part these opinions would have little foundation except the limited personal experiences of the respondents.

Leading questions

A factor that often biases the results of interview studies is the use of leading questions by the interviewer. A leading question is any question that, because of the phrasing of the question, leads the respondent to consider one reply more desirable than another. Let us say, for example, that we were interviewing a random sampling of voters concerning their attitudes toward federal aid to education. After establishing whether the respondent was familiar with the issue of federal aid to education, a reasonable question might be, "What is your opinion of federal aid to education?" A question that might be classified as moderately leading would state "Do you favor federal aid to education?" This question is a little easier for the respondent to answer in the affirmative than the negative. A more serious attempt to lead the respondent would result in a question such as "In view of the dangers of federal control, do you feel that federal aid to education is advisable?" Here the respondent is strongly motivated to give an unfavorable response to federal aid. Questions can be slanted even further by the use of emotionally toned words to which the individual is inclined to react for or against with little thought for the basic issue involved. Such a question might be "Do you favor federal aid to education as a means of providing each child with an equal educational opportunity?" In this case, the concept of "an equal opportunity for all" is likely to elicit favorable replies.

The respondent's frame of reference

Each person is the product of an environment that is unique. Words recall different experiences and have different shades of meaning for each of us. Unless the interviewer establishes a common ground for communication—a common frame of reference—these differences can seriously interfere with the communication process. If the respondent's frame of reference is different from that of the interviewer, his replies are likely to be misinterpreted. For example, if a group of mothers were asked "What do you think of the teacher your child has this year," one might answer in the terms of the teacher's personal appearance, another may think of the teacher's willingness to help on a P.T.A. committee, another may have never seen the teacher but may feel that her child is not getting proper reading instruction, while another may have had a conference with the teacher the day before about her child's misbehavior and think of nothing but this meeting in making an evaluation. Thus, we can see that unless the interviewer and respondent are using the same frame of reference, many difficulties can arise when obtaining interview data. In research, perhaps the most desirable solution to this problem is to specify the frame of reference wanted by the interviewer. The above question could be placed in a specific frame of reference by asking: "What do you think of the way your child's teacher handles parent-teacher conferences?"

Trial of the interview procedures

Although the interview can provide us with valuable data, the research worker must remember that it is a highly subjective technique. When this technique is used in research, all possible controls and safeguards must be employed if we expect to obtain reasonably objective and unbiased data. A careful pilot study is the best insurance the research worker has against bias and flaws in design. After the interview guide has been developed, a pilot study should be conducted to evaluate and improve the guide and the interview procedure and help the interviewer develop experience in using the procedure before any research data for the main study are collected. The number of subjects interviewed in the pilot study need not be large—ten to twenty are sufficient for most educational studies. The interviewer can usually determine from the progress of his last few pilot interviews whether more are needed to improve his procedures further. The subjects interviewed in the pilot study should be taken from the same population as the main study sample whenever possible and from a very similar population when research design does not permit drawing from the main study population.

The pilot study should be carried out with specific objectives in mind. The interviewer should determine from the pilot study whether the planned procedures actually produce the data desired. The interviewer should be alert to communication problems, evidence of inadequate motivation, and other clues that suggest a rephrasing of questions or revision of procedure. Several methods of opening the interview should also be tried and perfected. Unwillingness of the respondent to cooperate generally indicates that the techniques that have been established are not sufficient for motivation and maintenance of rapport. The pilot study also gives the interviewer an opportunity to evaluate his methods of recording the interview data, to determine if adequate information is being recorded, whether the recording method causes excessive breaks in the interview situation, and whether the mechanics of reporting can be improved.

During the pilot study the research worker also should assess carefully the methods he has planned to use for quantifying and analyzing his interview data. If the pilot study results indicate that data obtained cannot be quantified or are not falling into the areas anticipated, the interview procedures must be revised until satisfactory quantification and analysis are possible.

Tape recording of pilot study interviews is especially important even if the tape recorder is not to be used during the regular interview procedure. By playing back the interview, the interviewer can gain many insights into his handling of the questions and will be made aware of problems that may have escaped him during the interview situation itself.

The interview sample

In selecting the sample for the main study, care should be taken to use random sampling techniques. A serious weakness of interview studies done by graduate students is the usual necessity of using small samples. The research worker should remember that the dangers of a biased sample are particularly serious when only a small number of individuals can be included in the research. After a random sample has been selected, it is advisable to obtain some commitment of cooperation from these individuals before the interviewing starts. Every effort should be made to obtain the cooperation of all individuals initially selected. If some of the subjects selected refuse to cooperate, this refusal will almost certainly lead to some biasing of the research results. The random selection of substitutes for these noncooperating individuals does not remove the possibility of this bias.

The group interview in research

The group interview, involving an interviewer and a group of respondents usually ranging from six to twelve, has been used effectively under certain conditions. The principal advantage of the group interview seems to be that, through hearing the experiences of others, the individual's inhibitions are released and he is more likely to discuss openly his own problems and needs. The discussion also helps the respondent further develop his ideas and opinions. The group interview has been employed in many situations such as work with juvenile delinquent gangs, rehabilitation of prison inmates, and in the solving of various social and community problems.

Though adaptable to many clinical and social situations, the group interview cannot be applied to most educational research problems. Its major disadvantage for educational research is that although it may yield useful data concerning group structure and interaction, it provides relatively little objective data about the individual members of the group. The responses of the individuals in the group can, of course, be recorded but it is difficult to determine how many of their comments reflect their own feelings and how many reflect a tendency to follow the group leaders or fit the group social climate. The group interview situation also makes it impossible to obtain comparable data from all members of the group. Some members are highly verbal and will dominate the discussion and even if the opinions of some of the more reticent group members are obtained, it is impossible to determine to what extent they have been influenced by the statements of their colleagues. Thus, the group interview cannot be used as a device to increase the number of respondents in a study that calls for the use of the individual interview.

Educational studies that emphasize education as a group process and are concerned with group behavior rather than individual behavior can make effective use of the group interview.

The team interview

A relatively new procedure that can be adapted to many educational studies is the "Tandem Interview," or Interview Team technique. In this technique, two interviewers work with one respondent. Kincaid and Bright employed a man-woman team in an interesting application of this method.[8] The notes in their research were generally taken by the female member of the team but both worked as interviewers. This technique has certain advantages. It is effective in terms of time in that recording may be done without interrupting the interview, thus avoiding the usual breaks in continuity. In interviews of high-status respondents such as business executives or school administrators, this time-saving feature is important, because most personnel of this type are unwilling to spend too much time in an interview situation. This team-interview technique also gives the respondent the feeling that his time is being fully utilized.

Another advantage to having two interviewers is that each brings into the situation a different background of experience that insures a more thorough coverage of the topics to be covered by the interview. Still a further advantage observed by Kincaid and Bright was that, in cases where the respondent took a negative reaction to one of the interviewers, it was possible for the other interviewer to carry out the major portion of the interview efficiently. This is an important factor because such negative reactions can make it almost impossible to obtain the desired information from the respondent in the

[8] Harry V. Kincaid and Margaret Bright, "The Tandem Interview, A Trial of the Two-Interviewer Team," *Public Opinion Quarterly,* XXI (1957), 304–12.

regular interview situation. The interview team also works together in reviewing the report and preparing material for analysis. The chances of personal bias and unconscious selection of data are reduced considerably when two persons are responsible for preparing the interview report. Individuals in important positions are usually intelligent and verbal and are likely to produce a large quantity of complex information in response to the interviewer's questions. The team interview makes it possible to get a more thorough record of this individual's responses.

The team interview can also be used effectively in exploratory studies where the research plan depends on the interview situation to identify relevant variables for study. It is much more likely that such variables will be isolated if two interviewers apply their different points of view to the responses.

In many interview studies, the team technique would not be appropriate. For example, clinical investigations requiring identification between the interviewer and patient would probably be disturbed by the presence of another interviewer. Many interview studies of a general survey nature are such that the expense of using two interviewers is uncalled for and unnecessary. In interviews with persons who are average in intelligence or verbal fluency, it is usually quite simple for a single, trained interviewer to keep up with the responses.

MISTAKES OFTEN MADE BY GRADUATE STUDENTS

Descriptive Studies in General:

1. Student does not formulate clear and specific objectives.

2. Relates his data-gathering procedure to his objectives in only a general way and thereby fails to get quantitative data specific to his problem.

3. Selects his sample on the basis of convenience rather than attempting to obtain a random sample.

4. Does not plan his analysis until after his data are collected.

5. Structures his data collecting devices (questionnaires, interview guides, observation forms, and so on) so that biased results are obtained.

Questionnaire Studies:

1. Student uses a questionnaire in working with problems that can be better studied with other research techniques.

2. Gives insufficient attention to the development of his questionnaire and fails to pretest it.

3. Asks too many questions, thus making unreasonable demands on the respondent's time.

4. Overlooks details of format, grammar, printing, and so on that, if observed, give the respondent a favorable first impression.

5. Fails to check a sample of nonresponding subjects for possible bias.

Interview Studies:

1. Student does not adequately plan the interview or develop a detailed interview guide.

2. Does not conduct sufficient practice interviews to acquire needed skills.

3. Fails to establish safeguards against interviewer bias.

4. Does not make provisions for calculating the reliability of his interview data.

5. Uses language in the interview that is not understood by the respondents.

6. Asks for information that the respondent cannot be expected to have.

ANNOTATED REFERENCES

1. ARGYRIS, CHRIS. "Diagnosing Defenses against the Outsider," *Journal of Social Issues,* 1952, 8 (3), 24–34. This article discusses ways that are used to avoid research interviews or impede the collection of research data. Although referring primarily to the industrial interview situation, the points discussed have implications to other interview situations and will be useful to the graduate student using this technique.

2. BLUM, FRED H. "Getting Individuals to Give Information to the Outsider," *Journal of Social Issues,* 1952, 8 (3), 35–42. This paper describes the experiences of the author while carrying out a research project in an industrial plant. It deals with methods of becoming accepted by the group, methods of collecting data, problems of potential bias, and validating of information. It contains many suggestions and insights that will be helpful to the graduate student planning an interview study.

3. BRESSLER, MARVIN, and KEPHART, WILLIAM M. "An Experience with the Use of the Mail Questionnaire," *Nursing Research.* 1956, 5, 35–39. In this study, questionnaires were mailed to ten groups of one hundred subjects each with different inducements for returning the questionnaire em-

ployed with each group. Results are presented comparing previews vs. follow-up, airmail vs. special delivery, cash inducements and total cost factors. A study of this article will help the graduate student who is planning a questionnaire study to make sounder decisions concerning the factors discussed.

4. CANNELL, CHARLES S., and AXELROD, MORRIS. "The Respondent Reports on the Interview," *American Journal of Sociology,* 1956, 62, 177–81. This study reports data collected in several surveys concerning the reaction of respondents to being interviewed. These surveys covered considerably different topics and required interviews of different length. Many of the respondents reported the interview situation to be a pleasant one. The author discusses characteristics of the interview that appear essential for establishing and maintaining rapport.

5. FESTINGER, LEON, and KATZ, DANIEL (eds.). *Research Methods in the Behavioral Sciences.* New York: Dryden Press, 1953. This text contains an excellent chapter on collection of research data by interviewing and also contains information concerning sampling and analysis that will be useful to the student planning an interview study.

6. HYMAN, H. H., *et al. Interviewing in Social Research.* Chicago: Univ. of Chicago Press, 1954. This volume contains a wealth of data on the interviewer and reports much important research on the interviewer and the interview process. The main emphasis is upon the sources of error in the interview. Such variables as respondent's perception of the interviewer, interviewer opinions and beliefs, interviewer expectation, situational effects, effects of racial differences between interviewer and respondent, and many others are discussed, and research evidence is presented. This text is required reading for anyone planning an interview study. The final chapter on reduction and control of error merits very careful study.

7. KAHN, R. L., and CANNELL, C. F. *The Dynamics of Interviewing.* New York: John Wiley & Sons., Inc., 1957. This excellent text not only deals with interviewing procedures but provides a thorough coverage of the psychological factors related to the interview situation. Contains chapters on the psychological basis of the interview, techniques for motivating respondents, formulation of interview objectives, developing questions, probing in the interview situation, and interview methods. Provides recordings of actual interviews aimed at giving the student practical examples of how interview techniques are applied. The sections on formulation of questions and design of questionnaires are also useful to the student planning a questionnaire study. A careful study of this text is particularly recommended for students planning an interview study.

8. KENSKI, G. E., and LEGGETT, J. C. "Caste, Class and Deference in the Research Interview," *American Journal of Sociology*, 1960, 65, 463–67. This study demonstrated, through the use of asking mutually contradictory questions at different points in the interview, that persons of lower status tend to agree with an interviewer whom they perceive as having higher status. In the lowest status group, 32 per cent of the respondents gave mutually contradictory answers, which demonstrates the degree to which interview data may be distorted by social class differences between the interviewer and the respondent. This study, which is typical of several that have yielded similar results, should be read by any graduate student planning an interview research project.

9. PAYNE, STANLEY L. *The Art of Asking Questions*. Princeton, N. J.: Princeton University Press, 1951. This is an interesting and extremely valuable book concerned with the phrasing of questions. Most of the blunders made by students in phrasing questions for interviews or questionnaires are discussed. Anyone planning a research project involving interview or questionnaire techniques will profit from a study of this book.

10. SEE, HAROLD W. "A Primer in Research: Lesson II, Send It to the President," *Phi Delta Kappan*, 1957, 38, 129–31. This article reports very high returns in a questionnaire study dealing with requirements for the Master's degree, and, based upon an analysis of the returns, the author makes several recommendations and suggestions concerning procedure in questionnaire studies. Contains a number of valuable ideas for the graduate student planning this type of study.

11. SITGREAVES, R., and SOLOMON, H. "Research Methods: Status Studies and Sample Surveys," *Review of Educational Research*, 1957, 27, 460–70. This article contains a brief review of research methods involved in questionnaire surveys with special emphasis upon sampling techniques and errors. The extensive bibliography (103 items) will lead the student to other sources pertinent to his specific problems.

CHAPTER 11

The Methods and Tools of Descriptive Research (Concluded)

OBSERVATIONAL STUDIES

Most of what we know about the persons around us is the result of the casual observations that we carry on almost constantly in our daily activities. The observations that are conducted in order to obtain scientific information, however, are far different from these casual observations. The principal differences are that scientific observation attempts to gather _objective_ data and to reduce or eliminate the biases that distort most of our casual observations. The observational technique provides us with what is often the only logical approach available for the study of complex behavior. Much of the behavior that interests us in education, such as the role of the principal in the school situation, teacher-pupil interaction within the classroom, and teacher effectiveness is of a highly complex nature. The observational approach, which permits the direct study of complex behavior, seems an obvious choice for research in these areas. The practical difficulties involved in observational research, however, are of considerable magnitude and, as a result, relatively few observational studies are carried out in education.

Problems in observational research

The major problem encountered in planning and carrying out observational studies is to develop methods of obtaining objective information from the observation without losing the advantages of the observational technique in the process of objectification. It is not uncommon in observational studies to find the experimenter attempting to study complex behavior patterns but finding that the types of behavior that he can objectively observe and record are only slightly related to the complex behaviors he wishes to study. Thus, he is faced with the problem of getting objective data that is of little

value because of its limited relationship to the complex problems involved or getting data more closely related to the complex behavior
he is studying but finding it of limited value because of its subjectivity. Obtaining data relating to complex behavior that is objectively observable and yet pertinent to the problem requires careful
planning.

Another problem that must be faced in conducting the observational study is to determine the degree to which the presence of the
observer changes the situation being observed. In observations of
classroom behavior, for example, a change in the behavior of both
the teacher and class members usually occurs when an observer
enters the room. Classrooms in laboratory schools are often provided
with adjacent rooms fitted with one-way screens so that observations can be carried on without disturbing the situation. Occasionally, studies are conducted in which the observer visits the classroom a number of times before recording any observational data so
that the class will become accustomed to his presence and will react
normally when the research data are actually collected. Very often
the graduate student with limited control over the situations that
he wishes to observe finds it difficult to solve this problem satisfactorily.

The time factor often makes observational research difficult for
the graduate student. This method of gathering details is time-
consuming, and the student usually finds it difficult to make a sufficient number of observations of a sufficiently large sampling of
individuals to provide reliable data. In order to provide reasonably
sound data and permit reliability estimates, observational studies
usually require that at least two independent observers evaluate the
situation being observed. This again poses a problem for the graduate student who must often rely entirely on his own resources for
obtaining research data.

Developing the observation form

Significant observational studies require that the individual developing the study has a sound and inclusive theory concerning the
nature of the behavior he is observing. He must also understand how
the observations to be conducted relate to the traits or behavior he
wishes to study. Without this theoretical foundation and an extensive background of knowledge, the observational study often yields

inconclusive information that is difficult to express in quantitative terms. Thus, the first step after completing a review of the literature is to develop specific testable hypotheses concerning the behavior to be observed. The record form to be used by the observers must then be developed to provide specific items that will test the stated hypotheses.

After the specific hypotheses have been established, the next step is usually for the person developing the observation form to make a number of preliminary observations in order to identify observable behaviors that are related to his hypotheses. These behaviors are then listed on a tentative form. Early in the development of the form, the research worker must decide whether the behavior to be observed can be objectively defined. If the observer must draw involved inferences from the behavior, the chances of obtaining reliable data are slight. For example, in observing teacher-pupil interaction, it is rather simple to record reliably the teacher's spoken comments, more difficult to determine which comments contain sarcasm, and very difficult to determine the effect of these comments on the pupils spoken to.

In developing the observation form, the research worker often thinks of so many kinds of behavior that he would like to record that he produces a form that is almost impossible to use. It should be remembered that there is a limit to the number of different types of behavior that the observer can accurately record. The number that can be observed effectively is determined by the complexity of the judgment that must be made, the number of persons being observed, the frequency of the listed behaviors, and the level of training of the observer.

Recording observed behavior

Behavior to be scored on an observational rating form can be recorded in several ways. Perhaps the most common scoring procedure is to use a form that describes the behaviors to be observed in considerable detail so that the observer can check each behavior whenever it occurs. This form of scoring requires a minimum of effort on the part of the observer and can usually be developed so as to require the observer to make few inferences. This method is often employed in studies where the observer must record the behavior of a number of individuals simultaneously, such as an observation of participants in a faculty meeting or school board meeting. Some studies require that the observer not only record the behavior as it occurs, but also evaluate it on a quality scale. For example, the observer might be required to record each suggestion made by participants in a problem-solving conference and evaluate the quality of appropriateness of each suggestion. This type of observation obviously requires a higher level of inference on the part of the observer. The observer must not only record the behavior— he must also evaluate it, and this is much more difficult to do objectively.

Another form of observation involves checking the occurrence of a particular category of behavior, and then describing the specific action that has occurred. This approach is generally impractical if the behavior being observed occurs frequently or if the observer is responsible for recording data on several individuals. A further problem with this type of observation is that the descriptions eventually must be converted to quantitative data. A preliminary study will usually yield a system for classifying the behavior observed. This classification can then be set up as a checklist that is more convenient and more reliable than requiring the observer to record lengthy behavior descriptions.

A number of difficulties arise when rating scales are used in conjunction with the observation form. The most common mistake made by the research worker is the attempt to obtain excessively precise discriminations from the observer. Most human behavior studied in educational research cannot be reliably rated on more than five levels. The three-point rating scale, breaking the behavior observed into such categories as "above average," "average," and "below average" is often as fine a discrimination as can be made with satisfactory reliability. Five-point rating scales, however, are often used in educational research and can be employed effectively in observing well-defined behavior. It is almost never advisable to attempt to obtain ratings finer than a five-point scale. Furthermore, the more inference the observer must use in making the rating, the fewer rating levels should be employed. The "Officer Effectiveness Report" employed by the U.S. Air Force provides the ultimate example of attempting fine discriminations in the evaluation of characteristics that, at best, can only be differentiated roughly. This instrument, for example, requires the senior officer to make an evalu-ation on the individual's cooperativeness. Fifteen levels of coopera-tiveness are provided by the scale. It is doubtful that a complex behavior requiring as high a level of inference as "cooperativeness" can be accurately discriminated at more than three levels by most observers.

Rating errors

Another problem encountered in the use of observational ratings is that many observers have a tendency to place all or nearly all of their ratings at the high end of the scale. In studies where the re-search worker has an opportunity to train his observers thoroughly and has complete control over the situation, this is rarely a problem. In many observational studies, however, the research worker must rely upon observers over whom he has little control. For example, studies of teacher effectiveness often use the school principal as an observer. It is rarely possible in studies of this sort to train the observer sufficiently. This tendency of untrained observers to rate most individuals at the high end of the scale is called the "error of leniency." Another error common in observational ratings is the "error of central tendency." This error is caused by the inclination of the individual to rate the person he has observed at the middle of the scale. This error is often made in cases where some of the behaviors to be rated have not occurred during the observation. The observer, feeling the need to register some sort of information on the form, rates the individual at the average, or center, of the rating scale. Still another error frequently encountered is the so-called "halo effect." This is the tendency for the observer to form an early impression of the person being observed and to permit this impres-sion to influence his ratings on all behaviors involving the given individual. For example, if the observer forms an initially favorable impression of the person being observed, he will tend to rate the individual leniently in subsequent performance areas. An initially unfavorable impression can lead to the opposite effect. "Halo effect" is most serious when the observation requires the evaluation of abstract qualities rather than specific behaviors. It is much easier for "halo effect" to occur in ratings dealing with such characteristics as "cooperativeness," "integrity," and "interest in the job," than it is in ratings of such specific behavior as "shakes hands with the visitor," "rises from his chair when the visitor enters the room," and "offers the visitor a chair."

Ranking

Some observation forms, in order to obtain a relative evaluation of persons being observed while avoiding the pitfalls of the rating, employ a ranking system instead. In the ranking system the observer checks the occurrence of behavior and then, after completing the observation, ranks the individuals he has observed in order of merit. This procedure also has a number of weaknesses, the major of which is that it requires the observer to remember all individuals he has observed in order to establish their relative effectiveness. If the number of observations is small and takes place within a rather short period of time, this ranking can be reliable and accurate. A refinement of the ranking procedure is the paired comparison system of evaluation. In the paired comparison system, after completing the observations, the observer considers each pair of individuals separately and decides which person in each pair was superior in the rated behavior. The paired-comparison approach is more time consuming than the regular ranking procedure but usually leads to some increases in reliability.

Classifying data for scoring

During the development of the observation form, scoring procedures should be developed and tried. It should be remembered that observational data will usually have to be converted into some sort of numerical scores in order to permit a quantitative analysis. Single items usually deal with fairly specific behaviors, so it is frequently necessary to combine items into broader categories. Initial classification usually involves nothing more than grouping together items that seem to be related. These initial categories should be refined through trial and analysis of the observation form. Item analysis of the observer form serves several useful purposes. It permits the research worker to classify items into categories for scoring. It also reveals items that should be discarded, items not fitting into any scoring category, items having little or no variability (everyone responds the same way), and items that cannot be objectively scored (low agreement between raters).

Summary

In developing the observation form, the procedures can be summarized as follows:

1. Build a sound background of theory and knowledge in the area of your study.

2. Develop specific hypotheses relating the observable behavior to the variables being studied.

3. Develop items that are as objective as possible and require a minimum of inference to be drawn by the observer.

4. Be sure that the behavior observed is significant. If objectivity can only be obtained by observing behavior that is not significant to the variables being studied, then the observational technique will probably fail to provide useful research data.

5. Do not ask for more information than the observer can effectively watch for and record. It is safer to ask too little of the observer than too much.

6. Observing forms of behavior that occur infrequently requires a great deal of observation time and usually leads to unreliable information. Behaviors listed on the observation forms should be those that occur frequently enough in the situation being observed so that definite trends can be recognized in the behavior of the individuals being studied.

Training observers

After the observation form has been developed and tried out on a small scale to correct its more serious deficiencies, it should be employed to train the individuals who will conduct the observations required by the research. The first step in the training is to discuss the observation form with the observers, describing each item sufficiently to develop a thorough understanding of what is to be observed and how it is to be recorded.

Then, set up practice observations in which all observers complete the observation form. These practice observations should be discussed by the observers immediately after the observation. If appropriate, the situation should be tape recorded and played back immediately so that scoring differences between observers can be discussed and resolved. This technique, of course, cannot be applied to observations of behavior where speech is not the major factor, such as observations of social behavior among nursery school children. Tape recording, however, is very useful in training observers for situations involving verbal interaction such as counseling. In the more advanced observational studies, observers are often trained through the use of motion pictures that present practice observation situations. Although these methods are usually beyond the resources of the graduate student, the training system he develops for observers must involve some provision for immediate review of the training observations and for comparisons between the data recorded by the different observers. These comparisons lead to the development of a common frame of reference among the observers that is necessary if the observational data are to have satisfactory reliability. If each observer interprets and records the same behavior differently, it is obvious that no objective information will be produced.

During the training period, interrater reliability should be calculated after each ten practice sessions in order to estimate the degree to which observers are developing a common frame of reference. Interrater reliabilities should reach at least .70, and much higher reliabilities can be obtained if training is adequate and the observations are of specific behavior. During the training period, it is likely that some observers will be found who cannot develop a reliable frame of reference. Some persons seem to be unable to interpret the behavior they observe consistently, or in the same light as the rest of the group. After a reasonable training period, it is usually advisable to replace these persons with other observers.

During the training period, an effort should be made to further improve the observation form. Some items may be found for which the objective scoring procedures established do not work. Other types of behavior on the form will be found to occur so rarely as to contribute little or nothing to the overall record. Descriptions of behavior used in the observation form usually undergo considerable change during this period in order to make them more specific and usable.

Final planning

After the observation form has been perfected and observers have been trained, detailed plans for the actual collection of research data should be made. The research worker must remember at all times that objectivity is the essential element in scientific observation. Any steps leading to increased objectivity will generally improve the research. If observations are to be carried out in the classroom, as is often the case in educational research, the observer should be thoroughly briefed on such matters as when he should enter the classroom, whether the teacher should be contacted prior to the start of the observation, what should the teacher and class be told about the visit, where should the observer station himself in the classroom, when should he leave the classroom, and so on. If such details are ignored, the observer often becomes a disturbing factor and therefore changes the situation he wishes to observe. He may also interfere with the work of the teacher, thus losing the rapport necessary to obtain cooperation.

Whenever possible, two or more raters should be used in observational studies. The principal advantage of having more than one rater is that the two independent ratings permit calculation of interrater reliability. Also, the combined records of two or more observers will provide more reliable data than the record of a single observer. If only one observer is used, it is difficult to determine the extent to which the behavior recorded is a function of the situation and the extent that it is a function of the idiosyncrasies and biases of the individual observer. When more than one observer is used, each should work independently. If observers work together, one usually influences the others, and the judgments of this observer are therefore given heavier weight as they are reflected in the ratings of his colleagues. Also, when observers work together, each observer's ratings are contaminated by the judgments of the other observers, thus making reliability coefficients based on correlations between observer ratings spuriously high.

In carrying out an observational study, the research worker should take care to keep very detailed information on all aspects of the observational situation. Details should be recorded on such matters as the development of the observation form, the initial selection of observers, the training of observers, and the method used for setting up observation schedules. This information helps the person reading the research report to understand the precise situation under which the observations were conducted, gives other research workers insight into possible sources of bias and contamination, and makes it possible to repeat the study in order to check the results.

It is doubtful whether any observations that we conduct are completely free from bias. In the observation process the observer brings to bear all of his past experience, and, as this past experience will differ for each observer, it will lead to different perceptions of the situation, different emphases, and different interpretations. Biases, of course, have a much greater chance of operating when the observer is called upon to draw conclusions or make involved inferences from the behavior he has observed. Possible sources of bias should be looked for and eliminated if they are found. For example, it would be unwise to use an observer who was prejudiced against Negroes in a study in which he would observe the creative ability of Negro and white children in a nursery school. His bias would almost certainly lead him to see more creative behavior among white children and either ignore, misinterpret, or minimize the creative efforts of Negro children in the group.

Contamination is perhaps even more dangerous to the observational study than bias. The most common source of contamination is the situation in which the observer has knowledge concerning the performance of the subjects on one of the variables being studied, and this knowledge influences his observation of the other variable. Let us say, for example, that we are doing a study of the human relations skills of successful elementary school principals. Unsuccessful and successful principals could be identified by a composite evaluation made by teachers, parents, and school superintendents. It may then be possible to observe the performance of the successful and unsuccessful principals in faculty meetings and evaluate them on certain human relations skills. If, however, the persons observing the faculty meetings are aware of which principals have been classified as successful and which as unsuccessful, this knowledge will almost certainly influence their perceptions of the principal's behavior. This type of influence is called contamination because knowledge of one aspect of the study tends to corrupt by contact the data recorded in another aspect of the study. Contamination is an especially serious problem in Master's degree studies because one graduate student often collects all data involved in the study. If the student is aware of the dangers of contamination, however, he can usually avoid it. For example, if we are studying relationships between academic achievement and leadership in the classroom, observations of leadership behavior could be carried out before achievement data were gathered; or the achievement test could be administered, if necessary, but not scored until leadership ratings were completed.

Another point to consider in planning observational studies, particularly when observations are to be made over a long period of time, is that observers tend to drift apart in their frames of reference concerning the behavior they are observing. You may recall that the major goal of the observer training is to develop among the observers a common frame of reference upon which to base their observations. During the course of the study, efforts should be made to maintain this frame of reference. This may be done by having observers occasionally evaluate and discuss a practice observation such as was done during the training period. These discussions help the observers maintain the common basis for reporting the behavior they observe that is essential to objectivity and reliability.

SITUATIONAL TESTING

Situational testing employs situations developed by the research worker in which the subjects are assigned roles that they play to the best of their ability. The situations are aimed at bringing out specific types of behavior that are observed and evaluated. These situations are artificial in that the subject is generally aware of the fact that he is playing an assigned role. For the most part, situational testing has been developed by social psychologists for use in their studies of leadership and small group interaction. These techniques, however, are well suited for studying problems involving complex behavior, group interactions, and human relations skills that are often found in educational research. There are several types of role-playing situations that might be adapted to educational research. We will briefly discuss three of these: the leaderless group discussion, team problem-solving situations, and individual role-playing situations.

Leaderless group discussion

In the leaderless group-discussion situation, a group of subjects, usually six or eight, is given a problem by the research worker and asked to discuss this problem and arrive at possible solutions. Observers then record the behavior of the different group members. The leaderless group-discussion technique is said to have been developed originally around 1925 to study leadership behavior in the German Army.[1] Recently the leaderless group-discussion technique has been used to study decision making and interaction in various types of military groups, student groups, and groups of executive personnel in business. In education, this technique could be used to study such problems as decision-making processes in school board situations, leadership behavior among school children at different levels, and teacher interaction in faculty meetings.

Team problem-solving activities

Team problem-solving activities usually involve a situation where a team is presented with a problem that they are called upon to solve. These problems differ from the leaderless group discussion in that in addition to discussing solutions, the team arrives at a solution and attempts to carry it out. Problems involving the escape of the team from a prison compound or getting the team across a difficult physical barrier have been used in research by military psychologists. Observers may be assigned to evaluate total team activities or to evaluate the behavior of individual members of the team. This technique has been used for the most part in the study of military leadership.[2] This technique, however, could be applied to research in a number of educational areas such as studies of player interaction in team sports, studies of group behavior in high school clubs, and studies of work groups in parent-teacher projects.

Individual role playing

The individual role-playing situation is generally aimed at collecting research data in a situation where only one research subject is involved, usually in a key role. The situation may also involve actors who are trained to play other roles necessary to bring out the subject behavior that is to be evaluated. The subject is usually given material that describes the situation in which he is to work and sometimes discusses the nature of the problem he will attempt to solve and the identity of other persons who will participate. He

---

[1] H. L. Ansbacher, "History of the Leaderless Group Discussion Technique," *Psychological Bulletin,* XLVIII (1951), 383–91.

[2] E. Tupes, W. R. Borg, and A. Carp, "Performance in Role Playing Situations as Related to Leadership and Performance Measures," *Sociometry,* XXI (1958), 165–79.

studies this material prior to the start of the situation, arrives at his solution or method of handling the problem, and then attempts to carry out this solution in the role-playing situation. In observing his behavior in the situation, it is possible to evaluate his decisions; but more important, it is also possible to evaluate his skill in carrying them out. For example, the author recently participated in a study aimed at developing criteria for measuring the effectiveness of elementary school principals.[3] In this study each subject played the role of a principal in several different situations aimed at revealing different aspects of the behavior important in the elementary principal's position. Six situations were developed. In each of these the person being tested took the part of the principal. Actors were trained to take other roles called for. In one of these situations, the person tested was given the following instructions:

SITUATION NO. 1

Instructions to Principal

You are the principal of a large elementary school of about 1,000 pupils, from kindergarten to sixth grade, in a city of about 30,000 population. The schools in this city are up to date, progressive, and have a high rating. The people in the community are proud of their schools and support them enthusiastically.

There is a Mr. Jones waiting to see you about getting his son registered in school. Mr. Jones is a successful businessman who is active in civic affairs, is well liked, and has a lot of influence in the community. He is proud of his children (two of them are already in school) and he is interested in giving them every opportunity to grow and develop.

It seems that, when he attempted to enroll his son in kindergarten, the son was turned down because he was five hours too young. Miss Roberts was so busy enrolling new pupils that she didn't have time to discuss the matter with Mr. Jones and just told him that his son did not come up to the age requirement. Mr. Jones was a little disturbed and has asked you for an appointment to discuss the matter. He will probably try to get you to make an exception for his child.

[3] W. R. Borg and J. A. Silvester, *The Use of Role-Playing Situations to Measure Principal Effectiveness,* in press.

You have had problems before on the age requirements for enrollment so take a few minutes to think it through. The superintendent is out of town for ten days, and a decision has to be made before he returns.

Main Points:
1. Mr. Jones is an important man in the communi
2. Entrance age requirements or some other entrance requirements are necessary.
3. You are proud of your school and its high rating.
4. You can't afford to have the public unhappy about the school.
5. You have fifteen minutes to spend with Mr. Jones, and you should make a decision within the time limit.

The actor trained to play the role of Mr. Jones had the following instructions:

Instructions to Actor

You are a successful business man in a community of about 30,000 population. You are active in civic affairs and interested in the progress of the community. You are generally well liked and have considerable influence.

You are the father of three children and are very proud of your family and interested in their welfare. Two of your children are already in school and are well adjusted and doing very good work. You have your own set of cumulative records on each child that you keep up to date. These records are complete and show that your children are superior.

Your youngest boy, Edward, was just turned down when you tried to get him enrolled in the kindergarten because he was five hours too young. This disturbed you because the records you received from the private nursery school Edward has been attending show that his IQ is 136; he is well above the average in physical size and development; he is socially well adjusted; he is in excellent health; and is an active, alert, and happy boy.

You know he is ready for school and that he will make a good adjustment. You feel that it is in the child's best interest to start now, and if they won't take him into the public schools you'll have to enroll him in a private school. You don't want this extra expense and besides you are a taxpayer and have donated a lot of time and money for public welfare and feel that your children have a right to public education.

You think that the chronological age rule used to determine who is ready for school is old-fashioned and silly, and you know that your boy is more ready to enter kindergarten than 90 per cent of the children being enrolled.

You didn't like the way Miss Roberts turned you down when you tried to get Edward enrolled because she didn't take time to listen to the reason why you thought Edward was ready for school. So you decided to go to the principal about it. This bothers you because you are a busy man, and you don't like to waste time over something that seems so unreasonable and wrong.

You are not acquainted with the principal, Mr. Smith, but you are well acquainted with the superintendent of schools. You know the superintendent is a reasonable man and you tried to see him, but he is out of town for a few days, and this enrollment has to be taken care of now or it will be too late.

When you go to the principal's office, you present your problem and wait for his reaction.

There are several possible approaches the principal might follow:

1. He might dogmatically say no. If he does, threaten to make a public issue of it. You have rights as a taxpayer; your boy is superior, and so forth. Just don't take no for an answer. Don't hesitate to show your anger under those circumstances.

2. He may try to win you over without yielding—here again you should point out that your boy is better prepared for kindergarten than most of the children who were accepted because he has been in private nursery school and the test results show him to be superior.

3. He may refuse to yield but agree to study the policy and see how exceptions could be made.—But your boy is ready now and the policy could be studied and rules made for exceptions later.

4. He may accept Edward if it is kept quiet, as a special favor, and so on.—You don't want any underhanded admission because the boy is qualified to go in the "front door," on his own merits, and so on.

5. He may accept Edward without qualifications.—If he does, tell him that your neighbor has a boy that has been in the same nursery school that Edward attended. There is a complete set

of records showing that this boy is superior also. He is only fifteen days younger than Edward and his parents would like to get him enrolled also.

Keep in mind that you are an important man; that the records show that Edward is superior; that his experience in the private nursery school gives him an added advantage; that you think the chronological age rule is no good; and that other superior children should also be allowed in.

Situations such as the above seem to provide a better basis for evaluating some of the complex human-relations skills needed by a principal than any number of trait-oriented personality, aptitude, or interest measures.

A highly significant study using role-playing situations to study school-administrator behavior has recently been completed at Columbia University.[4] In this study, the subjects are introduced to a mythical school district through the study of the handbooks, motion pictures, and participation in meetings, and then play the role of a principal in attempting to solve administrative problems related to the school and district.

Advantages of situational testing

Situational testing has a number of important advantages for the study of complex behavior in education. Many studies have attempted to identify the factors relating to successful teaching or successful administrative behavior through the use of personality inventories and other paper-and-pencil measures. The results of these studies have been disappointing, probably because it is difficult to break down a complex behavior pattern such as that involved in the work of a teacher or principal and study it piece by piece. Role-playing techniques permit a study of the total behavior picture and seem more likely to give us insight into the characteristics required for success in complex activities.

The role-playing situation also has advantages over the observation of natural situations. By setting up the situation, the research worker can control, to a considerable degree, the types of behavior

[4] John K. Hemphill, Daniel E. Griffiths, and Norman Fredericksen, *Administrative Performance and Personality: A Study of the Principal in a Simulated Elementary School* (New York Teachers College, Columbia University, 1962).

that are likely to occur. This permits him to focus the observation on behavior that appears to be critical in the area being studied. In order to observe such critical behavior in a natural situation, it might be necessary for the observer to be present for weeks or even months. The artificial situation also permits much more careful training of the observers. Inasmuch as the research worker has a good idea of the types of behavior that will occur, he can develop observational rating forms that fit the situation specifically and can train his observers in the specific situations that they will later observe in the collection of research data. Because a number of subjects can be exposed to the same role-playing problem (although each, of course, will respond differently) it is much easier to obtain comparable data on the behavior through this technique than through observations of behavior in natural situations.

The principal criticism of situational testing is that the situation itself is artificial and therefore may not give an accurate indication of how the individual would behave in a natural situation. In using role playing situations in research, however, the author has been impressed by the degree to which the subjects appear to forget that they are involved in an artificial situation. Particularly in situations that involve emotional interaction between the subject and actors, it appears that most subjects become deeply involved in the situation, and many seem to forget, at least for the moment, that the situation is an artificial one. In the situations involving difficult human relations problems, some of the persons tested became very upset and went so far as to order the actor out of their office.

Perhaps the principal disadvantage of situational testing for the graduate student is the time involved in developing and carrying out a project using this technique. Small-scale situational studies, however, can be carried out by the graduate student. For example, parent-teacher conference situations could be developed and used by the graduate student in a study of teacher behavior. In research problems concerned with human relations, situational testing offers perhaps the best chance of producing meaningful data.

OBSERVATIONAL METHODS INVOLVING LESS CONTROL

Most of our discussion of observational studies to this point has been concerned with closely controlled scientific observation. In many educational studies, however, it is not possible to maintain this control over the observational situation. We will now discuss techniques that provide less precise scientific data and are to some extent less direct, as they are based on the observations and recollections of individuals whom we cannot train thoroughly or control closely. This type of observation is much more likely to be subjective and biased.

The anecdotal record

One technique used quite commonly in education is the anecdotal record. Anecdotal records are generally based on teacher observations and involve descriptions of behavior that the teacher considers typical of the individual described. With some training, teachers can produce anecdotal records of considerable value to the scientist. The anecdotal record should be an objective description of the child's behavior without interpretations by the observer. In preparing the instructions and forms for anecdotal records, the research worker should strive toward as great objectivity as possible. The most serious danger in anecdotal records is that the teacher will write these records while emotionally upset about the incident being described. For example, in compiling anecdotal records dealing with disciplinary problems and misbehavior, the teacher is much less likely to be objective than an observer who is not directly involved in the disciplinary situation.

Peer evaluations

This observational technique involves the evaluation of behavior by the individual's peers. Such evaluations suffer from most of the weaknesses of casual observation but often provide useful data if a fairly large number are collected. For example, in studying classroom behavior, the composite peer evaluations made by thirty children may be of considerable value. In this case, biases may have very little effect on the composite evaluation unless these biases are held by a large number of the class members. In a class of thirty children, two or three may intensely dislike child "A" and be highly critical in their evaluations. In all likelihood, however, someone else will be favorably disposed toward child "A" and the favorable evaluations will, to a degree, cancel out the unfavorable and permit the evaluations of the unbiased class members, who will usually be in the majority, to carry the greatest weight.

In collecting observational data through peer evaluations, it is often desirable to use a ranking system rather than a rating system. Rankings have the advantage of avoiding errors of leniency and central tendency that often occur in ratings.

Supervisory ratings

Ratings, such as those made of teachers by their principals or of principals by their superintendents, provide a commonly used method of gaining data concerning the behavior of subjects in educational research. Supervisory ratings, of course, are difficult to conduct on a scientific and tightly controlled basis. In some studies the supervisor makes special observations as part of the research plan, but as he has already formed an opinion of his subordinates prior to the time these observations are made this opinion will inevitably have an effect upon his observational ratings even if he tries to be objective. Under these conditions we may be sure that observed behavior that agrees with the observer's bias is most likely to be noted and recorded. "Halo effect" also operates strongly in this type of evaluation. In many cases, however, the behavior of the individual as seen through the eyes of his supervisor, although different perhaps from the objective behavior of the individual, still has an important meaning in educational research. Such observations, however, should not be confused with objective reality as the biases involved may cause them to be only slightly related to the behavior of the individual that would be recorded by objective and unbiased observational techniques.

The critical-incident technique

One form of observational rating that has been employed to a considerable degree in recent years is the critical-incident technique developed by Flanagan.[5] This technique, as usually applied, involves an interview with the supervisor of the individual to be evaluated. The interviewer attempts to obtain from the supervisor descriptions of the subject's specific behavior patterns that are considered to be critical to the skills being studied. Studies of leadership ability in

[5] John C. Flanagan, "The Critical Incident Technique," *Psychological Bulletin,* LI (1954), 327–58.

military situations, for example, have been done using the critical-incident technique. The author once had the opportunity to read hundreds of the critical incidents collected by Dr. Flanagan in his research on military leadership. In reading these incidents, it was apparent that many of the incidents recorded would not be considered critical in the eyes of the psychologist. Perhaps the most serious problem encountered in using the critical-incident technique is to obtain incidents from the individuals interviewed that seem to be truly critical to the behavior or skills being studied. If incidents can be collected that are truly critical—that truly differentiate between successful and unsuccessful behavior—then this method can provide a very useful research approach. The critical-incident technique seems to be well suited to many educational studies, particularly those involving qualifications of school administrators and teachers.

CONTENT ANALYSIS

"Content analysis is a research technique for the objective, systematic, and quantitative description of the manifest content of communication." [6] "Systematic," "objective," and "quantitative" are the key words in this definition. A systematic approach in content analysis requires a thorough coverage of pertinent content as it relates to a well-defined scientific problem or hypothesis. The first step, therefore, is to establish specific objectives or hypotheses to be tested by the research. A systematic approach also requires that the content to be analyzed be selected by some systematic means. Content analyses can be misleading or biased if the research worker does not use satisfactory methods for selecting the sample of content to be studied. In many content analyses, all content specifically pertinent to the research problem is studied. For example, an analysis concerned with the educational theories of a single author would usually be conducted by analyzing all of the writings of the author in question. Content analyses dealing with topics that can draw from a very large body of documentary materials, however, usually select material to be analyzed by some sampling technique. A study of trends in educational philosophy as reflected in newspaper editorials

[6] Bernard Berelson, *Content Analysis in Communication Research* (Glencoe, Ill.; Free Press, 1952), p. 18.

over the past fifty years would involve a very large volume of "raw material." In this case a sampling technique would be used to reduce the content to be analyzed to manageable size. Care would have to be taken to avoid obtaining a biased sample of the content available.

Objectivity in content analysis depends largely upon the classification procedures used. Specific and well-defined categories must be developed if the content analysis is to be objective. These procedures must have a high level of reliability so that different research workers of comparable skill could use the procedures independently and obtain very similar results. Estimates of reliability are often ignored in content analyses but should be calculated whenever possible.[7]

A method for presenting results in quantitative terms is essential to a scientific content analysis. In education, content analyses usually produce quantitative results in the form of numerical frequencies. Content fitting the various categories covered by the analysis is usually tallied in terms of frequency of occurrence. Occasionally content analyses of a qualitative nature are conducted on material that cannot be reduced to quantitative terms. Although such analyses make valuable contributions in literature and the arts, they are generally not applicable to problems encountered in educational research.

The raw material for the research worker using the content-analysis technique may be any form of communication (usually language), but other forms of communication such as music, pictures, or gestures should not be excluded. Textbooks, high school compositions, recorded language of preschool children, novels, newspapers, magazine advertisements, and political speeches are but a few of the sources available to the scholar.

Direct analysis

Most content analyses in education have been aimed at answering questions directly relating to the material analyzed. These analyses have generally been concerned with fairly simple classifications or tabulations of specific information. Content analyses of pupil compositions, for example, can give us a classification of grammatical

[7] Marvin Spiegelman, Carl Terwilliger, and Franklin Fearing, "The Reliability of Agreement in Content Analysis," *Journal of Social Psychology,* XXXVII (1953), pp. 175–87.

and spelling errors as well as information on the frequency of different types of errors. This information can be directly applied to the revision of English courses or the development of remedial programs. A content analysis of current textbooks in first year algebra can tell us such things as: What topics are covered by all books? What emphasis is placed on each topic? In what sequence are topics usually presented? What mathematical terms are introduced? What system of symbols is most frequently used? Such textbook analyses are often carried out by test publishing companies that produce standardized achievement tests in order that their tests can be constructed to have high content validity. Among the important early content analyses carried out in education were simple frequency counts of words in order to identify those words most commonly used in the English language.[8] Such word lists then formed the basis for the development of elementary reading textbooks and spelling lists. Other areas related to education that have been studied using content analysis include: analysis of propaganda, sociological effects of reading, treatment of the Negro in history textbooks, the Soviet Union in American textbooks, nationalism in children's literature, analysis of television programs, analysis of readability of books and newspapers, and social ideas in McGuffey readers.[9] It may be seen from these examples that the content analysis can be a valuable tool for obtaining certain types of information useful in the solution of problems relating to the educational process.

Indirect analysis

Many of the content analyses that are being conducted currently are somewhat less direct than those previously described. These studies often aim at getting new insights into complex social and psychological variables. They are much more difficult to carry out than the simple frequency studies and often require a high level of sophistication in psychology, sociology, or other behavioral sciences. Most of the complex studies reported in the literature have been carried out in areas other than education.

[8] Edward L. Thorndike, *A Teacher's World Book of the Twenty Thousand Words Found Most Frequently and Widely in General Reading for Children and Young People* (Revised ed.; New York: Teacher's College, Columbia University, 1932).

[9] See Berelson, *op. cit.*, pp. 199–220, for an extensive listing of research using content analysis.

An interesting study that illustrates the use of content analysis in an educational research problem somewhat less direct than the usual word counts, error studies, and textbook analyses was conducted by E. V. Estensen.[10] In this study, Estensen compared a series of McGuffey readers bearing copyrights in the 1870's with a selection of popular elementary school readers bearing copyrights in the 1930's. Comparisons were made on the motivational aspects of each reading selection in terms of the following classifications: economic motivation, nationalism, militaristic motivation, international understanding, and religious motivation. A number of significant changes in emphasis between the McGuffey series and the 1930 readers were found. Content analyses of this type can certainly give us some interesting and valuable insights into American culture as it relates to education.

Ralph Tyler's study of officer education at the USAF Air University provides a further illustration of content analysis applied to a broad and complex educational problem. The various officer training programs at the Air University had no clear-cut objectives prior to Tyler's study, and the relationship between the objectives that had been prepared and the needs of the Air Force had not been clearly established. One of the functions of Tyler's study was to develop statements of objectives for the various Air University courses. In order to do this, a large number of documents relating not only to the Air University programs but to many aspects of officer performance and job requirements were analyzed at the University of Chicago. One of the results of this complex analysis was the development of objectives that established the educational goals of the Air University on a very broad and comprehensive basis. These specific objectives formed a sounder foundation for further curriculum development and evaluation than had ever been previously available.[11]

The content-analysis technique is very well suited for small-scale educational research projects, and it is surprising that more students

[10] E. V. Estensen, "McGuffey—A Statistical Analysis," *Journal of Educational Research*, XXXIX (1946), 445-57.

[11] Ralph W. Tyler, *Analysis of the Purpose, Pattern, Score, and Structure of the Officer Education Program of Air University*, Maxwell Air Force Base, Alabama, Officer Educational Research Laboratory, May 1955 (OERL Technical Memorandum 55-56).

do not carry out content analysis studies. Education is almost wholly a communicative process, and nearly all of the communications that are employed in the educational process are adaptable to content analysis. Yet, little has been done beyond the direct studies of word frequency, spelling and grammatical errors, and textbook content. We know almost nothing about the more subtle effects of the different forms of educational communication upon the personality, goals, and values of our youth.

MISTAKES OFTEN MADE BY GRADUATE STUDENTS

Observational Studies:

1. Student does not sufficiently train his observers, and thus obtains unreliable data.

2. Uses an observation form that demands too much of the observer.

3. Fails to take adequate safeguards against the observer disturbing or changing the situation he is to observe.

4. Attempts to evaluate behavior that occurs so infrequently that reliable data cannot be obtained through observations.

Content Analysis:

1. Student selects content that is easily available but does not represent an unbiased sample of all content related to the research objectives.

2. Fails to determine the reliability of his content-analysis procedures.

3. Uses classification categories that are not sufficiently specific and comprehensive.

ANNOTATED REFERENCES

1. ADKINS, DOROTHY C. "Principles Underlying Observational Techniques of Evaluation," *Educational and Psychological Measurement,* 1951, 11, 29–51. This article provides a brief elementary treatment of the use of observational techniques and methods for obtaining objective evaluations based upon observations.

2. BALES, ROBERT S. *Interaction Process Analysis: A Method for the Study of Small Groups.* Cambridge, Mass.: Addison-Wesley Press, 1950. This book describes the development and use of a technique for measuring

interaction among individuals in small group situations. Although the graduate student will rarely find it possible to apply a technique of this complexity to his research, he will learn much about objective observation from the study of this body of methods. The sections on training observers, appraising observer reliability, and analysis and interpretation offer much information that can be applied to most observational studies.

3. BASS, B. M., GAIER, E. L., and FARESE, F. J. *Metagnosiometry: The Study of Changing Behavior in Groups.* Washington, D.C.: Office of Naval Research, Technical Report Number 6, February, 1956. This report describes a technique for measuring the behavior of participants in simple problem-solving situations. A major advantage of the technique is the level of objectivity and the lack of dependence upon observer ratings. The problems described are of a simple nature and the situations somewhat more artificial than those usually used in situational testing techniques. The student with strong interest in situational testing will find many interesting ideas in this report.

4. BERELSON, BERNARD. *Content Analysis in Communication Research.* Glencoe, Ill.: The Free Press, 1952. This book provides the student with a practical treatment of the use of content analysis as a research tool. Both quantitative and qualitative content analysis techniques are discussed along with many examples of their application to various types of content. Technical problems involved in content analysis, including reliability, sampling, and presentation of data are also covered. An extensive bibliography of content analysis studies published since 1950 is included.

5. GUETZKOW, H. *Groups, Leadership and Men.* Pittsburgh: Carnegie Press, 1951. This book describes the use of situational testing in the selection of personnel during World War II. It is one of the early experiments in situational testing and provides much useful background information for the student interested in this area.

6. HEMPHILL, JOHN K.; GRIFFITHS, DANIEL E.; and FREDERICKSEN, NORMAN. *Administrative Performance and Personality: A Study of the Principal in a Simulated Elementary School.* New York: Teachers College, Columbia University, 1962. The study described in this book is the most extensive use of situational testing in educational research that has been completed to date. Chapters dealing with the development and evaluation of the situational measures are particularly pertinent for students contemplating research in this area.

7. POOL, ITHIEL DESOLA (ed.). *Trends in Content Analysis.* Urbana, Ill.: Univ. of Illinois Press, 1959. An excellent source for the student planning a content analysis study. Discusses the qualitative and quantitative ap-

proaches, the research methods applicable to content analysis studies, and the application of content analysis techniques to several different fields of learning. Contains an extensive bibliography.

8. SPIEGELMAN, MARVIN; TERWILLIGER, CARL; and FEARING, FRANKLIN. "The Reliability of Agreement in Content Analysis." *Journal of Social Psychology,* 1953, 37, 175–87. This article discusses the problem of reliability in content analysis and evaluates current methods of determining reliability. The results of an experiment on the effects of discussion by a group of judges on reliability of content analysis is also presented. This is a useful reference for students planning a research project in which content-analysis techniques will be employed.

CHAPTER 12

Studying Relationships

INTRODUCTION

Many of the behavior patterns and cause-and-effect relationships that we wish to study in education and the other behavioral sciences do not permit experimental manipulation. For example, studies concerned with the effects of brain damage on human behavior cannot be carried out experimentally because this would require inflicting brain damage on a sample of human subjects. In addition to those problems that cannot be handled experimentally for ethical reasons, there are many field problems in education for which experimental manipulation would require such changes in the situation as to make the experimental findings of little practical value. Studies in such areas as school administrator behavior, community support for education, and popularity of high school students must usually employ causal-comparative, correlational, or descriptive methods because of the loss of natural conditions that occur if an experimental design is used.

CAUSAL-COMPARATIVE DESIGN

The causal-comparative method is aimed at the discovery of possible causes for the phenomenon being studied by comparing subjects in whom this variable or characteristic is present with similar subjects in whom it is absent. In using this method to study juvenile delinquency, for example, Gleuck and Gleuck located subjects who were juvenile delinquents and compared their behavior with that of similar subjects who were not juvenile delinquents.[1] Characteristics that were present more frequently among the delinquent subjects than among the nondelinquent subjects were examined as *possible* causes of juvenile delinquency.

In addition to seeking possible or probable causes, causal-com-

[1] Sheldon Gleuck and Eleanor Gleuck, *Unraveling Juvenile Delinquency* (New York: Commonwealth Fund, 1950).

parative design is often used to determine differences between defined groups or selected variables. Studies such as those comparing different racial groups or those comparing normal with handicapped groups are not aimed primarily at causes but rather at obtaining a better understanding of the relative characteristics of the groups compared. Such studies, of course, provide a form of descriptive data, but their comparative emphasis differentiates them from the descriptive study. A study by Howe, for example, compares the motor skills of mentally retarded and normal children.[2] This study has implications largely in terms of developing and adapting physical education to the mentally retarded child, and is concerned more with the effects of retardation than with its causes.

Causal-comparative studies bridge the gap between descriptive research methods and experimental methods. In its simplest form, the causal-comparative design involves identifying subjects with some particular characteristic and studying them in comparison with a normal or control group. A project, for example, that identified a group of "underachievers" in high school and studied their characteristics would be a causal-comparative design as test scores or other data collected would be compared with norms or other estimates of "normal" behavior. Such an approach, however, is much less rigorous because of the absence of a specific comparison group and is essentially similar to the descriptive study.

On the other hand, the selection of a closely comparable control group in causal-comparative research can produce results that approach the precision of a well-designed experiment.

STEPS IN DESIGNING THE CAUSAL-COMPARATIVE STUDY

The initial procedures of the causal-comparative study are essentially the same as those employed in other research methods. The review of the literature must be completed and the problem and hypotheses spelled out in detailed and specific terms.

Selecting subjects

Perhaps the most crucial step in designing the causal-comparative study is that of defining the populations from which samples will be

[2] C. E. Howe, "A Comparison of Motor Skills of Mentally Retarded and Normal Children," *Exceptional Children*, XXV (1959), 352–54.

drawn and setting up procedures for selection of these samples. The nature of the samples selected will not only determine the meaning and applicability of the results but may also determine whether meaningful results are possible. The first step usually is to define the group that possesses the characteristic we wish to study—for example, underachievers. The underachiever may be defined in general terms as a pupil whose achievement is less than would be expected from his aptitude. Our operational definition, however, must be much more precise. It must indicate the measure of achievement to be used, the measure of aptitude to be used, and the difference between them necessary to be considered indicative of underachievement. Such a definition might be: An underachiever is any pupil whose T-score on the total *STEP Achievement Battery* is five or more points lower than his T-score on the *California Test of Mental Maturity*.[3] Obviously, a study using the aforementioned definition of an underachiever will yield different results than one defining the underachiever as any pupil whose achievement test grade placement score is more than one year below his current grade placement. This latter definition, which is sometimes used, ignores the aptitude factor and will result in a sample that includes few pupils of high aptitude even if they are working well below their potential. Thus, studies that appear at first glance to be very similar may really be different because of differences in defining the samples.

Another problem that must be considered before selecting an underachiever sample would be whether underachievers obtained by applying our operational definition are likely to be reasonably homogeneous in terms of factors causing underachievement. Can we identify different types of underachievers that are probably underachieving for different reasons, or are the same causes likely to be operating for all? Is underachievement merely a symptom that may be common to a number of markedly different causal patterns? If this is the case, our findings may be difficult to interpret because a factor that may be very important for one type of underachiever may be unimportant for other types. Some children may become underachievers primarily because of emotional disturbances, some because of negative parental attitudes, some because of traumatic experiences in school, some because of sensory handicaps, and some because of reading retardation. If we were working with a behavior

[3] T-scores are specified so that direct score comparisons may be made.

pattern of this sort, our study would have a greater chance of producing meaningful results if a single subgroup were studied. In the previous example, the heterogeneity of the underachiever group could be reduced by taking only cases not suffering from physical handicaps or by taking only those who do have such handicaps. In either case a more homogeneous group is obtained. Findings obtained will be less generally applicable but will be more clear-cut and usable for the limited population from which our sample is drawn.

Another solution to the aforementioned problem that would be superior if sufficient time and money were available would be to select a large sample of underachievers without regard to possible types, and then see if the hypothesized types emerge. If different patterns do emerge, the sample can be divided into subgroups each of which may be studied separately. If different patterns do not emerge, the sample can be analyzed as a whole.

The fact that different types do not emerge does not necessarily mean they do not exist but may indicate that the data needed to bring out the differences were not collected. Obviously, causes that have not been hypothesized and for which data have not been collected cannot emerge. What we get out of a research project is limited to a considerable degree by what we have put into it in terms of hypotheses and measures. This again points up the need for very carefully thinking through the research problem before proceeding to collect data.

The research worker must now select a sample not having the characteristic being studied—in this example normal achievers—in order to permit comparisons. The population from which the control sample is to be taken is usually defined so as to be similar except for the variable being studied. This control group may either be selected at random from the defined population or control subjects may be matched with experimental group subjects on the basis of one or more variables. Random selection is usually preferred. The process of matching tends to eliminate the variables matched for by holding them constant. For example the Gleucks matched their delinquent and nondelinquent boys for ethnic origin, IQ, and age.[4] This procedure produces closely comparable groups with re-

_____
[4] *Op. cit.*

spect to these variables. Even if, for example, ethnic origin were an important factor related to delinquency, the Gleucks's study would not show this because, by matching for this variable, the research has eliminated any chance of it emerging as a possible cause.

Data collection

As the usual casual-comparative research seeks past causes for present conditions, there is often considerable emphasis upon biographical data. Knowledge of a pupil's family relationships, school behavior, and other biographical information during the time he was developing his current behavior patterns often tell us more than test scores and other data that describe his present personality, attitudes, or behavior. The latter type of information is also used, however, and the degree of emphasis placed upon the two types of data is determined by the nature of the study.

Analysis of causal-comparative data

Biserial correlations are often well suited to the analysis of causal-comparative data because the experimental and control groups usually form a dichotomy in terms of the characteristic being studied. Some thought is often required to determine the type of dichotomy involved. The student is especially cautioned to use the widespread biserial correlation if extreme groups are being compared, as is often the case in causal comparative research. For example, a study comparing very good with very poor teachers would require use of the widespread biserial correlation because the teachers of average ability have been left out.

The t-test and chi-square contingency table are also appropriate to determine the level of significance of differences between groups studied. A t-test that shows significant differences between the experimental and control groups in the magnitude of possible causal variables can be just as valuable as a correlation in appraising possible causes for the behavior of the experimental group being studied. In research where the aim of the comparisons is to better understand the nature of deviant groups, measures of difference such as the t-test are often better suited to analysis than the measures of relationship.

LIMITATIONS OF THE CAUSAL-COMPARATIVE METHOD

The causal-comparative method is most effective in exploring simple cause-and-effect relationships. If persons with damage to a specific portion of the brain always have a particular speech defect while persons not having such damage never have the defect, the brain damage may be accepted with considerable confidence as the probable cause of the speech defect. Unfortunately, most of the variables we study in education are highly complex and instead of having a single cause may have many contributing causes. For example, one set of factors may be important contributing causes to reading difficulty among some children and may be absent in other children with equally serious reading difficulties. If we select a group of good readers for comparison, it is doubtful that we will find a single characteristic that occurs frequently among the poor readers that does not occur at least occasionally among the good readers. Thus, we are faced with a situation in which a subtle and complex interaction among several variables may greatly increase the probability of a child having reading difficulties but does not insure that he will have such difficulties.

In all likelihood, there are a number of different kinds of reading difficulties just as there are probably different types of underachievers, and the confused picture would be somewhat clarified if the research worker could define and isolate one specific pattern of reading difficulty and study only subjects displaying this pattern. The tendency for educators to lump together subjects into such categories as juvenile delinquents, retarded readers, high school dropouts, and campus leaders for the purposes of causal-comparative research has been an important factor in the failure of such studies to provide clear-cut information on possible causes.

A research worker once suggested to the author that a causal-comparative study be conducted in which a group of successful air force officers would be compared with a group of unsuccessful officers in order to identify variables important to success. When one considers that the jobs of air force officers range from such activities as preparing and routing routine correspondence to designing complex electronic equipment, it becomes apparent that treating air force officers as a homogeneous group for the purpose of studying success and failure is ridiculous. A causal-comparative study of a specific type of air force officer such as bomber pilots, however, would be practical and might produce worthwhile results.

A serious limitation of the causal-comparative method is that the research worker must start with the observed effects and try to discover the possible causes or antecedents of these effects. In this process of discovery it is often difficult to determine whether a variable found to be related to the behavior being studied has been a contributing cause or has been a result of the behavior pattern. For example, the Gleucks's study of juvenile delinquency found that delinquent boys displayed more aggression than did nondelinquent boys.[5] We do not know the aggression patterns that were present in either group *before any* of the boys became delinquent. Thus, in attempting to interpret the findings we are faced with the questions: do boys who are more aggressive more often become delinquents; or do boys become more aggressive in the process of becoming delinquent; or does some third factor such as social frustration cause both the aggression and the delinquency? A similar dilemma has occurred in causal-comparative studies aimed at identifying possible effects of acceleration or grade skipping. These studies usually compare pupils who have been accelerated two or more years with pupils matched for intelligence who have not been accelerated. The results usually show higher achievement for the pupils who have been accelerated but the question arises: Did the accelerated students achieve more because they were accelerated or were they accelerated because they had developed patterns of high achievement before they were accelerated? Selecting the correct answer to such questions is very difficult and often impossible on the basis of causal-comparative data.

Because of the complexity of most educational studies, clear-cut cause-and-effect relationships almost never emerge. The causal-comparative method, however, by identifying possible causes can give direction to later experimental studies that are more likely to produce clear-cut results. The causal-comparative field study followed by the experimental-laboratory study is a productive sequence for the researcher to follow.

[5] *Op. cit.*

CORRELATIONAL RESEARCH

Introduction

Correlational studies include all of those research projects in which an attempt is made to discover or clarify relationships through the use of correlation coefficients. While causal-comparative research compares two groups in which the studied characteristic is either present or absent, correlational research usually compares members of a single group in which the studied characteristic is present in varying degrees. The basic design of correlational research is very simple—involving nothing more than collecting two or more scores on the same group of subjects and computing correlation coefficients. Many valuable studies in education have done little more than follow this simple design using the product-moment correlation coefficient. Many studies, however, involve much more complex forms of the basic design and employ partial and multiple correlation techniques in order to obtain a clearer picture of the relationship being studied. As is the case with most research, however, the quality of correlational studies is determined not by the complexity of the design or the sophistication of the correlational techniques used but by the level of planning and the depth of the theoretical constructs going into the development of the hypotheses. In the past, many correlational studies in education have involved little more than locating available scores on a group of pupils, and then correlating these scores in hopes that some meaningful relationship would emerge. Such studies cannot be classified as scientific research because they have no theoretical foundation and test no hypotheses. Instead they employ the prescientific trial-and-error approach. Occasionally such an approach will produce usable bits of information, but the chances of gaining significant knowledge are far less than if the individual employs careful research methods. Such trial-and-error techniques are not acceptable for thesis research in most colleges of education today.

Advantages of the correlational approach

The correlational approach is especially useful in attacking the problems of education and the other behavioral sciences. Its principal advantage is that it permits measuring a number of variables and their interrelationships simultaneously. The usual experimental technique, in contrast, permits the manipulation of only a single variable and is most applicable to the problems of the physical sciences in which simple causal relationships are found much more frequently than in the behavioral sciences. In the behavioral sciences, instead of a single direct cause, we are frequently confronted with situations in which a large number of variables are contributing causes of a particular pattern of behavior. Thus, the experimental method, which manipulates one variable and attempts to hold others constant, often introduces a high level of artificiality into research situations encountered in the behavioral sciences. In contrast, the correlational approach, though less rigorous, permits the studying of behavior in a far more realistic setting. The forms of physical control and manipulation often required in experimental design frequently change the behavior being studied to an extent that makes it doubtful whether the results have any implications to the field situations in which the behavior will normally occur. Partial correlation is often preferable to experimental design in situations where control is necessary, as it permits the statistical control of variables that we wish to hold constant and does so without changing the field situation.

Another advantage of the correlational approach is that it provides us with information concerning the degree of relationship between the variables being studied. Inasmuch as few behavioral phenomena can be logically divided into the type of all-or-none dichotomy most appropriate for the causal-comparative approach, the ability of the correlational technique to relate the degree to which the different variables concerned are related often gives the researcher an understanding of the way in which the variables are operating that cannot be gained through other designs. For example, causal-comparative studies involved with teaching ability generally start with the identification of a group of good and poor teachers. Comparisons are then made between the two groups on a number of dependent variables in order to identify possible causes for differences in teaching ability. It is obvious, however, that such a dichotomy is artificial because, within both of these groups of teachers, some will certainly be better than others, and these differences in degree are ignored when using the causal-comparative approach. In reality what we have in this population is not two groups of teachers of distinctly different ability but a single group ranging in degree of teaching ability from very poor to very good. Furthermore, certain characteristics might be more important at some levels of teaching ability than at others. A knowledge of the degree of relationships, as provided by the correlation coefficient, can therefore give us deeper insights into the relationships we are studying than are possible with research designs that do not yield some estimate of degree. In addition to the sounder insights given us by the correlation coefficient in relationship studies, this technique also permits carrying out prediction studies and making close estimates of the probable accuracy of our predictions.

TYPES OF STUDIES EMPLOYING CORRELATIONAL TECHNIQUES

Although all correlational studies are concerned with the discovery and clarification of relationships, they can be broadly classified as either relationship studies or prediction studies depending upon their emphasis.

Relationship studies

The relationship study is concerned primarily with gaining a better understanding of complex behavioral patterns and phenomena by studying the relationships between these patterns and scores on variables that are hypothesized to be related. This technique is especially useful for exploratory studies in areas when little or no previous research is available. In the study of a complex characteristic such as artistic ability, for example, a knowledge of the relationships between this talent and less complex variables such as nonverbal intelligence, spatial relationships, manual dexterity, and color perception start us on the road to an understanding of the nature of artistic ability. In a study of this sort, the researcher usually starts by attempting through a subjective appraisal to identify some of the specific variables that appear to be important in the complex characteristic or behavior pattern that is to be studied. Past research and a knowledge of pertinent theory usually gives the experimenter the insight he needs to identify such variables. Suitable measures are then selected or developed to provide scores on these variables, the measures are administered to an appropriate sample, and the scores obtained are correlated with a criterion such as a measure of performance on the complex characteristic being studied. Such exploratory research often involves no analysis beyond simple correlation coefficients but if designed with sufficient care and insight can increase our understanding of the behavior being studied.

Partial correlational techniques are sometimes employed in exploratory relationship studies. This approach is most valuable when we wish to rule out the influence of one or more major factors upon a particular behavior in order to clarify the role of less important factors. For example, let us say that we wish to understand better the determiners of academic achievement in the elementary school. A major factor influencing the level of achievement of a given child is his intelligence. Having first established the relationship between intelligence and achievement, a study in which the intelligence factor is held constant through partial correlation would be helpful in further clarifying our understanding of other variables relating to achievement. Motivation, for example, is related to achievement but if a motivation score is correlated with achievement without controlling intelligence, it will be difficult to estimate the true effect of motivation on achievement, as the student with high intelligence but with low motivation may well achieve more than students of average intelligence who have higher motivation. Once intelligence has been "partialed out" it is possible to see more clearly the relationship between motivation and achievement. The next step in such a study might be to partial out the effects of both intelligence and motivation in order to obtain a clearer picture of the influence of other variables such as study habits, socioeconomic status, vocational aspirations, and others.

Factor analysis is another tool that is of considerable value in helping us understand the relationships found in exploratory studies. In a factor analysis, tests that might measure different aspects of the complex characteristic or behavior pattern under study are administered and an intercorrelational matrix is computed.[6] The factor analysis is then carried out in order to determine whether "factors" can be identified that are related to the behavior being studied. The

---

[6] An intercorrelational matrix is a table on which all variables to be correlated are listed on both the horizontal and vertical margins. At the point where two variables intersect, the correlation between them is given; thus the matrix shows the correlation between each test and all other tests administered in the battery.

factors that emerge from a factor analysis are somewhat different than the test scores that are collected and used in the intercorrelational matrix. A factor is a basic behavior characteristic or pattern. The test, in contrast, may measure portions of a number of factors. Once factors have been identified, it is often possible to develop tests that are predominately measures of a single factor and are therefore more easily understood and interpreted than tests that measure certain elements of a number of undefined or only partially defined factors. Thurstone's classic study on mental ability factors is a typical example of the use of factor analysis in improving the understanding of complex variables.[7] In this study, Thurstone administered a battery of fifty-six tests to a sample of his students at the University of Chicago. The tests dealt with such variables as reading, word classification, word grouping, and figure classification. An intercorrelational matrix was then developed for the fifty-six measures, and a factor analysis was conducted. A number of major factors of mental ability emerged from this factor analysis and were identified by Thurstone as Verbal-Meaning, Number, Word Fluency, Perceptual Speed, Memory, Space, Motor, Inductive, and Deductive Reasoning. Based upon these results, Thurstone developed his *Tests of Primary Mental Abilities* aimed at measuring the various factors that had emerged. The factor analysis therefore led to the development of a series of valuable measures of mental ability in addition to contributing to our theoretical knowledge of mental abilities and our understanding of them.

Concurrent validity

Research aimed at establishing concurrent validity employs correlational techniques and is aimed at establishing the degree of relationship between tests or other measures being developed and concurrent criterion measures. The development of measures with concurrent validity is most important in those areas of psychology and education in which the currently available measures are valid but expensive, time-consuming, or difficult to use. If a group test could be developed, for example, that would identify persons with serious emotional problems as accurately as an interview with a clinical psychologist, this test would make it possible to conduct

[7] L. L. Thurstone, "Primary Mental Abilities," *Psychometric Monographs* (Chicago: Univ. of Chicago Press, 1938), I, 110–12.

research that would be prohibitively expensive if clinical interviews were used. Concurrent-validity studies usually require more knowledge than exploratory-relationship studies and often extend the knowledge obtained in exploratory studies. Concurrent-validity studies, in turn, are often preliminary to predictive-validity studies in research areas such as vocational interests in which predictive validity can only be established through long term research.

In any relatively new and developing science such as education, the development and validation of measuring instruments is an important task. Each new or improved instrument opens new avenues of research. Concurrent-validity studies are especially appropriate for graduate theses because they can be carried out in a relatively short time and offer a better chance of providing results of scientific significance than most other types of educational research that are within the resources of the graduate student.

Limitations

The correlational technique has some limitations as applied to relationship studies. In Chapter 6 we discussed the fact that correlations cannot be assumed to establish cause-and-effect relationships between the variables correlated. A theoretical limitation considered serious by many psychologists is that the correlational study attempts to break down complex behavior into simpler components. Although this atomistic approach is appropriate for many research areas in education and psychology, there is some question as to whether a complex characteristic such as artistic ability can be meaningful if broken into its elements. It is not uncommon to find artists who seem to possess all or most of the specific skills that appear related to artistic ability and yet are unable to produce creative art work. On the other hand, many of the recognized masters in the graphic arts have been notably deficient in some specific skill related to their media and yet have produced masterpieces. The correlational approach has failed in the study of some complex behavior patterns such as teaching ability where a great many studies have been done without materially advancing our knowledge. Another problem involving the use of the correlational technique to identify variables related to complex skills or abilities is that success in many of the complex activities that interest us can probably be attained in a number of different ways. For example, a study attempting to relate success of high school principals to specific independent variables might fail because of the lack of any set of characteristics common to all successful principals. For one group of administrators, for example, forcefulness might be significantly correlated with success, while, for another group of administrators who employ different administrative techniques, this characteristic might be negatively correlated with success. We know so little about certain behavior patterns and many of these patterns are so highly complex that only the most careful interpretation of correlational data can provide us with some understanding of the phenomenon being studied.

The "shotgun" approach

A serious weakness of many exploratory studies that use correlational techniques is that the research worker has employed the shotgun approach. The shotgun approach in correlational research involves the attempt to gain an understanding of a complex behavior pattern by administering very large numbers of measures to the research sample in hopes that some of the measures administered will turn out to be related to the behavior being studied. As a rule, measures are included even though the experimenter can think of no theoretical basis or establish no hypotheses to justify their inclusion. Although the shotgun approach sometimes yields significant relationships, it should be avoided by the research worker. Because of the large number of measures that must be administered, this approach is costly and inefficient. Finding tests that correlate with a given criterion is not enough because these tests may correlate for entirely irrelevant reasons, and, upon repeating the study, many of these correlations will normally disappear. The only situation in which this approach may be justified is when a quick research solution is required without regard to cost in an area where previous work is insufficient to form the basis for a more scientific approach.

Prediction and selection studies

Prediction studies, although aimed at the basic correlational goal of seeking relationships, are usually carried out in areas where a firmer basis of previous knowledge is present than is the case with exploratory relationship studies. Prediction through the use of correlational technique is based on the assumption that at least some of the factors that will lead to the behavior we wish to predict are present and measurable at the time that we make the prediction. For example, if we wish to predict the probable success of individuals in a management training program, we would normally start with variables that we have found in previous research to be related to later success in management positions. This type of test battery might include such factors as verbal intelligence, social attitudes, emotional maturity, and so on. The degree to which these predictor variables correlate with the specific behavior we are attempting to predict, of course, determines the accuracy of our prediction. In such an area as success in management positions, certain variables important to success could not possibly be predicted because they are not present at the time the prediction must be made. For example, the individual's abilities to work well with his superiors in the management hierarchy could not be predicted if these future superiors were unknown. Similarly, as success in some management positions is thought to be dependent to some degree upon the ability of the individual's wife to fit into the situation, it would not be possible to predict this variable if the individual were not married.

Much prediction research has been carried out in the field of scholastic success. Some studies have been aimed at short-term prediction of the student's performance in a specific course of study, while other studies have been aimed at long-term prediction of general academic success. A great deal of research has also been done to establish methods of predicting vocational success and success in various military specialities. As the cost of training new personnel for today's complex vocational skills increases, the saving to be realized by effective selection and prediction procedures also increases. For example, a selection system such as that employed by the U.S. Air Force for prediction of success in pilot training can save vast sums of money because it eliminates a certain number of persons who would fail during the training program. Because such training is extremely costly and because the cost of training the unsuccessful candidate up to the point of failure must be added to the per capita cost of training successful candidates, it may be seen that a prediction program that will reduce the number of failures can be of great value.

Long-term vs. short-term prediction

Generally speaking, prediction of events or behaviors that are to occur in the immediate future is easier and can be done more accurately than prediction of events or behaviors to occur in the more distant future. This is because in short-term prediction, more of the factors leading to success in the behavior being predicted are likely to be present. Furthermore, short-term prediction allows less time for important predictor variables to change or for the individual to gain experience that would tend to change his probability of success in the predicted behavior.

Types of correlations employed in prediction studies

Some predictions are based upon a single predictor variable. An example of this type of study is often found in short-term academic prediction. For example, an algebra prognosis test is often administered to pupils finishing the eighth grade to predict their success in ninth grade algebra. The proportion of prediction studies, however, that lend themselves to prediction based on a single variable are limited. Most attempts to predict future behavior are based upon scores on a number of predictor variables each of which is useful in predicting a specific aspect of the future behavior. For example, in prediction of college success, a single variable such as high school grade point average is less efficient in prediction than a combination of variables including high school grade point average, intelligence, socioeconomic status, motivation, and study habits. These more complex prediction studies, therefore, generally call for the use of multiple correlation and multiple regression equations.

Differential prediction

It is sometimes found that certain variables may be more effective in predicting the behavior of certain individuals or subgroups than in predicting the behavior of other subgroups. In a study to determine whether success in pilot training can be predicted from the cadet's interest in aviation, air force psychologists developed a test containing many items of general information about aviation. It was hypothesized that an individual interested in aviation would have gained the information needed to answer the questions while persons not interested would not have this information. The test was tried on a sample of aviation cadets and found to correlate moderately with later success in pilot training. It was then hypothesized that the test would be a more satisfactory predictor for individuals with low interest in reading than individuals with high interest in reading. This hypothesis was based upon the premise that the individual who did a great deal of reading might have gained much of the information called for without having a strong interest in aviation. On the other hand, individuals who had little interest in reading would almost surely not have the information on the test unless they had a strong interest in aviation. Further research proved this hypothesis to be correct.

Shrinkage

In using correlations for prediction, the usual procedure is to set up a test or battery of tests that we believe will predict the behavior with which we are concerned. These tests are then tried out on a sample in order to determine their predictive validity, that is, the degree to which they will predict the behavior that we wish them to predict. The correlation between the prediction made by the test and the later behavior of the individual gives us an estimate of the predictive validity of the test. This correlation, however, especially if it is based upon a predictive instrument of low-predictive validity and was validated on a small sample will almost certainly become smaller if we repeat the experiment with a new sample. The tendency for predictive validities to decrease when the experiment is repeated is referred to as shrinkage. Webb's study of success in dental school previously cited provides a good example of shrinkage.[8] His five predictor measures gave an R of .503 in his initial study. Upon repeating this study with another sample, this R shrank to .425. The validity of his best single predictor, predental grade average, shrank from .402 to .309.

Shrinkage is due primarily to the fact that when we initially validate our measures, some of them will yield significant correlations by chance. In other words, characteristics unique to the group of subjects we have tested tend to yield a maximum predictive validity for some of our predictive measures. Upon repetition of the study, however, these same chance variables are not likely to be present

[8] Sam C. Webb, "The Prediction of Achievement for First Year Dental Students," *Educational and Psychological Measurement*, XVI, No. 4 (1957), 543–48.

in our new sample, and in this case the correlation initially obtained becomes smaller or disappears. As it is not possible to carry out predictions on the basis of correlations that only apply to one sample of subjects, it is always advisable to conduct a cross validation of predictor instruments before using them in practical prediction situations. Thus, after preliminary validation of the battery, the predictive validity of each prediction instrument should be cross-checked using another sample, and those correlations that have dropped to the level that makes them impractical for inclusion in the regression equation should be eliminated.

INTERPRETING SIMPLE CORRELATION COEFFICIENTS [9]

Students often have a difficult time interpreting the correlation coefficient after computing it. Because correlations are expressed in decimals, students often assume that they are similar to percentage points. A simple correlation is a mathematical way of expressing the degree of relationship between two variables or, to state it another way, the amount that the two variables have in common. Although a correlation of .50 does not mean that the two measures have 50 per cent in common, the square of the correlation does give this "common variance." Two tests that are correlated .50 have $.50^2$ or .25 of their variance in common. The concept of common variance is a useful one in helping us interpret correlations.

Correlation coefficients are usually interpreted either with reference to their statistical significance in exploratory relationship studies or their value as predictive devices in prediction studies. These two interpretations are considerably different because a correlation that is highly significant is often of little or no value for most purposes of prediction. Statistical significance when referred to a correlation usually describes whether or not the correlation obtained is different from a zero at a given level of confidence. If the correlation is not significantly different from zero then it must be assumed that no relationship exists between variables. Most statistics texts include a table from which the statistical significance of a Pearson product moment correlation may be determined directly.

[9] The term "simple correlation coefficients" refers to those involving correlation between two variables. Multiple correlation and partial correlation involve more than two variables.

The level of statistical significance of the correlation is determined to a great degree by the number of cases upon which the correlation is based. For example, with 22 cases, a Pearson correlation of .54 is needed to be significant at the 1 per cent level. If we have 100 cases, however, a correlation of .25 is significant at the 1 per cent level, and with 1,000 cases a correlation of only .08 is significant at the 1 per cent level.

When we say that a correlation coefficient is statistically significant we mean that this coefficient is sufficiently high so that we may be reasonably confident that some relationship exists between the variables we have correlated. If the correlation is significant at the 1 per cent level, it may be interpreted as indicating that there is only one chance in one hundred that the correlation is due to chance errors in sampling. We have seen that if we have a reasonably large number of cases, the correlation coefficient may be significant even though it is quite low. The size of the correlation coefficient is indicative of the degree of relationship between the variables, and a low correlation indicates a low relationship even if the correlation is significant at the 1 per cent level. Relationship studies are aimed primarily at gaining a better understanding of the complex skills or behavior patterns being studied. In studies of this sort, low correlations are often useful because they give us clues about the nature of the behavior we are studying. These clues can then be followed up by prediction studies or by studies using experimental research designs.

Prediction studies are concerned with the use of correlation techniques to predict certain kinds of future behavior and require higher correlations than those usually found in exploratory relationship studies. In prediction studies, statistical significance is of little consequence because correlations must far exceed this point to be of practical value in most prediction problems. Correlations are also interpreted somewhat differently in problems involving individual prediction than in problems involving group prediction.

In individual prediction, we administer a test or battery of tests and on the basis of the test scores, predict the likelihood that certain individuals will succeed in the predicted activity. An algebra aptitude test, for example, is generally used for individual prediction. Another type of prediction used in educational problems is group prediction. In group prediction we predict, on the basis of our test scores, that at certain score levels a given percentage of our subjects will fail and the remainder will pass. For example, in establishing an intelligence cut-off point for selecting college students, it may be found that students below 105 IQ would have only one chance in ten of completing college. Students between 105 and 115 IQ might have three chances in ten of completing college, and students between 115 and 130 IQ might have six chances in ten of completing college. If we have a reasonably valid test to predict the behavior with which we are concerned, it is possible to predict how many persons between certain score intervals will succeed and how many will fail. The difficulty with group prediction is that we cannot predict *which* members of a given score interval will succeed and *which* ones will fail. Group prediction is often used in college admissions programs, the college usually adopts the principle that it is not feasible to accept ten students who score in a given intelligence range if it is known from past experience that nine of these ten will fail. Group prediction is also used in many of the training schools operated by the military services. The test battery used by the U.S. Air Force to predict success in pilot training is used to make group predictions. It is known from prediction studies of previous aviation cadets what percentage of cadets at each score level on the test battery will succeed in pilot training. Thus, it is possible for the air force to determine how many students at the score levels available must be entered into the program in order to have the number of graduates required to man the aircraft planned for at a given future date.

The correlation coefficient may thus be interpreted in terms of two major dimensions. First the correlation is either statistically significant or not significant. Secondly, the correlation has a meaning for prediction: either group or individual. The following rules provide the student with a basis for roughly interpreting correlation coefficients obtained in his research. These data are, of course, only a general guide but will be approximately correct for most situations. Let us assume that we are dealing with correlations based on one hundred or more subjects.

Correlations ranging from .20 to .35

Correlations at this level show a very slight relationship between the variables although this relationship may be statistically significant. A correlation of .20 indicates that only 4 per cent of the variance in the two measures that have been correlated is common to both. Correlations in this range may have limited meaning in exploratory research where relationships are being sought out using crude measures. Correlations at this level, however, are of no value in either individual or group prediction.

Correlations ranging from .35 to .65

Correlations in this range are statistically significant beyond the 1 per cent level. With correlations around .50, crude group prediction may be achieved. As a correlation of .50 between a test and the performance predicted only indicates 25 per cent common variance, it is obvious that predictions based on a correlation this low can be expected to be frequently in error.

Correlations within this range, however, are useful when combined with other correlations into a multiple-regression equation. Combining several correlations in this range can in some cases yield individual predictions that are correct within an acceptable margin of error. Correlations at this level used singly are of little or no use for individual prediction because they yield only a few more correct predictions than could be accomplished by guessing or by using some chance selection procedure.

Correlations ranging from .65 to .85

Correlations at this level make possible group predictions that are accurate enough for most purposes. As we move toward the top of this range, group predictions can be made very accurately, usually predicting the proportion of successful candidates in selection problems within a very small margin of error. Near the top of this correlation range individual predictions can be made that are considerably more accurate than would occur if no such selection procedure were used.

Correlations over .85

Correlations at this level indicate a close relationship between the two variables correlated. A correlation of .85 indicates that the measure used for prediction has about 72 per cent variance in common with the performance being predicted. Prediction studies in education very rarely yield correlations this high. When correlations at this level are obtained, however, they are very useful for either individual or group prediction.

THE TAYLOR-RUSSELL TABLES IN GROUP PREDICTION

The goal of many prediction studies is to develop measures with sufficient predictive validity to be used in practical selection programs in education or industry. The efficiency of a measure for selection purposes, however, is not determined solely by its predictive validity. Two other factors influence this efficiency in practical selection problems. The first is the selection ratio. This is the proportion of the available candidates that must be selected. A predictive measure gives better results if only the few candidates scoring highest need be chosen than if all but the few who score lowest must be chosen. In other words, the smaller the proportion of candidates that must be chosen, the more of those chosen will be successful. The other factor influencing the proportion of successful candidates who will be obtained by the selection system is the proportion of candidates who would be successful if no selection were applied. In most vocational applications, this is the proportion of employees hired for the given activity, prior to the selection system, whose work was satisfactory. In educational selection, it would be the number of students who succeeded in the given course of study prior to the use of selective admission. This number provides a base line, and a selection system, even one with low predictive validity, will improve to some degree the proportion of successful candidates.

The Taylor-Russell Tables combine the three factors of predictive validity, selection ratio, and proportion successful without selection. If these three factors are known, the research worker can predict the proportion of the candidates selected who will be successful. Table 5 is a sample page of the Taylor-Russell Tables, this sample being usable when 70 per cent of the candidates were successful prior to the selection system. A page is provided for each 5 per cent interval on this variable from 5 per cent to 95 per cent. After the correct page is located, the predictive validity is located in the left hand column under r. We then locate the selection ratio in the top row and read the figure at the intersection of the row containing the predictive validity and the column containing the selection ratio. For example, let us assume that a college of engineering has received

500 applications for admission to their freshmen class but can only take 250 students. They have a test battery that has been tried for two previous years when no selection system was used and found to

TABLE 5

SAMPLE TAYLOR-RUSSELL TABLE *†

(Selection Ratio: Proportion Selected on Basis of Tests)

r	.05	.10	.20	.30	.40	.50	.60	.70	.80	.90	.95
.00	.70	.70	.70	.70	.70	.70	.70	.70	.70	.70	.70
.05	.73	.73	.72	.72	.72	.71	.71	.71	.71	.70	.70
.10	.77	.76	.75	.74	.73	.73	.72	.72	.71	.71	.70
.15	.80	.79	.77	.76	.75	.74	.73	.73	.72	.71	.71
.20	.83	.81	.79	.78	.77	.76	.75	.74	.73	.71	.71
.25	.86	.84	.81	.80	.78	.77	.76	.75	.73	.72	.71
.30	.88	.86	.84	.82	.80	.78	.77	.75	.74	.72	.71
.35	.91	.89	.86	.83	.82	.80	.78	.76	.75	.73	.71
.40	.93	.91	.88	.85	.83	.81	.79	.77	.75	.73	.72
.45	.94	.93	.90	.87	.85	.83	.81	.78	.76	.73	.72
.50	.96	.94	.91	.89	.87	.84	.82	.80	.77	.74	.72
.55	.97	.96	.93	.91	.88	.86	.83	.81	.78	.74	.72
.60	.98	.97	.95	.92	.90	.87	.85	.82	.79	.75	.73
.65	.99	.98	.96	.94	.92	.89	.86	.83	.80	.75	.73
.70	1.00	.99	.97	.96	.93	.91	.88	.84	.80	.76	.73
.75	1.00	1.00	.98	.97	.95	.92	.89	.86	.81	.76	.73
.80	1.00	1.00	.99	.98	.97	.94	.91	.87	.82	.77	.73
.85	1.00	1.00	1.00	.99	.98	.96	.93	.89	.84	.77	.74
.90	1.00	1.00	1.00	1.00	.99	.98	.95	.91	.85	.78	.74
.95	1.00	1.00	1.00	1.00	1.00	.99	.98	.94	.86	.78	.74
1.00	1.00	1.00	1.00	1.00	1.00	1.00	1.00	1.00	.88	.78	.74

* H. C. Taylor and J. T. Russell, "The Relationships of Validity Coefficients to the Practical Effectiveness of Tests in Selection: Discussion and Tables," *Journal of Applied Psychology*, XXIII (1939), 565–78. Reprinted by permission of the American Psychological Assoc.

† For use when .70 per cent are successful without the selection system.

have a predictive validity of .60 when correlated with freshmen grades. During the previous two years, 70 per cent of the freshmen accepted had received passing grades. If the test battery is administered to the 500 applicants and the top 250 accepted, how many of these will succeed? If we enter the Taylor-Russell Table, using the page for 70 per cent success of previous students, a selection ratio of .50 (the number to be selected, 250, divided by the number available, 500), and a predictive validity (r) of .60, we find that 87 per cent, or 217 of the 250 selected, will be successful. If the predictive validity of the battery had been only .40, 81 per cent or 202 of the 250 selected would be successful. Thus, even with a battery of low predictive validity, the selection system yields 27 more successful candidates than the 175 (70 per cent of 250) that would be obtained if the 250 were selected by some random means. Thus, it may be seen that with a favorable selection ratio, measures with predictive validities lower than normally needed for group prediction can make worthwhile increases in the number of successful candidates selected.

MISTAKES OFTEN MADE BY GRADUATE STUDENTS

1. Student assumes the results of causal-comparative or correlational research to be proof of a cause-and-effect relationship.

2. Uses samples in causal-comparative research that differ on so many pertinent variables that comparisons of groups can yield no interpretable results.

3. Attempts to study possible causes of a broadly defined behavior pattern that actually includes a number of unlike subgroups. This usually leads to a jumble of confused and contradictory results with no clear relationships emerging.

4. Tries to build a correlational study around conveniently available data instead of collecting the data needed to do a worthwhile study.

5. Selects variables for correlation that have been found unproductive in previous studies.

6. Fails to make use of educational and psychological theory in selecting variables for study in correlational research.

7. Uses simple correlation techniques in studies where partial correlation or multiple correlation is needed to obtain a clear picture of the way the variables are operating.

8. Applies tables giving significance levels of Pearsonian correlation co-

efficients to non-Pearsonian correlations, which often leads to reporting nonsignificant relationships as being significant.

9. Uses the "shotgun" approach in exploratory relationship studies.

10. Fails to develop satisfactory criterion measures for use in correlational studies of complex skills or behavior patterns.

ANNOTATED REFERENCES

1. GLEUCK, SHELDON, and GLEUCK, ELEANOR. *Unraveling Juvenile Delinquency.* New York: The Commonwealth Fund, 1950. This classic study provides the student with an example of the causal-comparative method as used in a major research project. A number of critical evaluations of this study may be found by checking *Psychological Abstracts.*

2. GOOD, C. V.; BARR, A. S.; and SCATES, D. E. *The Methodology of Educational Research.* New York: Appleton-Century Co., 1941. Chapter 10 provides the student with a good coverage of causal comparative and correlational research methods, taking a somewhat different approach from this text.

3. HAMMOND, K. R., and HOUSEHOLDER, J. E. *Introduction to the Statistical Method.* New York: Alfred A. Knopf, Inc., 1962. Chapter 6 provides the student with a thorough but easily understood introduction to the theoretical and mathematical aspects of the correlation coefficient.

4. The following articles, all found in the 1961 volume of *Educational and Psychological Measurement,* provide the student with examples of different types of correlational research.
(*a*) Prediction Studies:
ANDERSON, H. E., JR. "The Prediction of Reading and Language from the California Tests," *Educational and Psychological Measurement,* 1961, 21 (4), 1035–36.
BERDIE, R. F. "Intraindividual Variability and Predictability," *Educational and Psychological Measurement,* 1961, 21 (3), 663–76.
(*b*) Relationship Studies not using Factor Analysis:
JACKSON, D. N., and PACINE, L. "Response Styles and Academic Achievement," *Educational and Psychological Measurement,* 1961, 21 (4) 1015–28.
MURSTEIN, B. I., and LEIPOLD, W. D. "The Role of Learning and Motor Abilities in the Wechsler-Bellevue Digit Symbol Subtest," *Educational and Psychological Measurement,* 1961, 21 (1) 103–12.

(*c*) Relationship Studies using Factor Analysis:

BECKER, W. C. "A Comparison of the Factor Structure and Other Properties of the 16 PF and the Guildford-Martin Personality Inventories," *Educational and Psychological Measurement,* 1961, 21 (2), 393–404.

COOK, D. L.; LINDEN, J. D.; and MCKAY, H. E. "A Factor Analysis of Teacher Trainee Responses to Selected Personality Inventories," *Educational and Psychological Measurement,* 1961, 21 (4) 865–72.

MCGUIRE, C.; HINDSMAN, E.; KING, F. J.; and JENNINGS, E. "Dimensions of Talented Behavior," *Educational and Psychological Measurement,* 1961, 21 (1) 3–38.

(*d*) Reliability Studies:

HOWELL, J. J., and WEINER, M. "Note on the Equivalence on Alternate Forms of an Achievement Test," *Educational and Psychological Measurement,* 1961, 21 (2) 309–13.

SILVER, R. J., and CASEY, E. W. "Stability of the Kuder Vocational Preference Record in Psychiatric Patients," *Educational and Psychological Measurement,* 1961, 21 (4), 879–82.

(*e*) Concurrent Validity Study:

FRENCH, J. W. "Aptitude and Interest Score Patterns Related to Satisfaction with College Major Field," *Educational and Psychological Measurement,* 1961, 21 (2), 287–94.

CHAPTER 13

Experimental Research in Education

INTRODUCTION

The experiment is the ultimate form of research design, providing the most rigorous test of hypotheses that is available to the scientist. While other designs such as correlational or causal-comparative can uncover possible relationships, the experiment is needed to establish cause-and-effect. Most experiments in education employ some form of the classic single-variable design. All single-variable experiments involve the manipulation of one variable followed by observing the effects of this manipulation on a second variable. The variable to be manipulated will be referred to in this chapter as the experimental treatment. It is often referred to as the independent variable, experimental variable, or treatment variable as well. The variable that is measured to determine the effects of the experimental treatment is usually referred to as the dependent variable or criterion variable. In this chapter we will use the term dependent variable to describe this measure. For example, let us suppose we wished to design an experiment to determine the effects of anxiety upon ability to memorize mathematical formulas. In this experiment the dependent variable would be the subject's performance in memorizing mathematical formulas, while the experimental treatment would be the steps taken by the experimenter to vary the amount of anxiety experienced by the subjects. In single-variable experiments, different groups are exposed to different experimental treatments while an attempt is made to hold constant all variables except the experimental treatment. Differences on the dependent variable that are uncovered between the experimental treatments can then be attributed to effects of the experimental treatment plus errors. Experiments in education may be carried out either in the field or in the laboratory. Some experimental designs are more appropriate for dealing with the less rigorous control possible in the field situation while others are more satisfactory in the laboratory situation. Whether in the field or the laboratory, however, many difficulties are encountered in applying experimental designs to most educational problems. The most difficult task in applying experimental methods to educational problems is holding all variables in the educational situation constant except the experimental variable that we wish to manipulate through our experimental treatment. In the physical sciences, where the classic single-variable experiment was first developed and where it has been most fruitful in the production of knowledge, the material worked with is much more adaptable to the rigorous requirements of the experimental laboratory. In the behavioral sciences and particularly in those experiments involving human subjects, it is doubtful whether the rigorous control of the physical science laboratory can ever be achieved.

A further dilemma that must be resolved in adapting experimental methods to educational research is that, as more rigorous controls are applied to the experiment, less carry-over can be expected between the experiment and related field situations. In other words, the behavioral sciences are constantly faced with the choice of obtaining rigorous laboratory control at the cost of realism or of maintaining realistic experimental situations, so that findings may be readily transferred into practical field application, but losing scientific rigor in the process. Most educational studies aim at a compromise between these goals—they attempt to attain sufficient rigor to make the result scientifically acceptable while maintaining sufficient realism to make the results reasonably transferable to educational situations in the field.

The experimental designs discussed here will be those that are most appropriate for use by research workers in education and the behavioral sciences. Many of the simple designs described can be combined or altered to provide designs of greater complexity. Nearly all experimental research in education being carried out at the present time, however, uses one or the other of the simple single-variable forms of experimental design you will find discussed in this chapter. You will also find a brief discussion of factorial designs, although this approach is too complex for most graduate students and for that matter is rarely used by experienced research workers in education.

ERRORS IN EXPERIMENTAL RESEARCH

In appraising the differences obtained between the scores of different groups on the dependent variable, it must be remembered that not all of this difference can be considered due to the effect of the experimental treatment. Part of the results are due to errors or uncontrolled variables that have entered into the experimental situation. In Chapter 8 we discussed sampling errors. Experimental designs, however, are subject to errors arising from the experimental treatments in addition to those arising from subject differences. Lindquist describes three types of errors. These are *Type S* errors that are associated with the sampling of the research subjects, *Type G* errors that are associated with the research groups, and *Type R* errors that occur between replications of the experiment.[1] An understanding of these errors can help the research worker to design experiments in which the effects of errors are reduced and can also help identify such errors and weigh their possible effect on research results.

Type S errors, which must be considered in all types of educational research, are those which arise because of the assignment of subjects to the research groups. Let us suppose that we wished to select random samples of ninth grade students from a population of 5,000 such students enrolled in a large school district. If we selected several samples of one hundred students from this population and calculated the mean IQ of each sample, we would find differences in these means. Some groups would have more bright students than others. Such variations can be expected to occur in random samples, and our statistical methods permit us to estimate the probable magnitude of such errors. When nonrandom techniques are used to assign subjects to different groups, such errors lead to sampling bias that can result in large errors because variables such as motivation, intelligence, and interest may be operating differently for different groups. The most serious problem in working with these nonrandom errors, however, is that we do not have statistical tools to estimate their probable limits.

[1] E. F. Lindquist, *Design and Analysis of Experiments in Psychology and Education* (Boston: Houghton Mifflin Co., 1953).

Type G errors are those that arise because of the many small differences that occur between the treatments given different groups. These errors usually have the same effect on all members of the same group but are present in different degrees for different groups. Such variables as time of day when tests were administered, interruptions during the experimental situation, distractions, changes in schedule, differences in ability of teachers working with different groups, and many others tend to make the total situation different for each group. Failure to control differences in teaching ability can be a very important source of error in educational experiments. In comparing the effectiveness of two different methods of teaching a foreign language, for example, the differences in skill of teachers using the different methods may be the major factor in rate of learning. Unless such variables are controlled, *Type G* errors can combine to produce completely misleading results. Many of the apparent contradictions found in the educational research literature can be explained by the presence of *Type G* errors in the research designs.

Type R errors are differences in the effectiveness of the treatment that are due to differences in the appropriateness of a given treatment for different subsamples studied. Thus, a democratic classroom atmosphere may lead to better achievement in one school not because of *Type S* or *Type G* errors but because of conditions in the environment and previous training of the subjects that make this method more appropriate. Upon replication in another school, this approach may result in lower achievement than the achievement in an authoritarian, teacher-centered atmosphere because of differences in the conditions that exist in the new situation. Discovery of *Type R* errors can often lead to further research aimed at identifying the conditions that led to the success of a particular method in one replication and its failure in other replications.

EXPERIMENTAL DESIGNS

The single-group design

The single-group design usually involves three steps. The first step is the administration of a pretest measuring the dependent variable. The second step is the application of the experimental treatment (independent variable) to the subjects, and the final step is the administration of a post-test measuring again of the dependent variable. Differences due to application of the experimental treatment are then determined by comparing the pretest and post-test scores usually using the t-test or analysis of variance for the analysis. F. T. Smith's study of changes in college student attitudes toward the Negro provides a good example of a study that employed single-group design.[2] In this study Smith administered his pretest, an attitude scale measuring attitudes toward the Negro, to a sample of 354 college students at Columbia University. Of this sample, he selected 46 students who were representative of the larger group tested. These students were then exposed to the experimental treatment that, in this case, was a series of favorable contacts with Negroes such as having dinner with a Negro family, visiting a Negro church, and meeting leaders of the Negro community in Harlem. These contacts extended over a four-day period. Smith's hypothesis was that these contacts with Negroes would change the attitudes of his research subjects in a favorable direction. Ten days after the last planned contact with Negroes, Smith post-tested his group using the same attitude measure and found that the mean attitude had changed significantly in favor of Negroes. Then, after waiting ten months, Smith administered still another post-test to determine how much of the favorable attitudes change had persisted.

The major limitation of the single-group design is that, as no control group is used, the experimenter must assume that changes between the pretest and post-test were brought about by the experimental treatment. There is always some chance, however, that one or more extraneous variables brought about all or part of the change noted between the pretest and the post-test scores. For example, in the case of Smith's study, let us assume that after the pretest was administered, but some time prior to the post-test, a Negro committed some especially vicious crime in Harlem and this crime received broad and highly emotional coverage in the New York newspapers. Smith then would have been faced with the problem of trying to determine how much of the attitude change observed on the post-test could be attributed to the planned application of the independent variable and how much was due to the crime over

[2] F. T. Smith, "An Experiment in Modifying the Attitudes Towards the Negro," *Teachers College Contributions*, No. 887, 1943.

which he had no control. Although situations such as highly pub-
licized crime quite obviously might have an effect upon the subjects,
there is also a possibility that some subtle factors unrelated to the
experimental treatment have operated on all or some of the research
subjects and have led to a change on the post-test.

Because of the assumption that the changes on the dependent
variable are not due to extraneous factors, the single-group design
is limited to the study of characteristics or behavior patterns that
are reasonably stable—that is, are not likely to change unless some
direct action by the experimenter is taken to bring about such a
change. The single-group design, for example, is often used for
studying changes in racial and religious attitudes of adults because
these attitudes are known to be quite stable in most individuals by
adulthood and are unlikely to change unless some significant effort
is made to change them. In fact, the attitudes are sufficiently stable
so that most of the research that has devoted considerable effort to
changing them has failed to bring about significant changes. The
single-group design is completely inappropriate for studies where the
dependent variable is not stable or where it is likely to change due
to maturation. For example, a study aimed at testing the effect of
teaching methods on the creative thinking of elementary school
children could not be done using the single-group method because
the abilities of children at this level are developing rapidly and a
significant gain between the pretest and post-test might be due
primarily to maturation rather than the effect of the teaching methods employed in the experiment.

In order to reduce the likelihood of external variables altering the
post-test results, most studies employing single-group design attempt
to keep the interval between the pretest and the post-test as short
as possible. For example, studies that attempt to measure the effect
of motion pictures upon racial or religious attitudes are frequently
designed so that the pretest is administered immediately before the
subjects are shown the motion picture and the post-test is administered immediately following the motion picture. Under these conditions, there is very little likelihood that extraneous variables have
entered into the situation. Such an approach, however, has its draw-
backs because immediate post-test scores are often a poor indicator
of the magnitude of permanent attitude changes brought about by
the experimental treatment.

In summary, the research worker should only use the single-group design when the dependent variable is reasonably stable, when the interval between the pretest and post-test can be kept short, and when it is impossible to obtain a control group.

Control-group designs

Nearly any study that can be conducted using single-group design can be carried out more satisfactorily using one of the control-group designs, which we will now discuss. The essential difference between the single-group design and the control-group design is that the latter employs at least two groups of subjects, one of which is called the control group and is included primarily to make it possible to measure the effect of external factors upon the post-test of the dependent variable. The treatment of the experimental and control groups is generally kept as close to identical as possible with the exception that the experimental group is exposed to the experimental treatment. Using control-group design, if external variables have brought about changes between the pretest and post-test, these will be reflected in the scores of the control group. Thus, only the post-test change of the experimental group that is over and above the change that occurred in the control group can be attributed to the experimental treatment. In simple control-group experiments, the mean post-test scores of the experimental and control groups are compared using the t-test to determine whether the experimental treatment has brought about a statistically significant change. Perhaps the most serious problem in applying the control-group designs to educational research is the control of *Type G* errors. When working with human subjects, small and very subtle differences in the treatment of the experimental and control groups that are unrelated to the experimental treatment can bring about large changes in behavior. Medical studies have found, for example, that if one group receives a pill and another receives nothing, the group getting the pill may report changes in physical condition that could not possibly be due to the chemical properties of the pill. Thus, the research worker should maintain as much similarity between the treatment of experimental and control groups as possible. In medical research, for example, if the experimental subjects are given a tablet containing a drug, the control subjects are given a tablet of identical appearance that contains some inert substance. If the experimental group is given an injection of a drug, the control group receives an apparently identical injection of distilled water. These apparently identical but medically inert substances are called placebos.

In educational research, whenever a placebo is appropriate it should be used. The principle underlying the placebo—keeping the apparent treatment of experimental and control groups as identical as possible—should always be followed as far as the nature of the study will permit.

PARALLEL-GROUP DESIGN WITH MATCHING

In parallel-group design, two or more groups are employed. In its simplest form, one experimental group and one control group are used. The research worker attempts to expose the two groups to as nearly identical treatment as possible with the exception that the experimental group is exposed to the experimental variable. Matching in such designs refers to an attempt on the part of the research worker to place his subjects into experimental and control groups in such a manner that they are closely comparable on a pretest that measures the dependent variable or variables correlated with the dependent variable. The main purpose of matching is to reduce initial differences between the experimental and control groups on the dependent variable. This leads to less heterogeneous groups and reduces *Type S* errors. Matching is most useful in studies where small samples are to be used and when large differences between an experimental and control group on the dependent variable are not likely to occur. Under these conditions, the small differences that do occur are more likely to be detected if sampling errors are reduced by the use of matching. The more closely the matching variable correlates with the dependent variable, the more effective the matching will be in reducing these errors. Thus, it is necessary, if matching is to be employed, to have available a matching variable that correlates highly with the dependent variable. This circumstance occurs in many educational studies. For example, in studies concerned with achievement gains that occur under different conditions of learning, alternate forms of the same achievement test can usually be used for the initial matching and for post-testing of the dependent variable. Inasmuch as these alternate forms usually correlate highly, standard error is reduced considerably by the matching technique. This increase in precision is reflected for example in the standard error of the difference-between-means formula used for correlated means vs. the formula used for uncorrelated means. The formula for the standard error of the difference between uncorrelated means is $\sigma_D = \sqrt{\sigma^2_{m_1} + \sigma^2_{m_2}}$ while the formula for the standard error of the difference between correlated means for matched groups is $\sigma_D = \sqrt{\sigma^2_{m_1} + \sigma^2_{m_2} - 2r_{12}\sigma_{m1}\sigma_{m2}}$. The two formulas are identical except for the last factor in the matched-group formula and, as this factor is subtracted, it always reduces the standard error (the size of the reduction increasing as the size of correlation increases).[3] Another advantage of matching is that it permits the division of experimental and control groups into subgroups on the basis of the matching variable in order to determine whether the experimental treatment has had a different effect on subjects at different levels. For example, let us consider an experiment aimed at determining the relative effectiveness of teaching algebra using an inductive method as compared with a deductive method. Subjects are given an algebra aptitude test at the outset, pairs of individuals who are closely comparable in aptitude are identified, and one member of each pair is randomly assigned to each of the two groups. This will produce groups that are closely comparable on the matching variable. At the conclusion of the algebra course (experimental treatment) an algebra achievement test could be given and the mean score of the group taught by the inductive method could be compared with the mean score of the group taught by the deductive method. Let us assume that in this hypothetical experiment, no significant difference was found in the overall comparison (see Table 6). Because of the data available on the matching variable, however, subgroups could be identified and a further analysis could be made. Based on scores on this variable, each group could be divided into three subgroups—high, average, and low aptitude students. Comparisons of these three subgroups might indicate that high aptitude students achieve more when taught by the inductive method, while low aptitude students achieve more when taught by the deductive method (see Table 6). Significant findings are often revealed in subgroup comparisons that would not even be suspected if the analysis were limited to overall comparisons.

[3] See Henry Garrett, *op. cit.*, chap. 9, for information on these formulas.

TABLE 6

COMPARISON OF INDUCTIVE AND DEDUCTIVE METHODS IN TEACHING ALGEBRA

	TREATMENT	
	Inductive Method	Deductive Method
High aptitude students Mean achievement (No. = 25)	78.6	67.2
Average aptitude students Mean achievement (No. = 25)	56.4	58.1
Low aptitude students Mean achievement (No. = 25)	41.5	51.2
Overall mean achievement (No. = 75)	58.8	58.8

Steps

The usual steps in carrying out a study using parallel-group design are as follows:

1. Administer measures of the dependent variable or of the variable or variables closely correlated with the dependent variable to the research subjects.

2. Match subjects in the experimental and control groups on the basis of the matching variables.

3. Expose the experimental group to the experimental treatment and if appropriate administer a placebo to the control group.

4. Administer measures of the dependent variable to the experimental and control groups and compare in order to determine the effect of the experimental treatment upon the dependent variable.

A study by Yang provides an example of parallel-group design with matching.[4] The purpose of this study was to determine whether a drug (Deanol) would bring about changes in the efficiency of the mental functioning of college students. A total of 150 subjects were taken from four sections of general psychology. The *School*

[4] John G. L. Yang, *The Effect of Deanol on Intellectual Efficiency and Experience* (Unpublished Master's thesis, Utah State University, 1961).

and College Ability Test (SCAT) was administered and subjects were matched on the basis of the initial test scores and placed in three experimental groups and one control group. The experimental groups received different dosages of the drug while the control group received a placebo. Over a period of seven weeks, subjects in the experimental group were administered Deanol while subjects in the control group were administered a placebo—small sugar pills that were identical to the drug in appearance. Subjects participating in the experiment did not know whether they were receiving the drug or the placebo. At the end of the third week and at the conclusion of the experiment, subjects were given different forms of the *SCAT* in order to determine whether differences developed among the experimental and the control groups.

Problems in matching

Most difficulties that occur in the application of parallel-group design with matching revolve around the matching procedure. The first question that must be solved by the research worker is to determine what variable or variables to use for matching. Matching on a number of variables that are correlated with the dependent variable will reduce errors more than matching on a single variable that is less highly correlated. In attempting to match on more than two variables, however, a difficult problem often comes up because of the impossibility of finding individuals who are reasonably well-matched on several variables. Under these conditions, the research worker must discard many subjects for whom satisfactory matches cannot be obtained.

Another related problem is to determine how closely to match the subjects on the matching variable or variables. For example, matching individuals within three or four points on IQ leads to a more precise matching than if a difference of ten points were allowed between pairs. This close matching, however, although leading to gains in precision, increases the number of subjects who cannot be matched. Many statisticians seriously question the value of any matching procedure that results in losing subjects because such a procedure may seriously change the nature of the sampling and lead to sampling biases. In the case of matching for IQ, for example, close matching of subjects at the high and low extremes is most difficult because there are far fewer cases at the extremes and therefore greater differences between adjacent scores. Thus, matching on normally distributed variables often leads to losing a disproportionate number of extreme cases, thereby reducing the variability, restricting the range, and making the sample less comparable to the population from which it was chosen.

The question of how to match is an important one in most educational research projects. The usual method that has been used in educational research is to employ the person-to-person matching technique just described, in which an attempt is made to locate two persons among those available who score within the matching limits defined by the study. After obtaining a pair of matched subjects, the experimenter uses random means for assigning one subject to the experimental group and his match to the control group. In working with established groups such as classes that have already been organized, this latter step cannot be taken—in other words, a random basis cannot be used for deciding which of each pair of subjects goes into the experimental group and which into the control group. This procedure leads to nonrandom groups, and, as we are working with groups that were not established on a random basis, an increase in *Type S* and *Type G* errors may be expected. Many biasing factors enter in in determining which pupils will attend one section of a given class compared with pupils attending a different section. For example, more bright students and more students from middle-class and upper-class families usually take an orchestra class. Thus, classes offered at the same period as the orchestra class will often contain fewer bright students and fewer middle-class and upper-class students than classes of the same subject offered at other times.

Another matching technique that is sometimes employed is to attempt to obtain a matching of the entire group in terms of mean and standard deviation on the matching variable rather than to match individuals. This procedure provides less precision than individual matching. Group matching is often used on established groups, and, usually, if the groups are not comparable in mean and standard deviation, the experimenter juggles a few subjects from one group to the other in order to obtain a closer match. The principal disadvantages of this approach are the loss of randomization caused by the usual juggling, the lack of random groups available at the start, and the smaller gains in precision as compared with individual matching.

The third method of matching that many statisticians consider superior to the first two is to place all subjects in rank order on the basis of their scores on the matching variable. After subjects have been placed in rank order, the first two subjects are selected (regardless of the difference in their scores on the matching variable) and by random means, such as flipping a coin, one subject is assigned to the experimental group and the other to the control group. The next two subjects on the rank list are then selected and again one is randomly assigned to the experimental group and the other to the control group. This procedure is continued until all subjects have been assigned. The principal advantage of this procedure over the previous two is that it provides a more random group and no cases are lost because of inability to match. Matching, of course, will be less precise than would be the case in close person-to-person matching, but the advantages of not losing subjects outweigh the disadvantages of the less precise matching.

Designs involving more than two groups

Parallel-group design with matching may also be employed with more than two groups. For example, a study may be designed to determine the relative effectiveness of four different methods of teaching remedial reading. Four experimental groups would be required, one for each of the different methods. In this case it may be desirable to match subjects on intelligence and initial reading level. With four groups to match instead of two, however, the matching problems mentioned earlier are magnified. In an individual matching situation, it would now be necessary to find four cases that match within the established limits instead of only two. The ranking method provides the easiest solution to the matching problem if matching is to be done on only one variable. In this case, instead of dividing the rank listing into pairs, it would be divided into consecutive groups of four, and again random methods would be employed to place the four individuals into the four groups. If matching on two or more variables is required, perhaps the simplest solution when several groups are involved is to assign each individual a composite score based on the combination of the scores on the matching variables, rank subjects on the composite score, and then proceed with matching. Any one of several methods could be used to combine the scores on the matching variables into a composite score. The most precise method would be to weigh the scores on the different matching variables in a multiple regression equation based upon the correlation between each matching variable and the dependent variable. In most cases, however, it will be sufficient to convert the raw scores on the matching variables to standard scores and combine the standard scores in order to arrive at a composite score for ranking purposes. This latter method would yield results reasonably close to those attained using the multiple-regression equation if the matching variables are all correlated at approximately the same level with the dependent variable. In practice, the only situation where the extra work of matching subjects on more than one variable is justified is when two or more variables correlate reasonably well with the dependent variable and do not correlate significantly with each other. If one of the matching variables correlates significantly higher than the other with the dependent variable, the results will probably be nearly as good if matching is based on this single variable only. Variables that do not correlate .50 or higher with the dependent variable do little to increase the precision of the experiment. Under most circumstances, such variables should not be employed for matching purposes. If only such variables are available, it is probably advisable to employ random techniques for setting up groups rather than using matching. When matching is employed in multiple group designs, subgroups may be set up in order to go beyond the overall group comparisons in the same manner described under parallel group designs. In the previous example, this might lead to a design such as is shown in Table 7.

Control-group design with random assignment to groups

The difficulties encountered with designs using individual matching have led in recent years to an increase in use of designs employing random assignment of subjects to the various groups. In matching, more comparability between groups is achieved on the matching variables, but the loss of randomness that occurs in most matching designs due to loss of cases may mean that, on those variables not matched, a biasing is introduced into the situation. Random assignment of cases to the various experimental groups usually

TABLE 7

THE RELATIVE EFFECTIVENESS OF FOUR DIFFERENT METHODS OF
TEACHING REMEDIAL READING

SUBGROUPS	TREATMENT			
	Remedial reading Method A	Remedial reading Method B	Remedial reading Method C	Remedial reading Method D
IQ over 130 Mean reading achievement gain	26.3	20.2	27.4	19.7
IQ 110–129 Mean reading achievement gain	21.0	16.6	18.3	15.9
IQ 90–110 Mean reading achievement gain	13.3	14.7	15.7	11.6
IQ 70–89 Mean reading achievement gain	7.1	11.3	12.6	6.7
Overall mean reading achievement gain	16.9	15.7	17.2	13.5

involves some mechanical system such as flipping a coin, drawing
names from a hat, or using a table of random numbers to assign
subjects to the necessary groups. This system, as contrasted with
matching systems, is just as easy to apply to ten groups as it is to
two. When random methods are used, the differences that occur
between groups so selected can be expected to follow the laws of
probability, which make it possible to estimate the magnitude of
Type S errors that might be expected. Random methods are also
based upon the assumption that, to a considerable degree, differences
between groups will "random out," that is tend to cancel each other
out. This assumption is dubious in the case of small groups where
large random errors might be expected to occur. In situations where
more than fifty cases are to be assigned to each group, however, this
assumption is reasonably valid, and, in situations where each group

will contain more than one hundred cases, random assignment will be preferable to matching for the great majority of research problems.

Steps

The steps involved in control-group design with random assignment are as follows:

1. Divide the sample into experimental and control groups on some random basis such as flipping a coin, using a table of random numbers, and so on.

2. Apply the experimental treatment to the experimental group. If appropriate, administer a placebo to the control group.

3. Test both groups on the dependent variable.

4. Compare the two groups with respect to their scores on the dependent variable. These comparisons most commonly employ analysis of variance or the t-test.

This method is preferable to matching when large groups are being used, because under these conditions the assumption that initial group differences will largely cancel out in the process of establishing random groups is reasonably valid. This method is also superior when a good matching variable is not available or when several experimental groups are necessary, which tends to make the matching procedure cumbersome and less effective in reducing sampling error.

Control-group design with random assignment and covariance analysis

This technique overcomes many of the difficulties of both matching and random assignment. The steps are as follows:

1. Subjects are randomly assigned to the necessary number of experimental and control groups.

2. Subjects are administered a pretest on a variable related to the dependent variable.

3. Experimental groups receive the experimental treatments; control group receives a placebo if appropriate.

4. All groups are measured on the dependent variable.

5. The final mean scores of each group on the dependent variable are adjusted for pretest differences (covariance analysis).

6. The adjusted final means are then compared to determine if differences are statistically significant.

The pretest variable in this case is comparable to the matching variable used in matched-group designs. In effect, the covariance analysis reduces the effects of initial group differences statistically by making compensating adjustments to the final means on the dependent variable. Matching reduces these same effects by mechanically assigning comparable subjects to each group. In using covariance analysis, no cases are lost and the laborious process of matching, which is often difficult to achieve under field conditions in education, is dispensed with.

Perhaps the most useful application for this design, however, is in studies where the research worker must deal with classroom groups that are already established. In this case, covariance analysis can reduce the effect of initial group differences that can only be achieved by the loss of large numbers of cases if matching is used. Use of established groups will still increase *Type G* errors and should only be used when random assignment is not possible.

It is possible, through multiple covariance analysis, to compensate for more than one pretest variable. The mathematics involved in this process is much more difficult than when a single pretest variable is used. Occasionally the research worker will design his study for covariance analysis but will find that his groups are very similar on their mean pretest scores. In this case, covariance analysis will not be necessary as the pretest means do not require adjustment, and analysis of variance may be used instead.

DESIGNS INVOLVING REPLICATION

In many educational studies, the basic design must be replicated a number of times in order to obtain a sufficient number of cases that have received each experimental treatment. In the hypothetical study of remedial reading methods diagramed in Table 7, for example, the small number of children usually taught in a remedial reading class (ten to fifteen) would not be sufficient to evaluate each method. If it were planned to divide pupils taught by each method into the indicated subgroups based upon IQ, still more cases would be needed in order that each IQ level under each method would include enough cases to reduce *Type S* errors to an acceptable level. It will be recalled that sampling errors are closely tied to sample size. If samples are too small, the experiment is often doomed to failure because the differences between the experimental treatments are almost sure to be nonsignificant due to large standard error. In experiments, such as illustrated in Table 7, an effort should be made to obtain at least thirty cases for each box. This would require a total of eight classes of fifteen students learning under each of the four methods or 480 subjects. If this number were not available, the needed number could be reduced by using three IQ classifications instead of four, accepting twenty as the minimum group size instead of thirty (realizing that this would increase sampling error), or eliminating one of the four treatments. Which combination of the aforementioned steps would be most advisable would depend upon the specific nature of the study. If large differences are anticipated between treatments, lowering the minimum acceptable number is most feasible. If subgroup differences are not expected to be significant or if one subgroup (such as subjects over 130 IQ) is disproportionately small, a reduction to three IQ categories is indicated. If one of the treatments seems considerably less likely to be productive than the other three, dropping this treatment may be advisable. Even with these reductions, however, it would be necessary to have more than one remedial reading class under each treatment so that, in effect, each experimental treatment must be replicated under the different conditions that prevail with different teachers in different classrooms. This is desirable, not only to increase the number of cases but to provide replications of the group design, thus reducing the likelihood of *Type G* errors. If four remedial reading classes with different teachers learn with Method A, there is much less chance that such group variables as teacher ability, favorable classroom, and so on will be different between treatments than if only one class receives each treatment. Replications of groups receiving the various experimental treatments tend to randomize *Type G* errors in the same manner that increasing the number of subjects tends to randomize *Type S* errors.

Counter-balanced designs

Counter-balanced designs are those in which the experimental variables are such that all of the different experimental treatments may be administered to the same subjects. The counter-balanced design usually is used when several experimental treatments are to be tested. In effect, it involves a series of repetitions of the parallel group design. In each replication, the experimental groups are shifted so that at the conclusion of the experiment, each group has been exposed to each experimental situation. The order of exposure to the experimental situation differs for each group although the sequence is usually the same. For example, let us examine an experiment designed to test the effects of alcohol and a tranquilizer upon verbal inhibitions.[5] The design of this experiment followed the pattern shown in Table 8. It will be noted that there are five different treatment levels. The first treatment (which was administered to Group A in replication 1) involves administration of a placebo followed by measurement on the dependent variable, in this case, a word association test including a number of socially taboo words. The second treatment involves consuming one ounce of alcohol thirty minutes prior to administration of the word association test. The other treatments involve consuming larger quantities of alcohol, the tranquilizer, and the two in combination.

TABLE 8

A SAMPLE COUNTER-BALANCED DESIGN

Replication	Placebo	1 Ounce Alcohol	2 Ounces Alcohol	T*	2 Ounces Alcohol + T
			TREATMENT		
1	Group A	Group B	C	D	E
2	E	A	B	C	D
3	D	E	A	B	C
4	C	D	E	A	B
5	B	C	D	E	A
	Overall mean	Overall mean	Overall mean	Overall mean	Overall mean

* T = tranquilizer.

Each row in Table 8 represents one replication. It will be noted that for each replication the groups are shifted so that Group A

[5] Ruth Southwick, *The Influence of Small Amounts of Alcohol upon Perceptual Inhibitions* (Unpublished Master's thesis, Utah State University, 1960).

first receives the placebo, then one ounce of alcohol, then two ounces of alcohol until, by the end of the fifth replication, each group has received each treatment. Each box would contain the mean score on the dependent variable for the group, treatment, and replication indicated after the testing was completed. The average mean for each column would give the performance of all five groups on the dependent variable under the treatment represented by the column. For example, in the third column each box would give the mean performance of a group after consumption of two ounces of alcohol, with the overall mean performance for this treatment given at the foot of the column.

Steps

The steps in carrying out the counter-balanced design are as follows:

1. Randomly assign available subjects to the number of experimental and control groups needed.

2. Expose each group to a different experimental treatment, including administration of a placebo to one group.

3. Measure all groups on the dependent variable.

4. Shift groups so that each group is exposed to a different experimental treatment.

5. Measure all groups on the dependent variable.

6. Repeat steps 4 and 5 until every group has been exposed to every treatment.

An experiment of this nature could be carried out using parallel group design in which case group members would be assigned by some random method from the available subjects, and the experiment would be complete after the first administration of the dependent variable (step 3). At the conclusion of the counter-balanced design experiment, each of the experimental groups will have been exposed to each of the experimental conditions, thus giving results comparable to several replications of parallel group design. The principal advantage of counter-balanced design over parallel-group design is that, when working with appropriate variables, it eliminates for all practical purposes the chances of *Type S* errors. This is because, upon completion of the experiment, each of the experimental situations has been administered to all subjects and therefore subject differences cannot exist excepting for changes that may have occurred in the subjects during the period required to carry out the experiment. The main limitation of counter-balanced design is that it may only be used when the experimental treatments are such that exposure to each treatment will have no effect on subsequent treatments. In the previous example, sufficient time was allowed between replications of the experiment so that the effects of the alcohol would have completely disappeared by the time the next replication was carried out. Unfortunately, there are relatively few educational experiments that may be adapted to counter-balanced design. Let us consider, for example, a study in which we are concerned with the efficiency of four different methods of learning poetry. One method might involve memorization of each single phrase followed by combining the phrases into lines, then into stanzas, then into verses, and finally into the entire poem. Another method might involve the line as the smallest unit to be memorized, the next method the stanza, the next method the verse, and finally the entire poem would be memorized as a single unit. This experiment could not be carried out using counter-balanced design because teaching the subjects one of these methods of memorization would almost certainly influence his behavior when the later memorization methods were taught.

FACTORIAL DESIGNS

The classic single variable experiment aims at holding all elements of the experimental situation constant except the experimental treatment. The problem of controlling variables in the experiment has made it difficult to set up such experiments in many educational areas without establishing a highly artificial situation. Correlational research permits measuring several variables and their interrelationships but does not permit the manipulation of variables, which is called for in an experiment. Factorial designs developed by R. A. Fisher permit manipulation of several variables in an experiment and appraisal not only of the effect of each variable but also of those effects due to interactions among the manipulated variables. Such designs are very well-suited to educational research. The statistical analysis needed to interpret the results of factorial studies, however, is complex and is usually not covered in courses in Educational Statistics. Factorial designs, therefore, are rarely used in educational research, and the discussion presented here is aimed at giving the student only enough insight so that he can read research that has employed these techniques.

It will be noted in Table 7 that when we divide the subjects of our remedial reading experiment into subgroups of different IQ levels we are, in effect, manipulating two variables (IQ and remedial reading method) instead of one. By comparing the mean achievement gain of each subgroup, we can estimate the effect of the different methods upon pupils in the same IQ ranges. For example, it may be seen in Table 7 that Method A has resulted in greater gains for the two top IQ groups, while Method C appears most effective for the two lower IQ groups. A comparison of the performance of the four subgroups in each method suggests that IQ has considerable influence upon learning under Method A, while having somewhat less effect on Method B. Thus, we have a situation in which the two variables, IQ and method, seem to interact. In other words, it appears that certain combinations of IQ and method produce gains that cannot be attributed entirely to these variables acting alone.

A comparison of the different mean scores in Table 7 using t-tests would give us considerable insight into the way that different methods operated at different IQ levels. Such an analysis, however, cannot tell us the effects of interaction between IQ and method, which might be very important. Thus, factorial design tells us much more about our data than we can obtain from simpler design and analysis procedures. The multi-dimensional analysis of variance techniques needed to analyze factorial designs are found in some of the references given at the end of this chapter. University courses dealing with this topic are usually offered by the departments of mathematics or statistics.

MISTAKES OFTEN MADE BY GRADUATE STUDENTS

1. Student permits differences to occur between the treatment of the experimental and control groups that lead to large *Type G* errors.

2. Uses too few cases, which leads to large sampling errors and insignificant results.

3. Fails to divide the main groups into subgroups in situations where subgroup analysis may produce worthwhile knowledge.

4. Matches his subjects in control group designs on variables that do not correlate sufficiently with the dependent variable.

5. Attempts to match on three or four variables, and in the process loses a large number of subjects who can't be matched.

6. Attempts to use counter-balanced design for problems in which each treatment tends to alter performance on subsequent treatments.

ANNOTATED REFERENCES

1. Cox, D. R. *Planning of Experiments.* New York: John Wiley & Sons, Inc., 1958. This text provides a comprehensive treatment of the principles of experimental design. Such basic designs as randomized block designs and Latin squares are treated in the first section of the book, while the latter section deals with factorial designs, incomplete block designs, fractional replication, and other advanced topics. Although the author has attempted to avoid statistical and mathematical technicalities, the average graduate student in education will find this text difficult. It is recommended for students with a strong statistical background who wish to learn more about some of the complex experimental designs. Many of these designs are appropriate for educational research but are not widely used at this time.

2. EDWARDS, A. L., and CRONBACK, L. J. "Experimental Design for Research in Psychotherapy," *Journal of Clinical Psychology,* 1952, 8, 51–59. Discusses the major problem of clinical research—because of the large number of variables that must be considered, single-variable designs are not adequate to deal with the clinical situation. Proposes the use of factorial design for complex research problems and illustrates how it may be used. Draws analogies between educational and clinical research, and contains many useful observations relative to statistical significance and research procedure. Especially useful to the student who is working with a problem that cannot be studied effectively using single variable designs.

3. LASAGNA, L.; LATIES, V. G.; and DOHAN, J. L. "Further Studies on the 'Pharmacology' of Placebo Administration," *Journal of Clinical Investigation,* 1958, 37, 533–37. This article presents data indicating that the subjective responses to placebos can mimic certain characteristics of "active" drugs such as peak effects, cumulative effects, and carry-over effects. Although this study is concerned mainly with medical research, the results have important implications for educational and psychological studies in which some form of placebo is called for. A number of implications for research are discussed. This article will give the student some appreciation of the subtle factors that often arise in research concerned with human subjects.

4. LINDQUIST, E. F. *Design and Analysis of Experiments in Psychology and Education.* Boston: Houghton Mifflin Co., 1953. This text aims at helping the student gain an understanding of the basic principles of experimental design and analysis in order to prepare him to devise designs needed for specific problems encountered in his research. Has a rather strong theoretical orientation, and places considerable emphasis on statistical treatment of research designs. Although an effort has been made to keep the content at a level that will make it understandable to the average graduate student, much of the analysis data will be difficult for students who do not have a strong background in statistics.

5. RAY, WILLIAM S. *An Introduction to Experimental Design.* New York: The Macmillan Co., 1960. Prepared primarily for psychologists, this text is a useful reference for research workers in education and the other behavioral sciences as well. Single-variable experiments are treated along with factorial designs. The first ten chapters provide the student with a somewhat more thorough treatment of elementary research design than is possible in a textbook in educational research methods, while the later chapters introduce the student to more advanced designs and require a higher level of statistical sophistication. This text is less technical than Cox (see Reference 1.) and provides the interested student with a foundation that will make transitions to the more advanced textbooks easier.

6. STANLEY, JULIAN C. "Controlled Experimentation in the Classroom," *Journal of Experimental Education,* 1957, 15, 195–201. This article provides an introduction to factorial design and presents two studies to illustrate how factorial design can be applied to educational experiments. The author then goes on to give some valuable suggestions on the design and conduct of educational experiments. Presented in nontechnical language and well worth reading for any graduate student in education.

7. WEITZ, JOSEPH. "Criteria for Criteria," *American Psychologist,* 1961, 16, 228–31. Discusses factors relating to the selection and use of criterion variables that may affect the research results. The author then analyzes data from a learning study using four different criteria and demonstrates that the results differ markedly depending upon the criterion. Implications of this difference are discussed.

CHAPTER 14

Action Research

INTRODUCTION

In recent years, some universities have accepted reports of action research projects in place of the scientific research thesis in partial fulfillment of the requirements for the Master's degree in education. Inasmuch as action research projects rarely meet the rigorous criteria for scientific research, this trend has been condemned by many research workers in education. It is the view of the author that action research has much to offer in the improvement of education and that an action research project may be more appropriate than a scientific research project for the Master's degree candidate who looks forward to a career of teaching in the public schools. In this chapter we will discuss the methods and goals of action research and draw some comparisons between "common sense" action research and scientific research as bases for solving educational problems.

WHAT IS ACTION RESEARCH

Action research emphasizes the involvement of teachers in problems important in their own classrooms and has as its primary goal the in-service training and development of the teacher rather than the acquisition of general knowledge in the science of education. It is research carried out by the person who feels a need for the results and is in a position to translate the results into action in the classroom. Although there are no necessary methodological differences between action research and other educational research, the emphasis of action research upon in-service training and solution of local classroom problems rather than acquisition of scientific knowledge has generally led to the use of less rigorous scientific controls in action research projects. A serious problem in education has been the lack of communication between educational research workers and teachers. This communication problem is caused partially by the tendency for research workers to prepare their findings in a form primarily for the consumption of other research workers and partially because very few teachers have the training required to understand and interpret research results in the light of their own classroom practices. Action research seems to offer some hope of closing the gap between the research worker and the teacher by helping the teacher take the first step towards developing an understanding of scientific methods and an appreciation for scientific evidence. Action research involves the application of scientific thinking to classroom problems and can provide a start toward making the teacher an educational scientist.

Perhaps the name "action research" is an unfortunate one because the procedures involved do not have the same goals as scientific research nor do they usually produce scientific knowledge. Largely due to this name, many educational research workers have attacked action research because it is not research according to the scientist's definition of the word. It appears to the author that action research should be strongly encouraged by educational scientists because this approach, though far short of scientific research method, provides the teacher with a sounder basis for solving his immediate problems than he has ordinarily used in the past. Action research with all of its limitations is still vastly superior as a problem-solving technique to the subjective methods and appeals to personal experience that are usually employed by teachers. The usual approach to a problem in the public schools is to discuss the problem in a faculty meeting. A committee is then appointed and this committee discusses the problem further, and makes recommendations to the faculty. No reference is made to research in the problem area, no effort is made to define the problem in specific terms, no procedure is set up to carry out the recommendations, and no measures are applied to evaluate their effect. Although many schools are more objective, the aforementioned description fits the problem-solving efforts of a great many. In view of the widespread use of subjective approaches to educational problems, there is much to be said for the view expressed by Bernard Corman that: "Any movement which will encourage a turn toward problem solving in teacher education needs to be nourished." [1]

[1] Bernard R. Corman, "Action Research: A Teaching or a Research Method?" *Review of Educational Research*, XXVII (1957), 545.

STEPS IN ACTION RESEARCH

Action research programs are usually initiated by administrative personnel in the school district in an attempt to improve the quality of teaching through the in-service training gained by the teacher in the process of carrying out an action research project. The first step in setting up the action research project is for the teacher or group of teachers to identify a problem that they perceive to be critical in their everyday teaching activity. The most widespread application of the action research approach has been in the field of curriculum development. Action research, however, has not been limited to curriculum studies. Work has been reported in many other educational areas such as children's social values, school administration, and others.[2] Actually, the action research approach can be applied to any educational problem.

Teachers often resist the findings of conventional research because these findings, to a degree, constitute a threat to the teacher. The teacher who has been using a particular method or set of procedures for many years and is complacent and satisfied with what he is doing is reluctant to accept research findings that suggest that he should make changes. Teachers are often strongly resistant to change, and this resistance is a contributing factor in the lag we find in education between research knowledge and field application. In the more mature sciences, the research worker and the practitioner who uses research findings have a common foundation of scientific training. Although amount and emphasis of training differ, both are oriented toward science as a method of solving problems. In contrast, the teacher usually receives little or no training in education as a science, does not look to science as a means of solving educational problems, and does not identify himself with the educational scientist. This lack of identification intensifies the threat of research to the teacher, and many teachers use such defenses as ridiculing research and refusing to admit that research findings have any application to teaching.

In selecting a problem for action research, the teacher often perceives the same threat. The teacher is asked to identify problems

[2] See the selected references at the end of this chapter for reports on action research studies in these areas.

causing him concern in his day-to-day work. Admitting that such problems exist is difficult for the insecure individual because he prefers to delude himself that there is little that can be done to improve the methods he is already using. Thus, unless the person coordinating the action research activities is successful in reducing the anxieties of the teachers involved, the action research topic chosen will often be unrelated to the teachers' basic problems, or the teacher will avoid the threatening situation by working on some trivial problem. A major difficulty of using the team approach in action research is for the team to identify an action research problem that all members consider critical and important in their own classrooms.

After a general problem has been identified by the teacher or teacher-group, the next step is a review of the literature. The type of exhaustive review of primary sources required in more formal educational research usually is not practical for the teacher. Most teachers lack the training necessary to understand and evaluate technical research articles. Furthermore, schools that are not close to a university do not have access to the journals required to carry out an exhaustive review of primary sources. Such a review, even if possible, would, in many cases tend to kill any enthusiasm the teacher might have for attacking his action research problem. Some review of the literature, however, is essential and should usually include a careful study of the best secondary source material in the area, which may be located by checking the *Encyclopedia of Educational Research, Review of Educational Research,* and current textbooks. One advantage of a team approach to action research is that the labor of conducting the review of the literature can be divided among members of the team, thus permitting this step to be carried out much more promptly.

The next step in the action research project calls for the teacher to redefine his general problem as established in step 1 (page 315) into specific testable hypotheses. The consultant or director of the action research program should attempt to guide the teacher to a point where his hypotheses are testable, specific, state a definite relationship, and are not in conflict with previous knowledge gained in the review of the literature. These requirements, it may be seen, are the same as those stated earlier for more formal educational research. Although it often requires considerable effort to guide the teacher to a point where he can establish hypotheses meeting the above criteria, such effort is essential to a worthwhile study. Fuzzy thinking in the establishment of hypotheses will almost certainly lead to frustration in later phases of the research and may well cause the teacher to develop negative attitudes toward research rather than help him take the first step toward becoming an educational scientist. A consultant with extensive training in educational research is almost essential at this point. If the project is to be carried out by a group of teachers, the consultant should carry out a series of discussions aimed at helping the group develop hypotheses. Several objectives can be attained in these meetings that will greatly improve the chances of a successful action research experience. First, teachers can be given experience in nailing down the problem. Examples of fuzzy thinking can be explored and clarified. Some progress can be made toward thinking objectively and in specific terms. Second, teachers can be helped to see the importance of establishing specific hypotheses as guideposts to their research. Third, the relationship between the hypotheses, the measures to be employed, and the method of analysis can be explored in order to give the participating teachers an overall appreciation of the research approach to problem solving. The consultant should stay in the background of these discussions but should raise critical points that will help the group gain the aforementioned insights inductively. A successful experience in the teacher's first contact with action research is extremely important as it will probably determine whether or not he will continue to use this more objective and systematic approach for the solution of future classroom problems that he will encounter.

The next step in the action research process is to set up the research procedures. Action research, being aimed at the specific problem of the teacher, usually uses the teacher's students as subjects for the research. This, of course, means that the usual sampling requirements of scientific research are almost never met in such projects. In action research projects carried out in a single classroom, the lack of a control group, the possible sampling errors, the small number of cases, and the presence of uncontrolled variables such as teacher attitude and ability combine to make the results of limited value from a scientific point of view. Such results, however, can still have meaning for the teacher carrying out the project and can lead to better teaching. If the action research is carried out by a team, however, so that the new methods or materials involved are tried in a number of different classrooms, the results probably will be sufficiently generalizable for use throughout the school district and may produce important implications that can later be tested more rigorously through scientific research.

Because action research has as its primary goal the in-service training of the teacher, it is desirable to call in a consultant to help teachers gain the necessary insights needed to plan, conduct, and evaluate their projects. Teachers usually need such help in selecting or developing measuring instruments to use in action research projects. Most teachers have had some elementary training in educational measurement, and if they have developed interest in their action research projects, they have the necessary motivation to profit from the in-service instruction they need for the further development of their projects. The teacher who decides to develop his own measuring instruments for an action research project will usually learn more in this process than he is likely to gain in a number of formal courses in educational measurement. Most of the larger school districts have someone on their staff, such as the school psychologist, who can help teachers in this phase of their project. If the school district does not have a qualified consultant in this field, one can generally be obtained from a college or university. Inasmuch as the results of action research are not usually generalizable as scientific knowledge, the procedure need not involve a rigorous research design and the design originally developed need not be adhered to. Frequently in the process of carrying out the action research, the teacher gains new insights into the project that may lead to changes in procedure that offer a better possibility of solving the teacher's problem. In scientific research, such insights would be applied to later research projects, but in action research, the procedure is usually changed while the project is in progress. In the scientific research situation, the research worker is usually outside the situation he is studying. He strives to be an objective and unbiased observer. In contrast, the action research worker is a participating part of the situation. His enthusiasm and ego-involvement in the situation, which lead to biasing and reducing the generalizability of his research findings, are considered by many to be desirable in action research as they increase the likelihood that the teacher is learning better ways of solving at least his own problems.

TABLE 9

DIFFERENCES AMONG FORMAL EDUCATIONAL RESEARCH, ACTION RESEARCH, AND THE CASUAL APPROACH TO PROBLEM SOLVING IN EDUCATION

AREA	FORMAL EDUCATIONAL RESEARCH	ACTION RESEARCH	CASUAL OR "COMMON SENSE" APPROACH
1. Training required	Extensive training in measurement, statistics, and research methods is needed. Much of the scientific research done in education is weak because of deficiencies of the researchers in these areas.	Only a limited training in statistics and research methods is needed because rigorous design and analysis are not usually necessary. More training in educational measurement is needed than most teachers possess. Even if teacher's research skills are low, good action research can be carried out with the aid of a consultant.	No training is needed. This is the same method used since prehistoric times to achieve faulty solutions to ill defined problems.
2. Goals	To obtain knowledge that will be generalizable to a broad population and to develop and test educational theories.	To obtain knowledge that can be applied directly to the local classroom situation, and to give the participating teachers in-service training.	To make changes in the current procedure that appear likely to improve the situation.

TABLE 9 (Continued)

DIFFERENCES AMONG FORMAL EDUCATIONAL RESEARCH, ACTION RESEARCH, AND THE CASUAL APPROACH TO PROBLEM SOLVING IN EDUCATION

AREA	FORMAL EDUCATIONAL RESEARCH	ACTION RESEARCH	CASUAL OR "COMMON SENSE" APPROACH
3. Locating the research problem	Problems identified by a wide range of methods. Research worker must understand the problem, but is usually not directly involved in it.	Problems identified in the school situation that are causing the research worker trouble or are interfering with the efficiency of his teaching.	Problems identified in same manner as action research.
4. Hypotheses	Highly specific hypotheses are developed that employ operational definitions and are testable.	A specific statement of the problem usually serves as the hypothesis. Ideally, action research hypotheses should approach rigor of formal research.	Specific hypotheses not established. Participants rarely progress beyond a fuzzy and ill-defined concept concerning the nature of the problem.
5. Review of the literature	An extensive review of primary source material is usually carried out, giving the research worker a thorough understanding of the current state of knowledge in the research area. This enables him to build upon the knowledge accumulated by others.	A review of available secondary sources gives the teacher a general understanding of the area to be studied. Exhaustive review of primary sources is almost never done.	Usually no review of the literature is carried out, although one or two secondary sources may be checked.

TABLE 9 (Continued)

DIFFERENCES AMONG FORMAL EDUCATIONAL RESEARCH, ACTION RESEARCH, AND THE CASUAL
APPROACH TO PROBLEM SOLVING IN EDUCATION

AREA	FORMAL EDUCATIONAL RESEARCH	ACTION RESEARCH	CASUAL OR "COMMON SENSE" APPROACH
6. Sampling	Research worker attempts to obtain a random or otherwise unbiased sample of the population being studied, but is usually not completely successful.	Pupils available in the class of the teacher or teachers doing the research are used as subjects.	Some casual observation of pupil behavior may be made by the teacher after the change decided upon has been in effect for a while.
7. Experimental design	Design is carefully planned in detail prior to start of the study and adhered to as closely as possible. Major attention is given to maintaining comparable conditions and reducing error and bias. Control of extraneous variables is important.	Procedures are planned in general terms prior to start of study. Changes are made during the study if they seem likely to improve the teaching situation. Little attention is paid to control of the experimental conditions or reduction of error. Because participating teachers are ego-involved in the research situation, bias is usually present.	If classroom testing of the decision is attempted, procedures are planned only in the most general terms. No attempt is made to establish common definitions or procedures among participating teachers.

TABLE 9 (Continued)

DIFFERENCES AMONG FORMAL EDUCATIONAL RESEARCH, ACTION RESEARCH, AND THE CASUAL
APPROACH TO PROBLEM SOLVING IN EDUCATION

AREA	FORMAL EDUCATIONAL RESEARCH	ACTION RESEARCH	CASUAL OR "COMMON SENSE" APPROACH
8. Measurement	An effort is made to obtain the most valid measures available. A thorough evaluation of available measures and a trial of these measures usually precedes their use in the research.	Less rigorous evaluation of measures than in scientific research. Participants often lack training in the use and evaluation of educational measures, but can do a satisfactory job with help of a consultant.	Usually no evaluation is made except for the casual observations of the teachers participating. The teacher's opinion as to whether the new procedure is an improvement or not depends almost entirely on whether the teacher approves of the change.
9. Analysis of data	Complex analysis often called for. Inasmuch as generalizability of results is a goal, statistical significance is usually emphasized.	Simple analysis procedures usually are sufficient. Practical significance rather than statistical significance is emphasized. Subjective opinion of participating teachers is often weighted heavily.	Subjective opinion of the participants is usually the only procedure used. No attempt made at objective analysis.
10. Application of results	Results are generalizable, but many useful findings are not applied in educational practice. Differences in training and experience between research workers and teachers generate a serious communication problem.	Findings are applied immediately to the classes of participating teachers and often lead to permanent improvement. Application of results beyond the participating teachers is usually slight.	Decisions reached are applied immediately in classes of participating teachers. Even if the decision leads to improvement, it is often changed later because no evidence is available to support its continuance. This approach leads to educational fads and "change for the sake of change."

The final step in the action research project involves data analysis. Action research projects rarely call for complex or sophisticated analysis procedures. Such simple comparisons as mean-achievement gains in the class prior to the implementation of the action research project and after completion of the project are often used. In addition to whatever objective data are available for analysis, the teacher should be encouraged to make a subjective analysis of the action research situation. The thinking-through process and introspection involved in such an analysis can help the teacher perceive what he has learned through his project and better apply the findings to his future teaching. Despite the lack of scientific rigor, the findings of the action research project generally should be shared with other teachers in the district who might be encountering the same problems. Some provision by the school district for sharing this knowledge not only leads to improved teaching procedures but will also afford recognition to the teacher who carried out the project.

Table 9 summarizes some of the differences that are usually found among formal educational research, action research, and the "common-sense" approach to problem solving. These differences, of course, are not always found when comparing the different approaches, but most would be found when typical examples of the three methods were compared.

MISTAKES OFTEN MADE IN ACTION RESEARCH

1. The teacher selects trivial problems to be attacked through action research.

2. The project is started before the teachers involved have thought through and specifically defined their problem.

3. The teacher fails to study and evaluate important secondary sources pertinent to the problem.

4. The teacher fails to obtain the assistance of a consultant or seeks assistance after irreparable blunders have already been made in the conduct of the project.

ANNOTATED REFERENCES

1. BARNES, JOHN B. *Educational Research for Classroom Teachers*. New York: G. P. Putnam's Sons, 1960. Contains case studies that demonstrate

how teachers can use an objective approach to attack problems in their classrooms. The book recognizes the limitations of the average teacher's training in statistics and research design and presents information in a clear and easily understood fashion.

2. COREY, STEPHEN M. *Action Research to Improve School Practices.* New York: Bureau of Publications, Teachers College, Columbia University, 1953. Discusses techniques for carrying out action research and compares action research with traditional educational research and the "common sense" approach to educational problems. A well-written book that will be very helpful to the student who wishes to carry out an action research project.

3. ———. "Curriculum Development through Action Research," *Educational Leadership.* 1959, 7, 147–53. Discusses the nature and goals of action research as contrasted with "fundamental research." Reviews the essential elements of the action research design with emphasis upon formulating hypotheses. An informative article by one of the principal advocates of action research.

4. CORMAN, BERNARD R. "Action Research: A Teaching or a Research Method?," *Review of Educational Research,* 1957, 27, 544–47. A brief review questioning the role of action research. An excellent bibliography is given, which the student may refer to if he is interested in specific aspects of action research.

5. HODGKINSON, HAROLD L. "Action Research—A Critique," *The Journal of Educational Sociology,* 1957, 31, 137–53. Examines the cases for and against action research. Raises a number of serious theoretical and methodological questions about action research. This article should be carefully studied and the arguments compared with those of Corey to provide the student with a well-rounded picture of the uses and limitations of action research. This article contains an excellent bibliography.

6. SHUMSKY, ABRAHAM. *The Action Research Way of Learning.* New York: Bureau of Publications, Teachers College, Columbia University, 1958. A thoughtful discussion of action research, how it is planned and carried out, and how it can contribute to the education and development of teachers. Particularly valuable is the insight into the teacher's attitudes about research and the discussion of the many subtle factors that can cause the failure of an action research program.

7. The following are examples of action research projects that the student may wish to examine to get better insight into the applications of this technique:

   (a) FOSHAY, ARTHUR W., *et al. Children's Social Values—An Action Research Study.* New York: Teacher's College, Columbia University, 1954.

   (b) HUGHES, MARIE M., *et al.* "Iron County Teachers Study Their Problems Scientifically," *Educational Leadership,* 1955, 12, 489–95.

   (c) LURRY, LUCILE L. "Core-Program Development through Action Research," *School Review,* 1955, 63, 469–76.

   (d) PURDY, RALPH D. "Action Research in County School Administration," *High School Journal,* 1954, 38, 47–54.

   (e) SMITH, MARY N. "We Improved Instruction by Means of Action Research," *Journal of the National Education Association,* 1955, 44, 229–30.

CHAPTER 15

Critical Evaluation of Research

INTRODUCTION

The research worker must build his research upon the knowledge accumulated by previous researchers, and a major goal of the review of the literature is to establish this foundation. Soon after starting his first review of the literature, however, the graduate student will discover that instead of a solid foundation, the previous research appears to provide a foundation of shifting sands. The findings of similar studies will often be contradictory, leaving the student at a loss to decide which, if either, to accept. This problem must usually be resolved by the research worker through a critical evaluation of the research. Every study reviewed that is pertinent to his problem should be critically evaluated in order that the research worker may determine the confidence with which the findings may be accepted and to resolve apparent conflicts in the results of different studies. Much of the educational research reviewed will have such serious flaws and biases that the results must be discounted entirely. Other studies, although basically sound, may have a single error in design or execution that makes a great difference in interpreting the results. Although the ability to review the work of others critically is essential to the research worker, it is equally important to the teacher or administrator who seeks solutions to his field problems by studying the available research data. The uncritical acceptance of research results by the practitioner can lead to unsound decisions and unjustified changes in educational procedures.

Mistakes, oversights, and biases may occur at any stage of the research process from the initial steps taken in problem definition to the final phases of statistical analysis. The research worker's effectiveness in detecting these errors is dependent for the most part upon two factors: his knowledge and understanding of the total research process in education, and his knowledge in the specific field of his review. Because of the importance of a general background in research techniques, this chapter has been placed near the end of the book. The student may profitably apply most of what he has already learned to the important task of critical evaluation. This chapter emphasizes those aspects of the previous chapters that are especially pertinent to critical analysis of research and brings together the pertinent facts so that the student will be able to refer to a single chapter for guidance when he starts his critical analysis of the research covered in his review of the literature. As he gains more knowledge and experience, his ability to carry out his important task will steadily increase. Let us now review some of the things the student must watch for in critically evaluating a research report.

FACTORS TO CONSIDER IN EVALUATING RESEARCH
Deliberate bias or distortion

The goal of research must be the discovery of scientific truth. Unfortunately, many persons who carry out educational research are more interested in obtaining evidence to support a particular viewpoint than in the discovery of truth. Whenever the researcher has reasons for wanting his research to support a particular viewpoint, the likelihood of bias is greatly increased. Occasionally, the individual will be so emotionally involved with his topic that he deliberately slants his findings or even structures his design to produce a predetermined result. Such cases of deliberate bias are usually easy to detect because the same emotional involvement that motivates the individual to bias his work is usually reflected in his research report. Studies that are introduced with the phrase "This study was conducted to prove . . ." must be considered suspect. The scientist does not carry out his work to prove a point but to get an answer. The use of emotionally charged words or intemperate language are the most obvious indicators of a biased viewpoint. For example, in reviewing the literature concerned with ability grouping the author found several articles that referred to ability grouping as "segregation." Inasmuch as this word has strong negative emotional associations for most of us, its use in this context suggests bias. One is not surprised to find that an article entitled "Must We Segregate?" is strongly biased against ability grouping.[1]

Many persons who are strongly involved emotionally with the topic of their research will not deliberately bias their research.

[1] C. A. Tonsor, "Must We Segregate?" *National Association of Secondary School Principals' Bulletin,* XXXVII (1953), 75–77.

Nevertheless, a strong likelihood of bias exists because the person may unconsciously slant his work in a hundred different ways. He may make certain systematic "errors" in sampling, in selecting measures, in scoring the responses of his subjects, and in analyzing and interpreting his results, which tend to favor the outcome he wants. Objectivity is always difficult to attain in research in the behavioral sciences and is probably impossible when the researcher is emotionally involved with his topic. Thus, the researcher should avoid working in such areas whenever possible.

If his position is such that he must do research in an area where he is involved emotionally, he should have his design checked by several other researchers for omissions or unconscious biases. The author was once directed to conduct a study comparing the effectiveness of air force second lieutenants who had received commissions through the U.S.A.F. Officer Candidate School (O.C.S.) with those who had received commissions through the R.O.T.C. Realizing some bias in favor of the O.C.S. graduate, he had the design carefully checked by other psychologists. One phase of the experiment called for a comparative rating of the effectiveness of officers from the two groups in drilling a company of basic trainees. Officers to be evaluated were to be instructed to report to the drill field in khaki uniform. Raters were not to be told the source of commission of officers being rated. One psychologist, upon reviewing these plans, pointed out that the officers who had graduated from O.C.S. would be immediately recognized as they were required to have their khaki shirts tailored to a close fit, while the R.O.T.C. Officers wore loose-fitting shirts, which they purchased from the post exchange. Although trying, at least on the conscious level, to avoid bias in this research, the author had "forgotten" this difference in uniforms when designing the research. This clue to source of commission would have permitted the raters to have reflected their biases in their ratings. In summary, the student should look for the following clues when attempting to locate possible biases of the research worker in a research report:

1. Does the phraseology used suggest that the research worker is inclined to favor one side of the question?

2. Is emotional or intemperate language of either a favorable or unfavorable nature employed?

3. Is the person in a position or does he belong to a group (racial,

vocational, religious, political, ethnic, and so on) that would make him likely to be predisposed in a given direction about the subject of his research?

Sampling bias

All of the points that must be remembered in setting up the procedures for selecting a sample for your own research should be applied to evaluating the sampling techniques used by other researchers. Sampling bias in one form or another probably weakens more educational studies than any other factor. Sampling techniques were introduced in Chapter 8. Let us review some of the sampling errors that should be looked for in evaluating the research of others.

1. *Did the study use volunteers?* Volunteer groups are rarely representative, differing at least in motivation level from nonvolunteers. Motivation is, of course, an extremely important variable in most educational research. A basic weakness of most questionnaire studies is that the persons responding are essentially "volunteers" who may differ greatly from the nonresponding subjects.

2. *Have subjects been lost?* Studies reporting large losses of subjects in one or more of the groups involved can usually be expected to have sampling bias. The reason for this bias is that subjects are not lost on a random basis. The subjects lost will generally be different from the ones who remain with the study until its completion. The nature and magnitude of these differences, and therefore their effect upon the research results, are difficult to estimate.

3. *In an effort to get subjects who differ in the variable being studied, have groups been selected who also differ in other important respects?* Causal-comparative studies often suffer from this form of sampling bias. Some of the early studies of relationships between cigarette smoking and lung cancer illustrate such bias. The "heavy-smoker" sample was obtained in large cities while the "nonsmoker" sample came from rural areas. These two groups were vastly different in many factors other than smoking such as living habits, amount of impurities in the air breathed, and pressures of daily life. With sampling biases of this magnitude, it would be difficult for such studies to link lung cancer to smoking with any degree of confidence.

4. *Are subjects extremely nonrepresentative of the population?* Few educational studies are able to employ truly random or representative samples of national populations. Yet, unless samples are extremely biased, the results often have important implications for the large population. For example, although no one would assert that a sample of poor readers taken from the different school districts in Los Angeles County were representative of the nation as a whole, a study involving this sample may well have national implications. This is because most American public schools have much in common, and pupils in one large heterogeneous area such as Los Angeles County who are having reading problems are probably quite similar to pupils in other areas of the country. As the sample becomes less heterogeneous and less representative, however, the general significance of the findings diminish. Subjects from a single district may lead to a less useful study because of unique district policies concerning reading instruction. On the other hand, such a study using subjects from an obviously nontypical school district, such as one with a large Latin-American population, may have no general implications because of the nonrepresentative nature of the group and the relationship between bilingualism and reading difficulties. Similarly, a study of attitudes toward Negroes, using a sample from New Orleans, or a study of attitudes toward smoking, using a sample from Salt Lake City, would produce little information of general significance, although such studies might throw much light on the situation in the area sampled.

In some studies a great deal more care is devoted to obtaining a representative experimental group than a representative control group. This difference probably stems from the erroneous notion of inexperienced researchers that the experimental group is far more important and that any subjects will serve for the control group. Because the performance of the experimental group must be weighed against the control group, a biased control group can obviously lead to erroneous results. Thus, careless selection of the control group should be watched for. In reviewing the research of others, it must be remembered that nonrepresentative samples do not produce data of general significance and often yield results that are misleading and can lead to serious blunders if applied to the general population. If such a study is read, the findings must be interpreted with the sampling bias in mind.

Have important variables been overlooked?

Many studies are found in education that have overlooked or failed to control important variables. Such studies usually produce misleading results because the influence of the uncontrolled variable upon the dependent variable cannot be assessed. For example, many of the early studies comparing the effectiveness of televised instruction with conventional classroom instruction failed to control teaching ability. The usual procedure was to select the best teacher available and give this person the full day to prepare his TV lesson. Progress of TV pupils was then compared with progress of pupils in conventional classrooms having average teachers who taught the usual four to six classes daily. The results, which were loudly hailed as proof that television had some intrinsic merit that greatly increased learning, were in fact nothing more than a demonstration that better teachers who have more preparation time do a better job. Better-controlled studies concerned with TV instruction showed little or no difference as compared with conventional classroom instruction.

Inasmuch as each of us brings a different background of perception and experience to focus upon a given problem, it is not surprising that one person may overlook the importance of a variable that is immediately apparent to another. The best way to avoid overlooking important variables in your own research is to have your design studied and criticised by several other researchers before starting to collect data. The previous research exposes the research worker to a number of different viewpoints about his research area and reduces his chances of overlooking or failing to control an important variable. Many such oversights can be traced to a careless and inadequate review of the literature.

Critical evaluation of measurement techniques

Many of the weaknesses and limitations of educational research can be attributed to the inadequacies of our measures. Many of the tools and techniques of educational measurement are crude and of doubtful validity. We have discussed the procedures for evaluating measurement tools in Chapter 5. Let us review these and related concepts with special attention to applying these methods to the critical evaluation of research.

A thorough check of all measuring instruments and techniques reported in all studies reviewed would be a very time-consuming task, and it is not recommended for the student doing his first review of the literature. The student should make such a check, however, of the measures used in any studies that are of major importance in his review. Any study that has yielded findings that make an important contribution to the area of the review or have an important bearing on the researcher's own design should be thoroughly checked. If standard measures are cited with which the student is not familiar, he should study a specimen set, consult the *Mental Measurements Yearbook,* and check other sources of information discussed in Chapter 5. If the measures used are new or have been developed for the research being evaluated, the student should obtain a copy and weigh the measure carefully against his knowledge of test development techniques and the theoretical constructs upon which the measure is based. The findings of research that the student reads can only be evaluated after the measurement tools that produced these findings have been carefully appraised, and the probable effects or flaws in these instruments have been considered.

Let us briefly summarize some of the questions that the student should ask when evaluating the measurement tools employed in research closely pertinent to his own topic.

1. *What reliability data are available?* The type of reliability calculated and the reliability coefficient should both be checked. Tests of very low reliability often lead to negative results even though the use of more reliable instruments would have given positive results. Thus, the student should consider carefully the possible effects of low reliability upon the reported results of studies he evaluates and should not reject a promising hypothesis from his own study because of negative findings based on small samples of unreliable measures.

2. *What validity evidence is available?* As discussed in Chapter 4, there are four important types of validity. The validity evidence should be studied carefully because interpretation of the research results hinges on the validity of the measures upon which these results are based. The absence of extensive validity data in a new measure does not mean the measure lacks validity but definitely limits the interpretations that can be made. Many inexperienced

research workers accept standardized educational measures at face value and assume that these measures are valid although little evidence is put forth by the test publisher to support this assumption. It is generally safer in the case of measures of dubious validity to consider the results reported to be tentative at best.

3. *Is the measure appropriate for the sample?* In evaluating the research of others, it should be remembered that even a well-standardized and generally accepted measure will have little value if applied to an inappropriate sample. A typical mistake made by inexperienced researchers is to use a measure that is more appropriate for some subsamples of the research group than others, therefore biasing results in favor of the subsamples whose background gives them an advantage on the measure. Occasionally, tests are employed that are either too easy or too difficult for the majority of the sample measured. For example, a study of achievement of children at different ability levels will have little meaning if the measures used have too low a ceiling, thus limiting the level of achievement that a superior student can display.

4. *Are test norms appropriate?* Many educational research projects compare the performance of the research sample with normative data that has been provided with the measure. If normative data are to be used, the comparability between the research group and the test norm group should be checked. Some tests, although generally applicable to the sample tested, have single items that are invalid. Some of the older intelligence tests, for example, have drawings of such objects as automobiles, airplanes, and telephones that are so different in appearance from the form familiar to today's children that the test item so illustrated has lost much of its validity. Such errors, although not immediately apparent to most adults, have a significant influence on test scores.

Many more subtle forms of measurement bias may also make significant differences in research findings. For example, the author recently encountered a questionnaire being used in an educational followup study in which the respondent was to rate various aspects of a school he had attended using five quality levels. The quality levels provided were "excellent," "superior," "very good," "average," and "below average." It will be noted that, on this scale, average is not located in the middle of the alternate choices. When asked why the choices were arranged in this way, the research worker stated that he had observed in previous questionnaires that more responses occur above the average line of the scale and he had, therefore, provided an extra classification on the above average side. He was surprised to find that the ratings he had obtained in this followup study were somewhat higher than those obtained in previous studies of the same school. When using the above quality levels, the mean response fell between the "superior" and "very good" categories as compared with a mean response between "average" and "very good" in previous studies. This suggested a higher evaluation of the course of study being followed up. Actually, however, the errors of leniency and central tendency (see Chapter 11) would lead most respondents to rate a course of study average or slightly above average if they had no strong feelings about it one way or the other. Because most people consider the average rating to be the one that falls in the middle, when the research worker changed the names of his categories, the respondents continued to check the middle category or the one adjacent to and higher than the middle. Thus, in terms of the mean position of the responses on a five-point scale, no change occurred. But in terms of the adjectives employed, there was an apparent improvement in the respondent's evaluation of the school. Use of unbalanced response choices in which more opportunities are available for a favorable response than for an unfavorable response will tend to yield responses with a favorable bias. The danger of such biases is well known to experienced measurement specialists and, therefore, errors of the sort described above are more likely to be found in measures developed specifically for the research project by an inexperienced researcher. If the use of such measures is reported in research projects pertinent to the student's field of interest, he should request copies in order that he may study them for biases of the sort previously described.

Observer bias

Human beings have a disturbing tendency to see what they want to see, hear what they want to hear, and remember what they want to remember. Observer bias has been recognized as a problem by workers in the physical sciences for centuries, and techniques to control such bias are routinely included in physical science experiments. Workers in the behavioral sciences have not only attempted to control observer errors but have studied these biases and found them to be much more subtle and complex than physical scientists had imagined.

Rostand [2] tells us a remarkable but true story that illustrates the dangers of observer bias, even in scientific areas such as physics that deal with phenomena that are much simpler, more concrete, and more adaptable to measurement than are the elusive substances of the behavioral sciences. This example deals with the N ray, which was discovered by a distinguished French physicist, René Blondlot, while investigating X rays that had been discovered a short time earlier by Röntgen. After discovering the N ray, Blondlot went on to study its characteristics. He found the ray increased the brightness of any luminous object. A Nernst filament was found to be a rich source of N rays and produced a radiation so intense that Blondlot doubted that anyone with eyes could fail to see it. In fact, of the many persons who were permitted to observe these rays, Blondlot reports only three or four who failed to see them. As his experiments continued, Blondlot discovered that the sun was a source of N rays. He learned that N rays could be stored in certain substances such as quartz and later reemitted. Further experiments revealed that external stresses caused certain substances to emit N rays. Finally, Blondlot set up a series of careful experiments using three independent measures that resulted in measuring the wavelength of the N ray. The results of measurements using the three different approaches were highly consistent. By February, 1904, successful photographs had been taken that showed the effect of N rays on an electric spark. Upon this discovery, Bordier, lecturer at Lyons Medical School, rebuked the few doubters who had not been able to see the N ray by pointing out:

'Such observers have only themselves to blame; no doubt they used faulty techniques or else the source of radiation was impaired; in any case, the existence of N-rays will never again be put in doubt, particularly now that their action has been recorded *photographically*, i.e. by a purely objective method.' [3]

Other researchers now began to report extensive findings from their experiments on the N ray. The experiments of one scientist revealed

[2] Jean Rostand, *Error and Deception in Science* (New York: Basic Books, 1960). Reprinted by permission of Basic Books, Inc.

[3] *Ibid.*, p. 18. Reprinted by permission of Basic Books, Inc.

that sound vibrations gave rise to N rays; another found N rays emitted from a magnetic field, another from liquefied gasses, and so on.

Charpentier, Professor of Biophysics at Nancy, discovered that N rays were liberated from the muscles and nerves of living animals and concluded that these rays might play a fundamental role in biology. Many further experiments were stimulated by this discovery. Because N rays were emitted from nerves, studies of the anatomy of the nervous system became possible and were started. This technique, of course, had very important implications for medical science. For example, research workers soon discovered that changes in N radiation occurred as a consequence of certain diseases of the nervous system.

In 1904, less than two years after Blondlot had reported his original work, an imposing body of knowledge had been amassed concerning the N ray. Yet, we hear nothing about N rays today. The fact is that *the N ray does not and never did exist,* and within a few short months after these later discoveries, the entire edifice erected by Blondlot and his colleagues had tumbled down.

Doubting voices had been raised from the very beginning of Blondlot's discovery and some specialist objections had never been silenced effectively. Still, no amount of doubting or criticism had been able to halt the triumphant progress of the new science. All the world had clearly observed a phenomenon that had never existed. Then, almost over-night, the hypnotic spell was broken.

The Nancy group and some of its faithful managed to put up some slight resistance, but the whole business was dropped and buried once and for all. N-rays, N_1-rays, and physiological radiations would never again grace the pages of scientific journals, in which they had cut so marvellous a figure. . . .

The most astonishing facet of the episode is the extra-ordinarily great number of people who were taken in. These people were not pseudo-scientists, charlatans, dreamers, or mystifiers; far from it, they were true men of science, disinterested, honourable, used to laboratory procedure, people with level heads and sound common sense. This is borne out by their subsequent achievements as Professors, Consultants and Lecturers. Jean Becquerel, Gilbert Ballet, Andre Broca, Zimmern, Bordier—all of them have made their contribution to science.

No less extraordinary is the *degree of consistency, and of apparent logic that pervaded the whole of this collective delusion;* all the results were consistent, and agreed within fairly narrow limits. . . .

While we have no evidence that flattery or deception was at the roots of the discovery of N-rays, we may take it that the urge to make new discoveries, so powerful in all men of science, played a considerable role from the very start. Coupled with this urge were *preconceived ideas, and auto-suggestion* together with the desire to break new ground.

The remarkable history of N-rays is full of morals both for the individual, and also for the social, psychologist.[4]

Although observations are sometimes deliberately biased by the researcher with an ax to grind, the more serious danger is from biases of which the researcher is unaware such as those that occurred in research on the N ray. These undeliberate and unconscious observer biases are often undetectable from the usual research report that appears in the professional journal. For example, an interviewer may unconsciously give the subject subtle signs of approval and disapproval to different responses that will tend to encourage the subject to give the approved answer whether it is true or not. Although the information available to the student is too limited for him to expect to detect many such biases, he should, nonetheless, search carefully for evidence of their existence, and weigh their possible effects when they are discovered.

The methods of descriptive research, especially interview and observation studies, are perhaps most susceptible to observer bias. Let us review some of the main sources of such bias that the student should watch for in critically evaluating descriptive research:

1. Does the interview guide contain leading questions? Is it structured in such a way as to give the subject clues as to the preferred answer?

2. Does the observer's or interviewer's method of recording behavior or responses permit undue emphasis upon behavior that is in accordance with observer biases or expectations? Use of tape recordings greatly reduces danger of this bias.

3. Do methods of recording behavior require that the observer or interviewer draw inferences about the meaning of the behavior he is observing? In general, the more inferences the observer must draw, the more the likelihood of bias.

4. Are questions asked that might threaten, embarrass, or annoy some respondents, thus leading them to give false or unsatisfactory replies?

In addition to the various forms of bias that can have an impor-

[4] *Ibid.,* pp. 27–29. Reprinted by permission of Basic Books, Inc.

tant influence upon research results, there are certain other factors that the student should be alert to in critically evaluating research literature.

Hawthorne Effect

In experiments involving human subjects, a great many subtle influences can distort research results. If the individual is aware that he is participating in an experiment, for example, this knowledge may alter his performance and therefore invalidate the experiment. A series of studies carried out at the Hawthorne Plant of the Western Electric Company first called attention to some of these factors.[5] In this study, the illumination in three departments in which employees inspected small parts, assembled electrical relays, and wound coils was gradually increased. The production efficiency in all departments generally went up as the light intensity increased. It was found, however, that upon decreasing the light intensity in a later experiment, the efficiency of the group continued to increase slowly but steadily. Further experiments, with rest periods and varying the length of working days and weeks, were also accompanied by gradual increases in efficiency whether the change in working conditions was for the better or for the worse. It appears that the attention given the employees during the experiment was the major factor leading to these production gains. This phenomenon is referred to by psychologists as the *Hawthorne Effect*. The factory workers who carried out the same dull, repetitive task month after month were stimulated and motivated by the attention and concern for their well-being that was displayed by the research workers. A new element had been added to their dull existence—not illumination or the other variables that the researchers were studying—but the researchers themselves. The term *Hawthorne Effect* has come to refer to any situation in which the experimental conditions are such that the mere fact that the subject is participating in an experiment or is receiving special attention will tend to improve his performance. Certainly, many educational experiments report changes and improvements that are due primarily to *Hawthorne Effect*. Studies involving methods, for example, in which one group of teachers continues with the same teaching methods they have

[5] Fritz J. Roethlisberger and W. J. Dickson, *Management and the Worker* (Cambridge, Mass.: Harvard University Press, 1940).

previously employed while another group is trained in a new method and receives considerable help and attention in implementing this method will usually result in changes in teacher performance or pupil achievement favorable to the new methods. Many school districts, in the process of trying out new methods, frequently set up a one year experiment in which the new method is introduced to a limited number of pupils. The results of such experiments are almost certainly influenced by *Hawthorne Effect* because teachers usually approach a new method with some enthusiasm, and the students, being aware that they are being taught by a new and different method, are also likely to display more interest and motivation than usual. The influence of *Hawthorne Effect* can be expected to decrease in the school situation as the novelty of the new method wears off, and, therefore, studies extending over a period of two or three years can be relied upon somewhat more in evaluating the effectiveness of a new technique.[6]

Placebos

A placebo is a chemically inert substance that is administered in the same manner as the drug or active substance under investigation. Placebos are employed in medical research and in educational and psychological studies in which the effects of various substances on human behavior are being tested. The purpose of the placebo is to make it impossible for the subject to determine whether or not he is receiving the active substance under study as this knowledge may have an effect upon his behavior. Many studies have demonstrated that if one group of subjects receives some sort of attention such as the administration of a drug, while the control group receives no comparable attention, some of those receiving the drug will react in various ways that cannot be explained by the chemical or medical effects of the drug. Although relatively little is known about the psychological factors causing such reactions, it seems likely that the human contact with the researcher and the subject's expectation that something will occur as a result of the substance he has received contribute significantly. The results of such studies that do not use placebos are always subject to doubt because the proportion of the results that are attributable to psychological factors and the proportion caused by the drug cannot be determined. The

[6] *Ibid.*

placebo, in effect, acts as a control permitting the psychological factors to operate. The physical or behavioral changes brought about by the active substance cannot operate in control group subjects because the active substance is not present in the placebo. Even when using placebos, it has been found that if the experimenter knows which subjects receive the active substance and which subjects receive the placebo, this knowledge can lead to observer bias or can result in the researcher unconsciously giving the subject subtle clues, such as watching for reactions more attentively in cases where the subjects have received the active substance. Therefore, most studies aimed at evaluating the effects of drugs or other substances now employ what is called the "double-blind" technique, in which neither the experimenter nor the subject knows when the active substance is being taken or when the placebo. Obviously, in order to attain this situation, the placebo must be identical to the active drug in those characteristics that may be compared by the subject, such as appearance and taste.

Although placebos play a useful role in helping control psychological variables, many researchers fail to recognize that the control attained is still subject to error. Medical studies have demonstrated that there is considerable individual difference in reaction to placebos. Some individuals tend to react to placebos while others do not. For example, some hospital patients will consistently report a reduction in pain following the administration of an inert substance while others will not. Persons may show either a positive or negative reaction to the placebo. Beecher found that the incidence of relief reported fifteen studies involving medical placebos ranged from 15 to 58 per cent. However, he also found thirty-five different toxic effects that occurred after the administration of placebos.[7]

Persons who react to placebos are referred to as *placebo reactors*. In small sampling studies, there is always a possibility that the control group will contain a larger number of *placebo reactors* than the experimental group. If this is the case, the results of the experiment may be negative even though the active substance being tested has a definite effect upon the experimental subjects. Some studies have shown that if *placebo reactors* are screened out, significant

[7] H. K. Beecher, "The Powerful Placebo," *Journal of American Medical Association*, CLIX (1955), 1602–5.

differences sometimes emerge that would not show up otherwise.[8] As yet we know very little about the degree to which some persons are consistently placebo reactors or whether such persons are different from individuals who do not react to placebos in terms of personality and other variables. Some evidence suggests that such differences do exist, and until we know more about placebo reaction, differences in this variable can considerably distort research findings involving small samples.[9]

Contamination

Faulty research design often permits contamination to occur in educational studies. It will be recalled that contamination refers to any situation in which data that should be kept independent to satisfy the requirements for sound research have in some way become interrelated. We have discussed various ways that contamination can enter the research design in previous chapters. Let us review some of these briefly:

Observer contamination

Observer contamination usually arises when the research worker has knowledge of the subject's performance on the dependent variable, and this knowledge influences his observation of the behavior of the subject on the independent variable. Let us suppose, for example, that we are doing a study of the relationship between the amount of conflict present in the home environment of the child and behavior in the classroom involving direct and indirect aggression. If the observer collected data on conflicts in the home prior to carrying out his classroom observations, there would be a strong possibility that his knowledge of the child's home environment would influence his interpretation of the child's aggressive behavior in the classroom. In other words, if he had hypothesized that chil-

[8] H. K. Beecher, A. S. Keats, F. Mosteller, and L. Lasagna, "The Effectiveness of Oral Analgesics (Morphine, Codeine, Acetylsalicylic Acid) and the Problem of Placebo 'Reactors' and 'Nonreactors,'" *Journal of Pharmacology and Experimental Therapeutics*, CIX (1953), 393–400.

[9] L. Lasagna, J. Mosteller, J. M. von Felsinger, and H. K. Beecher, "A Study of the Placebo Response," *American Journal of Medicine*, XVI (1954), 770–79.

dren coming from home environments involving conflicts would display more direct aggression in the classroom, he would tend to look for signs of direct aggression in these children and would be likely to see more direct aggression and interpret questionable behavior as direct aggression. Observer contamination, of course, is not limited to studies in which the person uses observational techniques. Any research situation that involves subjective evaluations, drawing implications, or making judgments on the part of the research worker is subject to this form of contamination. In any situation where a knowledge of one aspect of the research can influence the research worker in his appraisal of other aspects of his research data, the possibility of contamination is present.

Statistical contamination

Statistical contamination occurs when data that have in some way become related are treated as being independent in the statistical analysis. An example of statistical contamination was recently encountered by the author in the work of one of his doctoral candidates. The student was carrying out a study of characteristics related to success of elementary school principals. The design called for the participation of each person to be evaluated in six role-playing situations. In each situation, the subject was evaluated independently by two raters on a number of pertinent behaviors. These specific evaluations were combined in order to provide an overall evaluation of the individual as a principal. In carrying out his analysis, the student found a high correlation between observer ratings in the specific area of "human relations skills" and the overall evaluations of the individual's effectiveness. From this correlation, he concluded that "human relations skills" constituted by far the most important factor in the effective performance of elementary school principals. He had failed to realize, however, that because the overall rating also included the rating of human relations skills, which was the most heavily weighted of the specific rating areas, he was in effect correlating human relations skills with itself to the extent that it was part of the overall rating. Such correlations are, of course, spurious and indicate statistical contamination.

This chapter has attempted to alert the student to some of the factors that must be considered in critically evaluating the research of others. By carrying out the critical evaluations of research pertinent to his problem thoroughly and carefully, he will not only gain a sounder insight into this work but will also develop a better understanding of the entire field of educational research that will steadily improve the quality of his own work. At best, an introduction to research such as is presented in this text can do little more than start the student on the road to maturity as a research worker. After gaining this foundation, the student must work with more experienced researchers and do research of his own if he is to progress further.

This chapter is far from an exhaustive coverage of all the elements that must be considered in critical evaluation of research. Although guides and checklists are available, it is doubtful that a truly exhaustive evaluation could be written because scholars and researchers in the behavioral sciences are discovering new sources of research error and new methods of doing research almost daily.[10] Thus, even the experienced research worker will almost certainly overlook some errors and biases when he evaluates research. The goal of both the beginning graduate student and the research worker with many years of experience is thus the same in critically evaluating research—to do the best job that he can. The student who does a careful and sincere job, in this phase of his review of the literature, will find himself repaid by significant growth in maturity and research sophistication.

ANNOTATED REFERENCES

1. ALLEN, E. M. "Why Are Research Grant Applications Disapproved?" *Science*, 1960, 32, 1532–34. This article discusses why research projects submitted to the National Institutes of Health were disapproved, and, based on an analysis of the minutes of evaluation meetings carried out in 605 of these disapproved proposals, the author has constructed a table classifying the major reasons for disapproval. This article gives the student many insights into common shortcomings of research design as seen by scientists who sit on advisory boards and can assist the student in evaluating his own research ideas.

2. ANDERSON, K. E. (ed.). *Research on the Academically Talented Student.* Washington, D.C.: National Education Association, 1961. Although written primarily to present a review of research concerning academically talented

[10] See Appendix B for a checklist.

students, this pamphlet contains a great deal of interesting and insightful material concerning evaluation of research, including a section on the essentials of sound research that gives many valuable suggestions for developing and evaluating educational research.

3. ORLANSKY, H. "Research on the Series of Infant Care as Related to Personality," *Psychological Bulletin*, 1949, 46 (1), 1–48. This article provides a critical evaluation of research relating to Freudian and Neo-Freudian theories concerning the relationship between infant care and later personality development. The article provides an excellent example of how critical evaluation techniques can be applied to gain a clearer picture of the status of knowledge in the scientific field.

4. ROSENTHAL, R. "The Problem of Experimenter Bias," *American Psychologist*, 1959, 14, 424. (Paper read at the 1959 meetings of the American Psychological Association.) This paper describes three experiments carried out to determine the tendency of experimenters to obtain data in conformity with their expectations and also to learn the types of clues used subconsciously by experimenters to bring about this bias. It was found that both verbal and nonverbal visual cues were given by experimenters, with the verbal clues appearing somewhat more important. This study demonstrates that the expectations of the experimenter can have a highly significant effect upon the responses of the subject. Other important studies in this area in which the same researcher has participated include:
   (a) ROSENTHAL, R. "Projection, Excitement, and Unconscious Experimenter Bias," *American Psychologist*, 1958, 13, 345–46.
   (b) ROSENTHAL, R., *et al.* "Subjects' Perceptions of Their Experimenter under Conditions of Experimenter Bias," *Perceptual and Motor Skills*, 1960, 11, 325–31.

5. SELLS, S. B. "Psychological Aspects of Research Design," Taken from Collier, R. O., and Elam, S. M. (eds.), *Research Design and Analysis, 2nd Annual Phi Delta Kappa Symposium on Educational Research*. Bloomington, Ind.: Phi Delta Kappa, 1961. Sells emphasizes in this chapter (Chapter 5) the importance of situational variables in influencing research results in the behavioral sciences and the need for developing methodological tools for properly recognizing these variables. The value system of the experimenter and the subject and their frames of reference are also discussed as factors influencing the outcome of research in the behavioral sciences.

6. STANLEY, J. C., and BEEMAN, E. Y. "Restricted Generalization, Bias, and Loss of Power That May Result from Matching Groups," *Psychological Newsletter*, New York University, 1958, 9, 88–102. The authors discuss

some of the disadvantages of matching techniques in educational research and also discuss other designs, principally analysis of covariance, which overcome some of these disadvantages. A number of specific studies of mental deficiency are used to illustrate the main points of the article. This article will prepare the student to make sounder evaluations of research employing matching. Any educational researcher will profit from a study of this article before employing a matching design in his research project.

7. STINNETT, T. M. "Check That Statistic!" *Educational Record,* 1957, 38, 83–90. This article demonstrates ways in which the professional reader and the general public may be misled by biased reporting of statistical information. Many interesting examples from the field of education are given. The student who has been disturbed by the many shocking statistics about education quoted by public figures in the last few years would do well to study this article carefully. The type of critical questioning advocated by the author is one of the most important characteristics of a competent research worker.

8. VAN DALEN, D. D. *Understanding Educational Research—An Introduction.* New York: McGraw-Hill Book Co., Inc., 1962. Chapter 16 of this textbook presents a lengthy list of questions useful to the inexperienced research worker in carrying out an evaluation of a research project. The questions listed under *hypotheses, method of attack, presentation of data,* and *analysis of data* will be especially helpful in the evaluation of the research work of others.

9. WOLPE, JOSEPH, and RACKMAN, STANLEY. "Psychoanalytic 'Evidence': A Critique Based on Freud's Case of Little Hans," *Journal of Nervous and Mental Diseases,* 1960, 31, 135–48. This article provides an interesting example of how a critical evaluation may be carried out, and will help the student make the distinction among assumption, speculation, and scientific evidence.

CHAPTER 16

Processing Research Data

INTRODUCTION

After research data have been collected, it is necessary to process these data into a form that permits easy analysis. Tests must be scored, and scores must often be converted to standard form. Biographical data must be coded, and all data must be recorded in such a way that the analysis may be carried out rapidly and with minimum chance of error.

An important point for the student to remember in processing his data is that a systematic well-planned procedure is necessary in order to avoid errors and get the most out of the research data.

STEPS IN SCORING STANDARD TESTS

The first step in scoring standard tests used in research is to restudy the test manual and the test in order to be completely familiar with the test content and scoring procedure. Keys are provided with standard tests, and the key should be checked carefully against the test items to be sure that it is correct. Often, the handscoring keys supplied with standard tests are less convenient to use than a window key that the research worker can prepare for himself. After keys have been prepared, a definite scoring routine should be set up. In some tests, scoring may be done more quickly by scoring the first page of all tests before turning to the second page. On other tests, it is more feasible to score each test in its entirety before going to the next. The student can usually arrive at a satisfactory scoring routine by examining the test and answer sheet. When the graduate student is faced with a lengthy test-scoring job, it is usually advisable to work for periods of one or two hours rather than attempt to complete the entire job at one sitting. After an hour or two, most people become tired and bored, which leads to making mistakes. If the graduate student alternates periods of study or creative work with periods of test scoring and other clerical work, he will find the work less fatiguing and will make fewer errors. After all the copies of a test have been scored, the student should select every tenth copy for rescoring. When rescoring, he should tally each error, indicating its size and direction and, if possible, the item on which the error was made. After completing the rescoring of 10 per cent of the tests, the student must examine the error distribution and decide whether sufficient errors have been found to necessitate rescoring all copies of the test. A few small errors are usually found, and these have relatively little effect upon the research results. After all the copies of a given test have been scored and checked, the tests should be packaged and labeled, giving the date of the testing, the subjects tested, and other pertinent information that may be needed later to identify the data.

MACHINE SCORING

Many colleges and universities have test-scoring machines available and can supply test-scoring services at a low cost. The test-scoring machine saves the research worker a great deal of time and should be used to score standard tests whenever the student's finances permit. Some universities will permit the student to score his own tests on the machine during off-hours. If this is permitted, the student should do so because it provides him with valuable experience. Many test-scoring machines are also equipped with a graphic item counter that permits item analysis of the test with very little extra work. Item analysis is usually called for if the student has developed his own measure or if he is using experimental measures. The first step in using the IBM test-scoring machine is to check carefully all answer sheets to see that electrographic pencil marks are heavy and to erase random pencil marks that might cause the machine to give an incorrect score. The IBM key should then be checked and the test scored on the machine. Test-scoring machines can make errors so it is advisable to hand score 10 per cent of the tests and analyze the errors. One-point errors are often made by the person reading the score from the machine. Larger errors can be due to unfavorable atmospheric conditions or internal difficulties with the machine.

SCORING UNSTRUCTURED OR EXPERIMENTAL MEASURES

In many educational research projects, the research worker must develop some of his own measuring devices. Occasionally, he uses projective techniques, such as the *Rorschach Inkblot Test* or the *Thematic Apperception Test,* and must adapt the scoring procedures to the specific objectives he wishes to accomplish with these measures. Under these circumstances, the scoring procedures should be fully developed during a pilot study or a preliminary tryout of the measurement tools. The usual method of setting up scoring procedures for a new measure is to try out the measure on a number of subjects similar to those who will be used in the regular study. During this tryout, the research worker can make whatever changes in his scoring techniques that seem appropriate and may also make changes in the measure itself to correct deficiencies found in the administration and scoring of the preliminary form. After a scoring procedure has been developed, it is usually necessary to administer the measure to another preliminary group in order that an item analysis may be conducted. A measure should not be administered to a research sample until the research worker is fully satisfied with the scoring procedure and has completed the item analysis. Once the scoring of the measure for the research sample has been started, the scoring procedure must remain the same. In many cases, the graduate student does an inadequate job of developing scoring procedures, and then, during the scoring of the research data, he discovers changes that should be made. At this point, however, changes cannot be made because this would result in some subjects being scored on one basis and others on another basis. The alternative of rescoring all subjects on the new basis is also questionable unless the measure is highly objective because his previous scoring may effect the graduate student's perception of the subject's responses.

The greatest difficulties in developing scoring methods for exploratory measures are encountered in using measures that are somewhat unstructured, such as interview data, observational rating forms, and responses to projective tests. If one of these techniques is used, it is usually necessary that the measure be scored independently by two individuals. This will reduce the likelihood that the biases of a single observer will unduly influence the results and also will permit the calculation of interrater reliability.

It is extremely important to keep detailed records of scoring procedures used in experimental tests or on any test where the usual scoring procedures are not followed. This information should then be included in the research report, so that anyone reading the report can understand the scoring procedure and evaluate the results or replicate the study. The research worker, in developing a scoring system for such measures, should write down his procedure as a series of definite steps to be followed. He should also establish rules and definitions concerning the scoring procedure that will tend to help him score the same responses in the same manner on all of his tests. During the actual scoring of the measures, he should refer back to his written scoring procedures frequently, or there will be some tendency for him to drift away from these procedures as his experience with the scoring increases.

RECORDING RESEARCH DATA

After all the measures have been scored and scores have been converted when necessary into the form required, the data should be entered on a record card that lends itself to the planned analysis procedure. In studies involving relatively few cases such as those usually attempted by graduate students, the hand data card is generally the most efficient method of recording the research data. As a rule, a separate hand data card is prepared for each subject in the study. The hand data card contains all information concerning the subject. A sample hand data card with a key describing each entry is shown in Figure 8. The research worker can usually have the format mimeographed on 3×5-inch or 4×6-inch note cards at relatively little expense. He then writes in the pupil's name and copies the research data from the various tests, biographical forms, school records, and other sources. When he is finished, each card contains all of the information collected about one individual in the study. This method is usually superior to listing the data on summary sheets. With the summary sheet method, the students' names are usually listed alphabetically in the left-hand column of the sheet, and score entries are usually made in the row opposite the student's name. There is a greater chance of errors in reading scores from such a sheet than in reading them from the hand data card because it is easy to read the entry from the incorrect row or column on

I. D.	_____	Ach 9/60	_____
Sex	_____	Ach 5/61	_____
D. B.	_____	SSHA	_____
School	_____		_____
Group	_____		_____
F. O.	_____		_____
IQ	_____		_____

FIG. 8. Sample hand data card and key.

Key

I. D.	Pupil's identification number
Sex	1 = Boy; 2 = Girl
D. B.	Date of birth: first two digits give month, second two year (Example: 0250 = February, 1950)
School	1 = Harrison; 2 = Washington; 3 = Horace Mann
Group	1 = Experimental; 2 = Control
F. O.	Level of Father's Occupation using Warner scale
IQ	Total IQ on *California Test of Mental Maturity, 1957 Edition*
Ach 9/60	Achievement score on *STEP Science Test,* level 3, form A, administered 9/60
Ach 5/61	Achievement score on *STEP Science Test,* level 3, form B, administered 5/61
SSHA	Brown-Holtzman *Survey of Study Habits and Attitudes,* Raw Score

Other blanks may be used to record additional data.

the summary sheet. Hand data cards also simplify analysis in studies where the subjects are to be divided into a number of subgroups for different analytical approaches. With hand data cards, the cards for a given subgroup can quickly be pulled from the deck and data taken directly from them. These cards can then be returned to the deck for analysis of other subgroups or analysis of the overall sample.

The hand data card is too small to permit a complete description of each entry. Therefore, a key sheet describing exactly what is contained in each entry of the card is necessary. The student should use a hand data card large enough to permit a few more blanks than he expects to need because he frequently will encounter information that he wishes to add in the course of the study.

Test scores may often be recorded directly from the test answer sheet to the hand data card. Much of the material collected in educational research, however, must be coded in order to make it readily adaptable to analysis procedures. Descriptive data, such as sex, social class, homeroom teacher, and school attended are much easier to record if code numbers are assigned.

USE OF ELECTRONIC EQUIPMENT IN DATA PROCESSING

Coding and quantifying of information also permits the research worker to adapt his data to IBM cards for analysis by electronic data processing equipment with little additional effort. If the data on the hand data card are to be transferred to IBM punch cards, the column numbers are given on the hand data card instead of the abbreviated identification. For example, in Figure 8, instead of I. D., the first entry would be identified as column 1-3. This would indicate to the key-punch operator that the 3-digit entry in this column would be punched in the first three columns of the IBM card. If the data were to be transferred to IBM cards, the first identification number would be 001, because each column required must be accounted for.[1] Instead of "sex" the next entry would be identified as column 4 because only one digit would be required to record this information. Date of birth would be identified as column 5-8 because four digits are required to record the month and year. Eighty digits can be punched on the standard IBM punch card, and a single card will be sufficient to record the data collected in most small studies. Once data have been readied for the machine by punching on cards or entering on paper or magnetic tape, several steps are required before the electronic equipment can carry out the analysis procedures. Martin and Hall list the following steps that are necessary when a computer is used to solve a problem:

(a) The problem must be defined in logical or mathematical terms.

(b) This logical or mathematical formulation must be translated into an

[1] Three digits would be required if more than 100 and less than 1,000 subjects were used.

arithmetical procedure. (The translation from a mathematical statement into an arithmetical procedure is the subject matter of numerical analysis.)

(*c*) An explicit series of instructions to the computer (the program) must be prepared to direct the computer through each step necessary to solve the problem.

(*d*) The input data must be recorded in a form which the machine can read. (Readable media are punched cards, punched paper tape, and digital magnetic tape.)

(*e*) Finally, the problem must be run—and the computer produces answers.[2]

In some studies in which IBM analysis is to be employed, a mark-sense card can be used in place of the regular hand data card (see Figure 9). Scores are recorded on the mark-sense card using an electrographic pencil. These scores may then be transferred to a regular IBM punched card without employing a key-punch operator, thus greatly reducing cost. In using measures where each response must be transferred to an IBM punched card, such as information on a biographical inventory, a mark-sense card can often be used as an answer sheet. In this case the raw data can be made ready for analysis with very little clerical work. The research worker should avoid use of mark-sense cards to obtain raw data from elementary school children because children at this level make frequent mistakes and often have difficulty following the instructions that are usually more complicated if mark-sense cards are used. The use of electronic data-processing machines saves a great deal of time and effort in studies involving large numbers of cases or complex analysis procedures. As a rule, the bigger the research job the more is gained by use of electronic data processing. A student can calculate a product-moment correlation involving one hundred pairs of scores in about an hour by hand. If he has a desk calculator, this time can be cut to twenty or thirty minutes. Some of the most recent electronic computers can calculate hundreds of product-moment correlations per minute. It has been estimated that performing one million multiplications on a desk calculator would require an operator five years and cost $25,000. On an electronic computer, such as the LARC, one million multiplications can be done in eight seconds and would cost about fifty cents.[3] This figure, however, does not

[2] E. Wayne Martin, Jr. and Dale J. Hall, "Data Processing: Automation in Calculation," *Review of Educational Research*, XXX (1960), 523.

[3] Alton S. Householder, "Solving Problems with Digital Computors," *Computors and Automation*, V (1956), 6–9.

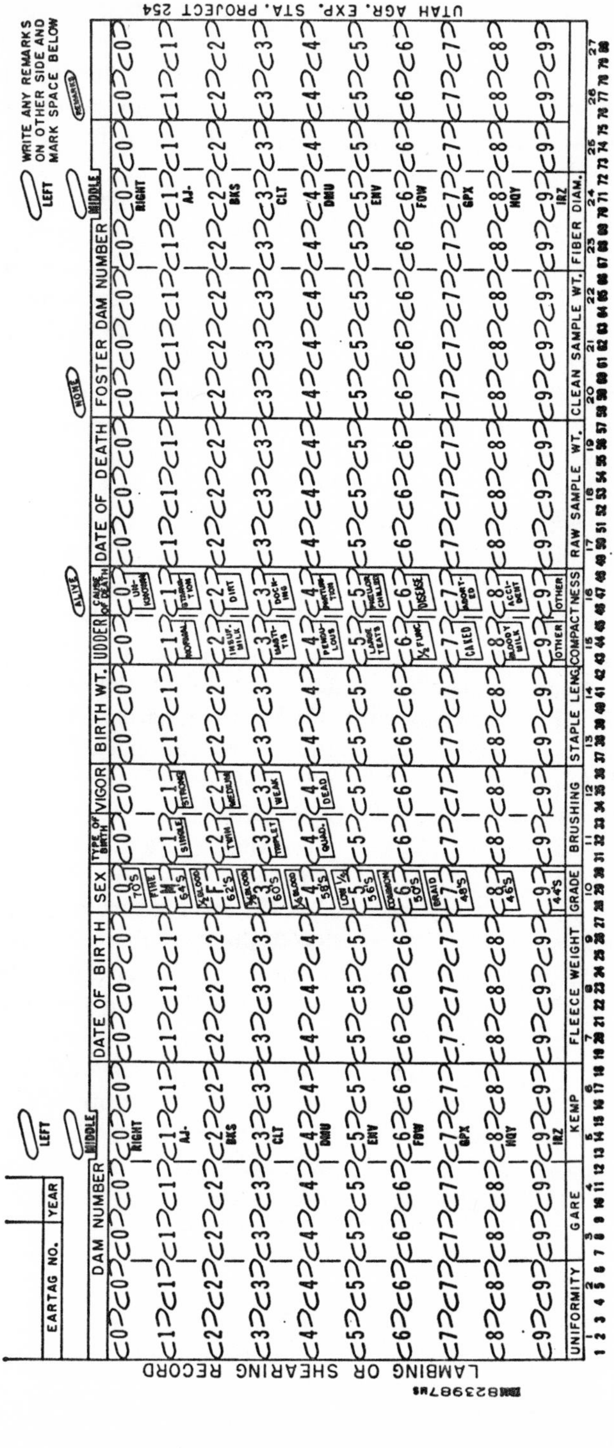

FIG. 9. Illustration of a mark-sense card.

include the expense involved in setting up the computer program and putting the material in a form the computer can use. Program libraries and exchanges have been set up so that much statistical work can be done at little programming cost. Some adaptation of existing programs is usually necessary, however, to fit the specific needs of the local problem.

Small studies or studies involving relatively simple analysis procedures can often be done just as efficiently using a desk calculator. This is because the cost of programming small studies involving a few subjects is the same as programming the same operations for a great many cases. Inasmuch as programming costs are high, the use of IBM for small studies is often inefficient. A study, for example, involving a number of breakdowns of the research groups into small subsamples followed by comparisons of the mean scores of these subsamples with the t-test, is often easier and cheaper to do with a desk calculator than with an electronic data-processing system because of the small numbers of cases involved and the large amount of programming required to obtain the necessary information by machine.

Another problem faced by the student who uses electronic data processing involves setting up satisfactory methods of checking results. Although the machines themselves rarely make errors, errors can be made by the person who punches the data on IBM cards or the person who programs the material into the machine. The machine merely follows a lengthy series of very simple instructions called a program, and if any of these instructions are incorrect, the results will be in error. Errors in programming are easy to make and difficult to locate. When data have been processed by machine such errors frequently go undetected unless the error is such as to produce ridiculous or very suspicious results. A situation that often leads to programming errors is found when the research worker knows how he wants his data analyzed but does not understand the operation of the machine, while the machine programmer understands the machine but often has little insight into the research worker's data. The result is often that the research worker asks for procedures that cannot be economically carried out by the machine, while the programmer suggests procedures for which he already has programs but that do not fit the requirements of the research.

A great many universities have electronic computers and offer courses in their use. Often, if the student can prepare his own program for the computer and can operate the computer, he is permitted to use the equipment without charge. The student who plans a career in educational research should get such training if available at his university, even if electronic equipment is not called for in his graduate research project. Within the next few years, virtually all analysis of major educational research will be done with electronic equipment. There is some doubt whether it is advisable for the student to turn his data over to the processing center of his university if he is not able to participate actively in the data processing. The student who processes his own research data on a desk calculator has a much better insight into what his data indicate— a better "feel" for the data. This insight often leads to discoveries that would be lost if the data were analyzed by electronic equipment under the supervision of a statistician who may know little about the nature of the data he is processing. The value of IBM for studies involving large numbers of correlations or a complex analysis procedure cannot be overestimated. Electronic data processing has opened the door to many research problems that never could have been attacked at all using other methods. The aforementioned precautions are given mainly to make the student aware of the fact that electronic equipment does not provide a panacea. Each research task should be evaluated carefully to determine what form of data processing is the most efficient for that task.

Whether analysis is carried out using a desk calculator or a high-speed electronic computer, the results should be checked to insure accuracy. When using the desk calculator, a series of checks at different points in the calculation may usually be made. Some desk calculators now provide a printed tape record of operations that is valuable in checking procedure. Most, however, do not have this feature, and the student must write down the results obtained at key points in his analysis in order to simplify checking. If such checks are not practical, it is advisable to make all calculations twice. Rechecking a major analysis procedure *in toto,* however, is a frustrating procedure because there are many places where an error may be made; and the graduate student who is not highly skilled in the use of a desk calculator may make a different error on each repetition, thus never obtaining a satisfactory check of his results. Checking the work of an electronic computer is usually much more difficult because the student has no data on intermediate steps. He can usually check the program by working out one example on a desk calculator. For example, if the computer has calculated a large number of correlations, he may work one of the correlations on a desk calculator to check the computer program. Generally, if the correct data are entered and the program is correct, the answer given by the computer will be correct.

After the student has completed his analysis, he should file his hand data cards, analysis data, computations, and raw data, labeling all material in such a way so that he can easily locate items he wishes to check.[4] In the process of the analysis, he will often wish to refer back to the raw data to check a particular score that seems doubtful. Also, retaining the raw data may make it possible for him to carry out future research in which these data will be used. Sometimes he will hit upon an idea for reanalyzing his data after he has completed the study that he originally planned. The reanalysis may yield new and interesting information that would be lost if the raw data had been destroyed at the end of the original analysis. If any of his results are challenged, the raw data provide the only fully satisfactory source for rechecking these results.

The process of checking will be greatly simplified if the student records his steps neatly and systematically and labels each step for future reference. The time consumed in keeping systematic records and labeling is well spent because the student will save the time of deciphering forgotten figures and reworking those that he cannot figure out.

MISTAKES OFTEN MADE BY GRADUATE STUDENTS

1. Fails to set up a systematic routine for scoring and recording data.

2. Does not record details and variations in scoring procedures when scoring data, and is then unable to remember what was done when called upon to describe procedure in his thesis.

3. Does not check scoring for errors.

4. Changes his scoring procedure when in the process of scoring his research data.

[4] Raw data are test answer sheets, observation forms, recordings of interviews, and other material as initially received.

ANNOTATED REFERENCES

1. GREGORY, ROBERT HENRY, and VAN HORN, RICHARD L. *Automatic Data Processing Systems: Principles and Procedures*. Belmont, Calif.: Wadsworth Publishing Co., Inc., 1960. A comprehensive discussion of electronic data processing systems and their use. Written primarily to introduce the layman to electronic computers and their applications. The first three chapters provide a brief orientation that will be sufficient for most graduate students. Later sections describe specific equipment, programming, and other topics for the student requiring a reasonably thorough understanding of the subject.

2. NETT, ROGER, and HETZLER, STANLEY A. *An Introduction to Electronic Data Processing*. Glencoe, Ill.: The Free Press, 1959. Provides the reader with an introduction to electronic computer systems, how they work, programming and machine language, and computer application. Written at a level that can be understood without special training in mathematics or knowledge of computer jargon.

3. WRIGLEY, CHARLES. "Electronic Computers and Psychological Research," *American Psychologist*, 1957, 12, 501–8. A brief introduction to electronic computers, tracing their development, describing their operation, and discussing their advantages and disadvantages when applied to research in the behavioral sciences.

The following articles provide a brief review of available equipment, programming systems, and computer applications. Extensive bibliographies are also provided with each article. The student interested in specific statistical programs adapted to a specific computer system should check these references thoroughly as a great many sources are covered.

1. MARTIN, E. WAYNE, JR., and HALL, DALE, J. "Data Processing: Automation in Calculation," *Review of Education Research*, 1960, 30, 522–35.

2. WRIGLEY, CHARLES. "Data Processing: Automation in Calculation," *Review of Education Research*, 1957, 27, 528–43.

The following articles are particularly pertinent to the use of electronic calculators and other data processing procedures in psychology and education.

1. APPEL, VALENTINE, and COOPER, GEORGE. "A Refinement in the Use of Mark-Sense Cards for Test Research," *Journal of the American Statistical Association*, 1955, 50, 557–60.

2. BASS, BERNARD M., and WURSTER, CECIL R. "Using 'Mark Sense' for Ratings and Personal Data Collection," *Journal of Applied Psychology,* 1956, 40, 269–71.

3. CAFFREY, JOHN, and WHEELER, FRED. "A Simplified χ^2 Formula for Rapid Computation of Certain Item-Analysis Data with IBM Punched-Card Equipment," *Journal of Experimental Education,* 1953, 21, 265–69.

4. DEEMER, WALTER L., JR. "The Use of Mark Sensing in a Large-Scale Testing Program," *Journal of the American Statistical Association,* 1948, 43, 40–52.

5. GADDIS, L. WESLEY. "Questionnaire Analysis Program," *Educational and Psychological Measurement,* 1959, 19, 435–37.

6. ———, et al. "An IBM 650 Program for Calculation of Means, Standard Deviations, and Product Moment Correlations in Test Analysis," *ibid.,* 1961, 21, 149–53.

7. IKER, HOWARD P. "Item Analysis on the Augmented IBM 650 Using a Continuous Criterion Variable," *Educational and Psychological Measurement,* 1960, 20, 153–62.

8. ———. "Item Analysis on the Augmented IBM 650 Using a Dichotomous Criterion Variable," *ibid.,* 1960, 20, 163–70.

9. ———. "Group Differences and Group Means with the Augmented IBM 650," *ibid.,* 1960, 20, 171–79.

10. KAHN, LESSING A., and BODINE, ADOLPH J. "Guttman Scale Analysis by Means of IBM Equipment," *Educational and Psychological Measurement,* 1951, 11, 298–314.

11. KAISER, HENRY F. "The Application of Electronic Computers to Factor Analysis," *Educational and Psychological Measurement,* 1960, 20, 141–51.

12. KAMMAN, JAMES F., et al. "Scoring Psychological Tests on Accounting Machines: A Follow-up Report," *Educational and Psychological Measurement,* 1959, 19, 421–23.

13. KATZ, LEO. "Punched Card Technique for the Analysis of Multiple Level Sociometric Data," *Sociometry,* 1950, 13, 108–22.

14. KEPHART, NEWELL C., and OLIVER, JAMES E. "A Punched Card Procedure for Use with the Method of Paired Comparisons," *Journal of Applied Psychology,* 1952, 36, 47–48.

15. MacLEAN, ANGUS G., and TAIT, ARTHUR T. "Some Computational

Short-Cuts in the Development or Analysis of Tests," *Journal of Applied Psychology,* 1954, 38, 260–63.

16. STAUGAS, LEONARD. "A Rapid Method for Scoring Tests Punched in IBM Cards," *Educational and Psychological Measurement,* 1954, 14, 101–5.

17. WARD, JOE H., JR. "Use of Electronic Computers in Psychological Research," *American Psychologist,* 1955, 10, 826–27.

The following series of articles deals with the use of computers in the behavioral sciences. These articles give the student a useful insight into the current and future role of computers in education and related sciences.

1. COLEMAN, J. S. "Analysis of Social Structures and Simulation of Social Process with Electronic Computers," *Educational and Psychological Measurement,* 1961, 21, 203–18.

2. GREEN, B. F., JR. "Using Computers to Study Human Perception," *Educational and Psychological Measurement,* 1961, 21, 227–33.

3. SAUNDERS, D. R. "How to Tell Computers from People," *Educational and Psychological Measurement,* 1961, 21, 159–83.

4. SEIBEL, R. "Computer Solutions to Some Noncomputational Psychological Problems," *Educational and Psychological Measurement,* 1961, 21, 185–201.

5. WARD, J. H., JR. "Markov Models and Monte Carlo Techniques," *Educational and Psychological Measurement,* 1961, 21, 219–25.

CHAPTER 17

Preparing the Research Report

INTRODUCTION

The purpose of this chapter is to give the graduate student a general guide for preparing his thesis, dissertation, or research article. The emphasis will be upon general principles of organization and presentation. Errors and weaknesses commonly found in theses and dissertations will be discussed. No attempt will be made to present detailed information on format. Most colleges and universities have established rules on style and format that must be followed closely, and for this reason, specific information on format in a book of this type is of little value to the student.

THE THESIS OR DISSERTATION

In carrying out your review of the literature, you will observe that all research articles are organized in essentially the same manner. Theses and dissertations follow this same organizational pattern, although, because these papers are less restricted in length, some topics are covered more thoroughly than in the published research article. Figure 10 is an outline giving the usual organization of the thesis or dissertation. Some variations in this outline will be found in the requirements of different universities.

When the student is ready to start writing his thesis, he should obtain, from his research committee chairman or from the Dean of the Graduate School, specific information concerning the format required at his university. Some universities prepare a style manual for graduate students, others refer the student to one or more of the published style manuals that are acceptable at the school in question. It is often wise for the student to ask his committee chairman to refer him to two or three outstanding theses in education recently completed at his school. An examination of these theses along with the prescribed style manual will give the student most of the information he needs to meet the style and format requirements. A study

Preliminary Materials

1. Title page
2. Preface and Acknowledgments
3. Table of contents
4. List of tables
5. List of figures

Body of the Paper

Chapter 1. Introduction

a. General statement of the problem
b. Statement of the hypotheses
c. Definition of terms

Chapter 2. Review of the Literature

a. Review of previous research
b. Pertinent opinion
c. Summary of the state of the art

Chapter 3. Method

a. Description of subjects
b. Description of measures employed
c. Research design and procedures

Chapter 4. Findings

a. Analysis techniques
b. Description of findings pertinent to each hypothesis
c. Other findings

Chapter 5. Summary and Conclusions

a. Summary of hypotheses, method, and findings
b. Conclusions
c. Implications

Reference Materials

1. Bibliography
2. Appendix

FIG. 10. Organization of the thesis.

of the organization, method of presentation, and language used in these theses will also give him some idea of the sort of thesis that his chairman considers superior. As his own thesis will probably be subjected to the same criteria used by his chairman to evaluate previous theses, this information can be very helpful in preparing his report.

Preliminary materials

Preparing the preliminary materials: title page, preface, table of contents, list of tables, and list of figures is essentially a matter of following the accepted format. In selecting a title the student should attempt to be brief while giving a specific description of what his study does. Let us say, for example, that he has done a study comparing the achievement gains of sixth grade pupils who had received a course in American history through closed-circuit television with the achievement gains of a matched group of sixth grade pupils who received the same course through regular classroom instruction. An appropriate title might be: "Regular and Televised Instruction in Sixth Grade American History." This title is reasonably brief and yet gives the reader some clue as to what the study does. Another title might be: "A Study Comparing the Achievement of Sixth Grade Students Instructed in American History through Closed-Circuit Television and Regular Classroom Procedure." This title tells what the study does but is too long. It also starts out with "A Study Of" which is superfluous. A third title for the aforementioned study might be "Teaching With Television." This title fails in that it does not tell what the study has done but merely identifies the broad area of the research. In doing your review of the literature, you will find such brief titles to be exasperating. They tell so little that it is necessary to check the article even though the majority will have nothing to do with the area of your review. Many reference books such as *Education Index* list only the title of research reports, and a general title that does not give the reader an idea of what the study has done is misleading and often is not indexed properly.

In preparing the table of contents and the headings for tables and figures, the main point that the student must remember, aside from the usual format requirements, is that such materials should follow parallel grammatical construction. In other words, chapter titles, headings, and titles of tables and figures should be prepared so that they are consistent and comparable in their wording and grammatical construction.

General considerations in preparing the body of the thesis or dissertation

Students often wait until all data have been collected and all analysis has been completed before starting to write their thesis or dissertation. It is much more efficient for the student to prepare some portions of his research report much earlier. It seems to be an almost inevitable feature of research that the student encounters some periods when he is extremely busy and some periods when he must sit and wait. These lulls in the research routine can be profitably used by the student to prepare drafts of the first chapters of his thesis.

Most students find that the easiest way to prepare a well-organized research report is to outline carefully each section before starting to write the report on that section. This outline may start merely as a listing of all major points that the student wishes to discuss in the section. These major points may then be placed in what appears to be the most logical order, and, finally, the subtopics to be discussed under each point can be added to the outline. This detailed outline helps the student a great deal in achieving a logical organization. It helps him identify and think through each point and usually provides him with subheadings for the section he is writing. If he has followed good procedure in planning and carrying out his study, he will have many guides that will help him organize his paper. For example, the outline of his research project, which is prepared early in the research sequence, will contain a detailed statement of the problem and hypotheses that can quickly be filled out to become part of the introductory chapter of his thesis. A well-thought-out set of subheadings help the reader a great deal in understanding the organization of the paper and make the paper more readable.

The introductory chapter

The introductory chapter usually starts with a general statement of the problem area, which has as its aim the general orientation of the reader. This statement should help the reader develop an appreciation for the problem, its place in education, and its importance and pertinence. The next section in this chapter is usually a specific statement of the objectives or hypotheses of the study. These may usually be taken directly from the research plan that the student developed prior to his data collection. The third section of the introductory chapter is devoted to definition of terms. This section is very important because educational terms such as underachiever, gifted child, core-curriculum, and many others are defined differently by different educators. A specific definition of the term as it applies to the reported research is therefore necessary in order that the reader will fully understand the meaning of the report and its significance.

The student can often prepare a reasonably complete rough draft of the introductory chapter early in the conduct of his study. Most writers find that if they prepare a rough draft and then set it aside for a week or two before revising it, they will see weaknesses that would not have been apparent if immediate revision had been attempted. Also, new points or different approaches often occur to the writer during the intervening weeks that can improve the report. If the student waits until he has collected and analyzed all of his data before drafting any of his paper, he usually does not have sufficient time to lay each section aside for this period of germination. Another advantage of drafting the early chapters of the thesis while carrying out the research is that a less demanding schedule of writing may be followed. Many persons find it difficult to write steadily for any period of time. It is much easier for them to write a few pages and then put the work aside and do something else. Such a procedure is often not possible if the student waits too long to start preparing his report.

The review of the literature

The purpose of the chapter reviewing the literature is to give the reader an understanding of the previous work that has been done in the area of the thesis in order that he will have the insight needed to understand the thesis and to fit its findings into the overall picture. In preparing to write this chapter, the first step is to make a rough outline. The coding system applied to the students note cards, during his review of the literature, is often useful as a basis for preparing this first outline. After a rough outline has been prepared covering the major topics of the review, the student should read all of his note cards and sort them into the topics contained in this outline. He must then decide upon the order in which these topics will be presented. After ordering his topics, he should review the cards dealing with the first topic until he is thoroughly familiar with their contents. Usually, in the process of rereading the cards he will get some additional ideas on how the topic should be presented. He can also organize the cards for the given topic into the order that he will present them and can decide which studies in this area are to be emphasized. Often he will find two or three studies in each topic that, being more pertinent and carefully done, can serve as the foundation of his review. The student may find several other studies that have been done in essentially the same manner and have produced similar findings. In this case, the student should pick out the best studies and describe them in some detail. The other studies are often dismissed merely by saying "findings of the above studies have been largely supported by a number of other studies that have employed essentially the same approach." These supporting studies may then be referred to in a footnote or referenced using whatever system the student has adopted for his thesis. This procedure has the advantage of presenting the pertinent findings and letting the reader know what other studies support these findings without laboriously discussing each study in detail.

The student should repeat the aforementioned procedure in each of the topics he wishes to cover in his review of the literature chapter. The review of the topics can then be combined in a rough draft that is well-organized and that gives the reader a brief yet reasonably complete picture of the status of research in the area reviewed.

A more difficult task in preparing the review of the literature chapter is to pull together all of the findings under the various topics discussed into an organized picture of the state of knowledge in the area reviewed. The process of combining and interpreting the literature is much more difficult than merely reviewing what has been done. In doing the review, the student should have gained some insights into his field that are not apparent to a person not carrying out a thorough review. These insights should be shared with your reader because they can make a significant contribution to his understanding of the field. This final section of the review is by far the most difficult to write because it requires that you have a thorough understanding of the research you have read.

A well-organized review of the literature followed by an insightful interpretation is not only of great value to the reader but its preparation greatly helps the research worker to develop his own understanding of the previous knowledge in his field. If the graduate student's schedule permits, a rough draft of the review of literature chapter should be prepared immediately after completing the review and prior to the start of data collection. At this time the material is most fresh in the student's mind, and the insights that he will gain by preparing his draft and interpreting the previous research may well lead to new ideas and improvements in his research design.

The student is cautioned against an article-by-article presentation in his review of the literature. Many students do little more than prepare an abstract of each article they wish to discuss, and then string these abstracts together without any attempt at continuity or logical organization. Such a review is excessively long and fails in its purpose of giving the reader an understanding of the field. Another pitfall the student should avoid in preparing his review of literature is that of presenting each study in essentially the same way. It is not uncommon, for example, to find reviews of literature in which the student treats each article in a separate paragraph and starts each paragraph with the name of the researcher who has written the described report. Such a stereotyped coverage of the literature, even if well-organized, is boring and tiresome to read.

Another error commonly made in preparing the review of the literature is excessive use of quotations. Generally, a research report can be made more interesting if quotations are used only when the material quoted is especially well written and can be inserted without spoiling the continuity of the presentation. Nothing is more tiresome or difficult to follow than a review of the literature that is merely an accumulation of quotations, each linked to the next with a sentence or two by the person preparing the review. Inasmuch as each quotation comes from a different context and has a different style, this technique invariably results in a report that is disjointed, poorly organized, and difficult to read.

Research procedures

The chapter on research procedures contains a description of the sample, the measures used, and the steps taken in carrying out the project. It is usually started with a detailed description of the sample. This description is needed in order for the reader to assess the generalizability of the research findings and also to determine the degree to which the research sample is representative of the population and is comparable to other samples to which he may wish to apply the research results. The specific information given in the description of the sample varies with the nature of the study, but often includes such information as the age range of the subjects, proportions of each sex if both males and females are used, IQ distribution, scores of the experimental and control groups on variables where comparability is important, urban-rural nature of subjects, education of parents, and others. The population from which the sample was drawn should be defined, and the method of selecting the sample should be described in detail. If a random sampling were employed, a detailed description of the procedure for selecting cases should be given. If a matching system were used, the matching criteria, why these criteria were selected, the number of cases lost because of inability to obtain a satisfactory matching, and the possible effect of the loss should be discussed in detail. In matching studies, some evidence of the comparability of matched groups, that is, an indication of the success of the matching, also should be given. If a stratified sampling were used, the criteria for identifying cases at each of the strata or levels should be described and the method for selecting the cases from those available in each level should also be described. If the study involves comparison of two large groups that are later broken into subgroups, the criteria for establishing the subgroups should be discussed. In most educational studies, it is desirable to describe in considerable detail the schools from which the sample was drawn. This might include descriptions of the curriculum, the socioeconomic groups served by the school, the experience of teachers participating in the study, the performance of the school or district on standardized achievement measures, and the special characteristics of the school or of the geographical area that may tend to make the sample different in some respect from similar samples drawn from other areas.

The next section of this chapter includes a description of all measures used to collect data in the research project. If well-known standard measures such as the *California Psychological Inventory,* the *STEP Achievement Tests,* or the *S.R.A. Youth Inventory* are used, this description can be quite brief. With well-known measures of this sort, a description of the scores obtained and what they purport to measure, a brief discussion of the evidence of reliability and validity, and the relationship of each measure to the hypotheses is usually sufficient.

If new or little known measures are used or if measures have been developed especially for the research project, a much more detailed description is required. This should include a description of the types of items used in the measure, reliability data, evidence of validity with particular emphasis upon construct validity, findings of other studies (if any) in which the measure has been used, and any other material necessary to give the reader a thorough understanding of the measure. If a measure has been developed for the study, a detailed description of how the measure was developed and stand-ardized should be provided. Very often, unless the measure is of a routine nature such as a biographical data sheet, a separate chapter in the thesis is devoted to the development of the measure. Measures are normally administered either to test one of the hypotheses of the study or to obtain descriptive data concerning the sample that may assist in the selection or description of the sample. In either case, the writer should explain in the discussion of each measure the reasons why the measure was selected and the specific purpose that is to serve in the research.

In using new or locally developed measures or when the scoring procedures of a standard measure have been changed to meet the needs of the study better, a description of scoring procedures is neces-sary. This description should be sufficiently detailed so as to make it possible for the person reading the description to use the scoring system if he so wishes. In most cases, the scoring procedure, keys, a copy of the measure, item-analysis results, and other standardiza-tion data on new measures are included in the appendix of the thesis.

In the final section of this chapter the writer describes the re-search procedures, usually starting by identifying the type of experi-mental design that he has employed such as: descriptive question-naire study, causal-comparative design, or correlational design. He then should present a detailed account of how this basic design was applied in his study. This description should be sufficient so that another research worker reading the report could set up an identical study. The description of the research procedures usually reviews the steps taken to collect the data, including any occurrences that may have influenced the results, such as changes in the schedule for administering tests, disturbances during the testing situation, or un-expected subject reactions. This section should also include a discus-sion of any steps taken to establish controls or reduce errors in the study such as administering measures to all groups simultaneously or at the same time of day, attempts to equate teacher ability, standardization of the testing situations for different groups, procedures employed to obtain makeups on students absent in the initial testing, methods of avoiding contamination, or controls employed to reduce or eliminate observer bias. If carrying out the study has revealed any flaws that might have affected the results, these should also be discussed so that the reader may consider them in his appraisal of the research findings and so that future research workers may avoid making the same mistakes. For example, if measures or techniques are employed that are found to be impractical or inappropriate for the sample, these should be discussed even though the research worker may have discarded the results obtained from them.

Research findings

The next chapter in the thesis or dissertation is concerned with the research findings. If a single analysis technique such as the t-test has been employed throughout the entire analysis, this technique and the reasons for using it are usually discussed at the beginning of the chapter on findings. If, on the other hand, the research is such that different techniques have been employed for testing different hypotheses, the description of and reasons for using each technique are usually included with the findings obtained from the use of the technique. Perhaps the best method to obtain clarity in the discussion of the findings is to organize this section of the paper around the hypotheses. After a brief introduction, the writer repeats the first hypothesis as it appears in Chapter 1, and then presents all findings pertinent to this hypothesis. This same technique is then repeated for each hypothesis and has the advantage of focusing the reader's attention on the hypothesis immediately before he reads the pertinent results. Tables and figures are useful in describing the research results and in showing trends that have emerged from the analysis. A table or figure can present the overall picture of the data more clearly and more economically than would be possible if no table or figure were used and, instead, each specific fact were discussed in the text. By using tables and figures, the writer is relieved of the responsibility of presenting a tedious recitation of all findings obtained and, instead, can emphasis those aspects of the results that seem to be most important or noteworthy. Students who are inexperienced in writing research papers often make the mistake of preparing a table, and then discussing every entry in the table whether significant or not. This approach results in a boring paper and defeats the purpose of using tables and figures.

The most important task of the researcher in writing this chapter is to identify and interpret the major findings. He should discuss possible reasons why these results occurred, fit them into the findings of previous research, suggest field applications, and make theoretical interpretations. Because the person doing the study has usually developed a deeper insight into his research problem than will be the case for most of the persons reading the study, his interpretations usually have greater depth than any that the reader could make for himself. In interpreting research results, a great deal of thought and careful study is required. One of the most common weaknesses found in the research writing of graduate students is that their reports present important and interesting findings but fail to provide a thoughtful interpretation of these findings. Often, the findings obtained from the analysis originally planned by the student will suggest other analysis procedures to the student that will either provide additional data concerning his hypotheses or in some cases provide interesting information not related to his initial hypotheses. In either case, the further analysis should be done. It is not uncommon for research workers to find that the most important results of their research are unrelated to the hypotheses, and these results come as somewhat of a surprise.

Summary and conclusions

The summary and conclusions chapter usually includes a brief statement of the problem, a description of the main features of the method omitting most of the details concerning subjects and measures, a listing of the main findings, and the writer's conclusions based on these findings. The summary should be as brief as possible consistent with a clear presentation of all important information concerning the problem, method, and findings. Findings are often listed by number with each major finding summarized in one or two sentences. The same method suggested for presenting the findings of the previous chapter may be used: that is each hypothesis may be listed, immediately followed by a very brief summary of the findings related to the hypothesis. The conclusions are usually presented in somewhat more detail. The student should be especially careful to draw all conclusions directly from the findings and to avoid over-concluding because this is looked upon by most research workers as a sign of immaturity and lack of scientific objectivity.

It is often desirable to add a section on implications. In this section, the writer can present interpretations, speculations, and ideas that would be out of place in the conclusions. Possible applications of the findings to the public schools or pertinent field situations may also be discussed, and such a discussion can be of great help to teachers and administrators in the field who may not have sufficient training to discover these applications for themselves.

Inasmuch as this final chapter is the one most often read by other persons, the writer should make every effort to make it clear and concise while covering all of the main features of the study.

Reference materials

The usual reference materials in a thesis or dissertation include the bibliography and appendix. The bibliography must list all references that have been referred to in footnotes or otherwise cited in the study and may also include pertinent references not cited.[1] The format of the bibliography should be decided upon when the student starts reviewing the literature so that the data on his bibliography cards will be recorded in the correct format. If this has been done, compiling the bibliography is a very simple matter because it merely requires selecting the bibliography cards that have been cited, placing them in alphabetical order, and copying the bibliographic data onto a sheet. If the bibliography cards have been carelessly compiled, the student will find it necessary to spend a considerable amount of time checking each card and making the changes necessary in order to get the reference in the accepted format. The most common fault found in the bibliographies of theses and dissertations is inconsistent format. The method of referencing a particular type of source should be consistent down to the last comma. Common errors include failure to use the same punctuation marks in different bibliographic entries, the use of the author's first name in some entries and initials only in other entries, the abbreviation of some journal titles while not abbreviating others, and the use of different abbreviations for the same journal title. Each bit of information, however, offers the op-

[1] Some universities require that bibliography be limited to references actually cited in the study.

portunity to make a mistake, and many mistakes will be made in a bibliographic reference unless the student exercises a great deal of care in preparing his bibliography.

Most theses and dissertations require an appendix in order to include items that may be of interest or importance to some readers but are not sufficiently pertinent to be included in the body of the paper. Materials commonly placed in the appendix include: (1) tables that are very long or that contain material not essential to understanding the study, (2) locally developed research aids such as forms and instruction sheets, (3) copies of the data-gathering instruments used in the study, (4) item-analysis data and other materials pertinent to measures, (5) scoring protocols and procedures, and (6) lengthy quotations that may be of interest to some of the readers, particularly if the source containing the quotations is not readily available.

PREPARING A RESEARCH ARTICLE

The graduate student has much to gain by preparing one or more research articles, based on his thesis or dissertation, immediately after he has completed his research paper. At this time, all phases of the research are fresh in his mind, and he can prepare the article for publication much easier than if he puts aside this task and does it later. Most persons who employ holders of graduate degrees in education are interested in their publications, and if the graduate student is able to list one or two publications, he will have an advantage over many of his colleagues.

The first step in preparing a research article is to decide what journal is most likely to publish work in your area. Journals that are likely to accept your article can easily be identified by checking the bibliography of your thesis to determine which journals have published articles pertinent to your research topic. Usually one or two journals will be found that have published most of the articles closely related to your research, and these are the ones most likely to accept your article. A factor that sometimes should be considered in selecting a journal to which the research article will be submitted is the publication lag. If the graduate student plans to seek a position in which research publication is especially important, such as an assistant professorship at a university, it may be to his advantage to submit his article to a journal that provides for early publication. Most journals in education have publication lags ranging from six months to two years. Some journals, however, will publish an article with almost no lag if the author pays an early publication fee. This fee is generally quite high; for example $30 per page in the *Journal of Educational Psychology*.

Once you have decided upon the journal in which you wish to publish, you should examine several recent issues in order to gain some insight into the format and usual length of articles accepted.

Although the research article follows the same general format as the thesis, it is much shorter. Brevity is essential in articles for publication in professional journals because the available space is very limited and the editor usually wishes to include as many studies as possible. In preparing a research article for publication in a journal, the general statement of the problem is usually shortened to a paragraph and is often omitted completely—the article then starting with a statement of the specific hypotheses. The review of the literature is also shortened a great deal with brief reference made only to those studies that are very closely related to the research being reported. The section on procedure is also shortened to some extent, usually giving only a brief description of the design, sample, and measures used. If, however, some of the procedures or measures employed are new or unusual, they should be covered in some detail. The section on findings makes up a considerably larger proportion of the research article than of the thesis, this section being shortened less when revised for publication. Even in the findings section, however, some shortening of the treatment as it was prepared for the thesis is usually in order. Tables are used extensively because they can present the findings in briefer form. Only the most important findings are discussed at any length in the text. The summary and conclusions should be presented in the thesis as briefly as possible, consisteı.t with clarity, and this section can thus be transferred with little change to the research article. The length of the bibliography is usually not restricted in research articles, and in preparing this section all of the important sources should be listed. A complete bibliography is, of course, of great help to future researchers who wish to carry out a review of the literature in the same area or wish to learn more about the topic dealt with in your study.

In some cases a thesis or dissertation deals with a subject that can be logically divided into more than one article, and such division usually makes it possible to prepare shorter articles that have a better chance of being accepted for publication. For example, if a student were doing a study of the characteristics of successful and unsuccessful nursing-school students, he may have collected some data dealing with personality characteristics, and other data concerning vocational aptitudes, interests, and intelligence. In this case, if sufficient important findings were obtained, it may be advisable to prepare two articles for publication—one dealing with personality characteristics of successful and unsuccessful nursing students and the other comparing vocational aptitudes, interests, and intelligence of the two groups.

After preparing a satisfactory draft of a research article, the student should have three or more copies typed double-spaced following the format of the journal to which he plans to submit his article. Some journals provide publication manuals that will be of consider' able help to the student in preparing an article in acceptable format. If he has decided to submit his article to one of the journals published by the American Psychological Association, he should purchase a copy of the A.P.A. publication manual.[2] Usually, however, an article meeting the format requirements of the journal can be prepared without a publication manual if the student carefully follows the format of articles published in a recent issue of the journal. He should be particularly careful to convert the form of his bibliography to the accepted format for the journal he has selected. The manuscript as submitted to the journal should be very carefully checked at least two or three times to be certain that no further changes are needed and no errors are present.

After the final manuscript has been prepared, he may check a recent issue of the journal to find out where his manuscript should be sent. A brief covering letter should be written, and stamps should be included for the return of the manuscript if it is not accepted for publication. Most journals require that two or three copies of the manuscript be submitted so that copies may be sent to different persons on the editorial board. After the editor receives the manuscript, a postcard is usually sent to the author acknowledging receipt, and the manuscript is sent to members of the editorial board who are

[2] Available by sending $1.00 to the American Psychological Association, 1333 16th Street, N.W., Washington 6, D.C.

most familiar with the topic covered by the article. There is usually a considerable lag before the author is informed whether the article is accepted; and after receiving this information, it may be a year or more before he receives the galley proofs. The galley proofs of an article are set up in type as it will appear in the journal. It is necessary that the author check the galley proof very carefully and correct any errors discovered.

If the student's manuscript is rejected by the first journal to which it has been submitted, this rejection will usually be accompanied by a statement of the reasons for the rejection. The article, however, may be revised and submitted to another journal. The fact that it has been rejected by one journal does not necessarily mean that it is unsuitable for publication. Many factors operate in the evaluation of an article such as changes in editorial policy, a particularly heavy backlog of accepted articles, personal biases of editorial board members, and others, any of which can result in an article being rejected even though it has merit.

MISTAKES OFTEN MADE BY GRADUATE STUDENTS

1. Student fails to prepare draft copies of information he must later include in his thesis while he still has it fresh in his memory.

2. Puts off all work on his manuscript until his study is finished.

3. Organizes his review of the literature chronologically instead of arranging his research articles into related topics.

4. Treats each study referred to in the "review of literature" in mechanical fashion, devoting about the same amount of space to each regardless of pertinence or importance.

5. Fails to integrate the findings of his review of the literature.

6. Uses too many quotations and selects quotations that do not make their point as well as the student could make it using his own words.

7. Provides an inadequate description of the research sample and measures used.

8. Discusses minor findings that can be presented better in a table, and fails to emphasize important findings.

ANNOTATED REFERENCES

1. The following four references will be particularly useful to the research worker in preparing his first article for publication in an education journal:

    (a) SHANNON, J. R. "Tips to Writers from Seventy-Five Editors of Educational Periodicals," *Journal of Educational Research,* 1950, 44, 241–68.

    (b) ———. "Art in Writing for Educational Periodicals: The Introduction," *ibid.,* 1951, 44, 599–610.

    (c) ———. "Art in Writing for Educational Periodicals: The Ending," *ibid.,* 1953, 46, 333–45.

    (d) ———. "Art in Writing for Educational Periodicals: The Main Body," *ibid.,* 1954, 47, 489–504.

2. AMERICAN PSYCHOLOGICAL ASSOCIATION COUNCIL OF EDITORS. *Publication Manual of the American Psychological Association, 1957 revision.* Washington, D.C.: American Psychological Association, 1957. This manual contains detailed instructions for preparing articles for the journals published by the American Psychological Association. Much of the material presented, excepting details of format, is equally appropriate as a general guide to publishing in other professional journals in the behavioral sciences.

3. ARKIN, HERBERT, and COLTON, RAYMOND R. *Graphs: How to Make and Use Them.* New York: Harper & Bros., 1936. This book presents a thorough and rather formal treatment of the construction of graphs, including a chapter on each major type of graph, with detailed information on the use, construction, and common applications of each.

4. BALL, J., and WILLIAMS, C. B. *Report Writing.* New York: The Ronald Press Co., 1955. Although written primarily as a guide for business men and engineers, this book contains chapters (on organizing facts and ideas, writing and revising, language, style, and the use of visual aids) that have much information pertinent to writing educational research reports. The third section of the book contains a number of brief and very well-selected supplemental readings by other authors that provide the student with a great deal of pertinent and interesting background material.

5. EMBERGER, M. R., and HALL, M. R. *Scientific Writing.* New York: Harcourt, Brace & Co., 1955. This text provides a detailed treatment on the subject of scientific writing. Each aspect of the usual research project ranging from definition of the problem to analysis and interpretation is

treated, and other topics, such as ways of directing the paper to the reader, scientific style, and format, are also covered. Each chapter is preceded by a brief outline of the chapter content so that the student may locate sub-topics with which he is particularly concerned.

6. McCann, L. E. "Presenting That Idea in the Professional Journal," *Phi Delta Kappan,* 1958, 39, 173–76. This article provides a useful guide to writing articles for professional educational journals. Most of the suggestions are more appropriate for preparing opinion articles than for research articles. Importance of orderly procedure and a good outline are stressed, and practical hints are given for finding the most appropriate journals to which to submit the article, procedures for submitting manuscripts, and other topics.

7. Modley, R., Lowenstein, D., *et al. Pictographs and Graphs: How to Make and Use Them.* New York: Harper & Bros., 1952. A well-illustrated and easily read coverage of the use of graphs with particular emphasis on pictographs. Chapter 6, "Cheating With Charts," deals with misleading charts and graphs and is especially recommended for study by the graduate student so that he may detect deceptive graphing practices in evaluating the work of others and avoid them in his own work.

CHAPTER 18

An Overview

EDUCATIONAL RESEARCH—PRESENT AND FUTURE

At present, educational research is in a period of great expansion. For many years the overwhelming majority of educational research was carried out by individual professors in colleges and universities and was supported largely by the research worker's personal resources or from small grants that usually covered nothing more than the materials and clerical assistance required. The trend in recent years, however, has been toward a great many more research projects and also larger and better-financed projects. Later in this chapter we will discuss some of the sources of financial support for educational research that have developed in recent years. The individual research worker is also, to a considerable degree, being supplanted by the research team because the scope of research projects and the breadth of knowledge required make it extremely difficult for a single individual to plan and carry out all phases of the project.

The expansion we are now experiencing in educational research is due to several factors. First, and perhaps most important, it reflects a gradual increase in scientific values within our society. The tremendous gains made in science and technology over the past twenty years have illustrated the power of scientific method to the average citizen to a degree far overshadowing his previous experiences. The impressive record of the physical sciences and medicine has led to an increased tendency in our society to look to science for the solutions to our problems. This tendency to look for scientific solutions has now expanded to embrace the problems of the behavioral sciences. It is reflected in the attitudes of businessmen who employ psychologists or sociologists to develop advertising programs, space age industries that employ behavioral scientists to design space capsules and study the effects of space travel on the psychology of the individual, and school teachers and administrators who increasingly recognize the need to understand the human being in the educational process and, for the first time, are looking to the educational research worker and behavioral scientist in large numbers in quest of the knowledge and understanding needed.

The increase in educational problems brought about by rapid technological change has also been an important factor in the expansion of educational research. Both laymen and educators have recognized in recent years that better educational methods and sweeping curriculum changes are needed to meet the educational challenges of a highly technical and rapidly changing society.

Problems of educational research

In many ways, our current resources in educational research are unequal to the demand placed upon them by the increased scientific orientation of our society and the need for solutions to our increasingly complex educational problems. Education is still in the process of transition from an art to a science, and the majority of the persons employed in the profession have little background in scientific thinking nor do they consider themselves to be scientists. Education has a number of "growing pains" that can be traced to our present transition from an art to a science. We can identify two groups in the profession: the smaller, containing persons strongly oriented toward research who consider education to be a science and are applying the available scientific tools to educational problems; and the larger, strongly oriented to deal with the problems of day-to-day teaching who are not familiar with educational research and do not regard the methods of education as being adaptable to scientific investigation. Communication has always been difficult between these groups, and this has contributed in turn to the wide gap that exists between educational research knowledge and public school practice.

Because of the lack of emphasis upon education as a science many educational research workers are poorly trained, and much of the educational research that has been done in the past has been poorly designed and executed. Thus, a major problem for educational institutions is to develop better training programs and to increase materially the output of educational research workers. When compared with almost any other field of endeavor, the percentage of educational resources that go into research is extremely small. It has been estimated, for example, that business and industry invest at least 5 per

cent of its budget in research. Education spends less than .05 per
cent for research.[1] In a recent report of the President's Science Advisory Committee, it was pointed out that:

> Education has a national budget second only to that of national defense.
> Yet only a small fraction of 1 per cent of this budget has been spent on
> research and development. This is one obvious reason for the failure of edu-
> cation to make technical advances comparable to those seen in other aspects
> of our national life.[2]

Inasmuch as the amount of money has increased more rapidly in
recent years than the number of trained research workers, the financial support available is adequate in terms of the personnel available
to do research, but, from a long term standpoint, it is far from adequate in terms of the amount of research that should be carried out
in education.

The future of educational research depends to a great degree on
how successful we are in solving the aforementioned problems. The
solution of one of these problems without making comparable gains
in the other problem areas will not lead us to the higher quality and
greater quantity of research needed in education. The cycle shown in
Figure 11 illustrates the interdependence of the various steps in the
educational research cycle. Each step in the cycle is related to all of
the other steps so that a gain in one leads to a gain in all. Forces are
at work in each step of the cycle that promise to lead to a great acceleration of educational research over the next few years.

Although it is difficult to identify all factors that have contributed
to the current cycle of expansion, the Cooperative Research Program
established in the U.S. Office of Education by Public Law 531 is
considered by many to have provided the initial impetus. Let us see
how this program has affected the cycle. The money made available
by this program has gone to educational researchers in colleges and
universities for the most part. This improved the competence of
many educational scientists on college faculties by giving them the
opportunity to attack significant problems with better designs and

---

[1] N. A. Fattu, "A Survey of Educational Research at Selected Universities," *First
Annual Symposium on Educational Research* (Bloomington, Ind.: Phi Delta Kappa,
1960), p. 6.

[2] Behavioral Sciences Subpanel of the President's Science Advisory Committee,
"Strengthening the Behavioral Sciences," *Science*, CXXXVI (1962), 240. Reprinted
by permission of *Science*.

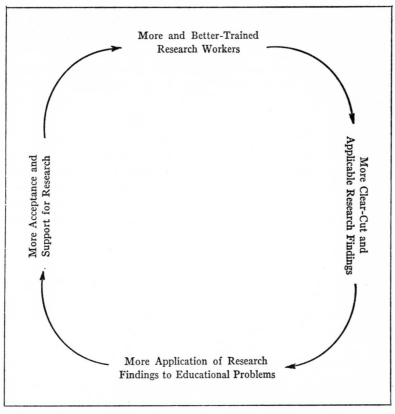

Fɪɢ. 11. Factors related to the expansion of educational research.

more thoroughness than was possible when the faculty member had to reply on spare time and his own financial resources. The more significant studies thus started also contributed to increasing the number of graduate students trained in research as money for graduate assistantships has usually been available in the Cooperative Research Program contracts. Students receiving research assistantships also received better training because they were able to participate in more significant projects. As was pointed out in a recent report concerned with the education of research workers in psychology:

Research training is achieved by doing research in a research environment; details of the procedures used by effective teachers of research vary in detail from one to another, and even the same teacher varies his procedure from one student to another. Only the apprenticeship relation, it seems, has the flexibility to allow for the great individual differences in attitude and procedure that characterize productive scientists.

In conclusion, therefore, we say that research is learned by doing and taught mainly by contagion. Research must first be going on if there is to be research training.[3]

To proceed to the next step in the cycle, better research has been achieved through the Cooperative Research Program, not only by providing money for better and more extensive studies such as Project Talent (see Chapter 1) but also by setting up high standards and supporting only research that meets these standards.

Some of the projects carried out under this program have already had an impact upon the public schools that will complete the cycle shown in Figure 11 and at the same time start the cycle again because this impact will lead to more financial support from school districts, states, private foundations, and the federal government.

There are many other activities and programs that are having an influence upon one or more of the factors that make up this cycle. Many of the larger universities have strengthened their programs in recent years. The following points that have been emphasized in the development of the Department of Educational Psychology at the University of Wisconsin illustrate this trend:

An atmosphere of high-level research endeavor must permeate the department of educational psychology. *Every* professor should be engaged actively and continuously in research, aided by graduate students specializing in his area. . . .

Doctoral candidates should realize early that the responsibility for learning is theirs. They learn some things in class, but much more outside class from the professor, other students, their own research, and especially the printed word. . . .

Participation in professional meetings by even first-year graduate students seems essential. This can begin at the local level with regular colloquia and faculty-student seminars, and then move to state, regional, and national levels. . . .

Pushing worthwhile materials to publication should be encouraged at every stage of the doctoral program. . . .

[3] American Psychological Assoc., "Education for Research in Psychology," *The American Psychologist,* XIV (1959), 179. Reprinted by permission of the American Psychological Assoc.

A considerable percentage of doctoral recipients should seek postdoctoral fellowships for one or more years to strengthen their research competency and pursue their research interests.[4]

The consideration of points such as these in the preparation of research workers will almost surely lead to a better program than most universities now have.

The cycle shown in Figure 11 not only illustrates factors leading to acceleration of educational research, it also illustrates their interdependence. Ideally, gains must be made in a balanced fashion to get the most out of educational research. For example, if Congress appropriated one hundred million dollars for educational research in the next fiscal year it is doubtful if any great acceleration of research would occur until enough educational researchers had been trained to utilize this money in productive and well-designed research programs.

In summary, the future of educational research rests jointly upon the federal government, which is the logical source of funds for research of national significance; the universities, which must bear the burden of training more and better educational researchers; and the public schools, which must better learn to translate research knowledge into classroom practice.

FINANCIAL SUPPORT FOR EDUCATIONAL RESEARCH

Introduction

The last twenty years have seen a tremendous increase in support for research in all fields. The number of foundations, many of which support research, doubled between 1955 and 1960. In 1957, the last year in which a survey was conducted, foundations granted over thirty-three million dollars to support scientific research.[5] Federal support has increased even more drastically. It is estimated that the federal government provided universities with fifteen million dollars in 1940 for research and development. In the fiscal year 1958 to 1959,

---

[4] Julian C. Stanley, "Helping Doctoral Students in Educational Psychology Become Excellent Researchers," *Newsletter of Division 15, American Psychological Assoc.* (1962), pp. 3–4. Reprinted by permission of Julian C. Stanley and the American Psychological Assoc.

[5] Ann D. Walton and S. E. Andrews (eds.), *The Foundation Directory* (1st ed.; New York: Russell Sage Foundation, 1960), p. 4.

this had increased to 440 million dollars, and will reach 1.2 billion dollars for the 1962 fiscal year.[6, 7] At this time over 70 per cent of all university research is federally financed. Both the proportion and the amount of research support in the physical sciences has been far greater than in the social sciences. Approximately 95 per cent of all university research in physics is federally supported as against only 25 per cent of research in the social sciences.[8] A good deal has been written on the advantages and disadvantages of this federal support but in the social sciences most authorities agree that the advantages have far outweighed the disadvantages and the net effect has been a significant gain in these sciences. The tremendous impact of federal research support is discussed by Darly who concludes that a major university today, public or private, engaged in graduate teaching and research, cannot maintain its stature without the present partnership with the federal government.[9]

Federal support in education

Federal support to educational research has been much less than in the physical sciences but has still been sufficiently great to effect tremendous changes. The major sources of federal support for research of a strictly educational nature is the Cooperative Research Program, The Title VI Program, and the Title VII Program of the U.S. Office of Education. The Cooperative Research Program received its first appropriation of about one million dollars in 1957. The appropriation for the 1962 fiscal year was about five million dollars. This program supports research in all areas of education. The Title VI Program supports research relating to improving the teaching of modern foreign languages. This program had a budget of over seven million dollars for research in this area during the 1962 fiscal year. The Title VII Program is devoted to research in the development and use of new educational media such as television and teaching machines. Over thirteen million dollars has been budgeted in

[6] J. C. Weaver, "Federal Aid to Research and Graduate Education," *Journal of Higher Education*, XXX (1959), 146–54.

[7] National Science Foundation, *Federal Funds for Science X, Fiscal Years 1960, 1961, and 1962* (Washington, D.C.: U.S. Government Printing Office, 1962), p. 13.

[8] Charles D. Kidd, "New Government—University Relationships in Research," *Journal of Higher Education*, XVI (1960), 3–6.

[9] John G. Darly, "The Impact of Federal Support on Higher Education," *The American Psychologist*, XIV (1959), 480–88.

this program since 1959, with about 4.75 million budgeted in fiscal year 1962.

In addition to the aforementioned programs, many other federal agencies support research in areas very closely allied to education such as educational psychology, developmental psychology, and educational sociology. For example, in areas of psychology such as learning and retention, speech and language, motivation, higher mental processes, and human development, all of which are closely related to education, the National Science Foundation reports research projects sponsored by many government agencies including the Office of the Surgeon General, U.S. Army, the Public Health Service, the Office of Scientific Research, the Atomic Energy Commission, the Office of Vocational Rehabilitation, and the Air Force Personnel Training and Research Center.[10] Some of these agencies designate specific areas in which they wish research to be carried out and invite scientists to submit proposals. Others accept research proposals related to the broad interest areas of the agencies, while still others consider all research proposals that promise to contribute significantly to the store of human knowledge.

Postdoctoral fellowships are available through the National Science Foundation and the National Institutes of Health to provide advanced training for research and to support scientists in conducting research. These fellowships are available in a wide range of subject fields, and no restrictions are placed upon the scientist in terms of specific areas that his research may follow.

Other sources of research support

In addition to federal support for educational research, research funds are also available through grants and postdoctoral fellowships supported by foundations, institutional research programs supported by universities, and educational research funds available in state departments of education and local school districts.

There are over twelve thousand foundations in the United States with total assets in excess of eleven and a half billion dollars. A recent survey indicates that the yearly grants of these foundations exceed six hundred million dollars with nearly half of this amount going to

[10] National Science Foundation, *Semi-Annual Report of Government Sponsored Research Projects in Psychology, Psychiatry, and Closely Related Areas* (Washington, D.C.: U.S. Government Printing Office, March, 1957).

education. The best source of information on foundations in the United States is *The Foundation Directory*.[11]

A number of postdoctoral fellowships supported by private organizations and principally aimed at supporting scientists in their research pursuits are listed in the yearly editions of *Fellowships in the Arts and Sciences*.[12] Many universities have institutional research programs supported at least partially in the university budget. Bureaus of Educational Research are found at nearly all of the major universities. Some universities have a centralized educational research council to consider proposals from faculty members and/or students. Such funds are particularly helpful to the new faculty member as they are often made available for pilot studies and small budget studies that would be unacceptable for support under most research programs sponsored by private foundations or the federal government. Such pilot studies, if productive, however, can lead to broader and more sophisticated research proposals that can obtain support from these latter sources. Many of our state departments of education include a research division, and some state departments also have research funds available to support research projects in the public schools of the state.

Most large school districts now employ research personnel and carry out research programs on problems of special interest to the district. Even smaller districts that do not employ full-time personnel to carry out research in the district are often willing to provide released time and some financial help for teachers or administrators in the district who wish to carry out educational research.

ASSISTANCE FOR GRADUATE STUDENTS IN EDUCATION

The amount of financial assistance available for graduate students also has greatly increased in recent years. Although undergraduate scholarships are based primarily upon financial need, the emphasis in programs of financial support for graduate students is on academic accomplishment. The amount of financial support is now sufficient so that it is doubtful that any student with a good scholarship record

[11] Walton and Andrews (eds.), *op. cit.*, p. 4.

[12] M. E. Shiltz, *Fellowships in the Arts and Sciences, 1962–63* (5th ed.; Washington, D.C.: Association of American Colleges, 1961).

need be deprived of graduate training because of financial considerations.

The usual types of financial assistance include the fellowship, the teaching or research assistantship, and the student loan. In each case, these forms of assistance may originate from the university's own income or may be sponsored by a private foundation, industrial organization, fraternal organization, or government agency. The amount of support available under different programs, of course, varies considerably. The fellowship usually does not require that the graduate student do any work or provide any services in return. The teaching or research assistantship requires a certain amount of work from the student, although usually this work is closely allied to his field and constitutes valuable experience. Student loans, which are perhaps expanding more rapidly than other sources of assistance, usually permit repayment over a long period and at low interest rates. Student loan programs sometimes have provisions for canceling part of the loan if the student meets certain conditions.

It is beyond the scope of this book to provide the graduate students with data concerning specific fellowships or scholarships. The sources and amounts of assistance, of course, change each year so that such information would quickly become out of date. If, however, the student refers to the annotated bibliography at the end of this chapter, he will find a number of sources that will be of help to him.

Federal and foundation support

To give the student some idea of the scope of assistance available, the following are a few of the major sources listed in *Fellowships in the Arts and Sciences, 1962–63*.[13]

1. *The National Defense Graduate Fellowship Program.* This program awarded 1,500 fellowships in the 1961–62 academic year with over one hundred being awarded in education. The National Defense Graduate Fellowship is normally a three year award providing a stipend of $2,000 for the first year, $2,200 for the second, and $2,400 for the third plus an additional allowance of $400 for each dependent.[14]

---

[13] Shiltz, *op. cit.*

[14] U.S. Department of Health, Education and Welfare, Office of Education, *National Defense Graduate Fellowships through Graduate Programs, 1961–62* (Washington, D.C.: U.S. Government Printing Office, 1961).

2. *National Science Foundation Graduate Fellowships*. These fellowships are given in some social sciences, including psychology, but not education. These fellowships are currently being awarded at the rate of 2,500 each year. Although most of the aforementioned fellowships have been awarded to graduate students in the physical sciences, other N.S.F. programs are available for the assistance of teachers and adminstrators in the public schools. Among these programs are summer fellowships for secondary school teachers in science and mathematics who wish to pursue advanced study in these areas. Stipends are computed at the rate of $75 a week with dependency allowance of $15 per week for each dependent. Tuition fees and a limited travel allowance are also paid by the National Science Foundation.[15] The National Science Foundation also supports summer institutes to provide additional training for high school and college teachers in science, mathematics, and engineering. Summer institutes have also been provided for elementary school supervisors and teachers. In-service institutes for high school and elementary personnel, designed to provide supplemental training in science and mathematics are offered during the regular academic year. These institutes are offered without tuition or fees, and funds are available for the cost of books and travel although stipends are not provided.[16]

3. *Woodrow Wilson National Fellowships*. Approximately one thousand fellowships per year of $1,500 are made to students who wish to enter graduate work in order to prepare for college teaching.[17]

The *Foundation Directory* is also an excellent source for graduate students seeking fellowships. A 1957 survey of 110 of the larger foundations indicated that 8½ million dollars was available through foundations for graduate fellowships during that year. The student should consult the field of interest index to locate foundations that grant graduate fellowships in his area of interest.

The most extensive source of student loans is the *National Defense Student Loan Program*. In this program, both financial need and scholarship are considered. Special consideration is given to students

[15] For information and application materials, write Secondary School Fellowships, American Association for the Advancement of Science, 1515 Massachusetts Ave., N.W., Washington 5, D. C.

[16] National Science Foundation, *National Science Foundation Programs for Education in the Sciences* (Washington, D.C.: U.S. Government Printing Office, March, 1961), 35 pp.

[17] Shiltz, *op. cit.*

who express a desire to teach in elementary or secondary schools and up to 50 per cent of the loan plus interest is canceled if the borrower becomes a full-time teacher in public schools. Students may borrow up to $1,000 a year over a four-year period with the repayment plan beginning the year after the borrower ceases to be a full-time student. Over $40 million was appropriated for this program during the fiscal year of 1960 and was distributed to 1,360 participating institutions. As of February 29, 1960, 125,000 loans had been made with these funds.[18]

Institutional support

A great deal of support for graduate students is provided by educational institutions themselves in the form of fellowships, loans, and assistantships. A survey of assistance available to graduate students at 106 institutions in 1955–56, showed nearly 25,000 fellowships had been granted with a value of over eighteen million dollars. Nearly 30,000 assistantships with a value of over thirty-five million dollars and over 30,000 loans with a value of nearly five million dollars were also awarded during that year.[19] Although more recent data are not available, these funds have probably increased significantly since 1956.

Many fellowships and assistantships go unfilled each year. Perhaps the essential requirements for obtaining financial aid for graduate work other than good scholarship are: (1) that the student know what aid programs are available, (2) that he plan his own work sufficiently in advance so he can obtain aid when he needs it, and (3) that he be persistent enough to keep checking the available sources until he receives the financial assistance he needs.

OPPORTUNITIES FOR CAREERS IN EDUCATIONAL RESEARCH

In recent years there has been a great increase in interest and appreciation of the potential values of educational research. A major factor slowing the expansion of educational research has been a shortage of trained personnel in this field. In addition to a tremendous

[18] M. E. Shiltz, *Fellowships in the Arts and Sciences, 1961–62* (4th ed.; Washington, D.C.: Association of American Colleges, 1960).

[19] Richard C. Mattingly, *Financial Aid for College Students: Graduate* (Washington, D.C.: U.S. Dept. of Health, Education, and Welfare, 1957).

expansion of educational research in universities, the demand for educational research workers has also increased because of many new types of jobs that require this type of training.

Let us review briefly some of the specific job areas in which persons trained in educational research are employed.

Universities and colleges

Twenty years ago nearly all educational researchers were employed by colleges and universities. A majority are still so affiliated. Large universities have, for many years, placed considerable emphasis upon research productivity in the employment and promotion of faculty members, and this emphasis is now being felt in smaller universities and colleges as well. Many university positions involve part-time research and part-time teaching because it has been recognized that adequate programs of graduate training in education cannot be carried out without faculty members who do research. Recent years have also seen the establishment of many new educational research bureaus at colleges and universities and the expansion of the established bureaus at the larger schools. Many university counseling centers also employ educational research workers to carry out local studies concerned with various problems related to the counseling service. In some universities, the Dean of Students Office also employs educational research workers to carry out studies concerning such matters as student dropouts, educational goals, and validity of student selection procedures.

Public schools

The new enthusiasm for educational research has now infected most of the larger school districts. Many large and medium sized districts now employ full-time research directors who plan and carry out research projects aimed at evaluating the educational effectiveness of the district and developing and validating new curricula, teaching methods, and educational programs. Some of the very large districts have well-staffed research bureaus that carry out studies in a wide range of educational areas. Smaller districts often employ a school psychologist or pupil personnel director, part of whose time is devoted to educational research projects of particular interest to the district.

Inasmuch as considerable financial support for research and development is available through federal programs and such private foundations as the *Fund for Advancement of Education,* educational research workers are often employed to direct a specific research or development project for which the school district has received financial support. Such special projects often lead to the district employing full-time research personnel after the special project has been completed.

State departments of education

The increased interest in educational research has also been reflected in state departments of education where research personnel are increasing rapidly. Federal research support is available to state departments of education through the Cooperative Research Program, and some of the projects currently being carried out indicate that the level of educational research in state departments has improved greatly. A few years ago, the research division in most state departments of education typically carried out no research but merely served as a statistical and record-keeping section concerned with such matters as average daily attendance and pupil cost.

Civil service

There are many opportunities for educational research workers in federal civil service. The Department of Health, Education, and Welfare employs educational researchers to monitor research contract programs and to carry out nationwide surveys of great importance in education. The Department of State also has a number of programs that require personnel skilled in educational research and development. The military services employ a great many civilian research workers in education and educational psychology. Some of these personnel are employed in centralized research units such as the Air Force Personnel and Training Research Center, the Personnel Research Branch of the Army Adjutant General's office, and the Naval Research Field Activities. Others are employed to carry out educational research and development in the many schools operated by the armed services. Because the teachers and administrators in these schools are usually military personnel with little or no professional training in education, the need for civilians skilled in educational research and development has long been recognized. Such personnel are often employed as educational consultants or in special research sections attached to schools such as the Training Analysis and Development Sections attached to many air force training facilities. There are also a great many research agencies and corporations that employ educational research workers. These organizations carry out educational research tasks under contract with the federal government or with private companies. The American Institute for Research at Pittsburgh, the Human Resources Research Office affiliated with the George Washington University at Washington, D.C., and the Systems Development Corporation at Santa Monica, California are illustrative of the various types of private research organizations that carry out educational research and employ educational research workers.

Business and industry

Many large corporations carry out extensive training and educational programs for their employees and frequently employ training directors and other personnel trained in educational research and development to direct and administer these programs.

Although this is far from an exhaustive treatment of the types of work open to educational researchers, it may be seen that a wide range of opportunities are open to the person with training in educational research.

SEEKING A POSITION IN EDUCATIONAL RESEARCH

The résumé

The graduate student who plans to seek a position in educational research should prepare a résumé several months prior to completion of his graduate work. The résumé should be prepared with considerable care and should be duplicated using the most finished process available. If possible, offset process should be used because it provides a neater copy than either mimeograph or ditto. The employer tends to judge the applicant not only by the content of his résumé but the care with which it is prepared. The résumé usually includes the following items:

1. *Biographical Data.* A photograph of the individual and a brief biographical sketch including name, address, age, marital status, and so on.

2. *Professional Experience.* A brief chronological description of any professional experience that the student has had.

3. *Educational Record.* This record should include a listing of all college and university courses taken at both the graduate and undergraduate level. Usually the course title, units of credit, grade, and professor are given for each course. The student may leave blank the grades for any courses in his program that he has not yet completed.

4. *Professional Affiliations.* It is advisable while still in graduate school for the graduate student to form professional affiliations. Because the majority of educational research workers are currently being trained in educational psychology, membership or student affiliate status in the American Psychological Association is desirable. Another organization that the student should affiliate with is the American Educational Research Association. He should also consider membership in the state education association and the regional psychological association, and should participate in their annual meetings. The early establishment of professional affiliations by the graduate student provides the employer with some evidence of the individual's professional maturity and his identification with the profession.

5. *Publications.* The graduate student usually lists his thesis and/or dissertation as a publication. If he has any other publications or has read any papers at professional meetings, they should be listed. If the graduate student is working toward the doctorate, it is advisable for him to prepare one or more articles based on the research findings of his Master's thesis as soon as possible and submit these to a professional journal for publication. Because journals publishing educational research have a publication lag, the student may have nothing to list that has actually been published. He should, however, list articles that are in preparation or have been accepted for publication, giving the title of the article and noting its status. Research publications are given a great deal of weight by most employers of educational researchers.

6. *Professional References.* The résumé should also contain the names and current addresses of at least three persons familiar with the student's professional training and ability. For most graduate students, these references are limited to his professors. It is customary

to request an individual's permission before listing his name as a reference.

Finding vacancies

The student should register with his university placement office at least six months prior to the time he plans to complete his graduate training. Many universities and public school districts begin looking for employees in December and January to fill vacancies for the following September. The student who is tardy in preparing his résumé and making his availability known will miss many opportunities. In addition to filing his records at the university placement office, there are several other steps the student may take to locate a suitable position.

Some professional placement bureaus specialize in jobs in the public schools or universities. These bureaus often advertise in the professional journals in education and may be located by checking recent issues of these journals. Before registering with a placement bureau, the student should make sure he understands the fees connected with these services.

Some professional organizations such as the American Psychological Association provide employment services. The American Psychological Association publishes a monthly Employment Bulletin to which the student may subscribe. This bulletin usually lists vacancies throughout the United States and overseas. The student may also, for a nominal fee, place a notice in the APA Employment Bulletin giving his qualifications and indicating his availability. Placement Bureaus are operated at the annual meetings of many professional organizations. Employers are present at these meetings to interview applicants.

The student may also correspond directly with school districts, universities, or other organizations that employ educational research workers. Such inquiries are usually accompanied with a copy of the individual's résumé. As there are more positions available at present in educational research than there are applicants, the student will often obtain a favorable reply to such direct inquiries.

Many positions calling for educational research workers are available in the various branches of the federal government. The student should check directly with federal installations in the area in which he wishes to work. He may also correspond directly with the Civil

Service Commission in Washington, D.C. and may obtain announcements of vacancies from the local post office. Many of the vacancies listed under "Research Psychologist" and "Educational Specialist" require persons with training in educational research.

ANNOTATED REFERENCES

1. BLESSING, JAMES H. *Graduate Education: An Annotated Bibliography.* Washington, D.C.: Office of Education, Bulletin 1961, No. 26. A survey of studies and commentaries published during the period 1957–60, but including earlier studies of major importance. Studies in such areas as enrollment, student assistance, standards, and types of graduate programs are covered. An excellent source for the graduate student who is seeking information on some phase of graduate education.

2. COREY, STEPHEN M. "The Support of Research in Education," *Teachers College Record,* 1957, 59, 129–36. This article discusses the Cooperative Research Program of the U.S. Office of Education, how this program began, and how it operates. Also discussed is the contribution of private foundations to educational research and some problems that have arisen with respect to such support.

3. MATTINGLY, RICHARD C. *Financial Aid for College Students: Graduate.* Washington, D.C.: U.S. Office of Education, 1957. This directory is based upon a questionnaire carried out by the U.S. Office of Education during 1956. Although much of the specific information concerning financial aid will have changed, this bulletin still provides an excellent source for graduate students seeking financial aid. Reporting institutions are listed alphabetically, and information on the field of study, number of awards, and average amount of award are given for each institution. Another section of the bulletin lists all institutions reporting financial aid by subjects so that the graduate students interested in receiving financial aid in education, for example, may check this index and learn which institutions offered such aid during the year of the survey. Students should remember that this source reports only financial aid originating at the institutions and does not cover fellowships, etc., originating outside the institutions from government agencies, private foundations, and so forth.

4. NESS, FREDERIC W. (ed.). *A Guide to Graduate Study* (2nd ed.). Washington, D.C.: American Council on Education, 1960. This is a valuable reference for graduate students. It provides a brief general treatment of such topics as the objectives of graduate education, how to select a graduate school, how to gain admission to a graduate school, and how to finance

graduate study. This reference also contains a description of graduate schools that offer programs leading to the Ph.D., including information such as when the graduate program was established, library facilities available, residence requirements, and admission requirements. Fees, tuition, cost of room and board in university dormitories, types of housing available, cost of housing, and first year aid available are also covered. For each field of study offering the Ph.D., a brief description of the program, including the specific area covered, the prerequisites for graduate study, the number of graduate students completing degree programs in recent years, and the number of staff members are given.

5. Ross, Sherman. "Educational Facilities and Financial Assistance for Graduate Students in Psychology: 1962–63," *American Psychologist*, 1961, 16, 808–28. Lists universities offering graduate training in psychology and financial assistance available at listed schools. Also gives information on other sources of financial assistance. Many of the fellowships and assistantships listed are available to students in educational psychology.

6. Shiltz, Michael Edmund. *Fellowships in the Arts and Sciences:* 1962–63. (5th ed.). Washington, D.C.: Association of American Colleges, 1961. This directory provides a descriptive listing of predoctoral and postdoctoral fellowships supported by funds outside of the universities. It also contains a chapter listing sources of financial support for summer study and another describing loan programs. A new edition is published each acadademic year, and the student is advised to obtain the latest. For each source of funds, the title of the program is given, the address to which students should mail inquiries, the purpose of the program, the fields in which fellowships are awarded, qualifications of recipients, periods of the award, stipends and other allowances, conditions under which the fellowships are available, application deadlines, and approximate number of awards to be made. The postdoctoral section contains some information on sources of support for postdoctoral research and study, although a more thorough coverage may be found in *The Foundation Directory*.

7. Walton, Ann D., and Andrews, F. E. (eds.). *The Foundation Directory*. New York: Russell Sage Foundation, 1960. This directory includes information on 5,202 foundations with assets over $50,000, making grants of $10,000 per year or more. The directory contains an alphabetical listing of foundations by state, giving the name and address of the foundation, donors, the date established, purpose and activities, and recent assets and expenditures. *The Foundation Directory* also has an index of Fields of Interest in which the student may look up educational research, fellowships, educational aids, student loans, and other topics related to his field of interest.

Appendix A

Questions to be asked by the student in planning a research project in education.*

A. Scope and Definition of Study
   1. Is your problem being considered broadly enough?
   2. Have you sufficiently limited your problem?
   3. What are the educational implications of your study?
   4. Have you governed your decisions by the experiences of investigators who have preceded you?
   5. How significant psychologically is a socially selected group such as "children who steal," "children who nail bite," "inmates of a correctional institution"?

B. Hypotheses
   1. What are the hypotheses?
   2. Are the hypotheses promising?
   3. Are the hypotheses clearly and precisely stated?
   4. Are the hypotheses stated in a form that permits them to be tested?
   5. Is it better to hazard a hypothesis or to ask a question?
   6. Has the study been restricted to one or a few principal hypotheses to be tested?
   7. Are your hypotheses independent of one another?
   8. Is it better to hypothesize causal factors or merely to hypothesize relationships?

C. Background
   1. Have you made a thorough, careful review of the literature pertaining to your problem?

D. Definitions
   1. Have proper distinctions been made between concepts?
   2. Have concepts been adequately analyzed so as to distinguish

* P. M. Symonds, "A Research Checklist in Educational Psychology," *Journal of Educational Psychology*, XLVII (1956), 101–9. Reprinted by permission of the Abrahams Magazine Service, Inc., New York, N. Y.

between small but significant differences in method, materials, subjects, setting, etc.?

3. Is there clear and unequivocal meaning in the use of your terms?
4. Are concepts adequately and accurately defined?
5. Do some of your concepts require restrictive definition?
6. Do the meanings of your terms change with changes in age, sex, socio-economic status, etc.?
7. From what (whose) point of view are you defining your terms?

E. Method of Study
1. Has a decision as to the method of inquiry been made?
2. Is there a relation between the data to be collected and the hypotheses which the study is trying to test?
3. Do you propose to collect your own data or will you make use of published data already gathered?
4. Are you planning to use a "shotgun" approach?
5. If you plan to study individual cases, have you given thought as to how you will go from cases to general conclusions?
6. Are the data necessary for your study available?
7. Are you in a position to secure the data necessary for a successful prosecution of your study?
8. Are there variations in the method whose results would be worth investigating?
9. When more than one investigational approach is available, is it worth while to compare the results using different methods?
10. Can you draw conclusions as to cause and effect from evidence as to relationship?
11. To what extent can you generalize from a single experimental situation?
12. Are you planning to draw general conclusions from a study limited in age, sex, social class, race, etc.?
13. Have you considered the desirability of studying the relationships covering the whole range of your population instead of studying contrasting extreme groups?
14. Is the range among your cases sufficient to permit you to demonstrate the relationships in which you are interested?

15. Is it possible that the differences or relationships in which you are interested might be due to differences inherent in the situation (personality differences, for instance) instead of or as well as the experimental factors you propose to study?
16. How do you propose to select your criterion groups?
17. Can you make detailed observations of individual subjects to supplement your mass data?
18. Would it be well to ask questions on both the positive and negative side of an issue instead of just one side?
19. Are you justified in assuming a constant motivation among your subjects?
20. Will your results be influenced by the order or position of your materials?
21. Have you considered the possibility of response sets in your subjects—i.e., a general tendency to respond, which might influence your results?

F. Design

1. Is the design of your study clearly formulated?
2. Have you taken into account the various hidden factors which might influence the results of your study besides the variables that you are specifically planning to study?
3. Have you taken into account the influence of age, sex, school grade, I.Q., socio-economic status, mental set, leakage among subjects, influence of examiner, emotional factors?
4. Have you taken sufficiently into account experiences other than your experimental variables that might intervene between your first and second test?
5. How may the influence of these variables be eliminated?
6. Have you made a decision with regard to whether it is better to control variables experimentally or to test the contribution of variables statistically?
7. Have you given sufficient thought to the necessity of controls?
8. Are you in a position to measure and/or control variables which might influence your results?
9. Does the design of your experiment permit you to randomize variables which you do not want to influence your results?

G. Sampling

1. To what extent will you be able to generalize your findings?
2. What are the criteria for selecting your cases?
3. Is sampling of materials, places, subjects, test items, etc., *adequate?*
4. How do you propose to select subjects for your study?
5. Are your proposed subjects representative of the population to which you intend to generalize your results?
6. What age level and age range do you propose to study?
7. Have you given sufficient attention to the sampling of tasks?
8. What factors may be biasing the selection of subjects?
9. Do you propose to use groups already selected by social processes, or do you propose to select groups by direct testing of the characteristics of individuals?
10. Would your results be more clear-cut if you selected groups which give promise of showing wide differences?
11. How stable will your findings be—that is, will they stand up when made under different conditions—when made with other subjects, materials, instructors, examiners, in other places, etc.?
12. Will you make your selections on the basis of known factors or on the basis of a random sampling?
13. Should you treat as a unit individuals over a wide age, grade, or cultural range?
14. Can you simplify your problem by limiting it to a narrower age range, grade range, geographical range, etc.?
15. Are you taking into account the subgroups in your total population?
16. How do you propose to group your subjects?
17. In studying the differences between two populations, are you sure the populations are differentiated on the variables which you assume differentiate them?
18. Are you determining your sampling, or are you letting others select cases for you?
19. If you depend on voluntary participation for your subjects, have you given consideration to what this will do to your sampling?
20. How do you plan to determine the equivalence of groups?
21. If not all of those whom you solicit return questionnaires, what does this do to your sampling?

H. Studying Personality

    1. Are you differentiating between manifest and covert personality trends?

    2. To what extent is it possible to consider motives and unconscious purposes?

    3. How do you propose to determine the values, attitudes, interests, motives, etc., that you plan to investigate?

    4. Will interviews be biased if the interviewer has access to other information about an individual?

    5. Can you depend on the subject's report to inform you about his motives, attitudes, problems, etc.?

    6. Are you sufficiently aware of the influence of dynamic mechanisms (repression, projection, denial, etc.) in the reports of your subjects?

    7. How are you going to ensure that your subjects express their true feelings and attitudes?

    8. If you plan to investigate underlying dynamics, are you prepared to establish close relationships with your subjects?

    9. Is the questionnaire or testing approach going to permit you to get at the inner dynamics?

    10. In a study using tests and other objective data, is it possible to question your subjects further to determine attitudes, beliefs, motives, etc.?

    11. Are you assuming that a verbal report of behavior is identical with the behavior?

    12. Are you assuming that a verbal report of attitude is identical with the attitude?

    13. Are you confounding a verbal report of memory with the actual facts?

    14. Is the recall of childhood experiences a safe index of the actual experiences?

    15. What is preferable for your study—the questionnaire or interview approach?

    16. In a study involving interviewing, have you considered the possibility of securing cooperation and frankness from your subjects?

    17. To what extent is the interviewer influencing the answers to questions?

    18. To what extent can you depend on self-testimony as compared with the testimony of others?

19. Are you assuming that inner expression of value, interest, and feeling are the same as the judgment of a person made by some other person?
20. Is one justified in attributing dynamic significance to behavior for the purpose of research?
21. Do you prefer the free response type of inquiry (so-called open-ended questions) where the answers to questions must be categorized, or do you prefer recognition type questions where the answers can be directly tabulated?
22. In using observation material, how can you be sure that your observations are representative?
23. Have you made sure that the items which you have selected to represent a given trait are not biased in some other trait?
24. In thinking about personality characteristics, are these general or do they relate to specific situations?

I. Tests and Measures

1. Are you using the appropriate measures?
2. How is the material in your test to be selected?
3. Are your measures independent?
4. Have you taken into account the difficulty level of your test?
5. Do you wish to use a time limit or work limit?
6. Have you considered the relative merits of recall and recognition types of items?
7. Have you given consideration to the best type of score for your test?
8. How will you construct a scale to measure attitude?
9. Do you have a large enough reservoir of items to be able to make a selection of items in terms of difficulty, validity, etc.?
10. How do you propose to make a composite of your measures? What would such a composite mean?
11. In using a questionnaire, do you propose to get a total score or merely to tabulate the answers to separate items?
12. To what extent are the responses of your subjects limited by the examiner or the directions?
13. Can you use a ready-made measuring instrument, or should you construct your own? If the latter, how will you determine its validity and reliability.
14. How valid are your measures?

15. Are there contaminating factors (age, sex, etc.) which might lessen the validity of the test you propose to use?
16. Do you propose testing the validity of your test on a new group?
17. Are your tests sufficiently reliable?
18. Do you propose to test the reliability of your measures?
19. Are you planning to use your time in scale-making, testing validity and reliability when it could more profitably be directed elsewhere?
20. Are there norms with which to compare the findings in the group that you are proposing to study?
21. If you plan to use content material (like the T.A.T.) as a measuring device, have you specified the variables you propose to measure?
22. Have you properly disguised your intentions in the test you propose to use?
23. Should a pre-test be given as well as a test at the close of your experiment?
24. Is a pass-fail score on a test item identical with a qualitative score based on a content analysis?
25. Is a point score which is the sum of factors used in the solution to a problem adequate as a measure when there is a possibility that the factors may differ in importance?
26. If you plan to study the extremes on your scale, would it be well at the same time to pay attention to the intermediate points?

J. Use of Judgment

1. If you plan to use judgments, have you specified the basis on which your judgments would be made?
2. In securing ratings, whom will you select as your judges?
3. If you plan to use judgments, are you sure your judges have the necessary intelligence, information, background, and other qualifications to permit them to make the judgments?
4. Can you depend on judgments to serve as a basis for selecting individuals as being mentally deficient, delinquent, schizophrenic, etc.
5. To what extent will subjective factors enter into judgments that you propose to make (or use), and how can these be avoided?

6. Which is better for your study—the overall judgment or a content analysis?

K. Content Analysis

1. How do you propose to determine your classification scheme?
2. Who is to make the classification scheme?
3. How reliable will the classification scheme be?
4. How do you propose to distribute material into the several classificatory categories?
5. Who is to distribute the items into categories?
6. Have you provided for determining the reliability of your classifications?
7. Have you sufficiently taken into account the subjective factor in analyzing content material?
8. Have you given attention to what sorts of behavior or responses will be included under such general categories as "resistance" or "rejection"?

L. Statistical Handling of Results

1. Do the conditions of your data warrant using the statistics which you propose to use?
2. Do your data satisfy the assumptions on which the statistical constants which you propose to use are based?
3. Have you enough cases to test fairly the significance of your statistical constants?

Appendix B

CHECKLIST *

Satisfactory	Unsatisfactory	Questions
		A. The Problem 1. Was the problem clearly defined? 2. Was a verifiable hypothesis formulated? 3. Was the hypothesis one that was logically deduced from some theory (or problem)? **B. The Design** 1. Was the statistical design employed in the investigation appropriate to the particular experimental methods, conditions, subjects, and hypotheses under test? 2. Was the population studied clearly specified? 3. Was the method, or methods, of drawing a sample from the population clearly specified? 4. Was a control group chosen in the same manner and from the same population as the experimental groups? 5. Were the various treatments (including control) assigned at random to the groups? 6. Did the experiment include a replication? 7. Was the level of significance necessary for rejection of the null hypotheses specified before the

* Taken from William W. Farquhar and John D. Krumboltz, "A Checklist for Evaluating Experimental Research in Psychology and Education," *Journal of Educational Research,* LII, No. 9 (1959), 354. Reprinted by permission of the *Journal of Educational Research.*

405

CHECKLIST (*Continued*)

Satisfactory	Unsatisfactory	Questions
		data were collected and analyzed?
		C. The Procedure
		1. Were the treatments and methods of collecting data described so that an independent investigator could replicate the experiment?
		2. Were the size and characteristics of the sample adequately described?
		3. Were the treatments administered so that extraneous sources of error were either held constant for all treatment and control groups or randomized among subjects within all groups?
		D. The Analysis
		1. Was the criterion of evaluation appropriate to the objectives of the study?
		3. Was the hypothesis one which was bility of the criterion measure given for the experimental sample?
		3. Were the statistical assumptions which are necessary for a valid test of the hypotheses satisfied?
		E. The Interpretation
		1. Were the conclusions consistent with the obtained results?
		2. Were generalizations confined to the population from which the sample was drawn?

Index

Index

Please renew/return this item by the last date shown.

So that your telephone call is charged at local rate,
please call the numbers as set out below:

	From Area codes 01923 or 020:	From the rest of Herts:
Renewals:	01923 471373	01438 737373
Enquiries:	01923 471333	01438 737333
Textphone:	01923 471599	01438 737599

L32 www.hertsdirect.org/librarycatalogue